SPAIN AND DEFENSE OF THE WEST
Ally and Liability

SPAIN AND DEFENSE OF THE WEST

Ally and Liability

ARTHUR P. WHITAKER

Published for the
COUNCIL ON FOREIGN RELATIONS

by
FREDERICK A. PRAEGER, *Publisher*
New York

BOOKS THAT MATTER

Published in 1962 by Frederick A. Praeger, Inc., Publisher
64 University Place, New York 3, N.Y.

Spain and Defense of the West
The first edition of this book was published in clothbound
form in 1961
by Harper & Brothers, New York, for the
Council on Foreign Relations

Library of Congress Catalog Card Number: LC 61-6234

Manufactured in the United States of America

American Book–Stratford Press, Inc., New York

PREFACE

THE CENTRAL THEME of my study is the evolving relationship of the United States and Spain under the agreements which they made in 1953 for the establishment of several joint air and naval bases in Spain as a part of the U.S. global defense system. Over the past seven years the relationship has become both broader and closer than was originally intended, at least by the United States, and it has had far-reaching repercussions both in the economy of Spain and in the economic policy of its government. In 1959 this evolution culminated in two spectacular events: in July, Madrid's commitment to the bold but hazardous economic reforms which are disarmingly described as a stabilization plan; and, in December, President Eisenhower's cordial visit to General Franco. Each of these events marked the end of one stage only to usher in another, and there is no reason to expect that the relationship will lose its dynamic character. On the contrary, its impact on the domestic situation in Spain is likely to be even greater from now on, if only because of the political and social as well as economic consequences of the stabilization plan.

The domestic situation in Spain is obviously of great importance and will accordingly be discussed at some length. To begin with the most obvious reason, the usefulness of the Spanish bases to Western strategy depends in large measure on the strength and stability, as well as the good will, of the government of Spain. At present, as for more than two decades past, that rule is in the hands of a dictator. General Francisco Franco seems firmly entrenched; yet, as always, the stability of his regime depends on two factors that have so far remained constant but now seem likely to become variable. These are the support that the regime receives from the country's principal power groups, especially the armed forces, and the weakness of the numerous opposition forces as a result of their internal divisions. In the next few years variations in both respects may be expected for a number of reasons. One of the most probable is the heavy impact the stabilization plan will have on both friends and foes of the regime if its austerity provisions are honestly enforced. Another reason lies in the political immobilism of the regime, for this, too, has begun to offend its friends as well as its foes and makes it increasingly an anachronism in an otherwise rapidly changing Spain.

Amid growing criticism of the regime, for example, within Catholic circles, the atmosphere is charged with the spirit of change. Yet General Franco can apparently think of no better solution than a restoration of the monarchy on terms that would in effect freeze the regime in its present form. A revolt is not necessarily indicated. Most Spaniards who lived through the Civil War are unwilling to risk a repetition of its horrors, and the younger generation has not yet taken over the direction either of the forces supporting the regime or of those hostile to it. Yet substantial changes are, I believe, sure to come before long. The main questions are, for Spain, what direction the shift will take and how far it will go, and, for the United States, to what extent it may be penalized for its increasingly close identification with the Franco dictatorship.

Spain's relations with other countries and with international organizations are also highly germane to my central theme. First place is necessarily accorded to Western Europe, for Spaniards are Europeans, though with a difference. Here, too, the dominant motif is change, as witnessed by Spain's recent *rapprochements* with West Germany and France. Yet there remains a large fund of antagonism to the Franco regime among Spain's neighbors. Despite that antagonism the United States has sought, so far unsuccessfully, to bring

about Spain's admission to NATO. This effort accords with
Washington's well-intentioned but rather undiscriminating
policy of promoting closer relations between Spain and her
European neighbors. The policy has, however, been sound
and successful in one case, that of bringing about Spain's
admission to full membership in the Organization for European Economic Cooperation in 1959, and now in its successor body, the Organization for Economic Cooperation and
Development.

Spain's relations with Morocco, which have so often played
a leading role in Spanish events, occupy an important place
in this study. From Morocco Spain's interests, or at least her
ambitions, have fanned out over the Arab world. They have
also been pressed in Latin America, and for a time in the
1950's the Franco government emphasized Spain's claim to
serve as a bridge between those two areas and, more broadly,
between Islam and the Christian West. Spain's ambitions and
efforts are considered here as they influence the new cooperation between Spain and the United States. These ties can, I
believe, be moderately useful to U.S. policy in the Mediterranean but are increasingly a handicap to it in Latin
America, where the victories of democracy over dictatorship
in recent years have created an atmosphere more and more
antagonistic towards the dictatorial regime in Spain.

In addition to conclusions on particular questions, I have,
in the course of my investigations, arrived at three recommendations of a general character. The first is that both the
concept and the policy of nonintervention ought to be re-
fined and clarified. In the present muddled state of the
question, generally intelligent and well-informed persons
hold that the policy of nonintervention permits the United
States to strengthen a dictatorship with economic, military,
and political aid, but prohibits it from putting any pressure
on that same regime to reduce the flagrant contradiction
between its own character and the ideals of democracy and
freedom which the arrangements made between them profess
to defend. Again, the same persons who unqualifiedly endorse
the requirement of economic reforms as a condition of aid

to a foreign country usually reject as "intervention" the suggestion that the need for political reforms might similarly be pressed.

My second conclusion is that we need to clarify the concept and scope of strategy. Too often this term is used as if it involved only military factors. In the protracted conflict in which the United States and the rest of the free world are now engaged with the Communist bloc, it is obvious that political, economic, and other factors must also enter into any sound strategy. They may even outweigh military ones in the final reckoning.

A third conclusion is that, because of the narrowly military concept of strategy that has dominated U.S. policy towards Spain, the United States has incurred an unnecessarily heavy political and moral liability, and that even now steps can and should be taken to diminish this liability. Some suggestions to this end are offered in the last chapter.

Any study of these complex problems is obviously replete with controversial questions. Most of these stem from the fact that the United States has become the virtual ally of a government that is not only the last survivor of the Nazi-Fascist era but is still today, seven years after the beginning of its association with the United States, an iron-handed dictatorship. While I have, in the course of my study, formed decided views on the various questions raised in this book, I have tried not to obtrude them but rather to examine impartially the origins of our present problems and to state the issues and the alternatives as clearly and as fairly as possible.

If my task has not been made easy, it has at any rate been made welcome by the repeated opportunities that I have had since 1924 to visit Spain, to observe her life under widely varying conditions, and to meet almost all sorts of Spaniards in all parts of the country. From the beginning of my scholarly activity I have had a keen interest in Spanish thought and public affairs, especially of the eighteenth and twentieth centuries, and in Spain's relations with the United States. My first visit in 1924-1925, like most later ones, was devoted to historical research, but much of my spare time was spent reading Ángel Ganivet, Miguel de Unamuno, José Ortega y Gasset, and others of the "Generation of 1898" that addressed itself so brilliantly to diagnosing the ills of Spain and prescribing for them. My second visit also was made during the reign of Alfonso XIII and the dictatorship of Primo de Rivera; my third fell midway in the brief span of the Second Republic; and my last four, between 1950 and 1959, have been during the Franco dictatorship.

I have thus seen Spain under all three regimes of the past thirty-seven years. While I was not in Spain during the Civil War, I returned for a new visit before the recovery from it and from World War II and the postwar ostracism was well begun. As a result, I have been able to appreciate the material reconstruction, truly remarkable in some respects, that was made during the 1950's, and also to observe the attitudes of Spaniards towards the regime that first made this reconstruction necessary and then carried it out.

My latest visit to Spain, and this entire study, were made possible by my appointment as a Research Fellow of the Council on Foreign Relations. The Council also smoothed my path for me in many ways, not only in the United States and Spain, but also in France, England, and Morocco, which I likewise visited in connection with this study because of their important roles in the international relations of Spain. I also wish to make special acknowledgment to the University of Pennsylvania's Foreign Policy Research Institute, which generously released me from my regular duties for the purpose of completing this study and, in particular, to express my appreciation to three of its members—Robert Strausz-Hupé, Director, William R. Kintner, Associate Director, and Hans Kohn—for their counsel and encouragement. It is likewise a pleasure to thank the University of Pennsylvania for granting me a research leave, which greatly facilitated the carrying out of my study.

In my efforts to study these complex problems of present and future policy I received valuable assistance and encouragement from a Study Group of the Council on Foreign Relations, under the able chairmanship of Charles M. Spofford. Its members, in addition to Mr. Spofford, were: Alfred W. Barth, Amory H. Bradford, Arthur H. Dean, Major General Harold C. Donnelly, USAF, William Ebenstein, E. Drexel Godfrey, Jr., Thomas J. Hamilton, Carlton J. H. Hayes, Richard Herr, Colonel William R. Kintner, USA, Hans Kohn, Charles Henry Lee, Herbert L. Matthews, Ben T. Moore, George S. Moore, Philip E. Mosely, William Reitzel, Vincent A. Rodriguez, Captain H. G. Sanchez, USN, Robert Strausz-Hupé, Theodore Tannenwald, H. Gregory Thomas, and Arnold Wolfers. The discussions of the group ranged broadly—and in them a wide variety of views was expressed. I hardly need add that neither the Study Group as a whole nor any of its members is responsible in any way for the views expressed in this study.

At different meetings of the Study Group a number of members and guests led the discussion of the various problems considered. I take special pleasure in expressing my appreciation, and that of the Council, to the following: Alfred W. Barth, Arthur H. Dean, Major General Harold C. Donnelly, USAF, Richard Herr, Paul C. Hoover, Colonel William R. Kintner, USA, and Captain H. G. Sanchez, USN. John C. Campbell, William Diebold, Jr., Gerhart Niemeyer, and John L. Snell also contributed to the discussion at individual meetings.

In preparing my study for publication I received helpful suggestions from Alfred W. Barth, John C. Campbell, and Colonel Lynn R. Moore, USAF, on individual chapters and points. I am grateful to Byron Dexter, William Ebenstein, and Charles M. Spofford for their reading of the manuscript as a whole. William Diebold, Jr., and Helena Stalson provided invaluable assistance in my research on Spain's economic situation and on U.S. aid programs in Spain. Otis H. Green and Ángel del Río were most helpful on the historical background of nationalism in Spain. I take special pleasure in thanking Philip E. Mosely, Director of Studies, who encouraged me to undertake this study and who reviewed and commented on the manuscript. He has been extraordinarily helpful throughout.

In addition, I take pleasure in expressing my appreciation to Ruth Savord, Donald Wasson, and Janet Rigney, of the Council's Library, for their constant assistance; to William Dean Howells, who prepared the digests of discussion at the meetings of the Study Group; to Lorna Brennan, who so ably copy-edited the manuscript and shepherded it through various stages of typing and proofreading; and to Elizabeth Valkenier, who prepared the index.

I should like to take this opportunity to thank many people of responsibility and experience in Spain and the United States, as well as in France, Britain, and Morocco, who devoted many hundreds of hours of their time to discussing with me the many and complex problems relating to my study. I regret that I cannot mention each of them by name. In some cases their official duties make this impossible, and there are obvious reasons why I cannot make proper acknowledgment to persons living in Spain.

In completing this study of Spain and its place in U.S. policy I want to thank the Council on Foreign Relations for its interest and support of my study. At the same time I wish to append the usual disclaimer: neither the Council, nor the Study Group, is responsible for the views expressed in it, for these are my own views, which I have arrived at in the course of my investigations and which I now present to the forum of public discussion, as a modest contribution to responsible thinking about the direction and goals of U.S. policy.

ARTHUR P. WHITAKER

Philadelphia, Penna.
September 6, 1960

CONTENTS

TABLES

MAPS

SPAIN AND DEFENSE OF THE WEST

Ally and Liability

Chapter I

THE MAKING OF AN ALLY:
FROM THE SPANISH CIVIL WAR
TO THE PACT OF MADRID

ON GENERAL FRANCISCO FRANCO's desk in the Pardo Palace, the story runs, stand two boxes, one labeled "Problems Time Will Solve" and the other "Problems Time Has Solved," and the General's chief occupation is transferring papers from the first box to the second.

Franco does have a talent for sitting out difficult situations, and its worth has been demonstrated time and again throughout his career. Its richest yield to date has been his agreement of 1953 with the United States, which brought his regime material aid and political respectability in return for letting the United States use and develop air and naval bases in Spain jointly with his government. Henceforth Spain was a partner in the defense of the free world.

Surely this Pact of Madrid, as the agreement has been called, represents one of the most striking reversals of relations between states in modern history, for, as a signer of the Anti-Comintern Pact of 1939, Franco had formerly been in the opposite camp as the partner of Adolf Hitler, Benito Mussolini, and the imperial government of Japan. The reversal is of quite a different order from those that have likewise brought West Germany, Italy, and Japan into the free-world camp since the end of World War II. All three of them had first been purged by defeat and revolution,

1

whereas Spain has not undergone either experience. She has remained at peace under the same ruler and the same type of regime as of yore, and, according to her spokesmen, follows the same domestic and foreign policies. It is the Franco regime's proudest boast, founded in the first instance on the Pact of Madrid, that the free world has at last come around to the course Franco has been following, and recommending to other countries, ever since the beginning of the Spanish Civil War.[1] That course is aimed against communism and Soviet imperialism.

There is an element of truth in this assertion, in the sense that the spread of the cold war, which was not foreseen in 1939 or in 1945, was mainly responsible for the desire of the United States, by 1953, to enter into partnership with Franco despite the antecedents and character of his regime. Yet this is by no means the whole explanation of the Pact of Madrid, and excessive reliance upon it has combined with other factors to foster a distorted view of the origin and significance of the pact and its long-range value to the United States. For example, as regards Spain, the pact is represented both as the culmination of Franco's undeviating policies of anti-communism and bilateralism, and also as lining "Spain" up on the side of the United States. The facts, however, are that Franco's anti-Communist slogan was an afterthought, adopted after the beginning of the Civil War; that he has at all times been quite ready to enter into multilateral arrangements whenever they were feasible and suited his purposes; and that, as we shall see,[2] what he has lined up on the side of the United States is only one-half of Spain.

Similarly, as regards the role of the United States, the events leading up to the Pact of Madrid are represented as beginning with Admiral Forrest Sherman's visit to Franco

---

[1] The leading example is Foreign Minister Alberto Martín Artajo's speech formally presenting the agreement to the Spanish Cortes, November 30, 1953, summarized below, Chapter II, pp. 53-56. See also Luis de Galinsoga, *Centinela de occidente* (Barcelona: Editorial AHR, 1956), and, as an anticipation of the fully developed boast, José María Doussinague, *España tenía razón (1939-1945)* (Madrid: Espasa-Calpe, 1950), pp. 361-376.

[2] See Chapter III.

in 1951 and the United States is said to have entered into the pact for exclusively military reasons. The first statement is accurate only in a technical sense, for the *rapprochement* crowned developments that had begun much earlier: in 1944 on the part of Spain, and in 1947 on the part of the United States. The second statement puts the emphasis in the right place but must be enlarged to accommodate the religious, humanitarian, political, and economic considerations that reinforced the weight of the new military factors.

Let us look at the record more closely.

Franco and World War II: Pro-Axis Phase

Outside the restricted circle of his unconditional champions, Franco's domestic policies have few ardent admirers. With his management of Spain's foreign relations it is quite otherwise. This has met with praise even from commentators who dislike everything else about his regime. Friends and enemies alike are impressed by the results of his management, which kept his country out of World War II, worked both sides of the belligerent street for its benefit, emerged politically stronger than before from the postwar ordeal of ostracism by the United Nations, and ended up triumphantly in a virtual alliance with the United States which in effect vindicated the basic policy of anticommunism that he had been following all along.

The item in this list of achievements that concerns us at this point is the one having to do with Franco's wartime relations with the Axis powers. Although the subject has given rise to no little controversy, it might not require attention here but for the fact that of late a myth about it has been gaining ground which ought to be disposed of in order to keep the record straight. The myth is that Franco was not really committed to the Axis cause but was only pretending to be, for Spain's advantage. The controversial period is the first half of the war, when the Axis powers seemed to be winning; no one has ever accused Franco of intentionally backing a loser.

That Franco aided the Axis to the best of his ability at that time, and stayed out of the war only because Spain was still too exhausted by her Civil War to fight another, was the virtually universal belief during the war; and just after its close, in 1946, the U.S. Department of State published a White Paper on Spain,[3] made up mainly of captured German and Italian documents, to prove the extent of the commitment. Subsequently, further revelations have shaded the degree of Franco's commitment, particularly by showing that he had reservations about becoming irrevocably linked with Germany and Hitler's ambitions. Partly on this basis, and partly also, no doubt, because the climate of opinion has changed since the United States took Franco into partnership, the myth has gained ground that his repeated professions of devotion to the Axis cause were never sincere, that he was only beating Hitler and Mussolini at their own game of double-dealing, and that he never had any intention of getting involved in the war. Perhaps it is no myth, but true and praiseworthy, that Franco's intentions towards the Axis powers were strictly dishonorable, but the fact is that he was eager to get into the war at one stage, in 1940, and stayed out only because Hitler and Mussolini were unwilling to pay the price he asked for coming in. And, as is well known, he actually did get into it later to the extent of sending his ill-fated Blue Division to fight with Germany against the Soviet Union.

Spain was already committed to the Axis when World War II broke out. In a sense the commitment began with Franco's acceptance of large-scale German and Italian aid during the Civil War. Many years later, even after he had become the virtual ally of the United States, Franco still publicly recognized that he had thus contracted a "blood debt" to the Axis powers.[4] But the commitment had also been formalized

---

3 *The Spanish Government and the Axis* (Washington: GPO, 1946).

4 *Ya* (Madrid), June 13 and 14, 1958; excerpts, in Spanish translation, from Serge Broussard's interview with Franco published in *Le Figaro* (Paris) on June 12 and 13. Franco's acknowledgment of the "blood debt" *(deuda de sangre)* to Germany and Italy occurs in the issue of *Ya* for June 13. Of course he denied that he ever intended to enter the war on their side and declared

by his accession to the Anti-Comintern Pact on March 26, 1939.

This was one of two agreements of long-range significance that Franco concluded in the last week of the Civil War, as Spain's international position was being regularized by the recognition of his government by France, Great Britain, and the United States, in that order. The second agreement, a nonaggression treaty with the Portugal of Dictator Salazar, signed on March 31, 1939, proved far more enduring. Later developed into the Iberian Pact, and still in effect, this treaty has been the most constant factor in Spanish foreign policy throughout the intervening period. Immediately, Spain's accession to the Anti-Comintern Pact was far more important than the treaty with Portugal; though not a military alliance, it did commit Spain to political cooperation with Germany, Italy, and Japan, and Spain gave them her cooperation and took part with them in anti-Comintern conferences through 1942.

Moreover, while Franco avoided even a bilateral type of military alliance on the ground that Spain must have five years of peace for recovery, he entered into a Pact of Friendship with Germany which assured the latter of a "more than favorable" Spanish neutrality in case of war. Signed on the same day as the Portuguese treaty, and like it a kind of nonaggression pact, the agreement with Germany was ratified shortly after war broke out (November 29, 1939). It was supplemented by secret pacts that gave Germany the use of naval facilities in Spanish ports and a "cooperative" role in relation to the Spanish police, press, and propaganda.[5]

Franco Spain also served the Axis by attacking democracy

(which was true) that he had made no agreement with them which could have obligated Spain to "take part in an armed conflict." When Broussard objected that Spain had in fact sent the Blue Division to fight against Russia, Franco replied that that was different, for "the war on the Eastern front was a crusade...analogous in many respects to our own [Civil War] crusade." It was at this point that he spoke of the "blood debt," which he also called a "moral debt."

[5] Herbert Feis, *The Spanish Story: Franco and the Nations at War* (New York: Knopf, 1948), p. 19.

and the United States as vigorously as it did communism and the Soviet Union. This phase of its policy was carried out mainly in Latin America through its Hispanidad program. Based on Spain's cultural ties with the eighteen Spanish American nations and representing a perversion of the relatively innocuous Pan Hispanism of the pre-Franco generation, the Hispanidad program was launched during the Civil War with Axis aid. It was intensified as soon as victory released additional energies for use overseas. Hardly a month after Franco's victory day, under the copious headline, "End of the Spanish War Entails for South American Peoples a Possible Change in Their Political Conceptions," the Falange's leading organ, *Arriba,* boasted that the progress of Hispanidad would damage the democracies and destroy the economic influence of the United States in Latin America. Leaving no doubt as to the implications of the Hispanidad program for the situation in Europe, the article pictured President Roosevelt's rearmament program as directed against Hitler's Third Reich in the service of "international Judaism." [6] Subsequently, *Arriba* and other Spanish journals denounced Western Hemisphere defense measures. Uruguay's leasing of a naval base to the United States was described as creating an American Gibraltar and signalizing the end of Uruguay's own independence and that of its neighbors as well.[7]

Instead of five years, Spain was granted barely five months for recovery before war broke out, from April 1, 1939, to September 3. Until November 1942, so long as the tide of victory ran in favor of the Axis, Spain played her chosen role of pro-Axis neutral throughout, though with varying degrees of vigor and in constant readiness to jump into the fray as soon as it was as good as won. What deterred her from entering sooner was not only her own weakness and the danger

---

6 *Arriba* (Madrid), May 3, 1939, as quoted in Emmet John Hughes, *Report from Spain* (New York: Holt, 1947), pp. 232-233. On Hispanidad, see Bailey W. Diffie, "The Ideology of Hispanidad," *Hispanic American Historical Review,* August 1943, pp. 457-482, and William B. Bristol, "Hispanidad in South America," *Foreign Affairs,* January 1943, pp. 312-321.

7 Hughes, cited, p. 232, n. 1.

of retaliation to which this and her geographical situation exposed her, but also her dependence on anti-Axis powers, particularly Great Britain and the United States, for essential imports such as petroleum, cotton, and foodstuffs.

The pro-Axis phase of Spanish policy is indelibly associated with Franco's brother-in-law, Ramón Serrano Suñer, first as minister of the interior and then, from October 1940 to September 1942, as foreign minister.[8] This phase falls into five periods, which were determined by the fortunes of war.

In the first period, from September 1939 to June 1940, Franco issued the traditional declaration of neutrality on September 4, and then secretly promised Berlin that in practice he would, as he had agreed, favor the Axis.[9] This promise he kept. Franco had been shocked by Hitler's eleventh-hour pact with Stalin, but he preferred the Nazi-Soviet frying pan to the democratic fire.

In the second period, from June 1940 to February 1941, the fall of France, which had left Britain fighting alone and apparently doomed, gave Franco the greatest freedom of action he was to enjoy at any time during World War II. Consequently, his record during this period probably provides the truest expression of his aims and ambitions. On June 14, 1940, while France was tottering to its fall and Hitler and Mussolini were in Munich conferring on its fate, Franco's government submitted to the German Ambassador a note declaring its readiness to enter the war—for a price. The price was Gibraltar, French Morocco, a slice of Algeria (the province of Oran), and additions to Spain's holdings on the west coast of Africa south of Morocco.[10] If the price seemed high to others, it was modest enough when measured

---

8 Serrano Suñer's own story is told in *Entre Hendaya y Gibraltar* (Madrid: "Diana" Artes Gráficas, 1947).

9 Hughes, cited, p. 20.

10 U.S. Department of State, *Documents on German Foreign Policy, 1918-1945*, Series D, v. 9: *The War Years, March 18-June 22, 1940* (Washington: GPO, 1956), pp. 620-621. On August 15, 1940, Franco wrote Mussolini that Spain was now "preparing herself to take her place in the strife against our common enemies" and urgently requested him to support Spain's aspirations. Mussolini promised to do so. Same, v. 10: *The War Years, June 23-August 31, 1940* (1957), pp. 484-486, 542.

on the scale of Franco's and the Falange's promises to restore Spain to her imperial glory of the sixteenth century.[11] As an earnest of his intentions in North Africa, Franco simultaneously moved his troops into the international zone of Tangier, and in November they took over its administration.

Any doubt that Franco's offer to enter the war was not made in all seriousness rests mainly on the assumption that Spain was still too exhausted to fight even a short war. The assumption is not justified, if we may trust a well-informed source, an appraisal of the Spanish army made by the German High Command, in August 1940. This report pointed to serious weaknesses in Spain's army of 340,000 men, such as severe shortages of both officers and ammunition. It also noted that all ranks possessed excellent fighting qualities ("generally willing, obedient, tough, and courageous"), and concluded that Spain was fit for limited employment in war and fully able to defend its homeland and external possessions, though without foreign help it could *wage a war of only very short duration.* [12] That was just the kind of war Franco expected to wage.

Franco was not given a chance to wage it. Hitler agreed to let him have Gibraltar, but was evasive about all his other claims, both on this occasion and later.[13] In October 1940 the two met, for the first and last time, at the French border town of Hendaye, where passengers from Paris to Madrid change trains because of the wider Spanish gauge. Here, agreements for Spain's participation in the war were roughed

---

11 Among the many expressions of this imperial spirit, special interest attaches to *Reivindicaciones de España* (Madrid: Instituto de Estudios Políticos, 1941), both because it stresses Spain's North African ambitions, and because its authors, Fernando María de Castiella and José María de Areilza, were in 1960, respectively, foreign minister and ambassador to the United States. Another and somewhat later example is José Corts Grau, *Motivos de la España eterna* (Madrid: Instituto de Estudios Políticos, 1946), consisting of articles published from 1943 to 1945.

12 *The War Years, June 23-August 31, 1940,* cited, pp. 461-464, "Note of the High Command of the [German] Army," August 10, 1940, "The Spanish Army at Present." (Italics in the original.)

13 William L. Langer and S. Everett Gleason, *The Challenge to Isolation, 1937-1940* (New York: Harper, for the Council on Foreign Relations, 1952), pp. 558-559.

out, but never perfected. Unable to exact his price, it was now Franco's turn to be coy as Hitler in the next few months pressed for his consent to "Operation Felix," an attack on Gibraltar by German forces crossing Spain from the Pyrenees. Mussolini was called in to support the suit, and Franco obligingly journeyed to Bordighera to be courted. The interview was pleasant, for he found his fellow Latin dictator congenial, but he still held out and so did the Axis leaders. Two weeks later (February 26, 1941) Franco canceled the Hendaye agreements by declaring them "outmoded."[14] That ended the second phase of his wartime policy.

What had kept Spain out of the war was Hitler's unwillingness to satisfy Franco's imperial aspirations. Morocco was the principal stumbling-block. For traditional and strategic reasons, it was highly important to Spain at all times,[15] and especially to a Spanish government of "Moroccan generals," of whom Franco was one. Yet Germany and Italy, too, had designs on Morocco; and there was the further complication of Hitler's fear of Pétain's reaction. If he took Morocco from France, the Vichy government might cast in its lot with Great Britain, which would then seize Morocco.[16] So Spain's price was too high, and, more than that, both Mussolini and Hitler, having already had a good taste of Franco's bargaining skill, feared, as Italian Foreign Minister Ciano put it in September 1940, that "the demands now put forward by Spain would be constantly increased in the further course of events."[17]

The third period, from February 1941 to June 1941, was the coolest one in Franco's relations with the Axis powers until they actually began to lose the war. His imperial aspirations, fired by the fall of France, had been balked by Germany. Hitler's pact with Stalin still galled him. And

---

14 Feis, cited, pp. 120-128.

15 For discussion of Spain's historic ties with Morocco, see below, Chapters III and IX.

16 Langer and Gleason, cited, p. 659.

17 *Documents on German Foreign Policy* . . . , cited, v. 3: *Germany and The Spanish Civil War* (1950), p. 933.

Mussolini had met with serious checks in North Africa and the Balkans.

Between June and December 1941 Hitler's attack on the Soviet Union made this fourth period, for Franco, one of jubilation comparable to the exultation which followed the fall of France. He could now talk of carrying on his anti-Communist crusade without stultifying himself. The danger of a German march through Spain against Gibraltar, his own plum, was averted, at least for a time, and, since he shared Hitler's confidence that the Soviet Union would soon be knocked out, a victorious termination of the entire war seemed in sight.

In this upsurge of confidence, Franco threw off all pretense of neutrality. On July 17, 1941, after warning the United States to stay out of the war if it wished to avoid a "catastrophe," he continued: "The Allies have lost [the war] . . . German arms are leading the battle . . . in which the blood of our youth is going to be mingled with that of our comrades of the Axis, as a living expression of our solidarity. . . . Our [Spanish National] Movement achieves in the world today an unsuspected vindication." [18] Accordingly, in September of that year Franco sent his Blue Legion of 14,000 "volunteers" to mingle their blood with the Germans' on the Leningrad front.[19] But Franco did not again press his imperial claims on French North Africa; the door was now firmly closed against them by the Vichy government's close collaboration with Hitler.

A fifth period, lasting from December 1941 to November 1942, opened with the entrance of the United States into the war, whereupon Franco shifted from "neutrality" to "nonbelligerency," implying still more active cooperation with the Axis. But the fortunes of the Axis failed to thrive. Mussolini's troubles multiplied, and, worst of all, Hitler's armies,

---

[18] Quoted in Hughes, cited, p. 233.

[19] According to Salvador de Madariaga, *Spain: A Modern History* (New York: Praeger, 1958), p. 577, the Blue Legion lost 8,000 of its men there. The remnant returned to Spain late in 1943. One of the legionnaires, Dionisio Ridruejo, a leading Falangist during the Civil War, broke with Franco soon after his return to Spain (see below, Chapter V).

frozen before the gates of Moscow, had failed to dispose of the Soviet Union in a short and glorious war and were evidently in for a long, grim one. Spain's exposed position, jutting out into the Atlantic, which was controlled by the United States and Britain, made Franco highly sensitive to the changing tides of war. When the Western Allies demonstrated their domination of the Western Mediterranean, as well as of the Atlantic, by their large-scale and successful landing in French North Africa early in November 1942, Franco began to hedge on his commitment to the Axis. Henceforth his energies were to be devoted almost impartially to working both sides of the street while keeping Spain untouched by war.

"Your Sincere Friend"

The Allied invasion of North Africa was preceded by a diplomatic incident that both illustrates the importance of Morocco to the Allies as well as to Spain and prefigures the American policy that led eventually to the bases agreement of 1953. The expeditionary forces of Great Britain and the United States were to make their landings on both flanks of the Spanish Protectorate, in French Algeria and French Morocco. The Allies knew they might encounter local resistance from the Vichy authorities and, in addition, Rommel's substantial German and Italian forces in and near Tunisia were too close for comfort. It was important, therefore, to the Allies that the Spanish army in Morocco, which now numbered about 150,000, should be neutralized. More than that could not be hoped for. Spain was tied to the Axis and awed by substantial German forces poised along her Pyrenees frontier; she had also developed close relations with Vichy on the basis of the personal friendship between Franco and Marshal Henri Pétain, who had been, in 1939-1940, the first French ambassador to Franco Spain.

In these circumstances Washington planners considered the possibility of seizing Spain's Canary Islands as a precautionary measure, but the American Ambassador at Madrid,

Carlton J. H. Hayes, protested "as energetically as [he] knew how" to President Roosevelt that this would be sure to "embroil us with Spain." [20] In the end, the first of two neutralizing devices chosen was modeled on one just employed at Madrid by Great Britain.[21] It took the form of a friendly and reassuring communication from President Roosevelt to General Franco, transmitted by Ambassador Hayes in writing to the Spanish Foreign Minister on November 2, 1942, six days before the Allied landings in North Africa began. The note not only pledged the United States to "take no action of any sort which would in any way violate Spanish territory." More than this, alluding to recent denunciations of the Franco regime in the American press, the note went on to say that the U.S. government "strongly deprecates any activities by purely private organizations or individuals within the United States which would seem intended to prejudice the growth of good feeling between the Spanish people and the people of the United States." [22]

This was quickly reinforced by a second neutralizing measure. On November 8, the day the North African landings began, Ambassador Hayes handed Franco a letter from President Roosevelt explaining that the operations were intended to forestall the military occupation of French North Africa by Germany and Italy. It began by stating that "your nation and mine are friends in the best sense of the word" and that "you and I are sincerely desirous of the continuation of that friendship for our mutual good," and concluded:

I hope you will accept my full assurance that these moves are in no shape, manner, or form directed against the Government or people of Spain or Spanish Morocco or Spanish territories—metropolitan or overseas. I believe the Spanish Government and the Spanish people wish to maintain neutrality and to remain outside the war. Spain has nothing to fear from the United Nations.

20 Carlton J. H. Hayes, *Wartime Mission in Spain, 1942-1945* (New York: Macmillan, 1945), p. 87.

21 *Memoirs of Cordell Hull*, v. 2 (New York: Macmillan, 1948), pp. 1190-1191. See also Doussinague, cited, pp. 70-74.

22 Hayes, cited, p. 88.

The salutation of the letter was, "Dear General Franco"; the valedictory, "I am, my dear General, your sincere friend." [23]

The purpose of these communications is what makes them germane to our present theme. Their purpose was to immobilize the 150,000 Spanish troops in Morocco and to forestall a Spanish attack on Gibraltar while the North African operation was being carried out. Hostile action on Spain's part was regarded as unlikely unless the operation failed, for Franco had passed up his best opportunity to attack Gibraltar in 1940 and 1941, when Britain faced the Axis alone. Yet, as General Dwight D. Eisenhower advised Washington in September 1942, if Spain should enter the war at this stage the results would be "most serious." [24] Hence the eventuality, however unlikely, must be guarded against.

Roosevelt's two communications to Franco therefore reflect a decision to give military considerations priority over political factors. In this sense they prefigured the position that was to be taken a decade later in concluding the bases agreement with the same regime. To be sure, by 1953 circumstances had changed in important ways: the war was now cold, not hot, and Franco's active cooperation, not his neutrality, was now sought. But essentially the policy decision was based on similar choices.

Did Franco foresee some new turn of this kind when, with the approach of victory in 1945, the United States for a time took a very different tack and joined in ostracizing Franco's regime? Was he confident that the wheel of U.S. policy would come full circle when another world crisis impended, as he was sure it soon would? We may never know the answer to

23 Same, p. 91. Similar friendly expressions were deleted from Roosevelt's letter to Marshal Pétain about "Torch"; Robert E. Sherwood, *Roosevelt and Hopkins: An Intimate History* (New York: Harper, 1948), pp. 644-648.

24 Dwight D. Eisenhower, *Crusade in Europe* (New York: Doubleday, 1948), pp. 92-93. Churchill thought it "reasonable to assume that Spain will not go to war with Britain and the United States on account of 'Torch,'" but was uneasy about what Germany might do through Spain; Winston S. Churchill, *The Second World War*, v. 4: *The Hinge of Fate* (Cambridge: Houghton Mifflin, 1950), pp. 528, 544, 596.

these questions, but we do know that Franco is a shrewd man, with a long memory and inexhaustible patience. As he pondered the problems of his ostracism in the withdrawn quietude of the Pardo Palace in his darkest years, just after the defeat of the Axis, he had reason to take heart for the future as he recalled President Roosevelt's communications of November 1942 and the policy imperatives that had so obviously dictated them.

Through Neutrality towards Strict Neutrality

For our purposes there is not much that needs to be said about the rest of the war period. On the American side the main lines of policy fixed by the end of 1942 were pursued until victory hove in sight, and the main concern was to implement the purpose of keeping Spain out of the war and reducing her usefulness to Germany. Spain's policy tended reluctantly towards the same result, but her task was more complicated, for two reasons. In the first place, while the tide seemed to have turned against the Axis, even after Italy was invaded and Mussolini ousted in 1943, belief in Germany's invincibility died hard. And until the Allied landing in Normandy, in June 1944, Hitler's forces stationed along the Pyrenees were a warning not to stray too far from the Axis camp. In the second place, what was to be done about Spain after the war was, to the Allies, a relatively minor question and one that could be taken care of in due course, whereas for the Franco regime it might be a matter of life or death.

In these circumstances, until the liberation of France reduced Spain's significance in the war to the vanishing-point, Washington's main concern was with such matters as manipulating the flow of oil to Spain as a means of shutting off the shipment of strategic materials, especially wolfram, to Germany.[25] Success in the control of Spanish trade was not fully

---

25 Wolfram, the source of tungsten, is used for making gun barrels, cutting tools, armor plate, and armor-piercing projectiles. A Spanish scientist, Fausto de Elhuyar, first isolated tungsten in 1784 and Spain has long been an important producer of wolfram.

achieved until the Allied invasion of France had cut the land routes. Whether it could have been achieved earlier through a relentless application of economic pressure on Spain, as was proposed by some on the American side, is a hypothetical question that need not detain us. But it is germane to the present study to note that, in preventing the trial from being made, the most telling argument, advanced by the British government in 1943, was that severe economic pressure might provoke serious internal disorder and even overturn Franco and that no alternative regime in prospect would be better than his.[26] This gloomy, not to say pessimistic, view seems to have communicated itself ultimately to the American side and, by taking permanent lodgement there, to have played no small part in the fashioning of subsequent policy.

The reluctance with which Madrid gradually disengaged itself from the Axis was apparent to all informed persons. The Spanish authorities still made no secret of their wish for an Axis victory. Equally apparent was Franco's determination to get as much as he could from both sides, particularly in the way of obtaining food, fuel, raw materials, and arms. Any head of government ought to do the best he can for his country, but it is worth noting that, when questioned why he was asking for arms, Franco explained that he needed them to maintain internal order and to strengthen Spain against forces that might be unleashed in neighboring countries after the war. Germany complied with his request for arms; at that time the United States turned it down.

Yet some fluctuating progress was made in 1943 towards Spain's disengagement from the Axis. In October Franco retreated by proclamation from nonbelligerency to neutrality. He also tightened his bonds with Portugal by concluding the Iberian Pact with Salazar. In view of Portugal's long-standing association with Great Britain and with Brazil, the only Latin American country to send an expeditionary force to Europe to fight the Axis, the conclusion of this pact seemed a definite

---

[26] Feis, cited, pp. 216-217.

step away from what remained of the Axis. So Hitler apparently regarded it, for almost at once he recalled his ambassador from Madrid.[27] Franco in turn recalled the remnant of the Blue Division to Spain.

Since Franco was following his usual equivocal course, there were items on the other side of the ledger as well. The one that attracted most attention was the so-called Laurel incident of October 1943, which took its name from the head of a Japanese puppet government set up in the Philippines; the incident was created by the sending of a cable from the Spanish Foreign Office congratulating Señor Laurel on his elevation. This action seemed a deliberate affront to the Allies, particularly the United States, but it has been plausibly explained away as a trick played on the Spanish Foreign Minister, who was well disposed towards the Allies, by some of his associates in the government, who were not.[28] In any case, the affair is significant rather as an indication of once-imperial Spain's continuing interest in world affairs and especially in the affairs of her former dominions, though in this case the congratulations to a puppet imposed by an Asian power were not easy to square with the official cult of Hispanidad.

Franco Courts Washington and Downing Street

In the judgment of Ambassador Hayes, Spain's neutrality had become positively benevolent towards the Allies by the spring of 1944. In stating this view he emphasized the fact that Spain reached the stage of benevolence "before we had gained any remarkable military success in Europe." [29] Whether or not this appraisal of the military situation does justice to the strength of the Allies' position at that time, the fact remains that, after the Allies' victories in France and Italy in the summer of that year, Franco's attitude towards them evolved rapidly and favorably.

27 Hughes, cited, pp. 256-257.
28 Same, pp. 259-260.
29 Cited, p. 239.

By December the evolution of the new attitude was complete and it found expression in overtures to both the United States and Great Britain. But before we examine them, let us take note of three other factors, in addition to the impending defeat of Germany, that doubtless helped to shape the Spanish government's new attitude. First, the liberation of Paris in August 1944 had brought Franco face to face with a very serious threat. Liberated France was sure to be hostile to his regime because of his close ties with Vichy as well as Hitler, and the scores of thousands of Spanish Republican refugees still living in southern France close to his borders were a special source of danger to him. In the second place, in August and September the Dumbarton Oaks meeting of the four principal Allies had laid the groundwork for a United Nations organization which was to be completed the following year. Here was another potential threat. The Soviet Union was sure to make whatever use it could of the new organization against Franco's regime, and the other principal powers were only too likely to follow suit unless Franco could find some way of disarming their hostility. In the third place, Franco was encouraged to make the effort by the "kind word" Winston Churchill had risen in the House of Commons on May 24, 1944, to speak about Spain and had expanded into many words and a tribute to Franco for not having done more to aid the Axis when things were going worst for the Allies. "I look forward to increasingly good relations with Spain," said Churchill, "and an extremely fertile trade between Spain and this country. . . ." [30]

With this encouragement, and under the prodding of the threats that were taking shape in liberated France, Franco's government bestirred itself to win favor among the victors. Its overtures were addressed not only to Great Britain, from which the encouragement had come, but also to the United States. True, Washington had not echoed Churchill's soft words of May 24 about Franco, but it had addressed him with kind words of its own in November 1942. In general,

---

[30] Quoted in Feis, cited, p. 254.

since the beginning of the Spanish Civil War it had generally developed its Spanish policy in concert with Britain and had even shown a certain deference towards the British as more expert in Spanish affairs and more deeply affected by them. Moreover, in November 1944 Spanish delegates had taken part in two international meetings in the United States—an unofficial business conference at Rye, New York, and a technical civil aviation conference at Chicago—and returned with "sincere and high appreciation . . . of the courtesies shown them" in the United States.[31]

Franco's overture to Great Britain was made in a letter to Churchill of October 18, 1944.[32] It took the form of a bid for Anglo-Spanish cooperation in defending Western Europe against Communist Russia, basing its bid on the calm assumption that Spain was a tower of strength for that purpose. Warning that the good faith of Communist Russia could not be trusted and that it was more necessary now than ever to unite the countries of Western Europe against "the insidious power of Bolshevism," Franco continued: "After the terrible test to which the European nations have been put," he told Churchill, "only three, among those of sizable population and resources, have stood out as being stronger and more virile: England, Germany, and Spain. But with Germany crushed, only one nation remains to whom England may turn: Spain." [33] Churchill rejected the proposal out of hand and stated that the British government based its policy firmly on the Anglo-Soviet treaty of 1942 and looked forward to permanent collaboration with the Soviet Union in the frame-

---

[31] Hayes, cited, p. 270.

[32] Franco's letter and Churchill's reply (undated) are printed in Samuel John Gurney Hoare, First Viscount Templewood, *Complacent Dictator* (New York: Knopf, 1947), Appendix A, pp. 305-310. Hoare was British ambassador to Spain at this time.

[33] Quoted in Vicente Girbau, "The Foreign Policy of Franco Spain (I)," *Ibérica* (New York), September 15, 1959, p. 4 (where the letter is erroneously dated December 8), and Alberto Martín Artajo, *Les Accords avec les Etats-Unis: Texte complet du discours prononcé par le Ministre des Affaires Etrangères M. Alberto Martín Artajo, au cours de la Séance Plénière des Cortès Espagnoles, le 30 Novembre, 1953* (Madrid: Bureau d'Information Diplomatique, 1953), p. 11.

work of the world organization then in process of formation.

Franco's Foreign Minister, José Félix de Lequerica, next sought a *rapprochement* with the United States through conversations with Ambassador Hayes, who was about to conclude his mission and return to the United States.[34] The terms of this overture were different. For one thing, they were more concrete and they were remarkably prophetic of the pact finally entered into in 1953. On December 5, 1944, when Hayes called on Lequerica to obtain Spain's *agrément* to the appointment of Norman Armour as his successor, Lequerica seized the opportunity to "expatiate upon his favorite theme, the desirability of the United States and Spain drawing together." The United States, said Lequerica, was "now obviously the greatest military nation in the world" and, if it was to play the proper postwar role, "it should realistically utilize Spain as a special bulwark in Europe." He contemplated the establishment of "special understandings between the United States and Spain—economic, political, military."

Any such "special understandings," Lequerica specified, should be "arrived at within the framework of any world organization that might be established after the war." This, together with the omission of any call to arms against the Soviet Union, differentiated the new approach to the United States from the one that had been rebuffed by Churchill. It also implied that the United States had a special interest in getting Spain admitted to the new world organization. Lequerica even pictured Spain as desiring to "play its part in discouraging any possible friction between North America and South America," that is, between the United States and Latin America. The versatility manifested by this last proposition was matchless, for, as long as it dared, the Franco regime had done its utmost, through the Hispanidad program, to turn Latin America against the United States.

Though not accepted by the United States any more than by Great Britain, these overtures represent the policy ad-

---

34 Hayes, cited, pp. 286-288.

hered to by Franco through the last phase of the war, for he had no alternative. Thus the dictator who had begun as a suitor to the Axis ended up a suitor to the powers that he had offered to help the Axis destroy. That his regime was not ground to pieces along with those of Mussolini and Hitler must be set down to his good management as well as good luck.

Franco's good luck consisted partly in the character of the victorious Allies, who did not punish him ruthlessly, as Hitler would have done if all the roles had been reversed. It consisted partly also in circumstances beyond Franco's control that gave him a small but adequate space for maneuver in his dealings with Hitler. These circumstances were the geographical, military, and other factors that had made it too risky for Hitler to dragoon Spain into the war against Franco's will and thus permitted him some freedom of choice.

Franco's good management consisted in the skill and prudence with which he exploited these slender opportunities. There is no doubt that he was as enthusiastic for the Axis as he could be for anything and that he would have entered the war on its side at the drop of a hat if he could have been reasonably sure of waging a short, glorious, and profitable war. But the Caudillo never let his enthusiasm run away with him. His course was coolly calculated and his calculations were based at least as much on the domestic situation in Spain as on external factors.

On the home front the decisive consideration was that he was the ruler of a deeply divided country; most of his subjects were a conquered people. This, even more than the exhaustion of the Civil War, was why any war he fought outside the peninsula must be short and glorious. If the troops he needed to maintain order at home were sent outside the peninsula and then became bogged down in a long war, he might have to cope with an uprising within Spain, especially if the Allies made a landing in Portugal or on his own weakly fortified and extensive coastline, along the lines of Wellington's Peninsular War against Napoleon. On the other hand,

the character of the faction that supported him in Spain
dictated the terms and conditions on which alone he would
dare enter the war. In the ideology of his regime two dominant strains were imperialism and nationalism: an imperialism, or "renewed will to empire," which could find its outlet
only in North Africa, a traditional focus of the Spanish "will
to empire" since the days of Ferdinand and Isabella; and
a nationalism which boggled at the thought of serving under
German or Italian command anywhere, especially in the
peninsula and against Gibraltar, and tolerated it, even in the
case of the Blue Division, only in repayment of the regime's
"blood debt" to the Axis.

The stiff terms that Franco set in June 1940 for Spain's
participation in the war are explained by these considerations, rather than by any supposed desire to conceal his peace
policy behind an impossibly high price tag. He was not reluctant, but eager, to enter the war on his own terms *at that
time*, for it gave every promise then of being the kind of war
he wanted and the only kind he could afford: short, glorious,
and profitable. But time was indeed of the essence. Soon
after Hitler's second thoughts about Italy and Vichy France
barred his acceptance of these terms, Franco decided that,
after all, the war might be a long one. From that moment
on he would have none of it. He had sense enough to see
that ultimate ruin faced him if the Axis lost, but he also saw
that he ran a great risk of hastening his ruin at home if he
jumped into the struggle prematurely. So he continued to
give the Axis all the aid he dared, short of war, until its cause
seemed lost, whereupon he shifted the "benevolence" of his
neutrality to the winning side, confident that this, together
with the usual inhibitions of democratic governments, would
save him from reprisal in their hour of victory.

One of the shortest but most revealing stories ever told
about Franco bears on this theme. In the summer of 1943,
when the tide had clearly begun to turn against the Axis,
one of Franco's closest friends asked him if he was not worried over what might happen to his regime if the Allies won.
Not at all, he said. Then what attitude would he take

towards the Allies? *"Pasar la cuenta,"* he calmly replied, "I'll hand them the bill"—the bill for his "services" to the Allies in denying Germany access to Spain for an attack on Gibraltar in 1940, and in not interfering with the Allies' North African campaign in 1942.[35] That such services were rendered, and should be paid for, became one of the most persistent myths—and talking-points—of the regime in later years, and was not without believers in other lands as well.

Ostracism

Instead of being taken into partnership by the United States and Great Britain and admitted to membership in the new general international organization, after the close of the war Franco Spain underwent an ostracism that was almost complete for two years; its effects are still reflected in the exclusion of Spain from NATO. The general conference that adopted the United Nations Charter at San Francisco in June 1945 also excluded Spain from membership. The great power conference at Potsdam adopted a similar resolution in July. At its first meeting the General Assembly of the United Nations endorsed this action, and at its second meeting the General Assembly adopted (December 12, 1946) a resolution recommending that its members recall their chiefs of mission from Madrid. Almost all of them, including all the principal powers, did so.[36] Despite Churchill's kind words about Spain in his speech of May 1944, even Great Britain, governed by a Labor government after July 1945, supported all these measures, and the United States did likewise. France and the Soviet Union called for still stronger action. This was not taken through United Nations channels, but on March 4, 1946, the United States, Britain, and France joined in a Tripartite Declaration which stated that the Spanish people

---

35 Hughes, cited, p. 269, says he got this story from a friend of Franco. Hughes was in charge of the information service at the American embassy in Madrid at the time.

36 The important role of the Latin American states, both in the adoption of the United Nations measures and in their subsequent abandonment, is discussed below, Chapter IX.

could not look forward to "full and cordial association" with them and their allies so long as Franco remained in control of Spain.[37] Like all the other measures, this one was aimed at encouraging a liberalization of that regime and a purging of its Nazi-Fascist elements.

Since the United States began to deviate substantially from this course in 1947, and had reversed it by 1952, the reader may wonder both why it was adopted in the first place and why it was later changed. Both questions are especially interesting because the same party and the same President were in office throughout the period from the adoption of ostracism in 1945 to the opening of the base negotiation in April 1952. Neither question can be answered fully here, partly because both are too complex for adequate discussion in a brief compass, partly because some of the most important records are not yet accessible.

As to the original policy of ostracism, however, the main reasons for its adoption by the United States seem to be clear beyond reasonable doubt. To begin with a negative proposition, we can disregard as preposterous the allegation that the ostracism of Franco Spain represented appeasement of the Soviet Union and that the United States was misled into joining in the policy by Communist agents and sympathizers who had infiltrated the government in Washington.[38] Not a shred of evidence has been offered in support of it. To appreciate its absurdity one need only recall that the leading exponent of anti-Franco feeling in the government was President Truman, who has never been accused of Communist sympathies and who had a special interest in the Spanish question. As will appear below, he subsequently abandoned the policy only because he concluded that it was the wrong way of doing the right thing.

On the positive side, the U.S. government's adherence to the policy of ostracism can be explained in terms of two kinds

---

37 Hughes, cited, p. 283.

38 This allegation was stressed by Spain's Foreign Minister Martín Artajo in presenting the bases agreements of 1953 to the Cortes. See below, Chapter II.

of pressure, one from its own people, the other from its allies and associates in Europe. During the Spanish Civil War public opinion in the United States about the Franco regime was divided, but a large and respectable body of it never wavered in the view that Franco was a tool of the Axis and the Civil War an Axis rehearsal for a general war. His record during World War II seemed to confirm this view and gained widespread acceptance for it. Washington's wartime dealings with him, like its Vichy policy, were barely tolerated by many influential segments of opinion as a matter of military necessity.

Relieved of that necessity by victory in 1945 and not faced by another until the outbreak of the cold war nearly two years later, the United States felt secure enough to carry out an extensive unilateral demobilization and to press for the liquidating of the remaining pro-Axis regimes, which included Juan Perón's in Argentina as well as Franco's in Spain. That these should be liquidated if the victory over the Axis was to be complete was generally agreed. The traditional U.S. policy of nonintervention inhibited direct action but not ostracism. As regarded Spain, the policy was adopted with general public support, which had no Communist inspiration and needed none. Many liberals only regretted that more could not be done to rid Europe of an odious dictatorship that had been set up with the direct support of Hitler and Mussolini.

Strong pressure in the same direction came from Europe itself. In liberated France, De Gaulle's government had taken a strong anti-Franco line from the start. In Britain, the leaders of the Labor government that replaced Churchill's Conservative cabinet while the Potsdam Conference was still in session took a less indulgent view of Franco's Axis associations. Indeed, just after the Labor party's victory one of its chief policy-makers, Harold Laski, threatened Franco with direct intervention. As it turned out, Laski's associates were unwilling to go to that extreme, but they gave ostracism far stronger support than it would have received from Churchill, and they persevered in that spirit long after the letter of the policy had been eroded and even after Washington had taken Franco to its bosom. The same anti-Franco line was followed by the smaller European countries; it was pursued most un-flaggingly by those that had been under the heel of Franco's comrade Hitler and in which the Socialist parties were strongest. This offers further disproof of the notion that Franco was ostracized in 1945 in order to appease the Soviet Union, for the West European Socialist parties have been among the sturdiest opponents of communism and of Soviet expansion.

The strong antagonism which most of Western Europe felt towards the Franco regime just after the war almost certainly helped to put starch into the United States' attitude towards Madrid, for in those days Washington was inclined to follow the lead of Spain's neighbors, especially France and Britain. in shaping its own Spanish policy. It had done so to a great extent during the Spanish Civil War, as Cordell Hull's memoirs show,[39] and to a lesser but still considerable extent during World War II. And as late as 1948 Acting Secretary of State Robert A. Lovett told a press conference that the government's attitude towards the exclusion of Spain from the Marshall Plan had been influenced by the wishes of Great Britain and France, whose interest in Spain was considerably greater than that of the United States.[40] Only after the beginning of the Korean War in 1950 did Washing-ton develop an independent policy towards Spain, different from and opposed to that of its principal European associates.

What Was Wrong with Ostracism?

There was just one fly in the attractively packaged demo-cratic ointment of ostracism, but that was enough to spoil the lot: the means could hardly have been worse adapted to the end. As stated most explicitly in the Tripartite Declara-tion of March 4, 1946, Spain's imposed isolation was designed to bring about "a peaceful withdrawal of Franco, the aboli-

---

39 *Memoirs of Cordell Hull,* cited, v. 1, pp. 481-482.
40 U.S. Department of State, Press Release, April 2, 1948.

tion of the Falange, and the establishment of an interim or caretaker government under which the Spanish people may have an opportunity freely to determine the type of government they wish to have and to choose their leaders. . . ." Nothing effective was done to back up this declaration. France closed the Pyrenees border (as Spain had already done a few days earlier) and, later, Spain was excluded from Marshall Plan aid, but whatever penalty this imposed was borne by the Spanish masses, not by Franco and his cohorts, who would be the last people in Spain to suffer privation. And if hard times led ultimately to a revolt, that would defeat a stated objective of the declaration, which was to achieve a change of government without again subjecting the Spanish people to "the horrors and bitterness of civil strife."

But how then would the "peaceful withdrawal" of Franco and the abolition of the Falange be brought about? There had been no slightest suggestion on the part of either Franco or the Falange that they might quit voluntarily, whereas the declaration made it clear that the three powers were not going to do anything further to get them out: "There is no intention," it said, "of interfering in the internal affairs of Spain." In short, this was simply an invitation to the subjects of an iron-handed, quasi-totalitarian regime to make a peaceful revolution, and an implied injunction to the Spanish power groups who were the supporters and beneficiaries of that regime to let themselves be dispossessed without striking a blow. And dispossession would be only the beginning of their woes, if one could judge by what was happening to former Fascists, Nazis, and collaborators all over Europe at that very time.

This kind of ostracism was not only fatuous; it was, to use a handy Spanish term, *contraproducente,* that is, it produced an effect opposite to the one intended. In short, it backfired. Instead of weakening, it strengthened Franco's hold on Spain. And the worst of it is that a complete misunderstanding of the way it strengthened him has created a legend within a myth that ever since has distorted and crippled the policies of other countries, including the United States, to Franco's further advantage. The legend is that the whole Spanish nation, incensed at Franco's ostracism, rallied to his defense in protest against this foreign meddling in Spanish affairs. The myth that cradles this legend is that the Spanish people have always been this way: no matter how much they may have fought among themselves, their fights are private and whenever an outsider tries to interfere, they always lay aside their differences and make common cause to drive him out.

This myth is arrant nonsense, and how it can be parroted by anyone who knows anything about the Spain of Franco's generation passes all understanding. Its falsity is proved to demonstration by the history of the Spanish Civil War. That started as a private fight, a civil war that was as completely Spanish as the nineteenth-century Carlist Wars; but immediately both sides moved heaven and earth to get all the foreign aid they could lay their hands on. And far from being new, this invocation of foreign aid to settle an internecine quarrel is one of the oldest and most familiar traits of Spanish history. Madariaga's name for it, "Don Julianism," suggests its antiquity, for Don Julián was the legendary Spaniard (Visigoth) who in 711 A.D. called in the Arabs from North Africa to help him right a local wrong, and thus opened Spain to Moorish conquest.[41] And modern instances abound.

The legend of the spontaneous national rally against Franco's ostracism is an equally hollow shell. Mass protests against it were staged in Madrid and other cities of Spain, but they meant nothing except that the production managers of Franco's political theater were doing their jobs well. Was there ever a time when a Hitler, a Mussolini, a Perón, or a Franco was not able to set up mass demonstrations for whatever purpose he pleased?

The fact is that Franco's ostracism tightened his hold over the groups already committed to him by making it clear that their fate was bound up with his, so that they must stand or fall with him. It was no monolithic mass over which he

---

41 Salvador de Madariaga, *The Fall of the Spanish American Empire* (New York: Macmillan, 1948), p. 195.

ruled, but a faction-ridden aggregation of power groups, like every Spanish regime of which we have any record. Even the Falange, misinterpreted abroad as the chief integrating force of a close-knit totalitarian regime, was itself still split into the factions that Franco had forced together in a shotgun wedding in 1937,[42] and others had split off since then. As Franco faced the unknown perils of the hostile postwar world in 1945, what he needed most of all was a rallying-cry to unite his disjointed forces against the subjugated other half of Spain, the forces described by him as Anti-Spain, which were still beaten and broken by the Civil War, but which at least had the advantage of a common cause in their defeat. Now, thanks to the way in which his ostracism had been mishandled, Franco was given that rallying-cry: the defense of Spain against foreign intrusion. With this device on his pennon, the Nationalist leader of Civil War days could safely ride again without fear of being unhorsed by the hosts of Anti-Spain around him, who liked him no better now than when they had fought him in the Civil War.

But the legend, which his regime has propagated sedulously, that all Spain had rallied to his side, has gained wide acceptance abroad. It is sustained by, and in turn sustains, belief in the myth that all Spaniards have always closed ranks against any foreign intruder. From this belief it is only a short step, easily and frequently taken, to assuming that they will always do so, and to basing policies towards Spain on this assumption.

Ostracism Revoked

Of the two United Nations actions against the Franco regime, the resolution recommending the recall of chiefs of mission from Madrid was not repealed until 1950, and another five years elapsed after that before Spain was admitted to membership in the United Nations as part of the famous "package deal" that brought in sixteen new members at one time. But even before the first of these bans was lifted there

---

42 See Chapter III.

had been many signs that the will to enforce Spain's ostracism was weakening, particularly in the United States and Latin America.

Franco, ever alert, was prepared to profit by the change. On the home front he took two steps in 1945 to blunt the edge of foreign criticism of his regime without making any real change in its nature. One step was his issuance, through his obedient Cortes or pseudo-parliament, of a "Spanish Bill of Rights" (Fuero de los Españoles). To give the gesture maximum publicity, the charter was promulgated on July 18, the anniversary of the beginning of the Civil War. It was an empty gesture, for the charter has been a dead letter from the start, but its emptiness was not apparent to foreigners for some time. His other step was a reorganization of his cabinet that shifted its emphasis from the totalitarian Falange to the more moderate Catholic Action group headed by Alberto Martín Artajo, the new Minister of Foreign Affairs.

This change was well calculated to make a favorable impression abroad, for the Falange, whose power was greatly exaggerated by most foreign observers, was regarded as the quintessence of totalitarianism of the Nazi-Fascist brand, whereas Martín Artajo represented Spanish Catholic elements vaguely akin to the Christian Democrats who were emerging as one of the principal political groups in postwar France, Italy, and West Germany. Actually, the shift involved in this cabinet reorganization was more apparent than real, for control still remained in Franco's hands, where it had always been firmly lodged. Nor was anything changed by the adoption in 1947 of the Act of Succession, which committed Franco for the first time to the ultimate restoration of the monarchy, for Spain remained indefinitely a kingdom without a king; Franco's powers were as great as ever, and indeed were confirmed by the adoption of this act.

In the field of foreign relations, even in the darkest days just after the war, when Spain's only friends were Portugal and Argentina, good use was made of the ties with them to assuage the hostility of Latin America, which had presented a solid front against Franco's regime at the United Nations

Conference in San Francisco. To this end the Hispanidad program was purged of its most objectionable wartime features and revised to stress its exclusively cultural and wholly irenic character. Moreover, its bias against the United States was converted into a bias in favor of the United States by broadening its objective to a spiritual *rapprochement* between Spain and *all* the nations of the new world. With the aid of the Institute of Hispanic Culture this expurgated edition of Hispanidad (the name remained unchanged) was earnestly and effectively disseminated by the new Foreign Minister, Martín Artajo, from beginning to end of his twelve-year ministry.[43] For a more direct approach to the United States in the interest of the more practical kinds of cooperation—political, economic, military—prematurely broached by Lequerica to Hayes in December 1944, Franco bided his time patiently, waiting for the postwar storm to pass.

Franco did not have long to wait. When a proposal to re-affirm the resolution of December 1946 on the recall of ambassadors from Madrid came before the General Assembly of the United Nations one year later, the United States took the lead in defeating it. To be sure, Washington held that the original resolution was still binding and continued to act accordingly. Besides leaving its embassy in Madrid without an ambassador, it withheld government grants and all other forms of assistance to Spain, prohibited sales of surplus government property to Spanish buyers, and cut its own purchases in Spain to the barest essentials. Moreover, this official policy naturally discouraged private banks and commercial firms in the United States from making loans or extending credits to Spain, and thus added to the latter's economic woes. Yet the failure of the effort to reaffirm the diplomatic sanction of 1946 enabled the Spanish government to contend, as it did with great force, that the ban against

---

[43] A collection of his speeches during the first decade is contained in *Hacia la comunidad hispánica de naciones: Discursos . . . desde 1945 a 1955* (Madrid: Ediciones Cultura Hispánica, 1956). The Preface, p. 8, states that this Hispanic community of nations is not opposed in any way either to inter-American solidarity or to Spain's role in Europe and the world at large.

it had in effect been lifted. Whether it believed this or not, it regarded the failure as the beginning of the end of its ostracism and was encouraged to hold on.

There had in fact been an undeclared revision of Washington's policy towards Spain by the autumn of 1947 and it went far beyond the change of front on the question of diplomatic representation in Madrid.[44] Although no authoritative statement of the new policy and the reasons for it has been published, they are believed to have been substantially as follows. The decision to change course was based on the conviction that the policy of ostracism had failed, since its chief results so far had been to strengthen the Franco regime, impede Spain's recovery, and make her cooperation less likely in case of another general war. Moreover, while a peaceful change of regime was still highly desirable from the point of view of the United States, it no longer seemed feasible since the Spanish opposition groups, both at home and abroad, now appeared to be divided among themselves and ineffectual. Consequently, it was decided to try a new tack: the United States would henceforth seek to normalize its political and economic relations with Spain and provide it with an opportunity to rehabilitate its shattered economy, develop its resources, and play its normal part in a general revival of international economic relations. But Washington would not have to bear the whole burden, for its new policy could be expected to stimulate private trade and credits for the building up of Spain.

Why this sudden softening towards Spain? What factors were responsible for it? And did the stress on the rehabilitation of the Spanish economy indicate a desire to include Spain in the Marshall Plan, which was then in process of adoption? Again we can only grope, for lack of official light, but the answers are not wholly obscure. The answer to the first question lies largely in the fact that by this time—the

---

44 Harry S. Truman's *Memoirs* (New York: Doubleday, 1955-1956; 2 v.), throw no light either on this revision or on the subsequent development of U.S. policy towards Spain to the end of the Truman administration in 1953.

autumn of 1947—the United States was in the thick of the cold war. Early in the year the Truman Doctrine had been proclaimed; [45] then Germany's partition was recognized as a fact of postwar life; shortly after that the rival Soviet and Western blocs were crystallized by the announcement of the Marshall Plan and Moscow's refusal to let its East European satellites participate in it; and in October the United States joined with Latin America in concluding the Inter-American Treaty of Reciprocal Assistance (the Rio Defense Treaty), which presaged the North Atlantic Treaty and NATO.

In this tense situation strategy took the upper hand over ideology and more weight was given to the help Spain might furnish in the next war than to any hindrance she had offered in the last. In any case, a certain boredom over the issues of World War II had set in. It had already speeded the decision to come to terms with Perón: why not do likewise with Perón's Hispanic cousin Franco, who could be more useful than Perón in the event of a new conflict?

As to who was responsible for the new policy, it was doubtless the work of many hands, but we are probably on safe ground in hazarding the conjecture that it was not the work of the State Department, which appears still to have preferred a Spanish policy conceived in the political terms described by its critics as ideological. The most likely author, it must be assumed, was the Pentagon, since it was most directly concerned with the new power challenge. But it also appears that the Pentagon must share the credit with certain members of Congress and with the so-called Spanish lobby in Washington. The history of this lobby remains to be written, but it is said by those who knew them both to have been more effective than the more highly publicized China lobby of that period.

From what we know of the congressional supporters of a softer policy towards the Franco regime, their motivations

---

[45] According to a newspaper report, the Truman Doctrine aroused extraordinary enthusiasm in Spain; John C. Campbell, *The United States in World Affairs, 1947-1948* (New York: Harper, for the Council on Foreign Relations, 1948), p. 38.

seem to have been religious, humanitarian, social, and economic, as well as military, but not political-ideological. The group, which numbered among its more active members Senator Pat McCarran and Representative A. E. O'Konski, represented in large part an influential Catholic view of the Spanish situation. The appointment of a Catholic lay leader of Martín Artajo's type to the headship of the Spanish cabinet was a plausible ground of hope for a softening of the regime. In any case the historic identification of Spain with Catholicism made the wretched lot of the Spanish masses a matter of special concern to charitable American Catholics. Their solicitude over it could hardly have been lessened by Franco's claims as defender of the faith. And whatever the motivation of these various groups, and whichever of them contributed most to the new policy, it is easy to understand why its major emphasis was placed on the economic relief and rehabilitation of impoverished Spain, for that was central to the realization of any and all their purposes, whether military, political, religious, or merely eleemosynary.

From Marshall Plan to Korean War

Though we cannot be certain, it seems probable that Spain's inclusion in the Marshall Plan was expected by Washington. At any rate, it was expected by Madrid, for the controlled press there talked about it as if it was "in the bag," and the Spanish government drew up optimistic plans for its use, together with a grim account of the nation's needs as a justification of its claims. According to this account, Spain's Civil War losses, which World War II had prevented her from making up, included two-thirds of the nation's transport, one-third of its merchant marine, and virtually all of its consumer goods, raw materials, and gold reserves; and, in addition, a terrific loss of manpower: one million killed and another half million in self-imposed exile. Moreover, since the war Spain had had to use all available foreign exchange for essential consumer goods and hence had been unable to import machinery, fertilizers, and other items

needed for recovery; as a consequence she had lost foreign
markets, with the foreign exchange they had produced, and
her situation was going from bad to worse. In order to cope
with this situation Madrid first asked for $451 million in
Marshall Plan aid for the first year but on second thought
raised the figure to $676 million.

Not a cent of Marshall Plan aid went to Spain. Its distribution was left by the United States primarily to its wartime
European associates to determine, and when they drew up
their European Recovery Plan (ERP), for this purpose, they
excluded Spain. Subsequently, on the initiative of Congress-
man O'Konski, the House of Representatives voted to impose
Spain's participation on the Economic Cooperation Administration (ECA), which had been set up to administer the
plan; but President Truman protested and the Senate up-
held him.[46] Already, however, Spain's situation had been
alleviated somewhat by two measures, both announced in
May 1948; their combined effect was described with considerable exaggeration as bringing Spain into ERP by the back
door.[47] One measure was a commercial agreement that re-
opened and regularized trade between Spain and France,
which was important to both nations. The other was an
agreement with the United States, Britain, and France for
the liquidation of German holdings in Spain amounting to
about $55 million.

These steps gave the Spanish authorities some encouragement. They derived much more from the multiplying signs
of a further thaw in the attitude of the United States. One
that particularly pleased them they found in the O'Konski
incident, mentioned above. They chose to regard the House
of Representatives, which had voted for the action in favor
of Spain, as expressing public opinion in the United States
more accurately and authoritatively than the Senate and the
President, who had blocked the House on this occasion. The

---

[46] William Adams Brown, Jr., and Redvers Opie, *American Foreign
Assistance* (Washington: Brookings Institution, 1953), pp. 149-150.
[47] *The Christian Science Monitor*, May 14, 1948.

other two, they were sure, would ultimately have to yield to the House and to public opinion.

This sanguine Spanish view gained plausibility from the multiplying visits of American legislators, businessmen, and diplomats to Spain. Among them were Senator Chan Gurney, Eric Johnston of the motion picture industry, James Farley of Coca-Cola, and Myron Taylor, whose visit to Madrid aroused special interest because of his long service as personal envoy of the President of the United States to the Vatican.

By 1948 these expressions of growing interest in Spain had produced two important results. In the first place, as an American observer in Madrid put it, "all this whoopla has made ineffectual (if they ever had any effect)" the efforts of the U.S. government "to encourage the adoption by the Spanish regime of liberalizing measures which would tend to bring Spain more in line with the political thinking and concept of the West." In the second place, the impression became widespread that the United States was moving towards an accord with Spain and that the Pentagon, though not making a public display of its role, was nevertheless a chief promoter of the movement. "In Washington," the Paris newspaper *Le Monde* told its readers in April 1948, after the flurry over Spain's exclusion from the Marshall Plan died down,

it is believed that the interest of the United States in the Spanish problem has not diminished, and it is asserted that Myron Taylor's visit to Spain is closely linked with this interest. The U.S. Department of National Defense attaches too much importance to Spain to allow the question of Franco to remain in abeyance and it will be brought up again in the near future.[48]

General Franco himself gave great encouragement both to the rumors about a movement towards a Spanish-American accord and to the movement itself. In July 1947 he said in an interview with an International News Service correspondent that Spain would be a better bastion of Western defense than France and that the United States could obtain the use

---

[48] April 7, 1948; report from its Washington correspondent.

of Spanish bases if it tried hard enough.[49] A year later, in an interview with a *New York Times* correspondent, he spoke in much the same terms, though without specifically raising the question of bases. Two points stood out: first, Franco expressed a decided preference for a direct, bilateral arrangement with the United States to Marshall Plan aid; and, second, he stressed the need for a Western alliance to combat the Soviet menace and affirmed Spain's willingness to participate in such an alliance.[50] The report of this interview as published in the Spanish press included the first of these two points but omitted the second, doubtless because Franco did not want the Spanish public to know that he had made a bid for membership in a multilateral Western alliance, a bid that might be turned down.

Franco was more hopeful of doing business on a bilateral basis with the United States, and he continued to work for this behind the scenes. A week after the *Times* interview just mentioned, an official of the Spanish Foreign Office broached the question of bases to the American embassy, indicating that Spain would be willing to provide the United States with bases in the Canary and Balearic Islands and with unspecified facilities in Spain itself.

This suggestion, which had not been encouraged by the embassy, was not followed up and no further progress was made towards a *rapprochement* between Washington and Madrid until after the beginning of the Korean War in June 1950. Until then, the forces in the United States that favored a new policy were held in check by the opposition headed by President Truman. There can be little question that the opposition was stiffened by the example of the Western European powers' rejection of Franco's bid for association with them in a Western alliance against the Soviet menace. When NATO was formed in 1949 they made a concession to military necessity by admitting Portugal despite the dictatorial character of the Salazar regime—the Azores were an im-

---

49 *The New York Times,* July 20, 1947.
50 Same, November 11, 1948; report of an interview with Franco by C. L. Sulzberger.

portant link in strategic communications—but Spain was excluded, apparently by unanimous consent.

The exclusion of Spain from NATO was based not only on the regime's past record—its Nazi-Fascist origin and wartime associations—but also on its present character. Spain's neighbors found the Franco regime far more odious than Salazar's and incompatible with an organization whose members were committed, by the Preamble of the North Atlantic Treaty, to the defense of "the freedom, common heritage and civilization of their peoples, founded on the principles of democracy, individual liberty and the rule of law," and, by Article 2, to "strengthening their free institutions." By the same reasoning Spain was likewise excluded from the Council of Europe, which was also set up in 1949 and was even more definitely dedicated to the strengthening of democratic principles.

Coming on top of Spain's exclusion from the Marshall Plan, ECA, and the Organization for European Economic Cooperation (OEEC), this Western European quarantine of the Franco regime on strong political grounds arrested the movement for a *rapprochement* between Washington and Madrid. The dismantling of the policy of ostracism continued through 1949 and the first half of 1950, however, as an American squadron visited the Spanish port of El Ferrol and Secretary of State Dean Acheson publicly advocated the repeal of the United Nations resolution on the recall of chiefs of mission from Madrid.[51] Reflecting the milder official mood, two of the largest New York banks, Chase and National City, made loans to the Spanish government, with Spain's gold reserve as security, and Standard Oil invested in a refinery at Escombreras, near the Mediterranean port of Cartagena.

But all this represented only a normalization of relations between the two countries and they might not have gone on to form a special tie but for the outbreak of the Korean War

---

51 On January 18, 1950, Acheson wrote Senator Connally that the United States was ready to support repeal; Richard P. Stebbins, *The United States in World Affairs, 1950* (New York: Harper, for the Council on Foreign Relations, 1951), p. 288.

in June 1950. That put a new face on the Spanish question, for it threatened to bring on a general war and at once shifted the priority from political to military considerations. However unwelcome Franco Spain might be as a political associate, it now seemed desirable and even essential to have the use of bases in Spain.

The Preliminaries of the Bases Agreement

It has often been said that General Franco is a poor strategist but an excellent tactician. Whatever one may think about the first part of this judgment, its second part is amply borne out by his management of the negotiations leading up to the bases agreement of 1953 with the United States. Before the outbreak of the Korean War, as we have seen, it was Franco who courted the United States, and, although Washington remained unresponsive, his overtures, begun in December 1944, were repeated time and again through both public and diplomatic channels. Once he sensed the thirst for oversea bases that was generated in Washington by the Korean crisis, he exchanged his own eagerness for a dignified reserve. Henceforth he let Washington make the advances. From the first preliminaries in July 1951 to the signing of the completed pact two years later, the whole negotiation was carried on in Spain, and the long delay in its completion was due mainly to Franco's insistence on securing better terms, which he finally got.

On the side of the United States this negotiation was part of a quest for oversea bases set off by the demonstration of Stalin's aggressive ambitions in Korea. Bases had already been obtained and "crash programs" of base construction started in French Morocco and several other countries of Africa, Europe, and Asia within bombing distance of the Soviet Union. For this purpose, one special advantage of bases in Spain was the reinsurance they would provide against the instability of France's internal situation. On Spain's part the negotiation represented a response to the need of the Franco regime for material and moral aid in rebuilding the country's shattered economy and gaining some measure of international respectability for itself. For both parties it betokened co-operation in the one major objective that they had in com-mon: resistance to the Communist threat.

The preliminaries began in July 1951 when Admiral Sherman, Chief of Naval Operations, went to Spain on behalf of the Joint Chiefs of Staff for an exploratory discussion of the question of bases with General Franco. Sherman's visit was, of course, made with the approval of President Truman. The motive force behind it came from the Pentagon, and particularly from the navy, which wanted naval facilities in Spain, including a base near Cádiz for its Sixth Fleet. The results of the exploratory talk between Sherman and Franco were mutually satisfactory and the second stage of the pre-liminaries then began with the sending of two technical missions from the United States to Spain. One was military, the other economic, and they were to lay the groundwork for the formal negotiation of a bases agreement.

There was strong but unorganized opposition to the nego-tiation in the United States, but none of a serious character was to be apprehended from Congress. On the contrary, both houses were now ready to do something for Spain even with-out the *quid pro quo* of a bases agreement. The Spanish lobby and its friends in Congress had done their work well. They had been ably seconded by José Félix de Lequerica, who, while foreign minister, had first broached the *rapprochement* idea in December 1944, had been sent to Washington as special envoy in 1948, and had become Spain's ambassador to the United States after the repeal in 1950 of the United Nations resolution on the recall of chiefs of mission. After earlier measures on behalf of Spain had been checked in one way or another, both houses late in 1950 approved an act appropriating $62.5 million for aid to Spain.[52] President Truman, still unsympathetic, interpreted this as merely an authorization, not a directive, but the funds were advanced to

---

52 Brown and Opie, cited, pp. 423-424: "Spain thus became the only European country to receive assistance through the ECA without having asked for it and without having to sign a bilateral agreement."

Spain by the Export-Import Bank in the course of the next few years. At any rate Congress had shown that it was well disposed.

On the other hand, the prospect of a military agreement between the United States and Spain aroused strong opposition among the United States' European allies and substantial opposition in Spain itself. Nowhere in Europe was the opposition stronger than in the United States' closest ally, Great Britain. There the Labor party, in power since 1945, harbored its original antipathy towards the Franco regime, for it had not shared in the transvaluation of values that had taken place in Washington in the interim. Speaking in the House of Commons on July 25, 1951, a little more than a week after Sherman's visit to Franco, Foreign Secretary Herbert Morrison said bluntly that, in a "frank exchange of views" with the authorities in Washington,

. . . we have expressed to them our conviction that the strategic advantages which might accrue from associating Spain with western defense would be outweighed by the political damage which such an association might inflict on the western community of nations.[53]

A more comprehensive analysis of the question by a French commentator likewise stressed the political objections to the projected bases agreement between the United States and Spain, and added several others.[54] France, he said, objected because the deal would upset the balance of power in the Mediterranean and complicate the situation in North Africa, in both cases to her disadvantage, and Britain feared that it might result in shifting control of the Mediterranean from her hands to those of the United States. The writer went on to cite many reasons why Spain would be of little value to the defense of Western Europe against a Soviet attack—an argument which reflected the widespread apprehension in Europe that the United States might be planning to withdraw its line of defense from the Rhine to the Pyrenees.

---

53 *New York Herald Tribune,* July 28, 1951.

54 E. J. Debau, "L'Espagne, forteresse européenne," *Revue des Deux Mondes,* December 1951, pp. 540-548.

The opposition in Spain cannot be documented or measured, because of the absence of freedom of speech and press, but there can be no doubt that it was strong and widespread, including elements addicted to the regime as well as its unconditional enemies. Among Franco's supporters, the agreement was most unwelcome to the more extreme exponents of nationalism, traditionalism, and Catholicism. Nationalists were offended by the concession of bases to a foreign power and the presence of foreign troops on Spanish soil; traditionalists, by the formation of a quasi-alliance which, they alleged, violated Spain's settled policy of neutrality and isolation; and Catholics by the concessions to, and contacts with, Protestantism implicit in the proposed relationship with the United States.

To some extent these were separate groups, though in many individual cases they overlapped. In any case they constituted a substantial phalanx of opposition which even Dictator Franco could not ignore. The strongest of them was the conservative Catholic group, led by formidable old Cardinal Segura of Seville, who openly protested against bartering the "Catholic conscience" of Spain for "heretical dollars." [55] This situation probably explains why Franco marked time on that agreement until he had completed the negotiation of a concordat with the Vatican, as he did in August 1953. Only after he had got this clean bill of health from the head of the church did Franco go on, the following month, to conclude the long-drawn-out negotiation with Washington.

The existence of this Spanish opposition to the agreement was obliquely admitted by Foreign Minister Martín Artajo,[56] who negotiated it on behalf of Spain. In explaining why it had taken so long to complete, one of the three reasons he gave was that time had to be given to prepare public opinion in "both countries" for the agreement. The other two reasons were: first, "obstructionist efforts on the part of other countries," meaning Great Britain and France, whom he accused

---

[55] Jean Créach, *Le Coeur et l'épée* (Paris: Plon, 1958), pp. 273-274. For Cardinal Segura and the Concordat of 1953, see Chapter VII.

[56] See Chapter II, p. 55.

of following a "maliciously anti-Spanish policy" ever since the end of the war; and, second, "the very widely different points of departure" of the two governments, the United States seeking to establish national bases of the type it had already obtained in conquered countries, while Spain insisted upon joint bases, jointly used and remaining under the flag and command of Spain.

All this may well be true, but it is not the whole story. The slow pace of the negotiation was probably due in some measure to lack of enthusiasm on the part of President Truman and Secretary of State Acheson for an agreement with the Franco regime. And the pace was inevitably retarded by the presidential election of 1952 and the change of administration which brought President Eisenhower into the White House and Secretary of State John Foster Dulles to the State Department in January 1953. Thereafter more animation was infused into the affair by Under Secretary of State Walter Bedell Smith, who, as an experienced military planner, had a keen sense of the strategic importance of the Spanish bases and was more willing than his predecessors had been to make concessions in order to obtain them.

Whatever the reasons, even after the preliminaries had been completed the formal negotiations dragged on for nearly a year and a half, from April 14, 1952, until September 26, 1953. They fell into two stages. In the first they were conducted by Ambassador Lincoln MacVeagh, who had been transferred to Madrid from Lisbon for the purpose; in the second phase, which began with the change of administration in Washington, by MacVeagh's successor, James C. Dunn.[57] The fact that Dunn was similarly transferred from the post of ambassador to France is a measure of the importance at-

---

57 Both MacVeagh and Dunn were career diplomats of long and wide experience. For the purposes of this negotiation Dunn had the advantage of having advocated, early in the Spanish Civil War, the policy of nonintervention, which had benefited Franco's side. Jean Créach, who was the Madrid correspondent of *Le Monde* during the negotiation of the bases agreement and claims to have been a friend of one of Franco's most intimate advisers, speaks highly of Dunn's conduct of the negotiation (*Le Coeur et l'épée,* cited, pp. 277-279).

tached to the agreement by the new administration. Throughout, the military aspect of the negotiation was entrusted to Major General A. W. Kissner, of the air force, and its economic aspect to George F. Train, who had been brought from the Lisbon embassy by MacVeagh and who remained on with Dunn. There was a similar division of labor on the Spanish side. Foreign Minister Martín Artajo had general charge of it, but was assisted by Lieutenant General Jorge Vigón and Minister of Commerce Manuel Arburua, as specialists in their respective fields.

The three-part Pact of Madrid was a model of diplomacy in the sense that it was a victory for both sides and a defeat for neither. Each government achieved its major objectives without surrendering anything that it considered essential.

Spain was the chief gainer. Her greatest single gain consisted in the mere fact that the agreement had been signed. Still excluded from the United Nations and NATO, still cold-shouldered by all her European neighbors save Portugal, Spain had now been accepted into active partnership by the West's leading power in circumstances that allowed Franco to claim with some plausibility that he had been right all along. In addition, Spain also obtained military and economic benefits that seemed very substantial at the time, and obtained them on terms that were gratifying to the national sense of dignity and honor. Hence the éclat with which the conclusion of the pact was celebrated in Spain.

There was no similar celebration in the United States, and no occasion for one. Its benefits, though also substantial, lacked the unique and decisive quality of Spain's. What the United States had gained was the right to add one more to its existing string of military base complexes designed to contain Soviet power and ambitions. Once the right was obtained, moreover, it showed no great haste in building the bases.

Chapter II

SPANISH BASES
AND AMERICAN STRATEGY:
THE PACT OF MADRID

FOR EACH GOVERNMENT the Pact of Madrid marked, as we have seen, a new departure in foreign policy. For the United States, it was a reversal of its earlier anti-Franco policy. For Spain, it meant the abandonment of neutrality and isolationism. In both countries the new departure was launched in the face of strong domestic opposition. And both governments were to find out before long that the new commitments of 1953 entailed even wider departures from past policy.

The Pact of Madrid

The three separate but interdependent agreements, called collectively the Pact of Madrid, were a Defense Agreement, an Economic Aid Agreement, and a Mutual Defense Assistance Agreement.[1] Signed on September 26, 1953, by Ambassador James C. Dunn for the United States and Foreign Minister Alberto Martín Artajo for Spain, they took effect upon signature. In American parlance they were executive agreements, not treaties, and hence did not require approval by the Senate.

The first and central document is the Defense Agreement,

---

[1] *The Department of State Bulletin,* October 5, 1953, includes the texts of the three agreements.

44

consisting of a preamble and five articles. It authorized the development, maintenance, and utilization of certain unspecified bases ("such areas and facilities . . . as may be agreed upon") by the United States, jointly with the Spanish government. It stipulates that the bases shall remain under the "sovereignty" and the "flag and command" of Spain and that "the time and manner of [their] war-time utilization . . . will be as mutually agreed upon." It authorized the United States to station in Spain the necessary supplies and equipment, operate the necessary facilities, and exercise the necessary supervision over personnel, facilities, and equipment. Finally, it provided that the agreement should remain in force "for a period of ten years, automatically extended for two successive periods of five years each," unless terminated according to a specified procedure.[2]

This rather vaguely worded document does not constitute a full-fledged military alliance since it does not specify the mutual obligations of the two governments in case of war. Nevertheless, it certainly constitutes a quasi-alliance. The provision for the bases alone would have made it that; but there was more. The Preamble associates the two governments in the "principle" of maintaining "international peace and security" in the face of "the danger that threatens the Western world," and Article I associates them in the "policy" of "strengthening the defenses of the West." Article I further committed the United States to the support of Spanish defense efforts by contributing to the effective air defense of Spain and by improving the equipment of Spain's military and naval forces.

The other two agreements were of indefinite duration,[3]

---

2 Under this procedure, the minimum initial period, nominally ten years, would actually be eleven and one-half years, if termination should take place at this point. Notice of intention to terminate may be given by either government only at the end of the first ten years and is followed by a six months' "consultation period"; if this does not result in their agreeing on an extension, termination becomes effective only after another year has elapsed.

3 The Economic Aid Agreement was to remain in effect at least until June 30, 1956. There was no such stipulation in the Defense Assistance Agreement.

though subject to cancellation on notice. They were more detailed than the Defense Agreement, but like it they left some of the most important matters to be settled later, unless, as may be the case, they had already been settled in a separate understanding not made public. They established a link between the Pact of Madrid and the U.S. Mutual Security Act of 1951, as amended, and each contained a provision that was unique to this pact: the agreement on defense assistance referred to the United Nations Charter, while the one on economic aid committed the dictatorial Franco government (along with the United States, of course) to the proposition that "individual liberty, free institutions, and genuine independence in all countries, as well as defense against aggression, rests largely on the establishment of a sound economy."

The Economic Aid Agreement was the longest of the three. In a preamble and ten articles it set forth both the principles which were to govern its fulfillment in accordance with the Mutual Security Act, and also the measures to be taken by the two governments in furtherance of its objectives. A three-part statement of "General Undertakings," set forth in Article II, obligated Spain, among other things, to "use its best endeavors" to stabilize its currency, balance its budget, create or maintain internal financial stability, discourage cartels and monopolies, encourage competition, and assist the U.S. government in observing and reporting on labor conditions in Spain. Next, both governments agreed to join in promoting international good will, eliminating tensions, and fulfilling their military obligations. Finally, the Spanish government promised to contribute within the limits of its resources to the development of its own defensive strength and that of the free world.

In one important respect, Franco's negotiators came off badly in this agreement. In most of the United States' arrangements of this kind it has been stipulated that 90 per cent of the counterpart funds in local currency generated by economic aid would be used for the economic development of the host country, and only 10 per cent reserved for U.S. administrative expenses in that country. The agreement with

Spain set aside 60 per cent of the counterpart pesetas to defray local expenses of the base construction program, in addition to reserving the usual 10 per cent for administrative expenses of the aid program, with the result that only 30 per cent was left for economic projects in Spain, instead of the usual 90 per cent.[4] Only in July 1958 did Spain receive the benefit of the more general practice; by that time the base construction program was nearing completion and idle counterpart pesetas were piling up in the Banco de España.

The Mutual Defense Assistance Agreement set forth the conditions governing the military assistance to be furnished Spain by the United States. Four of its seven articles obligated both governments: to make available to each other, and to such other governments as they might agree upon, such materials and services as might be agreed upon; to exchange patent rights; to promote peace; and to abide by the agreement until its termination on one year's notice. The other three articles imposed special obligations on Spain: to make peseta currency available; to admit U.S. personnel as part of the American embassy; and to cooperate with the United States in controlling trade with nations that threaten world peace.

Information on the initial cost of this Spanish operation was furnished by a State Department press release of September 26, 1953.[5] According to this, Spain was to receive $226 million for military and economic aid in the fiscal year 1954 under the Mutual Security Act. This sum included $125 million carried over from previous congressional appropriations, with the addition of $101 million appropriated in 1953. Of the $226 million, Spain was to receive $141 million in military end-item assistance and $85 million in defense support aid. This, of course, was only a beginning. A subse-

---

[4] The pesetas used for the construction of the joint bases were generated by U.S. aid to Spain under the Mutual Security Act. On the other hand, pesetas derived from sales to Spain under Public Law 480 were not used for military construction but for the economic development of Spain, although some of the projects they supported, such as road-building, were related to the bases program.

[5] Reprinted in *The Department of State Bulletin,* October 5, 1953, p. 435.

quent agreement fixed the amount of military aid at $350 million for a four-year period, 1953-1957. This did not include the cost of the bases, which was first estimated at $300 million and later at $400 to $420 million. As for Spain's contribution, the press release pointed out that a large portion of the peseta counterpart fund would be used for construction costs payable in pesetas.

The silence of the Defense Agreement regarding the type, number, and location of the bases in Spain was not broken immediately, but newspaper speculation on the subject was active and, as it turned out, fairly accurate. Most reports stressed the importance of the agreement from the point of view of air power. *The Times* of London was almost alone in finding that "the chief value [of the bases] seems to be naval." It noted that the American Sixth Fleet "has hitherto had no base on the scale of Malta or Gibraltar"; and "when enlarged, Spanish bases will firmly establish the United States as a Mediterranean naval power." [6]

American Views of the Pact

A balanced appraisal of the bases agreement and its strategic significance was provided by Hanson Baldwin, a leading expert on military affairs.[7] He noted, as "perhaps the greatest disadvantage of the Spanish agreement," the fact that its terms gave "no real clue to its exact meaning," while it committed the United States to "courses of politico-military action unknown to the American people at an unestimated cost in men, military equipment and dollars without the ratification of the Senate." He continued:

There is no doubt, however, that the geographic and strategic importance of Spain, her mobilization potential of 2,000,000 men, her relative social, political and geographic security as a base, and her strategic raw materials of potash, iron ore, zinc, lead and mercury are a major geopolitical asset.

Spain's bases help to seal the Western gateway to the Medi-

---

6 September 28, 1953.
7 *The New York Times,* September 29, 1953.

terranean; her Atlantic islands aid in controlling and protecting trans-Atlantic shipping lanes, and the Iberian Peninsula provides additional dispersed sites for light, medium and heavy bomber strips. And Spain, behind the rampart of the Pyrenees, provides a last line of defense if the rest of Western Europe should fall, and offers a springboard for offensive land, sea and air operations. Her bases are particularly important as an alternative to the great bomber strips in Morocco, surrounded by political and social unrest, and the great supply and air installations in France, which might be threatened by a Soviet advance across the Rhine or by a change in present French policies perhaps incident to German rearmament.

The Washington correspondent of the *New York Herald Tribune* noted the primacy of the Pentagon over the State Department in obtaining the agreement, and that of the air force over the navy in benefiting by it. He reported without comment three Pentagon views with regard to the agreement: the United States had no intention of retiring behind the Pyrenees in case of a Soviet attack; the Spanish bases would increase the United States' capacity of launching "powerful retaliatory blows" against Soviet aggression; and "Spain is certainly one country which cannot help but be on the side of the West in the event of Russian attack." [8]

A *Times* correspondent in Washington was more explicit about the uses to which the new bases would be put. The naval bases would be used for stockpiling fuel and making minor ship repairs; the air bases were "part of an over-all program of the Joint Chiefs of Staff aimed to supplement the power to retaliate with 'intercontinental atom bombing' in the event of war." Both kinds of bases had the advantage of not being too near the Soviet Union, "as are those of some of the North Atlantic Treaty powers"; the Spanish bases would be more defensible since attacks on them could be intercepted as they flew over Western Europe. According to this correspondent, official Washington denied that the agreement constituted an alliance and protested that it was not

---

8 *New York Herald Tribune,* September 27, 1953; report by James E. Warner.

aimed at bringing Spain into NATO; however, in case of an attack the United States could hardly fail to come to the defense of Spain. Clearly, he concluded, there must be supplementary secret agreements with Spain about the event of war.[9]

On its editorial page the *Times* was outspoken in expressing its distaste for the Pact of Madrid; however, the thing had been done and could not be undone. "We are now faced," it said, "with the necessity of swallowing a bitter pill —the military agreement with Franco Spain. Let us hope that the medicine will not do more harm than good." [10] The *Times'* aversion for the Franco regime, as well as for this quasi-alliance with it, was shared by a large part of the American public.

In other sectors of opinion, the pact had strong support, which was neither confined to the military nor based wholly on military considerations. Just before the pact was concluded, this school of thought found an able exponent in Carlton J. H. Hayes, former American Ambassador to Spain, in the form of a rejoinder to a protest by Salvador de Madariaga. One of the best-known Spanish writers of the present century, the representative of the Spanish republic in the League of Nations, and a refugee from Franco Spain, Madariaga had just published a letter protesting against the pact, which was being negotiated without the consent of the Spanish people and would cost the United States their good will for a long time. "When the regime falls, as fall it must," he warned, "the nation will refuse to acknowledge herself bound by an acquiescence given when she was gagged." [11] Hayes' reply asserted that ". . . our ostracism of the [Franco] regime only served to strengthen it with the Spanish people and to deny us what our military authorities deemed highly desirable, strategic bases for our naval and air forces in the defense of Western Europe." A common defense, he continued,

---

[9] *The New York Times,* September 27, 1953.

[10] Same, September 28, 1953.

[11] Same, September 16, 1953; letter from Madariaga, dated London, September 9, 1953.

is in the interest of the Spanish nation as a whole, and ". . . any future Spanish Government (short of a puppet one forcibly intruded by Moscow) will respect the agreement now being negotiated by our Government." [12]

Official comment in Washington was restrained in tone. The State Department's long press release was strictly factual, and Secretary of State Dulles' utterances about it are well represented by his succinct statement to a House committee in 1954:

During the past year [he said] the NATO defense system has been supplemented, so far as the United States is concerned, by a base arrangement with Spain. This will enlarge in an important way the facilities available to the United States air and naval craft in the western Mediterranean area. This has been desired for a long time. Now, the negotiations have been successfully concluded. This represents an addition to our over-all security.[13]

The Secretary's statement was both well worded for its purpose and compact. By invoking "defense" in the first sentence and "security" in the last, Dulles presented in as favorable a light as possible an arrangement which was politically unpalatable to many people in the United States and among its allies because of the antecedents and character of its new partner. The statement also contained direct allusions to important problems that have since proven their durability: Spain's role vis-à-vis NATO and as a Western Mediterranean power. It likewise contained an indirect but unmistakable allusion to the potential usefulness of the new Spanish bases for effecting "massive retaliation" by atomic bombing. The reference to the arrangement having been "desired for a long time" was a reminder that, though brought to completion by a Republican president, it had been initiated by the Truman administration. Finally, his tribute to the importance of the new facilities in Spain was

---

12 Same, September 21, 1953; letter dated September 17, 1953.

13 *The Mutual Security Act of 1954*, Hearings before the House Committee on Foreign Affairs, 83rd Cong., 2d sess., April 5, 1954 (Washington: GPO, 1954), p. 3.

tempered by his description of them as a supplement, an enlargement, an addition, to existing security arrangements.

Spanish Views of the Pact

Opinion in Spain, as summarized by one correspondent, seems to have been concerned with almost everything except the strategic aspects of the bases agreement. "Pride and hope," he wrote, "are the dominant feelings of most Spaniards now that their country is an ally of the United States." Even anti-Franco intellectuals, he continued, were pleased with the pact because it appealed to their national pride and they hoped that it would help to liberalize the government. The controlled press emphasized the purely defensive character of the pact and Spain's retention of sovereignty, command, and joint use of the bases. The fears of the previous year that such a pact would make Spain a number-one target for Soviet bombs had receded; "the feeling is that the economic benefits stemming from the accords will do the country a lot of good, whereas the threat of war is diminishing, and maybe the alliance will never have to become operative in the full military sense." [14]

Despite the existence of strong but necessarily muted opposition to the alliance, there seems no doubt that at the outset it did enjoy a rather widespread popularity. According to the then Foreign Minister, Martín Artajo, it had been feared by some and hoped by others that the conclusion of the pact might cause serious political repercussions within Spain. Instead, it became an occasion for the "popular apotheosis" of General Franco when he made his next public appearance in Madrid a few days later.[15]

---

[14] *The Christian Science Monitor*, September 29, 1953; report by Richard Mowrer.

[15] Alberto Martín Artajo, *Les Accords avec les Etats-Unis: Texte complet du discours prononcé par le Ministre des Affaires Etrangères M. Alberto Martín Artajo, au cours de la Séance Plénière des Cortès Espagnoles, le 30 Novembre, 1953* (Madrid: Bureau d'Information Diplomatique, 1953), p. 27. Franco's public appearance was on October 1, the anniversary of his assumption of full power as chief of state in 1937.

The dominant note of Franco's message transmitting the agreement to the Cortes was one of triumph, as was easily understandable. But it also contained two major themes that, whether understandable or not, were disturbing to American official observers. One was a strong strain of anti-Europeanism. Far from viewing the pact as a step towards the restoration of friendly relations between Spain and her European neighbors, Franco took this occasion to vent his spleen for their past efforts to oust him. This was his hour of triumph over them and he owed it to the attraction exercised by Spain over the "young nations" linked to it by historic ties, especially, in this case, the United States. The other theme was Franco's devotion to bilateralism: the message made it clear that he was not prepared to engage in international cooperation on any broader basis. This theme, too, might be only the expression of a grudge—the grudge he bore against his European neighbors for keeping Spain out of NATO. Whatever his reason for taking it, his position was firmly held. On both counts it seemed clear that by concluding the Pact of Madrid the United States had at best taken a first short step on the long and winding road towards bringing Spain into closer and more friendly relations with Washington's other partners in Europe.

Franco took substantially the same position in an interview with a representative of United Press, his first since the signing of the bases agreement.[16] The West, Franco declared, was now "completely assured" of Spain's help against Soviet aggression by virtue of his pact with the United States. Spanish membership in NATO was "out of the question for the time being"—as indeed it was, regardless of Spain's wishes. He also "ruled out direct military cooperation now with Britain and France." "For real collaboration," he explained, "it is necessary to create a state of cordiality, about which nothing so far has been achieved."

An exceptionally interesting statement of the official Spanish view of the bases agreement was provided by Foreign

16 *The New York Times,* November 5, 1953.

Minister Martín Artajo in a speech to the Cortes, which gave a comprehensive view of the significance of the pact for Spain's interests and policies.[17] Artajo was not seeking to persuade the Cortes; it needed no persuasion, for it has never been known to oppose any measure desired by the Caudillo. Rather, his speech was designed to celebrate Franco's triumph and give it maximum publicity both in Spain and abroad.

Artajo opened on a somber note, recalling Spain's ostracism at the close of World War II, and the Tripartite Declaration of March 4, 1946, in which the United States had joined with France and Great Britain in virtually outlawing Spain so long as the Franco regime remained in power. Describing that measure as "appeasement of Soviet Russia," he explained that the fundamentally well-meaning United States had been tricked into supporting it by the "anti-Spanish malice" of England and France, by "pro-Communist elements" in the administration at Washington, and by the latter's "almost complete ignorance" of the facts of life in Spain. He then went on to recount how Washington had "rectified its course" after its eyes had at last been opened to the truth that the "prophetic" voice of "clairvoyant" General Franco had been proclaiming all along: that the West was lost if it did not present a common front against the Communist peril as embodied in the Soviet Union.

From this point of departure Artajo moved by quick and easy stages to the Pact of Madrid, which he examined at length. Arrived at his peroration, he described Spain's postwar course as "at first difficult, then triumphant," a "victory," and an "indisputable success," which, "without doing the least injury to our sovereignty and independence, has restored our country to the important international position to which it is entitled, a position in which it is disposed to render once again, as it has done before, inestimable services to the cause of Christian civilization and the peace of mankind."

---

17 Speech of November 30, 1953, cited above, n. 15, p. 52.

In his discussion of the bases agreement Artajo expressed even more clearly than Franco the regime's resentment against its European neighbors, especially Britain and France. He attributed to them not only "malice" but also "injustice" and "bad faith." He gave the impression that Spain's "victory" in concluding the agreement with the United States had been won over them.

Significantly, Artajo ascribed the long delay in completing the agreement to three "fundamental reasons." For one thing, there had been a wide divergence between the respective "points of departure" of the two governments. At the outset the United States had wanted to apply in Spain an arrangement similar to those established in countries that it had defeated or liberated in the recent war—that is, a pattern of territorial concessions for its unilateral use. Spain, on the other hand, had insisted upon joint operation of the bases under the flag and command of Spain, as was ultimately agreed upon. In the second place, time had been necessary to allow the "evolution of a favorable opinion" in both countries. Artajo did not enlarge upon this statement as regarded Spain, but it is noteworthy that he admitted that opinion had to be prepared there as well as in the United States. As for the latter, he gave credit for the evolution mainly to unnamed "intrepid and tenacious congressmen, true friends of Spain, who exerted constant pressure on the administration of their country to carry forward the negotiations with ours." He did not mention the Pentagon in this connection, though he paid tribute to Ambassador Lequerica's "dialectical" as well as diplomatic skill. Finally, he noted, obstructionist efforts on the part of other countries "were not lacking." This was not explained, but Artajo was probably referring primarily to the British Labor government, which had publicly stated its opposition to the pact, and to France, which, under various cabinets, maintained a strong anti-Franco position throughout the negotiations.

In the third place, the Foreign Minister insisted that "the pact with the United States does not represent any alteration whatever in either our foreign or our domestic policy, for in striving for it we have not abandoned a single one of our fundamental directives." In the field of foreign policy, he specified Spain's continuing fidelity to three established policies: on all fronts, anticommunism; in Latin America, Hispanidad; and in the Arab world, a close friendship on the basis of traditional ties and Spain's support of freedom against "colonialisms of an imperialist type." On the home front, he said, the pact was even further from signifying any change in "our political evolution"; he added, "it is only just to say that the United States did not ask that any such change be made."

Finally, Artajo expressed unqualified satisfaction with the terms of all three of the agreements comprised in the pact. This is worth underlining, for only five years later he was to complain publicly and vigorously that the economic aid received by Spain under this pact was utterly inadequate, although he did not claim even then that it was less than had been promised. In his speech of 1953, however, he described the stipulated economic aid as the basis of one of the two "great 'opportunities,' to use an American term," that the pact offered Spain. This was the opportunity to "work for our economic and social reconstruction, by making use of the financial means that these agreements provide and which we need in order to accelerate the rhythm of production and obtain a better yield from our national effort, and, from our national wealth, increased revenue." What a triumph it would be "to push to their ultimate consequences the postulates of our Charter of Labor and thus give full dignity to the life of our working population, as is the ardent aspiration of so eminently social a regime as ours!"

Spain's expectations from the pact were great, and no one did more to encourage them than its Spanish negotiator.

The Bases Complex and Its Function

From the United States' point of view the heart of the pact was its provision for a complex of joint air and naval bases in Spain. The provision was vague but adequate. By 1959 the bases, together with their complement of communications and supply services, were virtually complete. How this operation was carried out, and how the value of the bases changed during the course of it, will be shown below. Only its military aspect will be discussed here. Its economic aspect, so important to Spain but only ancillary from the American point of view, will be discussed in a later chapter.

Since the bases in Spain form part of a system of U.S. oversea bases that girdle the globe, their value depends to a large extent on that of the system as a whole. At the same time, each part has its own particular uses. In Spain, the air bases have been designed primarily for launching B-47 medium-range bombers against the Soviet Union in case of aggression by the latter, and the naval bases for support of the U.S. Sixth Fleet in the Mediterranean. While there has been a good deal of public discussion of matters relating to land defense, such as Spain's manpower potential and the bastion of the Pyrenees, these have played a minor part in the arrangements actually adopted. This is essentially an air and naval operation, and it is hard to escape the impression that even the modest share that the Spanish army has obtained in it has been due mainly to its political importance as the principal prop of the Franco regime.

Four major bases form the core of the complex.[18] Three are air bases, located on the outskirts of Zaragoza in the northeast, at Torrejón, near Madrid in the center, and at Morón, near Seville in the south. The fourth is a combined naval air base and harbor at Rota, near the southern port of Cádiz. Rota also serves as the starting point of a 485-mile-

---

18 The Pact of Madrid did not specify the number and location of the future bases, and for some time a larger program than the one actually carried out was contemplated. In 1956 Secretary of the Air Force Donald A. Quarles told a House committee that the United States had at one time had a program of eight or nine bases but had decided that the four then under construction would suffice for the first phase and that additions to it could be considered later. He also said that the question was still undecided. *Mutual Security Appropriations for 1956*, Hearings before the House Committee on Appropriations, 84th Cong., 2d sess., February 10, 1956 (Washington: GPO, 1956), p. 834.

long oil pipe line (POL) that runs northward through Morón and Torrejón to its terminus at Zaragoza, supplying those bases with petroleum products. In addition, there are two minor air bases: at San Pablo, on the outskirts of Seville, a supply service and communications center; and at Reus, some ninety miles southwest of Barcelona, a fighter base. Of the foregoing, all except Rota were built on sites already in use by the Spaniards either as commercial airports or as air force fields. Only Rota was an entirely new installation; prior to the coming of the U.S. navy, it was a little fishing town and summer resort for Andalusians from cities such as Seville and Córdoba. (The bases are shown on the end-paper map.)

To complete the picture, mention should be made of two additional naval facilities and seven radar sites in various parts of Spain. The naval facilities are an oil storage and supply center at El Ferrol in northwestern Spain, and a similar but much larger center, together with an ammunition storage site, at Cartagena on the Mediterranean coast. The radar sites include one atop Puig Mayor, the highest mountain on the island of Mallorca, which performs the key function of filling the gap between the NATO radar sites in northern Italy and Gibraltar. The other six Spanish sites are on the mainland, and all seven are tied together by the Air Defense Control Center at the Torrejón base. They control both the U.S. and Spanish squadrons. All of them have equipment for identifying aircraft and maintaining direct ground-to-air radio communications; their main feature consists in search and height-finder radar capable of locating any aircraft within a radius of about three hundred miles.

At the end of 1958, U.S. military personnel in Spain for all purposes amounted, in round numbers, to 6,680, distributed as follows: air force, 6,000; navy, 600; army, 80. Six months earlier the total figure had been about 8,180; the decline, accounted for mainly by the air force, was presumably due to a change discussed below, in the use of the bases. These numbers have remained fairly constant though there may have been a slight increase as the radar sites and the

Rota naval base have been completed.[19] The military personnel are slightly outnumbered by their dependents, the two groups combined totaling just under 15,000 in mid-1960.

The management of the bases and of the rest of the military program in Spain presents an organizational picture which the layman may find confusing. To begin with, there is JUSMG (Joint U.S. Military Group); its chief, who is responsible for coordinating the whole military construction program in Spain, is subordinate to USCINCEUR (U.S. Commander in Chief, Europe) as the executive agent of the Department of Defense for administering this program. JUSMG has nothing to do either with the military assistance program which is administered by MAAG (Military Assistance Advisory Group), or with military operations, the control of which is vested, in their respective fields, in the Sixteenth Air Force and in Naval Operations. However, in order to coordinate relations with the Spanish government regarding the military program, both JUSMG and MAAG have the same chief. And this officer, under his JUSMG hat, is also the military contact of the American ambassador in Spain, who has over-all diplomatic responsibility for the conduct of U.S. policy in that country.

And this is not all. The Sixteenth Air Force, established on July 15, 1957, and the largest of all of the Strategic Air Command's oversea forces, administers not only the joint air bases in Spain but also the American air bases in Morocco. The latter, built under a "crash" program in 1951-1952, are approximately equal to the Spanish bases in number, strength, and geographical spread; the United States has, however, agreed to withdraw from the Moroccan bases by the end of 1963. To complete the picture, it should be noted that U.S. Naval Activities in Spain reports to CINCUSNAVEUR (Commander in Chief, U.S. Naval Forces, Europe) in London. The Commander of the Sixteenth Air Force reports directly to the headquarters of SAC at Offutt air base, Ne-

---

[19] In January 1960, more than 2,500 U.S. navy personnel, including marines and Seabees, were permanently based on Rota; *The New York Times*, January 17, 1960.

braska. Finally, the base construction program was carried out under an intricate organization that will be described below in another connection.

The Major Bases

The defense network in Spain is spread over the greater part of the country, but perhaps its most striking feature is the proximity of the four major bases to important urban centers. Torrejón, the nerve center of the whole complex, is only sixteen miles from Spain's national capital and largest city. The double air base of Sanjurjo-Valenzuela and the naval base at Rota are only six miles distant from, respectively, Zaragoza, the fifth largest city, and Cádiz, one of Spain's principal seaports. Seville, the fourth largest city, is separated by a somewhat safer thirty-seven miles from the major air base of Morón, but is almost cheek-by-jowl with the lesser base of San Pablo, which adjoins the city's commercial airport.

Just how this situation came about has never been fully explained, although considerations of transport, supply, communications, and terrain have been adduced to justify it. It is persistently reported that General Franco himself chose the Torrejón location, partly for its future convenience to the national capital when the Americans have gone and the base has become wholly Spanish, and partly for its immediate propaganda value as visible evidence that he had been taken into partnership by the West's greatest power. In any case the location of all the major bases so close to Spain's principal cities seems to have been unreservedly accepted by the Spanish government at the outset.

Since the successful launching of the Soviet sputnik in October 1957, Madrid has had second thoughts on this subject and, it has been rumored, on the whole question of its ties with the United States. On October 7, three days after the launching, Franco publicly drew a parallel between the Soviet system and his own, as proof that the regimes which succeed are those of an authoritarian character based on "discipline and order." And he coupled this with a slap at the United States for its "ingenuousness" in, as he asserted, giving in to Stalin's request at Potsdam in 1945 for the secrets of atomic energy. Five days later, Spanish Ambassador Areilza in Washington invited Soviet diplomats to a reception for the first time. Putting these facts together with evidence of the establishment of trade ties between Spain and iron-curtain countries, one correspondent speculated that Spain's "change of tune" might presage an abandonment of her alliance with the United States and a return to neutrality.[20]

That, of course, did not materialize. Privately Spain did insist upon a re-examination of the vulnerability of its cities in the light of missiles development, with a view to the relocation of the bases. The United States agreed to the re-examination but, after that had been completed, was extremely cool to the suggested relocation. The best available information indicates that the major bases will remain where they are for an indefinite period.

All three major air force bases are Strategic Air Command bomber bases, with additional facilities for fighter and support aircraft.[21] Up to the present they have been equipped with medium-range B-47 jet bombers, but they are capable of accommodating the largest aircraft. The principal runway at Torrejón is said to be the longest in Europe, with a length of 13,400 feet plus two 1,000-foot over-runs. The lengths of the two runways at Zaragoza are 12,200 feet (Valenzuela) and 9,923 feet (Sanjurjo) and of the Morón runway 11,800 feet.

Torrejón is where President Eisenhower landed and took off when he visited General Franco in December 1959. It is the headquarters of the Sixteenth Air Force, which comprises two air divisions, one in Spain and one in Morocco. Its mission is officially described as follows: to carry out the

---

20 *Manchester Guardian*, November 14, 1957.

21 A great deal of information about these bases (except as to the number of their military aircraft) has been published in various places. Most of the information given below will be found in various releases of the Office of Information, Sixteenth Air Force, and in dispatches in *The New York Times*, September 6, 1958, and January 6, 1959. I visited these air bases, as well as the Rota naval base, in February and March 1959.

operational functions of SAC; to provide SAC with essential support for its global mission; to serve as a full-time partner in "reflex operations" (the launching of bombers on fifteen minutes' notice); and to carry out the joint Spanish-U.S. air force defense program.

More and more, these bases have become self-contained units, with their own dining halls, social centers, recreation facilities, and churches, as well as living quarters. At first there was a severe shortage of housing for U.S. service families, but by early 1959 this was being remedied by a large-scale building program, about half on U.S. government account and the remainder on private Spanish account. As a result there has been decreasing contact between the American service personnel and the Spanish public; in this connection it may be noted that, in order to forestall charges of proselytism, churches on the bases are not open to Spaniards. In order to avoid other difficulties, service personnel are not permitted to wear uniforms when off base, except in line of duty. These and other precautions have been largely successful in holding down the number of "incidents" between American servicemen and Spaniards. Although there is a substantial fund of anti-Americanism in Spain today,[22] and the existence of the bases is partly responsible for it, most observers agree that it is not due in any large measure to difficulties with the American personnel. That phase of the operation appears to have been handled with skill and success.

The naval air station at Rota presents substantially the same personnel picture except that its degree of self-containment is even higher because of its greater isolation. Though Cádiz, clearly visible across the bay, is only six air miles distant, it is three times as far by road and it is not rich in the attractions sought by most American servicemen.

Stretching twelve miles along the northern shore of the Bay of Cádiz, and lying just east of the town whose name it bears and whose integrity it has respected, the Rota base

---

[22] Arthur P. Whitaker, "Anti-Americanism in Spain," *Orbis*, Fall 1959, pp. 313-331. See also Chapter III, n. 3.

has been described as "the mightiest American naval installation in Europe." [23] It has a 12,000-foot runway but does not operate bombers. According to the official description, its mission is confined to the operation of fleet reconnaissance, the support of fleet communications and an aircraft replacement pool, the occasional basing of carrier aircraft units, and similar functions. Its chief purpose is to support the nuclear striking power of the Sixth Fleet. As the starting point of the pipe line to Zaragoza, Rota has a POL pier completed and in operation that will accommodate two tankers at a time. A mile-long breakwater, a 1,000-foot pier, and dredging operations, all completed by mid-1960, will enable it to accommodate the largest ships of the U.S. navy.

The three major air bases were virtually complete and fully operational by early 1959. Housing facilities were still in various degrees of completion at all the bases. Some of the housing was on-base, some off-base, and considerable numbers of U.S. military personnel were still scattered around in Spanish-owned houses and apartments. Bomber crews on duty were of course housed in close proximity to their planes, ready to take to the air within fifteen minutes after the receipt of a warning.

In December 1958 it was estimated that the total cost of the four bases when completed would be about $255 million. Partly because of rising wages in Spain this estimate was substantially exceeded.[24] In the end, the four bases accounted for the greater part of the total of about $420 million spent by the United States on its military construction program in Spain down to the end of 1959. Counterpart pesetas contributed about one-third of the cost, the balance being paid directly by the United States.[25]

23 *The New York Times*, January 17, 1960.

24 By early 1960 an unofficial estimate put the cost of Torrejón at $100 million and Rota at $120 million (*The New York Times*, January 17, 1960). Earlier it had been estimated that they would cost about $71 million and $103 million, respectively.

25 Testimony of Stuart H. VanDyke, regional director, ICA, in *Mutual Security Appropriations for 1959*, Hearings before the Senate Committee on Appropriations, 85th Cong., 2d sess., July 14, 1958 (Washington: GPO, 1958), pp. 191, 193.

Pace of Construction

In at least one case, that of Morón, the percentage of completion cited above may leave an exaggerated impression of the readiness of the base to perform its appointed mission. Like the other joint air bases in Spain, Morón exists primarily for the purpose of getting atomic bombing planes airborne on fifteen minutes' warning. Yet as late as the spring of 1959 the runway at Morón was still crossed by a Spanish railway line which was in regular use several times a day. To be sure, steps had been taken to remove this serious hazard by building a new line outside the runway area, but just after being completed it was washed out by floods in December 1958. When I visited Morón in March 1959 no work appeared to have been done to repair the damage, and the original railway line across the runway was still functioning as usual. Precautions had of course been taken to prevent a Spanish train from crossing the runway when the bombers needed to use it, but no precautions could eliminate the risk of a train breaking down on this stretch of track—and Spanish trains are notorious for frequent breakdowns. On March 9, 1959, *Stars and Stripes* published an article on this "unique problem," complete with a photograph of a U.S. air force jet plane waiting for a Spanish train to clear the track. The tone of the article was generally lighthearted but it concluded: "Last month two F-100's declared an emergency because of minimum fuel as a result of two go-arounds ordered by ground control approach and tower personnel because a train was on the end of the runway. They finally landed safely."

Perhaps amusing unless a war emergency should arise, but possibly disastrous then, this situation highlights an important point about the bases program, namely, the lack of urgency that characterized their construction from the start, in August 1954. It was decided that, unlike earlier programs in Morocco and elsewhere, the Spanish program should not be carried out on a "crash" basis, and this ruling has been adhered to ever since. In the absence of documentation the reasons for this policy can only be divined, but chief among them at the outset were a lessening of international tensions, and hence of the sense of urgency, that followed Stalin's death in 1953; public criticism in the United States of the wastefulness of crash programs in general; and the fear that such a program might cause a severe shock to Spain's very weak economy and thus reduce the value of the alliance by discrediting its government and provoking strong antagonism among its people.

Moreover, from the beginning the comparatively leisurely pace of the construction of the bases has been a faithful reflection of their role in U.S. strategy. It cannot be too often repeated that their role cannot be properly appraised except by regarding them as a part of the whole far-flung system of U.S. oversea bases. From this point of view the value of the Spanish bases has always been prospective and relative rather than immediate and absolute. With reference to neighboring countries they provide an alternative against the day when other bases now in use might no longer be available, and Spain at large might provide a safe haven for refugees from other areas of Europe rendered untenable by enemy action. So far, neither contingency has occurred, though the former is certain to arise as regards Morocco now that the United States is committed to evacuate its bases there by the end of 1963. With reference to the oversea base system as a whole, one of the two chief functions of the Spanish bases is performed by all the bases—that of complicating the Soviet Union's military problem by their number and wide dispersal. For the other chief functions of the bases in Spain—retaliatory bombing from the air bases, support of the Sixth Fleet by the naval base—there have always been available elsewhere sufficient alternatives to remove any great sense of urgency about the completion of the Spanish bases.

Modest though it was, the pace set for the construction of the bases was not maintained. Apparently, one of the chief factors was that a large part of the equipment had been used in carrying out the crash program in Morocco and its condition and diversity of makes created many replacement problems. Another lay in the task of training Spanish workers for unaccustomed jobs. Still another was the complexity of the organization. To put the matter as briefly as possible, the construction program was successively subinfeudated by the U.S. Department of Defense to the Department of the Navy; by the latter to its Bureau of Yards and Docks, which served as construction agent for the Secretary of the Air Force; and by the Bureau of Yards and Docks to its Officer in Charge of Construction, or OICC, who was under the over-all control of the chief of JUSMG, an air force officer. This, however, was only the beginning, for the OICC engaged as its prime contractor a firm which, under the name of Brown-Raymond-Walsh, had been formed for the purpose by three separate firms in the United States: Brown and Root of Houston, Texas, Raymond International of New York City, and the Walsh Construction Company of Davenport, Iowa. And Brown-Raymond-Walsh then engaged subcontractors who did the actual work.

Most of the program would have been delayed even longer if the Spanish government had not expedited the construction of the vitally important petroleum pipe line. In the extraordinarily brief period of three months it obtained all the necessary rights of way from owners of thousands of properties along its 485-mile-long route from Rota to Zaragoza. Until it was completed, the air bases would be of relatively little use; Spain produces no petroleum and its other facilities for transporting petroleum products are quite inadequate. Even in 1958, after Spain had received substantial American aid towards improving its railway system, a SAC source stated that "a wing of B-47's consumes in an afternoon more fuel than the entire Spanish railroad tanker fleet can transport in a month." As for transportation to the air bases by water, that is possible only in the case of Seville, and even in this case the principal base, Morón, then requires an overland haul of nearly forty miles.

Missiles Development and Oversea Bases

Only half-finished as late as mid-1957, the air bases in Spain did not become fully operational until the following year. By that time the cumulative effect of recent developments in weapons and strategy was not only changing the nature of their use but was also stimulating a reconsideration of the utility of oversea bases in general, including those in Spain.

As regards the Spanish bases, the change in their use was summed up in a few lines by Benjamin Welles:

Until a few months ago the Strategic Air Command used to send full wings of forty-five B-47 bombers, plus crews and ground staff, overseas in rotation for periods up to three months. This left too many valuable planes exposed at each base too long for safety. . . . Recently this was changed. Smaller bomber groups— perhaps up to fifteen—now fly overseas [from the United States to Spain] on three-week tours, then fly home again.[26]

This succinct statement reflected the change that was taking place in the strategic functions of American oversea bases in general, as a result of recent technological developments on both sides of the iron curtain. The Soviet Union had acquired first the atomic and then the hydrogen bomb. It had greatly increased its capabilities of delivery through the development and large-scale construction of long-range bombers and submarines. And in October 1957 it had capped the climax by launching the first sputnik, which gave plausibility to the claim that Moscow had also developed an intercontinental ballistic missile (ICBM). Even earlier, during the Suez crisis of 1956, Moscow had begun menacing with annihilation the countries in which American oversea bases were located. In the United States, weapons progress included all varieties but was headed by the development of an intermediate-range ballistic missile (IRBM, range 1,500 miles) and an atomic-powered submarine that would soon be capable of firing, even when submerged, the Polaris missile of

---

[26] *The New York Times*, September 9, 1958.

a similar range. It also included a great improvement in the means of refueling even the fastest and heaviest jet bombers in flight.

The net effect of these changes was to reduce the value of the oversea bases, change their role in the global defense system, and even raise the question whether, on balance, it was worthwhile to retain them. Their value had been impaired by technological advances in the United States as well as the Soviet Union. For example, the progress of the United States in refueling in flight lessened its initial dependence upon oversea bases and raised the question whether they might not soon serve mainly as landing fields for pre-strike and post-strike ground refueling. Likewise, the bases had been rendered far more vulnerable by the progress of the Soviet weapons system, which could be offset only partially by the "hardening" of the bases through the construction of underground shelters.

Mainly because of Soviet progress in weapons, there occurred at this time an accentuation of the political problems that have always existed in some degree even in the friendliest countries as a result of the American military presence there. For example, this new threat explains Spain's request, already mentioned, for a reappraisal of the vulnerability of those cities located near the bases, with a view to the possible relocation of the bases. These and other developments, such as the current upheaval in the Arab world, have brought about a reassessment of the whole oversea base system.

The debate was by no means one-sided. Strong arguments, both military and political, were advanced in favor of retaining oversea bases. One military argument ran as follows: despite the rapid pace of missiles development, bombers will continue to make up a large part of the striking force of the United States through the early 1960's; it is virtually certain that during that period there will be no substantial increase in the range of bombers, which therefore will require the use of oversea bases; consequently these bases will continue to be indispensable at least through the early 1960's. Other military arguments—valid for a longer future, if not indefinitely—cited the complications that oversea bases raise for the enemy in terms both of attack and defense, and the greater efficiency even of atomic-powered submarines when served by overseas-based submarine tenders. The political argument in their favor held that the withdrawal of the United States from its oversea bases would destroy the morale of its allies.

One expert who took part in the restudy of the bases system has rendered a verdict highly favorable to retaining oversea bases. But he urges a change-over from their original function, that of giving the "great deterrent" of atomic air power "credibility and effectiveness," to a new purpose, that of "valid capability for limited military action on the boundaries of Eurasia." [27] The original function of the bases, Hoopes believes, will still be required for several years to come, until current technological advances, such as the improvement of Polaris and the availability of the ICBM, enable the United States to dispense with oversea bases in maintaining the great deterrent; and it should, he holds, dispense with them at the earliest possible moment in order to obtain greater freedom of action and at the same time allay the "atomic fear" that now poisons its relations with its allies as well as with uncommitted peoples. During this transition period, Hoopes predicts, the oversea bases will remain "very important" to the maintenance of the great deterrent, for they continue to be a "major strategic asset" and "the cement in our system of alliances." In his opinion, however, the emphasis should be shifted gradually to their second function, that of providing support in limited wars and maintaining a "favorable local power balance in selected areas."

Some experts regard Hoopes' findings as unduly skeptical of the oversea base system. Yet, even if one accepts his conclusions at face value and applies them to the bases in Spain, it seems clear that the latter will retain for several years to come their value in relation to the first function, that of sup-

---

27 Townsend Hoopes, "Overseas Bases in American Strategy," *Foreign Affairs*, October 1958, pp. 69-82.

porting the great deterrent. It likewise seems clear that they will have considerable and perhaps increasing value for an indefinite period in relation to the second function, that of maintaining "a favorable local power balance in selected areas." The areas which the Spanish bases could be most useful in defending are Western Europe and North Africa.

There remains the possibility that the bases in Spain may some day be supplemented or supplanted by missile-launching sites, but up to the present Spain has not been included in any authoritative list of the countries in which such sites have been proposed. Naturally, Communist propagandists, such as Radio España Independiente, have asserted that Spain is included, and that such sites have already been built there.

The Spanish Armed Forces

By its nature as well as its terms, the Pact of Madrid gave Spain's armed forces a key role in their country's new relationship with the United States. They still retain this role, although the relationship has undergone some rather important alterations.

From the point of view of the United States the pact was a necessary evil: an evil because of the character of the Franco regime, but necessary as the only means of gaining access to valuable bases in Spain. Hence the nature of the pact: it was a strictly military *quid pro quo* arrangement, with the United States providing aid in return for Spanish bases. Moreover, the entire American aid program to Spain was aimed, directly or indirectly, at achieving or supporting military objectives, and its main bulk was at first channeled directly to meet the wishes of the Spanish armed forces.

Subsequently the relationship has changed as the U.S. government has broadened its economic action and sweetened its political attitude towards Franco Spain. Yet fundamentally the policy has not changed. Solicitude for the bases still provides its two major premises, which are, first, that continued use of the bases must be assured by promoting stability in Spain, and, second, that Spain must be compensated for the use of the bases. Given the character of the Franco regime, any program carried out on these premises could not fail to maintain the Spanish armed forces in their key role in the relationship established by the Pact of Madrid. For they are the regime's chief prop, the best guarantor of its stability, and the strongest claimant to whatever compensation it receives for the use of the bases.

Policy-makers in Washington are not blind to these obvious facts. In public they prefer to talk as if the only function of the Spanish armed forces under the Pact of Madrid were to defend Spain, and especially the bases, against enemy attack. But every informed person knows that the Spanish military also perform the indispensable function of maintaining domestic stability against all comers. It is only natural, therefore, that since the original four-year agreement on American aid expired in 1957 the aid has been continued unhesitatingly from year to year. At present it seems more likely to be increased than diminished.

The first shipment of military matériel under the Mutual Defense Assistance Program reached Spain in February 1954, six months before the construction of the bases began. By April 1956, 130 shiploads of such equipment had been delivered, including more than 1,000 trucks and trailers and "substantial numbers" of tanks, antitank weapons, field artillery pieces, and antiaircraft guns. Two months earlier American Ambassador John Davis Lodge had officially presented a squadron of F-86 Saberjet fighters; they were taken over by a hundred or so Spanish pilots who had been trained on American planes. By this time many Spaniards had received American instruction in other lines of military operations, some in Spain and hundreds of them in the United States.[28]

After the completion of the initial four-year program of military aid amounting to $350 million, during which Spain's most urgent needs were met, its scale was reduced considerably. For example, in the fiscal year 1960 the program called for only $32 million. The aid, still substantial,

28 *New York Herald Tribune*, April 15, 1956.

was more varied and now included some of the most modern weapons, such as equipment for a Nike battalion and an Honest John battalion as well as some Sidewinder missiles. By the end of 1958 Spain had received at least sixty M-47 tanks as the nucleus of an armored division. The program also provided for the loan of naval vessels and the continuation of the training program. In the fiscal year 1959 the program had provided for training nearly six hundred Spanish military personnel in the United States and about seventy in third countries or at U.S. bases overseas. During fiscal years 1954-1958, a total of some 4,800 Spaniards had received American military training in Spain.

By agreement with the Spanish government U.S. military assistance has been allocated among its armed forces as follows: air force, 40 per cent; army and navy, 30 per cent each. The preference shown the air force has been justified mainly on the grounds that, when the allocation was made, defense against possible air attack was Spain's major problem; in order to prepare against it, the Spanish air force must be equipped with jet planes, which are expensive.

If the allocation had been made on the basis of size, the lion's share would have gone to the army, always much the largest of Spain's armed services. For a variety of reasons its exact strength at any given time is hard to ascertain, but at the end of 1958 it was believed to number almost 250,000.[29] To this figure should be added the nearly 45,000 members of the Guardia Civil (Civil Guard, a national police force) which would come under army command in case of war. By contrast, the air force numbered at this time only 43,000 and the navy 39,000. The fact that the big army was equated with the microscopic navy in this aid program, and both were subordinated to the air force, strongly suggests that no serious thought was being given to the much-discussed possibility of

---

[29] The army's nominal strength is about 400,000, but this figure is based on the assumption that the draftees, who make up the bulk of it, serve a full two-year term; in fact they serve only eighteen months and in some cases even less.

"tapping Spain's reservoir of manpower for the defense of the West."

What of the quality of the Spanish armed forces? Would modern equipment and training be enough to bring them up to the level of, say, the Germans, the Americans, and the Russians? Some forty years ago that noted Spanish authority on Spain and its people, José Ortega y Gasset, said that his fellow countrymen make fine fighters but poor soldiers. During the Spanish Civil War a German general in Spain thought they made very poor soldiers until trained by German officers, when they did rather well.

Despite the resoluteness and success with which the contending armies in that war killed each other off, doubts about Spanish military capabilities persisted in the United States. They were voiced, rather than answered, in a colloquy that took place in 1957 at a Senate committee hearing on aid to Spain. The participants were Senator Wayne Morse, a member of the committee, and Brigadier General John S. Guthrie, of the Defense Department. Said Senator Morse:

Can anybody in this witness group tell me how much help you think we would get from Spain . . . from the standpoint of the battle-efficiency of any Spanish troops, the battle-efficiency of the Spanish Air Force? . . . Building the bases and working out economic contracts with Spain I am for, but I don't know why I should be voting to build up supposedly a military establishment in Spain when such military experts as I have talked to, when they let their hair down, always smile.

To which General Guthrie ruefully replied:

As you can see, I don't have any hair to let down, Senator. Perhaps General Norstad . . . can enlarge on the NATO side of it; although Spain is not a member of NATO, it is important in the NATO concept.[30]

General Norstad did not enlarge on Senator Morse's point, but members of the American military who are well ac-

30 *Mutual Security Act of 1957*, Hearings before the Senate Committee on Foreign Relations, 85th Cong., 1st sess., June 4, 1957 (Washington: GPO, 1957), pp. 404-405.

quainted with their Spanish counterparts have spoken
highly, both in print and in private, of their ability and
spirit. In this generation, they say, when reminded of Ortega's
quip, that the Spaniards they have seen are good soldiers as
well as good fighters. Their only serious reservation is expressed in the description of the average Spanish officer as a
"week-end soldier," meaning that the low pay scale obliges
most Spanish officers to take on a second job in order to make
both ends meet. The general official opinion is well represented by a statement made in 1956 before a House committee by E. Perkins McGuire, Deputy Assistant Secretary of
Defense:

> I can speak from the military point of view. We enjoy excel-
> lent relationships with Spain . . . the MAAG chief [Military
> Assistance Advisory Group in Spain] . . . is very enthusiastic
> about the Spanish military people and the way they are coop-
> erating.[31]

By 1958 a rapidly changing situation had substantially altered the requirements and the desires of the Spanish military and their government. To put it in a nutshell, they
were now urging the United States to promise more aid for
a smaller but stronger military establishment. One major
reason was the loss of Spain's protectorate in Morocco, which
had become independent in March 1956. For the Spanish
military, the loss of Morocco, long its special province, had
dealt a double blow: it was a blow to their morale, and it
called for a substantial reduction in their numbers. Another
major change was the sharp increase in military budgets that
took place in Spain as in other countries in the middle and
later 1950's, mainly as a result of the growing complexity and
cost of modern equipment.

This was one of the two main grounds on which former
Foreign Minister Alberto Martín Artajo was protesting by
early 1958 that the volume of U.S. aid was now "wholly in-

---

[31] *Military Security Appropriations for 1957*, Hearings before the House
Subcommittee of the Committee on Appropriations, 84th Cong., 2d sess.,
June 6, 1956 (Washington: GPO, 1956) p. 280.

adequate" to the needs of Spain.[32] Artajo had, of course, negotiated the agreements of 1953, but now he was highly critical of their terms. He complained that in four years under this *quid pro quo* arrangement Spain had received only one-tenth as much as she would have received gratis under the Marshall Plan. So seriously did he take Spain's present predicament that he called for a "fundamental revision" of the "pacts of '53" in regard to the supply of arms and the defense of the air bases. Though no longer a cabinet member, Artajo was widely regarded as speaking for the Spanish government on this occasion, and his speech, originally delivered before the American Chamber of Commerce (February 5, 1958), was extensively reprinted in the Spanish press.[33] As a sign that the speech was to be taken seriously, and not regarded as the product of a passing whim, it was also published in Spain's leading scholarly periodical in its field, the *Revista de Estudios Políticos.*

In October 1958 the Spanish Minister of War, Lieutenant General Antonio Barroso, visited Washington in an effort to obtain increased aid; his aim was to strengthen the Spanish armed forces, while reducing their numbers. Specifically, according to newspaper reports, Barroso's plan was to cut the army from eighteen to twelve divisions, modernize five of these, and convert two of them into "pentomic" divisions of the most advanced American type, that is, five-unit divisions with atomic capabilities. It was estimated that this would cost more than $100 million. In addition, General Barroso's plan called for a large increase in the soldiers' pay, better

---

32 Alberto Martín Artajo, "El primer lustro de los convenios hispanonorteamericanos," *Revista de Estudios Políticos,* March-April 1958, pp. 5-18; also reprinted separately. The reference here is especially to pp. 11 and 14-15. Artajo's other main argument was the economic one, that precisely because Spain's pace of economic development had accelerated greatly since 1953, she needed increased economic aid which, in his opinion, the United States ought to furnish.

33 *The Christian Science Monitor,* February 24, 1958. While in the United States nearly two years earlier, Artajo had already spoken to much the same effect, without then proposing a drastic revision of the agreements of 1953 (*The New York Times,* April 17, 1956, reporting Artajo's speech at Fordham University).

housing, and special training. With these inducements he hoped to transform the army from a sprawling and ever-changing aggregation of draftees serving nominally for two years, but actually for only fifteen months or so, into a more compact professional force serving for much longer periods on a voluntary basis. General Barroso buttressed Spain's claims to increased aid by stressing the importance of her role in protecting both Gibraltar and, through the Canary Islands, West Africa. In support of his contention he cited Winston Churchill as to the Canaries and West Africa—not as to Gibraltar.[34]

In Spain the Barroso plan expressed government policy, of course, but in army circles it met with some opposition. This protest was voiced in private conversation early in 1959 by a retired officer of great distinction. He objected mainly on two grounds: the build-up of only five divisions was un-dermining the morale of all the rest; and the reduction in the size of the army was shortsighted since Spain needed at least as large a force as before. These views are believed to represent a substantial body of opinion among the Spanish military, who like most other groups in Spain cling to tradi-tion and do not like to be cut down, even in the name of effi-ciency. Nevertheless, in accordance with the Barroso plan, the reduction of the army's size was begun on January 1, 1960, with the deactivation of three divisions.

The Barroso plan was not unrelated to the ever-recurrent question of Spain's admission to NATO, according to a well-informed American correspondent.[35] In reporting the plan and General Barroso's impending departure for Washing-ton, Welles wrote:

In recent months there have been increasing unofficial sug-gestions by legislators, particularly in the United States, Britain and West Germany, that Spain's large pool of military man-power should not indefinitely be denied to NATO whose ground forces are seriously depleted by French and British troop trans-fers.

---

[34] *The New York Times,* October 6 and 20, 1958.
[35] Benjamin Welles, *The New York Times,* October 6, 1958.

Spain's admission to NATO for this purpose would confer important advantages upon her armed forces. For one thing, it would require an even more extensive modernization of them than was called for by the Barroso plan. Likewise, it would probably forestall the proposed reduction in their size.[36] In addition, Spain's NATO contingents would presumably be sent to West Germany and in any case would necessarily be in close contact with the NATO partners, who have the best armed forces in Western Europe.

Such large-scale contacts with free Europe, it is true, might ultimately weaken the loyalty of the Spanish military to the present regime. But that was a long-range political problem and, as such, of more concern to Franco than to the military. To them, Spain's admission to NATO would be a handsome compensation for the material and moral reverse they had suffered in the loss of her Moroccan protectorate. It would also offer Spain the best lever for utilizing her greater potential bargaining power vis-à-vis the United States, now enhanced by the approaching evacuation of its Moroccan bases.

There is still no certainty that Spain will some day be admitted to NATO, but her chances have improved so greatly in the past two years that the eventuality has become a major factor in looking to the future of Spain's armed forces and her military ties with the United States. As matters stand in mid-1960, Spain's admission to NATO appears to be a matter of great and perhaps crucial importance for the future development of her armed forces. The formation of a new multilateral tie would not necessarily weaken the existing bilateral tie with the United States. On the contrary, it would be more likely to result in a substantial increase in U.S. military aid under the pact, for without such an increase Spain could hardly hope to bring her armed forces up to NATO standards.

---

36 For a high-ranking Spanish officer's views on the future of Spain's armed forces in relation to her admission to NATO, which he thought "probable," see Lieutenant General Alfredo Kindelán Duany, "En el umbral del caos," *Ejército* (Madrid), March 1958, pp. 11-15.

U.S. Policy to 1960

Despite occasional grumblings in Congress over the rising cost of base construction, the U.S. government has forged steadily ahead along the policy line laid down in the Pact of Madrid. More than that, it has broadened the scope of a relationship that was at the outset narrowly limited to military cooperation to include new factors of general economic and political support. In most instances the initiative seems to have come from the executive branch, but Congress has seldom lagged behind and has sometimes taken the lead, particularly in the matter of economic and technical assistance, for which year after year it approved larger appropriations than the executive had asked for. It is true, all such measures continue to be justified in terms of the military tie with Spain, and specifically of the bases program. Where the change has taken place is in the concept of what is necessary and proper for the United States to do in support of its bases program in Spain, and this concept has been noticeably enlarged. The limited liability pact that the United States negotiated in 1953 has fast been shedding its limitations. That may have been inevitable, but its inevitability was not foreseen.

At the outset, economic aid was tied closely to the base construction program. By 1957 the shoe was on the other foot, for the purpose now was to help Spain meet a serious economic situation marked by inflationary pressures and balance-of-payments difficulties. When Assistant Secretary of State C. Burke Elbrick presented the economic aid proposal to a Senate committee in these terms, one member, Senator Allen J. Ellender of Louisiana, objected. "Now, why is that necessary . . . ?" he asked. "We were led to believe, and it is in the record, that the base construction in Spain would prime the economy of Spain. However, now we are requesting aid grants for Spain. What has happened to make us take a new course?" Replying, Elbrick took the usual line: whether the proposed course was a new one or not, "this aid program for Spain is very closely connected with the base program. . . ." [37]

The broadening of the U.S. economic commitment was highlighted by its participation in the Spanish stabilization plan of July 1959. The plan was concerned with the Spanish economy at large, without specific reference to the air and naval bases, and the initiative in drawing it up had been taken by the International Monetary Fund and the Organization for European Economic Cooperation—both of them technical international organizations that had no concern whatever with the bases. Yet not only did the United States promote and support the stabilization plan, but it is committed to making it a success. This is a far cry from the limited liability concept.

In the political field, the attitude of the United States towards Spain has changed from the coolness of 1953 to the camaraderie expressed in President Eisenhower's visit of December 1959. We cannot be sure of the inner workings of this change, or even whether the change has been more apparent than real. During most of this period this aspect of policy was determined by the late Secretary of State John Foster Dulles, and he was not very communicative about it. One measure of the shift is found in the attitude of the United States towards Spain's admission to NATO.

While the available evidence is not conclusive, it appears that at the outset this was not advocated by the executive. At any rate, when the Pact of Madrid was announced, the impression was that the pact was intended not as a prelude but as an alternative to Spain's joining NATO. In 1955, however, Dulles told a House committee that "the State Department would be sympathetic to" Spain's admission.[38] And in 1957 that was made the official position of both the State Department and (by joint resolution) of both houses of Con-

37 *Mutual Security Appropriations for 1958*, Hearings before the Senate Committee on Appropriations, 85th Cong., 1st sess., July 29, 1957 (Washington: GPO, 1957), p. 269.

38 *Mutual Security Act of 1955*, Hearings before the House Committee on Foreign Affairs, 84th Cong., 1st sess., May 25, 1955 (Washington: GPO, 1955), p. 17.

gress. This did not necessarily imply any special friendship for or approval of the Franco regime. During these years, however, Dulles had developed the practice of stopping off in Madrid to see Franco on his return from NATO Council meetings in Paris. These meetings did signify something more than a coolly correct attitude towards a militarily useful but politically uncongenial ally. On occasion a note of cordiality was sounded in Dulles' public statements after the meetings.

Proof that a change had in fact taken place came from two visits that President Eisenhower made to Europe in 1959. On the first, in August, he took time out from a busy schedule in London to receive Foreign Minister Fernando María Castiella, who had made a special trip to see him. Castiella would not have been welcome in London otherwise, since he had said some decidedly unpleasant things about Great Britain in a book published in 1941 when he was a fire-eating Falangist, and the British government had refused to receive him as ambassador in 1951.[39] The purpose of his visit was to deliver a cordial letter from Franco to Eisenhower; the latter replied in the same vein.[40] The net effect was to put Spain in the international limelight and increase the prestige of the Franco regime at home and abroad. The Madrid newspaper *ABC* crowed that "from a military standpoint the United States considers Spain the most important of its allies in Europe, except perhaps the United Kingdom."

A second visit to Europe took President Eisenhower to Madrid in December 1959. Aside from some Arab potentates, he was the first chief of state to visit Franco since Hitler and he had met at Hendaye early in World War II. The original omission of Madrid from Eisenhower's itinerary made its inclusion two days later all the more striking.[41] Its inclusion

___

39 The book in question was *Reivindicaciones de España* (Madrid: Instituto de Estudios Políticos, 1941) written by Castiella and José María de Areilza, later Spain's ambassador to the United States.

40 Both letters were published in *The New York Times,* September 3, 1959.

41 Same, November 12, 1959.

was explained on grounds of military expediency and the bases program, as is customary in any question relating to Spain. From all reports President Eisenhower's visit turned out in much the same way as elsewhere, except that apparently he worked in an atmosphere of greater cordiality in Madrid than he had in Rome or Paris.

An incident that attracted attention related to the *abrazo* or formal embrace that is customary among Latin peoples of Europe and America, both as between personal friends and on formal occasions. It was noted that when Eisenhower was met by Franco at the Torrejón air base, there was no *abrazo;* when the President left on the next day, they exchanged not one but two *abrazos.*[42] So seemingly trivial a matter might have passed unnoticed but for the fact that high officials of the U.S. government had quite recently declared that in its dealings with the Latin American states the United States should make a distinction in favor of democracy and against dictatorship by greeting democratic leaders with an *abrazo,* while giving dictators only a formal handshake.

A joint communiqué issued at the end of the brief visit noted that "gratifying progress" had been made in the "implementation of the economic and defense agreements" of 1953.[43] It also confirmed Franco's support, already signified in his August letter, of Eisenhower's policy of seeking cautiously to relax tensions with the Soviet Union, while maintaining a "firm defense posture." Both men were apparently highly pleased, Franco because this defense posture is the key to the American bases program and to U.S. aid to Spain, and Eisenhower because the Spanish government had proved most cooperative and the people of Madrid had given him a rousing welcome. "Flushed with happiness" over it, he "clasped the short Spanish chief of state twice warmly" just before leaving, and declared that the friendship and active

---

42 Same, December 22 and 23, 1959; reports by Benjamin Welles.

43 Same, December 23, 1959; "Statements by Eisenhower and Franco," including their joint communiqué and farewells by each of them.

cooperation between the United States and Spain would become steadily stronger.[44]

It is not surprising that Franco's supporters, including the controlled Spanish press and radio, were jubilant over the President's decision to visit Franco and over the visit itself, which they pictured as a tribute to the regime.

The Spanish Ambassador to the United States, José María de Areilza, described the President's visit as "again demonstrating to the world the international prestige of Spain, of its Chief of State, and of our foreign policy." [45] Altogether, it seems that a marriage of convenience can lead to a honeymoon, even though it be delayed for six years.

Nevertheless, at least by mid-1960 the honeymoon atmosphere had not greatly relaxed the United States' hold on the pursestrings of its aid to Spain. General Barroso's visit to Washington in October 1958 had apparently brought Spain a little more money and some modern arms, but no pentomic divisions. A year later reliable sources indicated that the current policy of the United States was to maintain the existing force levels in Spain, at least for the time being. Some provision would be made for modernization, but none for advanced weapons systems.

Viewed broadly, the main objectives of U.S. policy towards Spain at the present time seem to be:

The development and use of the military facilities in Spain for the common defense of the West;

The maintenance of Spain's non-Communist orientation and its close relations with the United States;

The improvement of Spain's capability to defend the Iberian peninsula;

Increased acceptance by the Spanish people of the im-

---

44 Same, December 23, 1959. One detail worth noting is that Eisenhower's phrases, "peace with justice, friendship in freedom" and "peace and friendship and freedom," which he used in his response to Franco on his arrival at Madrid, were faithfully reproduced in Spanish translation by the Madrid newspapers; *ABC,* December 22, 1959, p. 48. This is not really surprising, for Franco does not object to the use of the word "liberty" or "freedom" and indeed claims the Spanish people already have freedom, and democracy as well.

45 *Ya* (Madrid), December 30, 1959.

portance of collective security and international cooperation, both political and economic;

The improvement of relations between Spain and the NATO nations, for two purposes: to tie Spain as closely as practicable into Western plans for regional defense, and to obtain Spain's admission to NATO as soon as appropriate, though without necessarily committing the United States to bring Spain's forces up to NATO standards;

The maintenance of internal stability in Spain to the extent required for the accomplishment of the other objectives.

If the above analysis is correct, clearly the bases still remain the key to U.S. policy towards Spain. And, clearly, the U.S. government is satisfied on the whole with the results of its seven-year-old "marriage of convenience" with the Franco regime. Likewise, it has no intention of dissolving the tie, whether because of the new threat of recent and prospective missiles developments to the bases in Spain, or for any other reason. On the contrary, it envisages, without quailing, the possibility that the tie may involve it in further activities and commitments.

Any such involvement seems most likely to arise in connection with Spain's relation to NATO and the maintenance of its internal stability. The problem of Spain and NATO concerns many countries, and it entails, on the part of the United States, commitments of a political and moral as well as a military and financial kind. And the maintenance of Spain's internal stability has far-reaching implications in at least the political and economic fields. The problems implicit in both these objectives will be discussed below, as well as the large "political bill" which, as Cyrus L. Sulzberger has pointed out in sobering detail,[46] is a part of the price the

---

46 *The New York Times,* February 9, 1958. Sulzberger specified these items in the bill: The Catholic Church in Spain still mistrusts the United States. The army is jealous of the highly paid and well-equipped Americans, resents the presence of foreign troops in Spain, and "numerous younger officers favor a return to Spain's traditional neutrality." Intellectuals and university students see the United States as the Caudillo's main prop. All this is grist for Communist propaganda mills and the United States is losing its oldest Spanish friends, the intellectuals and liberals, who may dominate Spain when Franco is gone.

United States pays for its access to bases in Spain. As the close-
ness of its association with the Franco regime has grown,
so has this bill.

Chapter III

HOW MANY SPAINS?

PERHAPS THE MOST distinctive feature of the bases agreement between Spain and the United States is its mutuality. Their relationship is not one of landlord and tenant but of partnership in a joint enterprise. This is written into the agreement in the most explicit terms. It is also made manifest in the operation of the bases. While the United States provides nearly all the tools and weapons and would unquestionably carry out, if need arose, any retaliation against Soviet aggression—the primary purpose for which the bases were created—they were nevertheless built with Spanish aid, they remain under the flag and command of Spain, and at all the principal bases Spanish air or naval units function day in and day out alongside those of the United States.

Since the arrangement is in effect a partnership, its long-range viability and worth to the United States depend to a great extent on the character of its Spanish partner. In appraising this, one must consider not only the government of Spain but its people in a wider sense, and not merely their present-day situation and behavior but also the more enduring features and trends exhibited by the historical record of their development.

This task could be dispensed with perhaps if one could assume either that there will be no change in the present regime during the life of the bases agreement, which may be extended to 1973, or that, no matter what changes may occur in its regime, Spain can never afford to give up the advantages of its bases agreement with the United States. No prudent planner would make either assumption. The present regime is a personal dictatorship—not the most stable form of government—and the dictator, born in 1892, is well on in years. As for the advantages to Spain of the bases agreement, Moroccan nationalism has recently sacrificed similar advantages for the satisfaction of getting the armed forces of the United States out of that country; anyone who thinks Spanish nationalism is not capable of doing likewise does not know the Spaniards. Moreover, almost any conceivable successor to Franco's regime would have no need for one of the chief advantages the latter has derived from the bases agreement, that of political respectability.

Consequently, any study of the quasi-alliance with Spain must be addressed to a wide range of questions about the character, compatibility, and capabilities of its Spanish partner. Answers, so far as they can reasonably be projected, to these comprehensive questions depend on many factors, and these will be dealt with in this and the following chapters. In any case it can be said at once that the current situation, measured by Spain's performance over the preceding century and a half, is highly abnormal in its political immobilism.

Compatibility

What more suitable facet of Spain's past for us to begin with than its relations with the United States? As we scan its pages we at once encounter a paradox: from their beginning, during the American Revolution, the people-to-people relations between the two countries have generally ranged from good to excellent; until quite recently, their government-to-government relations, when not cool, have most often been contentious.

We must not let this paradox trick us into assuming that all would have been well if only the two governments could somehow have been forgotten and the two peoples brought face to face. The benevolence of the individual contacts that have taken place is subject to two important qualifications.

In the first place, until Spain first became a happy hunting-ground for masses of American tourists only a few years ago, individual contacts between the two peoples were relatively few, as compared, for example, with the contacts of each with the peoples of France, Italy, England, and Germany; they were also limited largely to intellectuals and artists. In the second place, as soon as they moved outside the circle of personal relations, even these select few were prone to accept the "black legends" of their respective countries about each other. These were deeply rooted in historic religious and political differences and nurtured by more than a century of sporadic but sharp contention between the two governments.

Beyond these superficial contacts, however, American intellectuals have shown a long-standing interest in Spain, and also a readiness, which has had no counterpart in that country, to revise the traditional indictment of Spain. The depth and duration of the Spanish tradition in the literature of the United States is impressive. A recent scholarly study of the subject comes to two stout volumes.[1] No comparable work on the United States has been or could now be produced in Spain. For in the nineteenth century Spanish writers took little interest in any foreign country—the great vogue of the now obscure German philosopher Karl Krause is only an apparent exception—and, when they began to look abroad after the disaster of 1898, their attention was fixed mainly on Europe north of the Pyrenees.

In the United States, on the other hand, the roster of writers in the Spanish tradition includes many of the great and near-great names, from Washington Irving, Bryant, Longfellow, Prescott and Mark Twain to Ernest Hemingway. Two of these, Irving and Prescott, produced important historical works. In addition, some of the best contributions to the history of Spain were made by American historians, among them Henry C. Lea, Julius Klein, and Roger B. Merriman. Some of the nineteenth-century historians were quite unsympathetic to Spain, but from the turn of the century

---

[1] Stanley T. Williams, *The Spanish Background of American Literature* (New Haven: Yale University Press, 1955; 2 v.).

Edward Gaylord Bourne and others aided greatly in revising the black legend in Spain's favor. First among specialists and then, by the 1920's, among a wider American audience, the Spanish cultural renaissance represented by the "Generation of 1898" excited admiration and hope for Spain's future. This, together with the fact that most Spanish intellectuals were Republicans, reinforced the sympathy that most American intellectuals felt for the Spanish republic at the outbreak of the Civil War.

Spain has not repaid the compliment. For obvious reasons —the loss of Louisiana and Florida to the United States early in the nineteenth century, the Monroe Doctrine, the Ostend Manifesto, the war of 1898 over Cuba—Spaniards have not felt much sympathy for the United States even when they have thought about it at all. Hence they readily laid the foundations of Yankeephobia in Spanish America in the late colonial period and built on this theme in later times, especially during the first half of World War II. But, in general, Spain's interest in foreign countries has been centered largely on Western Europe, and the few Spanish writers in this century who have occupied themselves seriously with the United States have on the whole deepened the hue of their country's unfavorable legends about it, an outstanding example being the scorching attack on the "Yankee peril" just after World War I by Luis Araquistain, one of the chief spokesmen of the rising generation of Spanish liberals at that time.[2]

In the late 1930's and early 1940's a flood of Hispanidad propaganda strengthened the Spanish bias against the United States. Since then, in the new atmosphere created by the *rapprochement* between the two governments, kind words have been spoken about the United States by Spanish writers such as Julián Marías and Rafael Calvo Serer.[3] In

[2] *El peligro yanqui* (Madrid: Publicaciones España, 1921).

[3] Julián Marías, *Universidad y sociedad en los Estados Unidos* (Madrid: Langa, 1954), and "Spanish and American Images," *Foreign Affairs*, October 1960, pp. 92-99; Rafael Calvo Serer, *La fuerza creadora de la libertad* (Madrid: Rialp, 1958). In the *Foreign Affairs* article cited, Marías, a leading young intellectual who lives in Spain but has visited the United States, says that "the

the late 1950's the United States even enjoyed a kind of literary vogue in Madrid, but the most popular North American writers were those who emphasized the seamy side of their country's life. Outside intellectual and official circles, one of the strongest influences in shaping the Spanish image of the United States in recent years has been the clandestine, Communist-operated Radio España Independiente.

When all is said and done, reciprocal attitudes in the two countries, and relations between them, have been determined mainly by political and military considerations that have found their focus in the interests and policies of their governments. This has been unfortunate, for the two governments, when they were conscious of each other's existence at all, were at loggerheads throughout the first century and a quarter after the beginning of American independence.

The antagonism continued at a high pitch most of the time from the birth of the American republic for the next half-century.[4] Throughout that period Spain was one of the three most important nations in the world to the United States, next to England and France. Spain's importance was due mainly to her presence in America. Until about 1820 she had by far the greatest colonial empire in the new world.

American image in Spanish minds," which was favorable about 1950, has suffered an "obvious deterioration . . . from 1954 on," partly because of misinformation due to the Spanish censorship, but also for other reasons (see especially p. 96).

[4] An interesting by-product of the recent *rapprochement* between the United States and the Franco regime is the fairy tale, propagated in Spain and given some credence by uninformed persons in the United States, to the effect that Spain helped the United States win its independence. The story rests on the inadequate basis of two distorted facts: that Spain made some small loans to the United States and went to war with England in 1779. The loans were, in fact, made to keep the war going so that England and the United States would wear themselves out, to Spain's benefit, and Spain entered the war against England for objectives that were either irrelevant or injurious to the American cause. Unlike the France of Louis XVI, Spain refused the United States an alliance, never sent a single soldier or warship to its aid, and even refused to recognize its independence until after England had recognized it at the end of the war. See especially Juan F. Yela Utrilla, *España ante la independencia de los Estados Unidos* (Lérida: Gráficos Academia Mariana, 1925; 2 v.), and Samuel F. Bemis, *The Diplomacy of the American Revolution* (New York: Appleton-Century, 1935).

For most of that time two of her provinces, Louisiana and Florida, hemmed in the United States along its entire western and southern borders.[5] The same facts largely explain the antagonisms between the two countries, for Spain felt that her American empire was threatened by the Americans, who in turn believed that they had a destiny to fulfill and that Spain barred their way.

In the light of these facts it is also easy to understand why the United States had no qualms about annexing the former Spanish provinces of Louisiana (1803) and Florida (1819-1821) or why its people overwhelmingly favored the Spanish Americans in their long and bitter struggle for independence that began in 1810. Fearing reprisals by the reactionary great powers of Europe, the American government remained officially neutral throughout that struggle. But at the first favorable opportunity, in 1822, it took the lead in recognizing the independence of the new Spanish American states, and it backed up that policy in 1823 with the Monroe Doctrine. However much or little these political acts affected the outcome, by 1825 the wars of independence were virtually ended and Spain had lost all her vast continental dominions, from California and Texas to Cape Horn.

With the disruption of the Spanish empire in America, the importance of Spain and the United States to each other diminished greatly; it did not rise again noticeably until the onslaught of the cold war, a century and a quarter later. Even the war of 1898, despite its impact on domestic developments in each country, was merely an episode in their relations with one another. It did, of course, symbolize a long line of irritations and controversies resulting from Spain's retention of Cuba, which, with Puerto Rico, was all she had salvaged from the wreck of her American empire early in the century. But the war was not the result of deliberate plan-

---

5 The early and, for the United States, most critical phase of this conflict has been described in Samuel F. Bemis, *Pinckney's Treaty* (Baltimore: Johns Hopkins Press, 1926); Arthur P. Whitaker, *The Spanish-American Frontier* (Boston: Houghton Mifflin, 1927), and *The Mississippi Question* (New York: Appleton-Century, 1934).

ning on either side. It took both by surprise and was over almost before it started. In its immediate effects it neither cleared the atmosphere nor made it much worse. Indeed, by 1902 a few Spaniards were already speculating on the possibility of an eventual alliance with the United States.[6]

Over the long run, of course, Spain's loss of the last remnants of her American empire diminished friction by reducing contacts. Now for the first time in their history Spain was no longer a close neighbor of the United States, and the two had little to quarrel about. On the other hand, there was little to bring them together. As a result, on the political-diplomatic-military level, there has never been a time when the two countries meant less to each other than in the first three and a half decades of this century, down to the outbreak of the Spanish Civil War. Thus, although the United States took part in the conference of 1906 at Algeciras, Spain, which settled the Moroccan crisis of the preceding year, Spain's own interest in Morocco, important to herself, passed almost unnoticed in the United States, where the conference was regarded as, so to speak, a banquet at which Spain's role was that of *maître d'hôtel*.

When the Civil War broke out, the United States had no Spanish policy. This may explain why it followed the lead of Britain and France and why its own policy subsequently went through such marked gyrations between 1935 and 1953. While these were going on, relations between Washington and Madrid reached their lowest point since the war of 1898. At a tense moment in September 1941, Spanish Ambassador Juan Francisco de Cárdenas, about to return to Spain for a visit, called on Secretary Hull. "I spoke to him," says Hull, "as bluntly as I had ever spoken to any diplomatic envoy." Hull told him, among other things, that "your Government's course has been one of aggravated discourtesy and contempt in the very face of our offers to be of aid." He pinpointed the target of his complaint as "the coarse and extremely offensive methods and conduct of [Foreign Minister] Serrano

---

6 Rafael Olivar Bertrand, "Perfil internacional de España de 1900 a 1909," *Cuadernos de Historia Diplomática* (Zaragoza), v. 4 (1958), p. 19.

Suñer in particular and in some instances of General Franco." [7]

The puzzlement that one senses in Hull's outburst is instructive for the past. The sequel is even more so for the future, for the diplomatic revolution which has since made General Franco the virtual ally of the United States is a salutary reminder that a coincidence of needs is a stronger cement than mutual esteem and good will. Now, for the first time since the American Revolution, the United States had need of Spain. This time Spain needed the United States. And the mutual recriminations of a few years before were filed away in the archives.

Isolationism, Nationalism, and the "Two Spains"

Over the centuries Spain has been no more fortunate in her relations with her European neighbors than with the United States. Since the eighteenth century her experience with "Europe" has nourished a strong trend towards isolationism, which in turn is partly a product of Spanish nationalism.

Except for the British Isles, perhaps every country in Western Europe has been fought over by foreign armies as much as Spain. But Spaniards think their country has been exceptionally unfortunate in this respect, and what they think is the important thing. They base their opinion not only on the number, duration, and intensity of such conflicts on Spanish soil but also, and even more, on the fact that these were essentially foreign conflicts. As one of them put it over a hundred years ago, Spain has for centuries been the dueling-ground of Europe.[8] All agree that the chief exhibits are the War of the Spanish Succession (1701-1714), which grew out of the resistance of England and Holland to Louis XIV's effort to place his grandson on the throne of Spain; the Peninsular War (1808-1813), which was a consequence

---

[7] *Memoirs of Cordell Hull*, v. 2 (New York: Macmillan, 1948), p. 1187.

[8] Mariano José de Larra (1809-1837), as quoted in José Ortega y Gasset, *El espectador*, v. 2 (Madrid: Calpe, 1921), pp. 198-199.

of Napoleon's duel with England; and the invasion of Spain in 1823 by the Duc d'Angoulême's 100,000 "sons of St. Louis," by which the liberal regime recently established there was destroyed as, so we are told, a warning from the Holy Alliance to liberals in other European countries. Some would conclude the list with the Spanish Civil War as a duel between the Axis and the Soviet Union, but most Spaniards know that this was a conflict of Spanish vintage.

The worst of the lot, from Spain's point of view, was the Peninsular War, for this major disaster wiped out all the substantial progress made by Spain in the eighteenth-century age of enlightenment and left the country a wreck at home and stripped of most of its empire. It was a traumatic experience from which Spain did not recover for generations. Among its ill effects, it was the starting-point of Spain's isolation, confirmed by the French invasion of 1823.

In the decades that followed, Spain's isolation was only partly a matter of choice; it was partly also a necessity imposed upon her from without. Because of her weakened state she decided that her best protection lay in leaving the game of power politics to the great powers. For the same reason they left her to her own devices. Otherwise she might not have adhered to her wise decision as closely as she did, for her commitment to isolationism was never by any means complete. Thus, while Spain remained outside the system of great-power alliances of the late nineteenth and early twentieth centuries, she did participate in the scramble for Morocco, first through a treaty with France in 1904 and then as a party to the multilateral agreements reached at the Algeciras Conference of 1906.

The fact is that, even at its strongest, Spanish isolationism has been qualified by older tendencies towards imperialism and internationalism, and by the concept of a world mission, all of which have retained their vitality. Hence Spain's membership in the League of Nations and the United Nations; hence also Franco's adherence in 1939 to the Axis' Anti-Comintern Manifesto and his bid after World War II for association with the West in the defense against the Soviet

Union. Spain is no Sweden or Switzerland, but a bundle of conflicting policy trends, and the choice among them is dictated by the circumstances of each case. The isolationist trend has been strong for over a century. For a time after World War II it was intensified by a natural reaction to Spain's ostracism. But Spain's record was so mixed that, when fortune favored Franco with the chance of a virtual alliance with the United States, he was able to seize it without doing too much violence to tradition and public opinion in Spain.

The isolationist trend and its fluctuations appear to be in large degree a function of nationalism, which was one of the chief original ingredients of the Franco regime. The relationship can only be described in tentative terms since, while a great deal has been written about Spanish nationalism, no comprehensive study has been made of it. Nevertheless, some of the major outlines of its development seem to be fairly well established and they are worth noting here because of their relevance to our theme.[9]

To begin with, while modern Spanish nationalism is a variation on the nationalisms that have developed in Western Europe generally since the French Revolution, it has several distinctive if not unique features. For one thing, it contains a stronger element of xenophobia than most other varieties. The explanation, I believe, lies in the extraordinary strength of regionalism. It would be little exaggeration to say that even today most of the Spanish people are Spaniards only in opposition to foreigners; in their internal affairs they are not so much Spaniards as Castilians, Catalonians, Basques, Andalusians, and so on. Partly for the same reason, nationalism also developed more slowly in Spain than in

---

[9] The literature of this subject is far too diffuse to be discussed here, but it should be said that, in addition to the writers mentioned in the text and notes, the following are a few whose works should be consulted: Claudio Sánchez Albornoz, José Pemartín, Ramiro Ledesma Ramos, Eduardo Jiménez Caballero, Ramón Menéndez Pidal, and Onésimo Redondo. I am much indebted to Ángel del Río, director of the Hispanic Institute in the U.S., Columbia University, and Otis H. Green, University of Pennsylvania, editor of the *Hispanic Review*, for suggestions on this subject; neither is responsible for anything that I have said on the subject.

most European countries. The strength of regional loyalties has actually made the growth of nationalism a source of disunity rather than unity, for in some parts of Spain the idea became identified with a particular region rather than with Spain as a whole. As a result, both Basque nationalism and Catalan nationalism first emerged in organized movements under that label in the late nineteenth century. Other retarding factors were the force of traditionalism and the weakness of that pillar of modern nationalism in most of Europe, a strong middle class.

Indeed, some authorities date the emergence of modern Spanish nationalism as late as the "Generation of 1898." This term, used loosely to describe a highly heterogeneous intellectual movement headed by Joaquín Costa, Ángel Ganivet, Miguel de Unamuno, and José Ortega y Gasset, was stimulated, though not started, by the shock of Spain's disastrous defeat in its war with the United States. The chief common aim of these writers was to find a way to regenerate Spain and, in this connection, to define and express its national character and purposes.

With important qualifications, theirs was an open nationalism, which aimed at regenerating Spain with the aid of foreign precept and example. Most of them were liberals, at least by Spanish standards. To illustrate the latter qualification, we may note that Ortega y Gasset, who became a founder of the republic in 1931 and whose influence is still strong in Spain, had already adumbrated by 1914 [10] the theory of leadership by an elite which was later more fully stated in his internationally famous books, *Invertebrate Spain* (1921) and *The Rebellion of the Masses* (1932). At the same time that he disavowed nationalism, which he identified with imperialism, he demanded "nationalization of the

---

10 José Ortega y Gasset, *Vieja y nueva política* (Madrid: Renacimiento, 1914), pp. 31-32: "I am not speaking now to the masses; I am addressing myself to the new privileged men in an unjust society—to the physicians and engineers, professors and merchants, industrialists and technicians—I am addressing myself to them and asking for their collaboration. . . . Let us traverse the countryside in an apostolic campaign . . . let us first become the friends of those whose leaders we are later to be."

army, nationalization of the monarchy, nationalization of the clergy . . . , and nationalization of the worker." [11] The views he expressed on this occasion are all the more important because he was the spokesman of an organization, the League for Spanish Political Education, several of whose members—such as Manuel Azaña, Américo Castro, Salvador de Madariaga, Ramiro de Maeztu, Antonio Machado, and Ramón Pérez de Ayala [12]—were to play leading parts in Spain's political and cultural life in the decades ahead.

But Spain is full of contradictions and Spanish nationalism is also marked by other distinctive features which ill accord with some of those just described. One of the most striking is its identification, in the minds of many Spaniards, with Roman Catholicism. The identification was established in modern Spanish nationalism by one of its chief exponents, Marcelino Menéndez Pelayo, whose great erudition and eloquence, combined with boundless patriotism and unbending religious orthodoxy, gave him enormous influence over the development of Spanish thought in the late nineteenth century. His concept of Spanish nationalism was summed up in the epilogue to one of his most famous books, *Historia de los heterodoxos españoles* (1880-1881): "Spain, evangelizer of half the world; Spain, hammer of heretics, light of [the Council of] Trent, sword of Rome, cradle of Ignatius [Loyola] . . . ; this is our greatness and our unity: we have no other."

Menéndez Pelayo's clarion call went echoing down the decades, to become the bannerhead of *Acción Española,* the journal of a group that, under a similar name, helped to destroy the anticlerical republic and shape the ideology of the Franco regime. In 1933 it quoted with unreserved approval this profession of nationalist faith and added its own elaboration of the theme.

In Spain [it said] it is not possible to deify the nation, and one cannot conceive of an integral patriotism that is not born in a

11 Same, pp. 53-54.
12 Same, pp. 67-69; list of members of the League.

Catholic breast. . . . A sound patriotism, one that loves the fatherland in space and time, can be felt only by those Spaniards who feel themselves united with historic Spain, with its defense of Christianity against Islam and of the unity of Christianity against the sects. . . . A Spanish heretic . . . has only two choices, either to renounce his heresy for patriotism . . . or to renounce his patriotism for heresy. . . .[13]

The editor of *Acción Española,* Ramiro de Maeztu, developed these ideas more fully in a book, *Defensa de la hispanidad* (1934). Combining them with ideas of an authoritarian and functional state that Maeztu had been one of the first twentieth-century writers to state "with any intellectual dignity," [14] his book on Hispanidad became the bible of many of Franco's followers, who during the Civil War were generically and appropriately called Nationalists. Even among them Maeztu's Catholic nationalism had no monopoly. Its most serious rival was the original Falange group founded by José Antonio Primo de Rivera, which, under Nazi influence, developed, during and after the Civil War, a strong secular and even pagan strain. It represented the kind of Spanish nationalism that *Acción Española* had declared inconceivable, for it was a nationalism that deified the nation and was not born in Catholic breasts. Only Franco's strong hand was able to make this ill-matched team pull together. Neither Maeztu nor the younger Primo de Rivera lived to see that interesting performance, for both were put to death by the Republicans at the beginning of the Civil War. If they had lived, the team might have been less manageable.

A more important rift in the fabric of Spanish nationalism is the one referred to by the familiar phrase, "the two

---

13 *Acción Española* (Madrid), August 16, 1933, pp. 440-441.

14 Salvador de Madariaga, *Spain: A Modern History* (New York: Praeger, 1958), p. 573, n. 2. The reference is to Maeztu's *Authority, Liberty and Function in the Light of the War,* published first in London during World War I, and later in Spain as *La crisis del humanismo.* Hispanidad is a neologism, and Madariaga says that Maeztu invented it; in fact, it was an imitation of the term *argentinidad,* invented a generation earlier by the well-known Argentine writer Ricardo Rojas.

Spains." Although it is widely used, there is no general agreement as to the precise meaning of the term. Since Menéndez
Pelayo's time it has been most often used to denote the rift
between "progressive anticlerical and Catholic-conservative
Spaniards." [15] But Ortega y Gasset applied it explicitly to
the dichotomy of "official Spain" and "vital Spain," [16] and
Ramos Oliveira clearly implies it in his contrast between the
"organically healthy" and "organically diseased" areas of
Spain.[17] Other variants of this term could be listed, and, as
will be shown below, the recent history of Spain has given
these words a new meaning today.

In any case, the superficial dualism of the "two Spains"
concept is rejected by some Spanish observers as a misleading
oversimplification of a highly complex problem. As one acute
commentator has recently said, Spain is historically divided
not only in two parts, but into countless numbers of parts,
for each of its halves is in turn divided and subdivided "as
far as the eye can reach." [18] No one who has given more than
a glance to the individualistic, regionalistic, and otherwise
variously fragmented Spanish people is likely to deny that
the statement is true as far as it goes. But if it goes no farther
than this it is only a counsel of despair to the observer who
seeks to bring some kind of order into the chaos of his observations of Spain.

The writer just referred to realizes this. After having rendered the "two Spains" approach futile by multiplying it
to infinity, he comes forward with the proposition that the
Spanish people do possess a certain unity in the form of
unique national traits. Taking as his text Américo Castro's
statement that in every Spaniard "there is a *quid ultimo*

---

[15] Richard Herr, *The Eighteenth-Century Revolution in Spain* (Princeton University Press, 1958), pp. 443-444.

[16] See below, p. 102.

[17] Antonio Ramos Oliveira, *Politics, Economics and Men of Modern
Spain, 1808-1946* (London: Gollancz, 1946), p. 219.

[18] Camilo José Cela, "Sobre España, los españoles y lo español," *Cuadernos* (Paris), May-June 1959, p. 9. One of the first and best-known living
writers on Spanish national character is of course Salvador de Madariaga;
his *Englishmen, Frenchmen, Spaniards* (London: Oxford University Press,
1928), is a classic in the field.

that is Spanish and nothing else," [19] he asserts that this *quid* exists in "all the thousand faces of Spain," adding quite plausibly that, without it, "the phenomenon of Spain could not be understood." His own application of this idea begins with the propositions that the commonest vice of the Spaniard is envy and that a virtue which animates him but also renders him impotent for great undertakings is disobedience, contrariety, the habit of being *against* things. The rest of the article is in the same vein: stimulating, persuasive, and highly subjective.

Interpretation in terms of national character is also preferred to the dualism of the "two Spains" by another Spanish commentator.[20] In Andia's opinion (though he does not put it in so many words), it would seem that the "two Spains" exist not as two separate, mutually antagonistic groups of Spaniards but as a split personality in each individual Spaniard, no matter what group, party, or region he belongs to. He cites, as an example, the widespread acceptance of a "monstrous contradiction," best defined by Miguel de Unamuno, that destines the Spanish peoples to hypocrisy—a contradiction arising from the clash between their nationalistic assumption that the Spaniard is an *hidalgo,* who bases his behavior on superior moral values, and their profound pessimism about the future of Spain. To give only one more example, Andia holds that nothing could be more equivocal than "Spanish religiosity." In fact, he suggests, religion in Spain may be only "a compensatory system of collective security against a bad conscience." In this connection he quotes the "exaggerated but eloquent" saying that "Spain is a pagan country with Catholic superstitions."

In a longer view, the case for interpreting the present sit-

---

19 Américo Castro, *España en su historia* (Buenos Aires: Editorial Losada, 1948), pp. 12-13.

20 Julián Andia, "España como futuro," *Cuadernos* (Paris), March-April 1959, pp. 29-33. According to an editorial note, Julián Andia is the pseudonym of a well-known Spanish intellectual. Some identify him as Enrique Tierno Galván, who is not only a leading intellectual and professor of political science at the University of Salamanca, but also second in command of the quasi-political party Unión Española discussed in Chapter V.

uation in Spain in terms of the "two Spains" concept of liberalism versus conservatism, as those concepts took shape in the nineteenth century, seems a doubtful one at best. If understood in that sense, the term oversimplifies a complex situation by exaggerating the unity of each of the contending sides. It has also become something of an anachronism. New issues have arisen, the lines of division on some of the older issues have become blurred, and the specific content of both liberalism and conservatism has changed. One or two examples must suffice here. Strong anticlerical elements exist within the Franco regime as well as among its opponents. The present regime has shown more social consciousness than some of its critics. Some of his adversaries would unhorse Franco only to establish an authoritarian regime of another kind. And the regionalism which cuts across the lines of the "two Spains" is much stronger than when those lines were first drawn in the early nineteenth century.

Nevertheless, a "two Spains" pattern does exist today. It is new and even simpler than the older one, and Franco himself has been responsible for establishing and perpetuating it. Its simplicity lies in the fact that the two parties are easily identifiable and are separated by a definite line. They are, respectively, Franco's regime, which he calls Spain, and the opposition, which he dubs "Anti-Spain." Before we describe this new pattern more fully, we should prepare the way by examining two other enduring factors in Spanish life: the pronunciamento and guerrilla warfare.

Pronunciamentos and Guerrillas

Two of nineteenth-century Spain's principal gifts to the world have been the words "pronunciamento" and "guerrilla." As commonly used in English, one is a figure of speech, the other a pleonasm. For pronunciamento signifies not only the proclamation with which a military uprising is started, but also, and even more, the uprising itself, and guerrilla, which means "small war" in Spanish, must often be coupled with some such word as "war" to give it meaning in English.

Both terms reflect the turmoil that marked the life of Spain during most of the nineteenth century, and then broke out again in the twentieth. The Civil War of 1936-1939 was the culmination of a century and a quarter of civil conflict, and Franco's uprising only the last of a long line of pronunciamentos. Of these, there had been forty-three between 1814 and 1923, of which thirty-two failed and eleven succeeded.[21] If these figures mean anything, Franco had one chance in four of winning, but, as events turned out, he was favored by an international situation without a counterpart in the earlier struggles. He may also have been favored by technological changes in warfare and by the increasing professionalization of the military, but that is less clear.

What seems beyond question is that this prolonged turmoil first wrecked the promising recovery that Spain had begun in the eighteenth century and then brought about a redistribution of political and economic power that virtually insured Spain's failure to achieve internal coexistence—what the Spaniards call *convivencia,* or the ability to live together with a reasonable degree of harmony and satisfaction. Beginning with the Peninsular War of 1808-1813, the army and the church became for the first time independent power groups, frequently in competition or conflict with each other. The monarchy lost its moral authority, never to regain it. The Liberals, who might conceivably have filled the power gap, set a precedent in 1820 by seizing power through an army pronunciamento and later bungled their best opportunity for reform, in the 1840's and 1850's. And the oligarchy, taking advantage of a mismanaged Liberal agrarian reform measure to consolidate their central position under the new regime, used their power for their own class interest while the nation drifted into Moroccan adventures, the disastrous war of 1898 with the United States, and the even more disastrous sharpening of social tensions brought on by

---

21 Ramos Oliveira, cited, p. 40.

the growth of industry and an urban proletariat in northern and northeastern Spain.

Most other European countries in this period faced problems similar to Spain's. France had her revolutions, her men on horseback, and her church-state controversies, and suffered invasion, defeat, and the Paris Commune of 1871. Yet she weathered these storms so successfully that Frenchmen now look back to the generation before 1914 as *la belle époque*. Granted that the rose-colored glasses of nostalgia have much to do with this, yet rare are the Spaniards who look back with any such nostalgia to that period in their own history. Rather, if they recall that age at all, they subscribe to the verdict of Ortega and his associates, handed down in March of 1914, that Spain was then a moribund nation, sick unto death not only in its ruling classes but throughout its social structure. That the ailment was grave and general was abundantly demonstrated by the sequel. But what were its causes? Ortega found them in the Restoration, which since 1876 had imposed the "terrible" dead weight of "official Spain" on "vital Spain" (Ortega's concept of the "two Spains"), crushing its vitality under a collusive system of alternating Conservative and Liberal rule, maintained by force and fraud for the enrichment of a favored few. This, he said, was justified by the regime's supporters on the ground that, after the civil wars of the nineteenth century, it had brought Spain "peace and order." But it was, he held, the peace of death.[22]

The middle class as such was not mentioned by Ortega as an active force, but his summons to remedial action was addressed to members of its constituent groups. Others have attributed Spain's misfortunes more directly to the lack of a strong middle class. While they may be right, there have been other factors as well, no less potent. Among these have been the strength of rival groups, particularly the army and the church; factional rivalries among the Liberals; and the unfortunate association of the Liberal movement with Free-

---

[22] Ortega y Gasset, *Vieja y nueva politica*, cited, pp. 12-15, 18.

masonry, with the French Revolution and, despite the opposition of many of them to it, with the Bonapartist intrusion into Spain in the first decade of the nineteenth century.

All these factors, and others as well, were brought into focus by the sporadic Carlist Wars between 1833 and 1876. The immediate issue was the succession to the throne. But the Carlist cause also represented authoritarianism, militant Catholicism, and the hostility of rural folk to urban dwellers. Its professional military leaders provided the best examples of guerrilla warfare that have been seen in Spain since the Peninsular War. Finally beaten, the Carlists were far from broken, and the danger that they might rise again exerted a perpetual blackmail against any genuinely liberal government in Spain; their important contribution to Franco's victory in the Civil War is noted elsewhere.[23]

It is little wonder, then, that the Liberals failed to provide the Spanish people with effective leadership in the century before World War I, although they held office time and again throughout this period. Indeed, for four decades after the Restoration of the Bourbon monarchy in 1876, they regularly alternated in power with the Conservatives under the "Box and Cox" system established by their chief leader, Práxedes Mateo Sagasta, and his Conservative counterpart, Antonio Cánovas del Castillo.

This is not to say that the Liberals were completely sterile. They fathered several measures typical of nineteenth-century European liberalism, even including some of an anticlerical character, such as the abolition of entailed estates, the guild system, monasteries, tithes, the expropriation of church property, and the establishment of freedoms of the person, of speech and the press, and a representative government under a constitutional monarchy. For a brief period, largely by default of the monarchists, the Liberals were even able to set up the First Spanish Republic, in 1873 and 1874. But on the whole they fell short of providing sustained national

---

23 See below, pp. 116, 165.

leadership, for the crippling effect of the objective handicaps they faced was magnified by their own shortcomings. Before the Restoration they were as intolerant as their Conservative opponents.[24] Under the Restoration they virtually abdicated leadership by joining the latter in maintaining the *status quo* through a system of rotation in office. And at all times they showed themselves as ready as anyone to resort to the pronunciamento.

From Parliamentary to Military Dictatorship

By the close of the nineteenth century the Liberals had become indistinguishable from the Conservatives. Both were in effect agents of the oligarchy in operating a regime that Joaquín Costa described as a parliamentary dictatorship disguised as a constitutional monarchy. As symptomatic of the liberalism of this period we may note that one of its new leaders, Conde de Romanones, was a major stockholder in an iron mining company whose operations near Melilla led, in 1909, to clashes with Moroccan tribesmen, whereupon the Madrid government sent in the Spanish army to protect the company's interests.[25] The upshot was a resumption of large-scale hostilities in Morocco, in the course of which the Spanish forces suffered the first of two military disasters (the second came a dozen years later) that led in 1923 to a new pronunciamento and the replacement of the parliamentary dictatorship by the military dictatorship of General Primo de Rivera.

The first of the fiascos in Morocco blighted the career of the Conservatives' best hope in this generation, Antonio

---

24 José Miranda, "El liberalismo español hasta mediados del siglo XIX," *Historia Mexicana* (Mexico City), October-December 1956, pp. 193-199. The author is a Spanish Republican exile.

25 Ramos Oliveira, cited, p. 143. Olivar Bertrand, cited, pp. 46-53, gives a useful summary of the Moroccan hostilities and their repercussions in Spain, with bibliographical data. He does not mention the economic interest of Romanones in Morocco, but he does state that the Liberals were even more active than the Conservatives in promoting Spain's claims and interests in the area (pp. 29, 49).

Maura, who was prime minister at the time. The call for more troops was violently resisted in Barcelona. Already notorious as a center of terrorist activities led by anarchists and other extremists, Barcelona now fell under mob rule for several days, with a substantial loss of life and property, principally church property. When order was restored, one of the scapegoats singled out for retaliation was a certain Francisco Ferrer, a railroad clerk; though he had neither participated in nor directly incited the violence, Ferrer was well known as a nihilist and a Freemason. His was guilt by association. A military court condemned him to death. In the face of strong public protests, Maura confirmed the sentence and Ferrer was shot.[26] The outcry against this gross injustice forced Maura out of office and into retirement, though it should be noted that he was already at odds with the young King, Alfonso XIII, whom he held in check, and with the oligarchy, whose whole system of control he threatened by his campaign for honest elections.

Maura was an aristocrat, not an oligarch, but that neither endeared him to the masses nor fitted him to lead them. As he frankly avowed, his whole concept of policy was one of reform from above. Reform from any source would have helped, but that was not the kind Spain needed at that juncture to help it adapt its regime to the profound changes which were taking place in Spanish society behind the Restoration's mask of immobilism.

Many of these changes were in response to Spain's increasingly close contacts with her European neighbors. With the aid of foreign capital, the textile industry was booming in the Barcelona area, and the iron industry in and around Bilbao. Spain's exports of raw materials and foodstuffs were growing apace. Those of iron ore reached their all-time high just before World War I, and have never approached it since. Fanned by the Generation of 1898, new winds of doctrine were blowing across the peninsula and there was a great stirring among the opposition groups, from center to extreme

---

[26] Ramos Oliveira, cited, pp. 145-146, and Olivar Bertrand, cited, pp. 49-51.

left, from moderate Republicans, who were found in all the cities, through the Socialists, whose citadel was Madrid, to the Anarcho-Syndicalists, strongest in Barcelona. The youngest of these groups had been in existence since the 1880's, but all of them flourished as never before in the decade preceding World War I.

The oldest political group of all was also bestirring itself. This was the army, which was threatening to become a state within the state or, as it ultimately did, to take over the state. From the beginning of the Restoration, its position had been strong, as evidenced by the fact that this was brought about by a general, Martínez Campos, who then added to his laurels by negotiating an agreement, in 1878, to end the first Cuban war for independence. The army's position was further strengthened through the support of Alfonso XIII, who came to the throne in 1902; like the present "Young Pretender," Don Juan Carlos, he had been educated in Spain's military schools. In 1907 the army won an extraordinary concession through the passage of the Law of Jurisdictions, which gave military courts jurisdiction over all cases involving offenses against military officers and institutions. Significantly, the impetus to this surrender of the civil to the military authority was provided by a Barcelona newspaper cartoon that had offended the susceptibilities of the military.[27]

The army's next long step forward came after the outbreak of World War I, during which neutral Spain profited handsomely by the wartime stimulus to her trade, but suffered domestic political tremors presaging the military coup of 1923. When the turbulence reached earthquake intensity in 1917, the army officers were prepared to deal with it through their newly formed committees of defense *(juntas de defensa)*. These were an unexpected offshoot of the same syndicalist ideas, preached by Sorel's Spanish disciples, that had already begun to revolutionize the Spanish labor movement and were later to spread to other occupational groups

---

[27] Madariaga, *Spain: A Modern History,* cited, p. 173; Ramos Oliveira, cited, pp. 142-143.

and social spheres. As Madariaga has said, the syndicalist "tenets of particularist association, abstention from politics, and direct action" appealed strongly to Spaniards.[28] Originally a sort of guild or professional association whose purposes were confined to military matters, committees of defense soon became instruments for direct control of the government by the army.

Twice during the crisis of 1917 the committees of defense dictated changes of government. After its peak had passed and a threat of revolution through a general strike had been put down, they also demanded and obtained an increase in the military budget. Apparently this was too much even for the army's best friend, Alfonso XIII. At this point he drew back and for the next six years used his extensive powers to support at least a semblance of constitutional government under civilian control.

The effort was doomed. Its end came in the wake of Spain's second major military disaster in Morocco, where in July 1921 a large Spanish force was almost annihilated by the tribesmen of the Riff. The reaction was slow but sure. Amidst charges by civilians that king and army were responsible for the disaster, and countercharges by the committees of defense that it was a final demonstration of the incompetence of constitutional government, a parliamentary commission of inquiry plodded ahead with a painstaking investigation of the whole affair. Just as its report was about to be published, the Cortes was sent packing by a military pronunciamento.

On September 13, 1923, the Captain General of Catalonia, General Miguel Primo de Rivera, rose in arms, announcing that his purpose was to free Spain from the corrupt and bungling rule of "professional politicians." Several of the leading army officers rallied to his support at once. After an interval of hesitation just long enough to meet the decencies, the King, too, gave the pronunciamento his blessing. On September 15, Primo set up his military dictatorship in

---

28 *Spain: A Modern History,* cited, p. 316.

Madrid, grasping all the reins of government in his hands.[29]

The new dictatorship, which lasted until January 30, 1930, marked the end of political rule by the oligarchy, whose agents, the "professional politicians," had been the chief target of the pronunciamento. On the other hand, Primo de Rivera's economic policy favored one segment of the oligarchy, the great landowners, possibly because he was one of them. It bore heavily on the other two main segments, mercantile and industrial, particularly in the field of labor relations, for Primo showed a special solicitude for industrial workers in the urban and mining areas. This was something new in the history of Spanish social policy, and it led to some new political alignments. While continuing to persecute the revolutionary Anarcho-Syndicalists, Primo won the collaboration of the Socialists under the leadership of Francisco Largo Caballero, who was to become the firebrand of the Second Republic. And the Socialists grew so rapidly under his patronage that they emerged as the strongest single party in Spain soon after the republic was established.

With the aid of an able finance minister, José Calvo Sotelo, whose assassination sparked the Civil War in 1936, Primo de Rivera put Spain's finances on a sound footing in his early years, made great improvements in the railroad and highway system, and almost succeeded in making the trains run on time. He won his greatest success in Morocco, where he obtained the cooperation of France. His relations with England were good, and with Mussolini's Italy cordial, though he made no effort to implant a full-fledged Fascist system in Spain. His censorship was galling to the intellectuals and his condemnation of Miguel de Unamuno to exile in the Canary Islands gave great offense to a wider circle. Otherwise his police state was hardly more oppressive than the Restoration had become in its later years.

Whatever its merits and defects, Primo's regime suffered from one weakness, but that was a fatal one: it failed to retain the support of the armed forces. Most of Primo's fellow

---

[29] Ramos Oliveira, cited, pp. 185-190; Madariaga, *Spain: A Modern History*, cited, pp. 338-340.

officers proved fair-weather friends. When the weather turned foul, with the first premonitions of the world-wide economic depression, which came early to Spain, the army was quick to appease public discontent by throwing him to the wolves. It was they who forced Primo to resign in January 1930. An easy-going Andalusian who had not taken adequate precautions, he yielded without a struggle, perhaps because his health was gone, and died in Paris three months later.

Primo's provisional successor was another general, but as the ferment continued to mount the army leaders sought to avoid too close an identification with the regime. And when the municipal elections of April 1931 indicated a strong trend of urban opinion against the monarchy, they sacrificed the King. Not that they raised a hand against his sacred person; they merely told him that they could not answer for the maintenance of public order if he remained on the throne. Without abdicating, he left the country rather than risk a civil war. But the civil war came just the same, and when it did it was more terrible and prolonged than a war fought in 1931 could conceivably have been. This was because in the interval between 1931 and 1936 the heterogeneous agglomeration of countless classes, factions, and cliques called the Spanish people had been driven by circumstances to group themselves in rival camps approximating the fabled "two Spains."

Spain and Anti-Spain

Spain is still divided by the rancors of the Civil War and General Franco has done his part to keep them alive. The most striking recent example of his contribution is provided by his speech of April 1, 1959, at the dedication of the imposing Civil War monument in the Valley of the Fallen (Valle de los Caídos). Describing his side's role in the war as a "crusade," he said:

That glorious epic of our liberation cost Spain too much to be forgotten. The struggle between good and evil never ends, no matter how great the victory. . . . Anti-Spain was beaten and routed, but is not dead. . . . This is no time to relax. . . . You [veteran reserve officers of the Nationalist army] must maintain with exemplary purity the brotherhood forged in the ranks of the crusade and prevent the enemy, who is always lying in ambush, from infiltrating your ranks. The [Nationalist] dead did not sacrifice their lives in order that we might rest.[30]

We have Franco's own word for it, then, that he is still waging a cold war on the Anti-Spain that he defeated in battle two decades ago. At that time it included more than half the Spanish people. Whether the proportion is larger or smaller today no one can say with certainty. But we do know—and this is more important—that by "Anti-Spain" he means not only these people, the Republicans or "Reds," as he calls them, but also the things they stood for, including above all democracy and representative government operating under a free political party system.

Individual Republicans who repent and do penance can hope for Franco's conditional forgiveness, though to none of them has he ever entrusted a post of authority. Under heavy foreign pressure he has recently adopted liberal economic policies that were followed by the republic, after being rejected by him for many years. But in the political sphere he still maintains his proscription of the core principles of the republic, even of the constitutional monarchy that preceded it. Since democracy is the universal talisman of the mid-twentieth century, he claims of course that his regime is democratic in the best "organic" sense, but Communists make the same sort of claim for their system. The fact is that, as democracy is understood in Western Europe and the United States, the Franco regime is as resolutely antidemocratic as it is anti-Communist.

This alone, if there were nothing else, is enough to keep Spain a deeply divided country so long as Franco rules it. For, as we have seen, Spain has a strong, deeply rooted liberal tradition a century and a half old. Its forms of expression have changed from age to age, and today it expresses itself

---

30 Text of Franco's speech to the Alféreces Provisionales, *Levante* (Valencia), April 2, 1959.

in an aspiration for democracy. But the basic idea has always been the same: the right of a people to govern themselves and to live as free men under the rule of law. The Spanish liberals have, as we have seen, bungled many an opportunity since 1810, but their record is one of achievement as well as failure. On balance, has any kind of Spanish regime made a better record? In any event, for the liberal forces in Spain no defeat has been final, and today they constitute the core of that Anti-Spain against which Franco finds it necessary to continue the "crusade" he launched in 1936.

Many Spaniards who survived the Civil War would like to bind up its wounds, and most of the younger generation are bored by so much talk about a conflict that is hardly more real to them than the time of Napoleon. There is no better proof of the popularity of the idea of national reconciliation than its adoption by the Communists as one of their principal talking-points. Yet Franco's summons to an unending crusade against Anti-Spain must evoke a powerful response somewhere among the Spanish people, for it is the keynote of a regime that he has maintained against all comers, domestic and foreign, for upwards of two decades.

Why Franco's "crusade" still makes so strong an appeal is not easy to explain. One of its sources may be the strain of absolutism that is so marked a feature of the Spanish character. It exists among liberals and progressives as well as conservatives and reactionaries. Years ago Ortega y Gasset saw in Cánovas del Castillo's motto, "neither victors nor vanquished," not a magnanimous, statesmanlike desire for national reconciliation after the civil wars of the nineteenth century, but rather a shameful surrender of principle.[31] Or perhaps waving the bloody shirt is good business for the many vested interests that have grown up in and around the Franco regime and depend upon it for their well-being if not for their very existence. Most recently, as even his Communist critics admit,[32] Franco has hedged a bit on his crusading principle by suggesting that the time has come for a

---

31 Ortega y Gasset, *Vieja y nueva política*, cited, pp. 24-27.
32 Radio España Independiente; monitored broadcast, February 9, 1960.

"dialogue," but this hint has so far remained a mere word, unaccompanied by any relaxation of controls on freedom of speech and action that would give it reality. The "two Spains" pattern that emerged from the Civil War remains substantially intact.

The Civil War and the "Two Spains"

Always an oversimplification, the "two Spains" concept was brought into closest correspondence with reality, not during the republic of the 1930's, but by the Civil War that destroyed it. When the monarch fled in 1931, the existing fragmentation only increased. Such unity as had existed among the advocates of a republic vanished the moment it was established. Moderates were content with the political victory, but to men of the left this was only a first step. "Now," they said, "we must have our social revolution." And within each wing there were further deep divisions, as between Catholic and anticlerical moderates, and between Socialists and Anarcho-Syndicalists. The Republic's enemies were similarly split until the Civil War and Franco forced them to coalesce.

War is the cement of coalitions, and Franco's continuation of his cold war within Spain has maintained a semblance of the "two Spains" pattern since 1939. Its maintenance has been due also to the fact that the Civil War, in giving birth to the Franco regime, endowed it with certain features which could not subsequently be altered without imperiling its existence. These included the myth of its anti-Communist origin, which was put to antidemocratic uses; its chief policies and institutional arrangements; and a spirit of intolerance even sharper than had been displayed by the regimes that emerged from Spain's earlier civil wars. All these features took shape early in the struggle.

The military uprising that opened the Spanish Civil War on July 18, 1936, was neither aimed against communism, as Franco later claimed, nor instigated by Fascist Italy and Nazi

Germany, as his enemies alleged.[33] His first pronunciamento made no mention of communism. In fact the government that he attacked was a representative republic of the familiar Western type, in which the Communists were a minute splinter group. Instead, at its outset his "National Movement," as he has always called it, was just another of the long line of *cuartelazos* or military revolts that have peppered the history of Spain since 1820.[34] Almost at once a complex of circumstances changed the character of the war profoundly and placed a lasting imprint on the regime to which it led. Needing foreign help, both sides took it where they could find it: Franco in Germany and Italy, the Republicans mainly in the Soviet Union. As a result each side soon became identified with either the Axis or communism, thus giving credibility to Franco's role as the paladin of anti-communism, a posture which he adopted early and has continued to exploit ever since.

What sparked the army's revolt of July 1936, if not resistance to communism? While there were many contributing factors, central to them all was the resentment of the army officers over being shorn of political power by the republic. For nearly a century before the republic replaced the monarchy in 1931, the army had been Spain's principal political power group, though for nearly half a century before 1923 it had operated behind the mask of an ostensibly constitutional monarchy, decked out with the usual paraphernalia of a representative parliament and political parties. Then the mask was thrown off and the officers made Primo de Rivera dictator, only to oust him in 1930 in favor of another general. All the while, as in Mussolini's Italy, a complaisant king was permitted to keep his throne.

---

33 Madariaga, *Spain: A Modern History,* cited, pp. 481-482. Madariaga holds the left-wing Republicans equally responsible for the outbreak of the Civil War. Our concern here is not with the question of responsibilities but with the character of the Franco regime.

34 It is interesting to note that Herbert Matthews, who had once taken a different view, admitted this in his book, *The Yoke and the Arrows* (New York: Braziller, 1957), p. 13: "This was a military *pronunciamiento* in the good old Spanish style. . . ."

In forcing the second change, however, the Spanish military had overplayed their hand and had discredited the entire monarchical regime, which collapsed within a year. On their advice Alfonso XIII went into exile, but that did not save them: politically speaking, the army fell with the monarchy. Civilians not only controlled the new republic, to the exclusion of the army. They also deprived the officers of many privileges and perquisites and eased large numbers of them into retirement.

The republic made the mistake, however, of stopping short of a thoroughgoing purge. Its program only irritated the armed forces without reforming them. They were left virtually intact to strike a counterblow that they had begun to plan even before the republic was well established. There were other mistakes as well, both of commission, such as its doctrinaire and highly divisive assault upon the church,[35] and of omission, such as its failure to cope with urgent social and agrarian problems or even to maintain a minimum degree of public order. All this has been admitted by the republic's well-wishers. As for its critics, one of the more temperate of them, writing recently with the imprimatur of the Franco regime, has explained the "lost opportunity of the republic" on three general grounds: the sectarianism of its leaders; the abstention of the conservative classes; and the lack of political and civic education on the part of the masses.[36] However that may be, the result of five years of Republican rule was to assure the disgruntled army officers of strong support from the church and the upper classes for their blow against the republic.

Clearly, Franco's rebellion did not create the schism in Spanish society which he has perpetuated. But he could have done a great deal to heal it. He was obligated to make the effort by the very name "Nationalist" that he gave to his

---

[35] Madariaga, *Spain: A Modern History,* cited, pp. 393-394, 405-406, describes the republic's anticlericalism as one of the chief reasons for its failure. Gabriel Jackson, "The Azaña Regime in Perspective," *American Historical Review,* January 1959, pp. 282-300, lays less stress on this factor.

[36] *Ya* (Madrid), February 14, 1959; interview with Fermín Zelada.

forces, and, if vigorously sustained, such an effort might have met with some success. For one thing, Spain's divisions in previous civil wars had in each case been followed by reconciliation. True, this had been an exceptionally bitter and destructive conflict; yet, after the only comparable civil war of the past century in the Western world, the north and south of the United States did not perpetuate the victor-vanquished pattern, and within a decade after Appomattox the nation was more closely knit than before the war. While the Spanish people have never been as united as the Americans, they had better possibilities of reunion after their Civil War, since in Spain the division between the belligerents did not follow clear-cut geographical or economic lines. Even its religious and social lines, though clearer, were sufficiently blurred to leave the door open to reunion after the shooting war was over.[37] Most important of all, if Franco had let it, the National Movement as originally constituted (army, church, Falange, and monarchists) could have promoted reunion, whether by following the policy of "integration and comprehension" advocated by Pedro Laín Entralgo, Dionisio Ridruejo, and other leaders of the Falange in its early years,[38] or in some other way.

Franco, in the event, opted for perpetual war between Spain and Anti-Spain. He then made institutional provision for its continuance under his command. After narrowing the National Movement to the Falange by making the latter the "political expression of the Movement" and Spain's only party, he then reduced the Falange itself to a bureaucracy administering his personal regime. All other parties were prohibited and at the end of the war even Freemasonry was outlawed because of its political association with republicanism.

Franco's own explanation of his choice, as stated to the

---

37 Ramos Oliveira, cited, pp. 579-581, argues persuasively but not quite convincingly that the "conflict between the two Spains" did achieve geographical expression on the basis of the presence or absence of a strong middle class.

38 Dionisio Ridruejo, "Un pensamiento generacional," *Cuadernos* (Paris), July-August 1959, pp. 27-35.

German Ambassador in 1937, was quite simple. The only practical alternative to his personal rule was, in his opinion, a "return to the monarchy," which was "absolutely out of the question for the foreseeable future." "Only after the completion of the reconstruction of Spain, which would take a long time, could one consider whether a certain continuity could not be established by reintroducing the monarchy." So strongly did Franco feel on this point that, as he said in this same conversation, he was deterred from putting one of the most active monarchists to death only by the fear that this would alienate the Carlist-monarchist Requetés, who were some of his best soldiers.[39] Again, Alfonso XIII, then in Rome, had provided the first funds to finance the rebellion. But, when he sought to return to Spain on the outbreak of the war, Franco sent him a passport made out to "His Excellency Don Alfonso de Borbón." The former King took the hint and stayed in Rome. His third son, the present Pretender, did enter Nationalist Spain, only to be expelled. For this Franco was not responsible, as he was for the rejection of Don Juan's later efforts to join the Nationalist navy.[40] Obviously, there was not room enough in Spain for both the Caudillo and a member of the royal family.

In the same conversation with the German Ambassador, Franco also talked of his plans for fusing the monarchists and the Falange into a single party. He himself would be its leader and the Falange would be its core, for it had the soundest program and the largest following in Spain. He might have added that for him the Falange had a further attraction. It was a quite new party, had only gained its large following since the start of the war, and, as he himself remarked, had had no strong leader since the murder of its founder, José Antonio Primo de Rivera, at the beginning of the war. It would therefore provide Franco with the most

[39] U.S. Department of State, *Documents on German Foreign Policy, 1918-1945*. Series D, v. 3: *Germany and the Spanish Civil War* (Washington: GPO, 1950), pp. 267-269.

[40] Jean Créach, *Le Coeur et l'épée* (Paris: Plon, 1958), pp. 185-189. The author, former correspondent of *Le Monde* (Paris) in Spain, heard this story from Don Juan himself.

serviceable instrument he could hope to find or fashion for the future government of Spain.

In April 1937 Franco did in fact fuse the Falange, already joined in 1934 to the proletarian, Nazi-inspired JONS,[41] with one of the monarchist groups, the Traditionalists of Navarre. After a brief resistance, soon overcome, the product of this fusion of disparate elements, still bearing the Falange label, served Franco docilely and well, first to the close of the shooting war and afterwards in his permanent cold war against Anti-Spain, which the Falange, by its very origin, is dedicated to combat.

Many factors doubtless contributed to Franco's choice, among them, the intolerance typical of Spaniards, the outlook of a Spanish soldier shaped in the ruthless warfare of Morocco, and the examples of Mussolini and Hitler and their authoritarian systems manipulating power through a single party. No less decisive were Franco's fear of what might happen to his regime if more than one party were permitted, and his belief in his mission as a providential, indispensable leader. When I questioned him in 1959 about this sense of mission, Franco talked about it freely, describing how it had first taken definite shape in his mind during his Moroccan service in the 1920's and had been confirmed by divine interventions on his behalf during the Spanish Civil War. His conviction showed no sign of weakening in 1959. Perhaps its most succinct expression has been achieved in the minting of Spanish coins styling him "Caudillo of Spain by the grace of God."

Whatever Franco's reasons for persisting in his crusade against Anti-Spain, the consequences for the whole country were grave. In 1950, on the eve of the first public overture from the United States, Spain still had the aspect of a conquered country, a country conquered by its own armed

---

41 The initials stand for Juntas de Ofensiva Nacional Sindicalista. The founder of this group, Ramiro Ledesma Ramos, was the son of a village schoolteacher; as a student at the University of Madrid he had had a "flair for quoting Nietzsche and Kant" and an "enormous passion for proletarian justice," and was a "frank admirer of Hitler"; Emmet John Hughes, *Report from Spain* (New York: Holt, 1947), p. 24.

forces. The garrison-state atmosphere created a widespread feeling of insecurity and mutual suspicion. Half a million Spaniards were still in exile, others left as opportunity offered, and capital, too, took flight. Government controls paralleling the political monopoly of the Falange choked private enterprise. The Spanish economy had not recovered even its modest level of the 1920's. Except in a few industrial fields to which the government devoted special efforts at heavy cost, production lagged well behind that of three decades before, although the population had been growing steadily. A dozen or more years after the end of the Civil War it was clear that without foreign assistance it would be a long time before Spain could complete her recovery. The turbulence of the unruly republic had been replaced by peace and order, but the price had been high. One part of that price was a national schism that the country's government seemed bent on perpetuating.

Chapter IV

THE CAUDILLO AND HIS SUPPORTERS

THE FRANCO REGIME is still an iron-fisted dictatorship, as it has been from the start. Its manners have become milder and a glove has been drawn over the mailed fist. The change is reflected in the quip that the *dictadura,* or hard dictatorship, has evolved into a *dictablanda,* or soft dictatorship. But the mailed fist is still there and is used whenever occasion requires, as the people of Barcelona were forcibly reminded in May 1960 when General Franco visited the city. Amid demonstrations of the regime's military might various concessions were announced, and at first all went well. One evening, however, a crowd in the Palace of Music defied the authorities by singing a hymn to the Catalan flag in the proscribed Catalan language, whereupon the police fell on the crowd, beat and arrested a score of the ringleaders, and reportedly tortured some of them. Most of them were released two or three days later, after a sharp protest to Madrid from the Abbot of Montserrat, but the most prominent of them, young Dr. Jorge Pujol, was court-martialed and sentenced to seven years' imprisonment. Pujol, a moderate, heads a youth movement of Catholic Catalans.

Politically, a regime of this character could be nothing but a liability as a partner in the defense of the free world, but the U.S. alliance with it was originally based on military considerations; from this point of view, Washington appears satisfied that Franco is a useful ally in the light of its experience under the pact of 1953.

But will Franco's regime continue to be useful? And will it continue? Dictators are notoriously undependable, and dictatorships unstable. Is there anything in the Spanish case that differentiates it from the common run of such regimes? Franco has been in power more than twenty years—longer than any other Spanish ruler since the eighteenth century. How is this feat to be explained? The answers to these questions should throw light on a further question, one of direct practical interest to the United States: What is the outlook for its alliance with Spain, whether under the Franco regime or any likely successor to it?

While Franco is a close approximation to an absolute personal dictator, his regime is nevertheless based upon and could not stand without the support of certain key elements in Spanish society. No dictator was ever strong enough to stand for twenty years with his feet firmly planted in mid-air. Any dictator who lasts so long must also, I assume, have the psychological support of a widely accepted idea or myth.

Franco has had, in the main, the support of four power groups and one phantom. The power groups are the armed forces, the church, the "oligarchy," and the Falange. Of these the first has been the regime's chief warranty and the last its most docile instrument. All four have served him well, thanks to Franco's clever coachmanship, which up to now has kept them pulling, however reluctantly, under his reins, sometimes in double tandem, sometimes in relays. The phantom, born of the terrible Civil War and its million dead, is the fear that Franco's removal might bring about a repetition of the horrors of that ordeal. Once compelling and almost universal, this fear still provides his regime with strong support, although its foundations are being eroded by the passage of time, which is dimming memories of the Civil War among those who lived through it and bringing to maturity a new generation who know it only by hearsay.

Before examining the regime's chief supporting groups more closely, it will be helpful to take a look at the govern-

mental framework within which they act. Since in a sense
Franco *is* the government, the survey will be a rapid one
except as regards Franco himself, in whose person are combined the four functions of chief of state, prime minister,
generalissimo of the armed forces, and Caudillo or chief of
the "Movement" and its corporate representative, the Falange. The only important institution that he does not rule
is the Catholic Church in Spain, still headed, as it has been
for many centuries, by the Archbishop of Toledo as Primate
of Spain. But, as we shall see, Franco has his own ways of
influencing the church.

The Government: Structure and Functioning

Franco ordinarily refers to his system simply as "the
Regime" *(el Régimen)*. What does he mean by this term? By
the Law of Succession of 1947, Spain was declared to be a
Catholic, social, and representative state which "in accordance with tradition" formed itself into a kingdom. Franco's
subsequent public utterances have ratified the terms of this
description, though not without attaching some glosses of his
own. He not only insists that his regime is representative,
but has discovered that it is an "organic democracy" as well.
In official cant, the term "the dictatorship" is reserved for
Primo de Rivera's regime, all references to which are in the
laudatory vein an early Christian might employ in speaking
of John the Baptist.

The fact is that Franco has gone far beyond his illustrious
predecessor of the 1920's in centralizing in his own hands all
control over the nation's life. In recent years there has been
a rising chorus of complaint, swelled by his own adherents,
that he has not institutionalized the government of Spain.
In the sense in which it is meant, the complaint is well
founded. And yet no one can deny that Franco has done a
remarkably thorough job of institutionalizing his personal
dictatorship. He makes and can unmake the nation's fundamental laws, subject only to the approval of the Cortes, which
is automatic, and of a popular referendum, which is easily

managed, as in 1947. The representative assembly, or Cortes, represents no one so much as Franco himself. He is the head of the country's only political party, which is also its bureaucracy. Labor, capital, the press, and the universities are under the thumb of cabinet ministers and other functionaries whom he appoints and dismisses at will. The armed forces, on whose loyalty the whole structure rests, are under his direct command. His regime is thus the ultimate in personalism, and its personalist character does some odd things to the traditionalism to whose preservation the regime is ostensibly consecrated.

By way of illustration, let us look at some of the chief features of the regime, beginning with its two most famous fundamental laws, the Fuero de los Españoles, or Charter of the Rights of Spaniards of July 20, 1945, and the Law of Succession, of July 28, 1947. *Fuero* is a term redolent of Spanish traditions handed down from the middle ages, and its constitutional significance and historical associations are the Spanish equivalent of Magna Carta. Accordingly, Franco's Charter of 1945 provides an ostensible guarantee of personal rights and immunities that Thomas Jefferson himself would have applauded. The only trouble is that, as Madariaga puts it, "The Charter of Rights is the most mendacious document ever penned. It guarantees every right which the government tramples upon daily. . . . There is not a single article of this Charter that is not in itself an insult to the nation whose daily experience gives it the lie." [1]

The Law of Succession of 1947, which also capitalized on the appeal to tradition and has likewise so far proved a hoax, is an even more notable instance of Franco's ingenuity. It committed him for the first time to the restoration of the monarchy and met the demand for institutionalizing the regime to the extent of setting up a Council of the Realm which, sitting with the cabinet, would nominate his successor, and a Council of Regency to serve in case of an interregnum. The law even specifies the qualifications of the future

---

[1] Salvador de Madariaga, *Spain: A Modern History* (New York: Praeger, 1958), p. 596.

monarch: he must be male, a Spaniard, at least thirty years of age, and must swear to uphold the fundamental laws of the realm.[2] The vagueness of these qualifications put Franco in a position to play off possible candidates for the throne against one another. As no deadline for the restoration was set, he could go on playing this game as long as he lived—as he apparently intends to do. Moreover, the appointment of high church and army officials to the two councils binds those groups more closely to his regime.

Franco's master stroke was to incorporate in this law for the ultimate restoration of the monarchy an article confirming his own position as chief of state for an indefinite period. He then had the law approved not only by the Cortes but by the extraordinary device of a popular referendum. According to the government, this plebiscite ratified the law by an overwhelming majority. In round numbers, some twelve million of the thirteen million votes cast were in favor of it. Franco could now claim that he was Caudillo not only by conquest and the grace of God, but by the will of the Spanish people.

The apparatus of government is headed, under Franco, by a Cortes, or parliament, and a cabinet. The Cortes, too, is a traditional Spanish institution whose history reaches back into the middle ages. Once roughly equivalent to the English Parliament and the French Estates General, it is older than either. In modern times its history extends from the famous Cortes of Cádiz, which adopted the constitution of 1812, to the Civil War of 1936-1939.

By a fundamental law of July 18, 1942, Franco revived the name of the Spanish Cortes. But his Cortes is neither a representative nor a legislative body, and the cabinet is not responsible to it but to Franco. Of its 585 members he hand-picks one-third directly. The rest nominally represent corporate groups (economic and municipal), but these are controlled by Madrid. The Cortes only advises, and votes

---

[2] At that time, these included the Charter (Fuero) of 1945, the Charter of Labor (1938), the law establishing the Cortes (1942), and the Law of Succession itself.

without debate. It has never been known to oppose Franco's will.

The cabinet, too, is traditional in the sense that it has been a familiar institution in Spain for over a century. Before Franco, however, its primary association was with parliamentary, constitutional government, whereas his cabinet is responsible to him alone. He appoints and dismisses its members at will. He has appointed virtually new cabinets about once every six years, though individual members have frequently been continued from one cabinet to the next. The senior post, that of minister of foreign affairs, was held continuously for twelve years by Alberto Martín Artajo until he was dropped in the cabinet overturn of February 1957. The ministers usually serve as long as Franco chooses to keep them; few have been permitted to resign.

The cabinet is Franco's most important institution, for, with the exceptions noted below, most of the powers of government are concentrated in its members. As his agents in their respective departments, they give detailed effect to his policy decisions and carry his authority into the remotest nooks and crannies of Spanish life. This is not to say that the system works perfectly—far from it, for the Spanish bureaucracy preserves the spirit summed up in the time-honored phrase, "I obey, but I do not execute," and it also has at least the usual quota of human and particularly bureaucratic frailties. Favoritism is so common that the regime has been described as government by *enchufe,* meaning connection, pull, influence.[3] Sterner critics describe it as a tyranny tempered by corruption. Nevertheless, it is the most efficiently centralized government Spain has ever had—even the absolute monarchy at its eighteenth-century peak did not have the technological means to match it—and the cabinet is Franco's central control room for most aspects of his rule.

The present cabinet contains eighteen members, whose assignments are, with one exception, of the kind met with in most contemporary governments, such as Foreign Affairs,

---

[3] Literally, *enchufe* is an outlet to plug in an electric lamp, radio, or other appliance.

Finance, Commerce, Interior (Gobierno), Public Works, and the armed services (three ministries, one each for War, Navy and Air). The exception is the secretary-general of the Movement, i.e., the uniquely Spanish Falange. The presence of its secretary-general betokened, however, not a rise in the Falange's political fortunes but its decline to an all-time low. In fact, since 1957 most of the members of the cabinet have been unfriendly to the Falange and have opposed its policies. The principal posts have recently been held either by members of the armed forces, who checkmated the Falange's recent bid for power between the summer of 1956 and January 1957, or by members or sympathizers of the Opus Dei, a Catholic lay institute, whose religious orientation sets it poles apart from the Falange.

Insofar as one can generalize about the rather amorphous cabinet which Franco appointed in February 1957 its trends in both the economic and political spheres have run counter to Falangist principles. This is important because its appointment was Franco's way of meeting a political and economic crisis that had developed in the preceding months. The great majority of the new cabinet ministers are monarchists. At least two of those mainly concerned with economic questions—Minister of Commerce Alberto Ullastres and Minister of Treasury Navarro Rubio—are advocates of a new departure in economic policy, stressing sounder finance, greater freedom for private enterprise, and closer economic ties with foreign countries. None of these policies jibes with Falangist ideas. The only militant Falange member, José Luis Arrese, Minister of Housing, clashed with Navarro Rubio and was dismissed by Franco when the controversy became public in March 1960. In his place Franco appointed José María Martínez Sánchez-Arjona who, though likewise long active in the Falange, conspicuously lacked Arrese's crusading zeal.

Whether or not the Falangists have been happy with the new cabinet of 1957 is relatively beside the point, since their organization is Franco's creature and has no independent political power of its own. What is much more important is the fact that the choice of this cabinet was Franco's way of solving a crisis compounded of ferment in labor and student circles, feuds within the regime, and a general malaise brought on by the threat of runaway inflation; and that he has made only one cabinet change down to mid-1960. In the meantime he has adopted the stabilization plan of July 1959, advocated by the cabinet's economic specialists, but he has not moved an inch closer to a restoration of the monarchy, which the great majority of the cabinet members are said to favor. Moreover, there is every reason to believe that Franco's conversion to economic reform has been due less to the persuasions of his ministers than to the inexorable pressures generated by Spain's deepening economic crisis, reinforced by the advice of international organizations and foreign governments—foremost among them the United States—whose help he had to have.

No such pressure has been put upon him with regard to the monarchy or any other political question affecting his regime. And on such questions he has not budged. The contrast illustrates the fact that, supremely important though the cabinet is as an administrative control center, it is not in any real sense a policy-making body. Franco makes policy and the ministers only execute it, but it is they who take the blame when things go wrong.

Of the many matters administered through the cabinet, labor is one of the most important. It is the subject of one of the regime's fundamental laws, the Charter of Labor, promulgated in March 1938 while the Civil War was still going on. Well aware that organized labor was the backbone of the opposition to his Movement, and looking forward to the postwar period, Franco combined the carrot with the club in this Charter, based mainly on Socialist ideas worked over by the Falange. The Charter regiments labor in government-controlled syndicates, denies workers the right to strike, and prohibits all other labor organizations. On the other hand, labor enjoys job security and government protection in the matter of wages, hours, and working conditions, for management too has been forced into the syndicates and deprived of most of its former freedom in dealing with the workers.

The vertical syndicates, built up from local units in offices, plants, and factories, combine management and labor with the nominally impartial government and head up in the Ministry of Falange. Franco still boasts that his syndical system is the best means of averting class conflict and achieving social justice. The system has, however, come under heavy fire from many quarters, including the Catholic hierarchy, and the slight relaxation of its controls granted in 1958 has by no means satisfied either capital or labor. It has done little if anything to abate the class conflict or promote social justice. It is important mainly because the syndical organization has over the years created vested interests that may play a significant role in the struggle for power when the present regime changes.

Through his cabinet, Franco controls nearly all areas of Spanish life. The universities, for example, are regulated by a law of July 1943 administered through the Ministry of Education. Reflecting the inner contradictions of the regime, this law purports to make the universities strongholds of both Falangism and Roman Catholicism, which are mutually antagonistic. So far, the latter has had the edge, especially through Opus Dei. A considerable number of faculty members belong to neither group; among them are some even who are known as opponents of the regime. These facts betoken not tolerance on the part of the regime but rather its contempt for mere intellectuals, combined in recent years with a fear of offending influential foreign opinion by the persecution of well-known university figures. Even the university students are regimented in a single syndicate, the SEU (Sindicato Español Universitario). In this case, too, enforcement is lax, for other student organizations, nominally clandestine, also exist.

The press, for which the regime has anything but contempt, is controlled through the Ministry of Information under minute regulations, rigorously enforced ever since the adoption of the first press law in 1938. In addition to an all-but-universal censorship, newspapers are required to follow prescribed news and editorial policies; their editorial staffs are subject to appointment and dismissal by the minister. Even loyal Catholic Action's *Ecclesia,* the only uncensored periodical in Spain, was once forced to dismiss an editor who had offended the regime.

Finally, the rule of law is not the rule. The judiciary is generally reputed to be the most nearly honest segment of a corrupt regime. But the judges are subject to harassment by the minister of justice through reassignment and otherwise, and the judicial system is corrupted at its source by the regime's lack of respect for its own fundamental laws, including the Charter of Rights of 1945. Whenever the government chooses to regard a case as involving state security, the case is tried before a military court. If, as sometimes happens, the military court deals too leniently with the offender, the government has the case retried and imposes a judgment more to its own liking. A recent instance is the case of Julio Cerón Ayuso, a young Spanish diplomat charged with the crime of attempting to bring about the establishment of a democratic federal republic in Spain. In early November 1959 he was convicted and sentenced by a military tribunal to three years' imprisonment. Then, reportedly on direct orders from the Pardo Palace, the Special National Military Tribunal for Extremist Activities reconsidered the case, and on December 23 it raised the sentence to eight years.

Executive Agencies: INI and Suanzes

Even in administrative matters the cabinet is not Franco's sole channel of authority, as illustrated by the role of the INI (Instituto Nacional de Industria) of Juan Antonio Suanzes, who has headed it ever since its founding in 1941. The case also shows how policy is made in Spain. Suanzes and Franco have been friends since their childhood in El Ferrol. As they grew older, Franco formed a lasting admiration for the talents and character of his companion, his senior by one year and at first more successful. Both wanted to become naval officers. Only Suanzes was accepted; he had a rapid rise in the select engineering branch, specializing in naval construction. Although Franco had to be content with an army appointment, he too won rapid promotion, so that there was no ground for jealousy. Their paths parted for several years only to meet again during the Civil War.

In the meantime Suanzes' course had strengthened him in Franco's esteem. Appointed in 1932 director of a semi-private, partly British-owned firm engaged in building ships for the Spanish navy, he resigned in 1934 because he was unable to bring about the nationalization of the British share. The outbreak of the Civil War two years later caught Suanzes in Republican-controlled Madrid, where he had gone into the elevator manufacturing business. He escaped, joined the Nationalist forces, and soon turned up at Burgos, the wartime headquarters of Franco's government. At first employed in his special field of naval construction, in January 1938 Suanzes was raised to cabinet rank as minister of industry. Only eighteen months later he was dropped, because, it is said, he was unable to check corruption in his ministry; but his personal integrity seems never to have been questioned.

In any case Franco's respect for Suanzes was undiminished. Only two years later, in 1941, he followed his old friend's advice in making the important decision to found INI, and then entrusted it to his care. Suanzes has directed INI ever since. From 1945 to 1951 he was again a cabinet member, as minister of industry and commerce. All along, whether in the cabinet or out, he remained until 1959 one of Franco's most trusted economic advisers.

The relationship between the two men has been reinforced by other ties. Their wives are intimate friends, and, like Franco, Suanzes is both a devout Catholic and a model family man. In 1958 a foreign visitor who ranged widely through government offices in Madrid noted that the only ones that showed a religious influence were Suanzes' INI offices, all of which displayed crucifixes and religious pictures. A distinguished economist as well as a perceptive observer, this visitor was impressed by Suanzes' evident dedication to improving the lot of the common man—a purpose not shared, according to Suanzes, by any member of the cabinet—and by his ready sense of humor and combination of an unphilosophical cast of thought with shrewd and quick intelligence. Another expert observer noted about this time, after talking with Suanzes, that he was "mildly Falangist."

This is the man who is believed to have been the chief architect of Franco's economic policy for nearly twenty years, insofar as he had a settled policy. That policy was largely conceived outside of the cabinet and to a considerable extent carried out through executive agencies, such as INI, not under cabinet control. The policy was one of autarky under rigid government control, and its main goal was industrialization.

This policy was easy to defend during Spain's enforced isolation of World War II and its general ostracism in the next five years. From the start, however, there was bitter resentment in business and banking circles against many of the government-sponsored enterprises through which Suanzes implemented this policy. The outstanding example is INI's big and costly steel plant at Avilés, which competes with Spain's private iron and steel industry centered in Asturias and the neighboring Basque country. Suanzes still believes that Avilés and his whole program were indispensable. Fifty years from now, he asserts, no one will remember what they cost, but all will remember that Franco and Suanzes began the industrialization of Spain. Nevertheless, as the circumstances that had been invoked to justify his system changed in the 1950's and the tide of Spanish opinion mounted against it, Suanzes at last gave way. By the end of 1958 he was already admitting privately that the time for autarky and a government-directed economy had passed.

Franco himself moved more slowly. When at last he made his decision, it was again not based solely, or perhaps even mainly, on the advice of his cabinet. Instead, in the winter of 1958-1959, he held a kind of national inquest on the economic problems at issue, conducted among the country's leading economic organisms, such as the banking community, the syndicates, and the head of INI. All of them, including Suanzes, recommended a far-reaching liberalization of economic policy. After Franco had been won to this view, the cabinet dutifully endorsed the change. Franco then took the plunge into the new course by negotiating the international arrangements of July 1959.

Franco, the Man and the Caudillo

Franciso Franco y Bahamonde was born December 4, 1892, in El Ferrol. He has rarely left Spain except for service in Spanish Morocco, and, as we have noted, heads up nearly every important Spanish institution in his fourfold role of chief of state, prime minister, generalissimo, and Caudillo. Nevertheless, it is a favorite quip among his opponents that Franco is built like Napoleon and is no more Spanish than the Corsican was French, because Franco is a *gallego*, or native of Galicia in northwestern Spain.

There is an element of truth in the quip, but not a large one. Franco's physical resemblance to Napoleon breaks down at a vital point: his health is excellent and he has already outlived Napoleon by fifteen years. As for Galicia, it once seemed more Portuguese than Spanish, but it has been a part of Spain for many centuries and contains Spain's oldest and most famous national shrine, Santiago de Compostela. Galicia does indeed have its regional peculiarities, but particularism is less marked in Galicia than in some other parts of Spain, as in the Basque country and Catalonia.

Franco's personal idiosyncracies and deviations from what is generally regarded as the Spanish norm may be due in some measure to his Galician antecedents. He differs most in being cool, calculating, and deliberate. A story often heard in Spain illustrates these qualities. When Franco, then a young man, took over the command of the Foreign Legion in Morocco, so the story runs, there was great discontent among the enlisted men over their treatment, especially in the matter of food. Franco investigated personally and while he was questioning individual soldiers during a meal hour, one indignant legionnaire emptied his mess kit in his face. Franco, the story continues, calmly wiped his face and went on as if nothing had happened; when he had completed his inspection he cashiered the mess officer and had the offending soldier taken out and shot.[4] One may conclude from this story that Franco is also immoderate and ruthless; these qualities, unlike some others, are not un-Spanish.

In most respects, Franco is Spanish to his fingertips. To be more precise, he is a typical product of the Spanish army officer class, to which he has belonged since his early teens. Like most of its members, he is authoritarian, nationalistic, conservative, and Catholic. He also shares his fellow officers' strong sense of the army's mission to rule the country in time of crisis, though, again like most of them, he would prefer a monarchy for normal times.

In some respects, of course, Franco is an exceptional Spaniard. Otherwise he would not be where he is today. He is exceptionally courageous and astute. These qualities, exhibited from the beginning of his career in hard fighting with Moroccan tribesmen, earned him a promotion to the rank of general at the very early age of thirty-three. He was thus in line for the leadership over the rebel forces when an army revolt which he had helped to engineer opened the Civil War a dozen years later. Exceptional also has been Franco's good fortune. For example, when the Civil War began, he was outranked by two other rebel generals, José Sanjurjo and Emilio Mola; both were soon removed from the scene by death. Again, just after World War II, when his regime was seriously threatened by a combination of domestic and foreign pressures, Franco was saved by the coincidence that his Spanish enemies—some Republicans, others monarchists—were unable to unite, and the principal foreign powers, including the United States and Great Brit-

---

4 This is the story as it was told to me in Spain in 1959. It is related in greater detail with some slight differences in *The Yoke and the Arrows* (New York: Braziller, 1957), pp. 62-64, by Herbert Matthews.

ain, were unwilling to carry their pressure to the point required to make it stick.

There are other ways in which Franco differs from the general run of his class. Whereas Franco has been publicly and solemnly committed ever since 1947 to the ultimate restoration of the monarchy, and most of the officers want it restored now and in some traditional form, he has made it clear—notably in a speech of May 1958 to the Cortes—that he plans both to rule as long as he lives and also to bind his successor to the fundamental principles of the Movement. In addition, the Movement, though broader than the Falange, has Falangist connotations that make this condition unwelcome to many army officers. Obviously, Franco likes his job. Whether or not he likes the Falange as much as his stand on this question would seem to indicate, he apparently thinks it good politics to play up the party, and perhaps also to play it off against the army and other sectors of the regime, in accordance with his divide-and-rule tactics.

Another example of Franco's untypical views relates to social policy. In this field Franco has committed himself to a broader view of the government's social responsibilities than is held by most army officers. Again the motivation is necessarily in doubt; he may hold these views either from conviction, as he claims, or in order to keep the masses in line, as other dictators have done, or under pressure from Catholic leaders, as some of them believe, or again in furtherance of the Falange line, for the Falange still retains a flavor of national socialism and poses—not very convincingly, to be sure—as the champion of social justice and the workingman against capitalist exploitation. Contrary to Suanzes' reported assertion, some members of the present cabinet seem to be genuinely concerned over the lot of the Spanish masses, but the one whose concern is most apparent, Secretary-General Minister Solís, is reported on good authority to be less than enthusiastic about the Falange.

In this connection it should be noted that capitalism is one of two important subjects on which Franco has continued to take a strong public stand which is at odds with that of the United States. The other is representative democracy with its corollary, the political party system. Franco's hostility to both has been publicly stated on many occasions both before and since he signed the Pact of Madrid. One of the most recent and important was the formal inauguration, on April 8, 1959, of the first stage of an ambitious irrigation system in Aragon. Early in his speech Franco pointed out that seventy years had elapsed since the imperative need for irrigation systems of this type had been recognized, but nothing effective had been done to meet it until his own regime came to power. The failures of preceding governments, he asserted, had been due to the inherent and inescapable vices of the political party system and of capitalism, whose baneful influence had paralyzed all these essential projects even when the government was headed by "the glorious General Primo de Rivera." [5]

There can be no doubt of Franco's genuine and deep aversion for the party system. The same cannot be said of his professed hostility to capitalism. He must profess it in order to please some of his supporters, but he has to belie the profession in order to please others and keep his regime going.

Perhaps Franco's dictatorship could not have survived so long in any climate of opinion other than the average Spaniard's mortal terror of another civil war. In a more immediate sense, however, he has been kept in power by the support of four major groups or sectors of Spanish society, and by his astute and forceful management of them.

These four groups are the armed forces; the Catholic Church; the oligarchy of big businessmen, bankers, and landowners; and the Falange. They do not form a solid phalanx. There are, it is true, some interlocking ties among the first three, but these are mainly of a personal or family character. No love is lost between any of them and the Falange, and none of the four groups is a monolithic bloc. Consequently, Franco manages them, not like the chairman of a harmonious

---

[5] *ABC* (Madrid), April 9, 1959, contains the text of the entire speech.

board of directors, but rather like a lion tamer or perhaps a supreme political manipulator who plays off one group or faction against another for his own ends. He has, as we shall see, employed the same tactics in handling the opponents of his regime. "Divide and rule" has been one of his principal devices for keeping an unruly nation under his thumb for more than two decades. The particularistic character of Spanish society, with its sharply marked regional, class, and occupational distinctions, has contributed greatly to his success.

The Armed Forces

In any account of power groups in Franco Spain, the armed forces must come first. For the prime question about any power group is "What kind of power does it have?" In the Spanish context the decisive kind is not political bargaining power or moral authority or any kind but physical force. Of the latter, in Franco Spain, the army, navy and air force have a near-monopoly. In other situations, other groups may predominate, as the labor unions did for a time under the republic of the 1930's, or the Argentine *descamisados* under Perón; but anything like that is outside the very nature of the Franco regime. There is no real freedom of bargaining or debate. Political parties are banned, associations of all kinds regimented, and meetings of whatever kind subjected to police control. Workers and employers alike are bound to the captive syndicates. As for moral authority, even the Catholic Church is permitted to exercise it only within prescribed limits, and what the regime once had of it in earlier years has been dissipated long since. While all governments may rest on force in the last instance, Franco rests on it from first to last.

Among the armed forces, which dominate the Spanish scene, the army is by far the strongest of the three. Moreover, army units are widely distributed in strategic positions throughout the country, including the Balearic and Canary Islands and the remnant of Spanish Morocco, whence it began the Civil War. Military officers hold the key posts of captains general in all provinces, and the army is strongly represented in the present cabinet. It has, as we have seen, a long-established tradition of intervention in the public life of the country.

According to a well-informed French observer, André Fontaine, the only force in Spain that could turn Franco out is the army, and it could do so overnight if it chose.[6] My own observations in Spain tend to confirm this opinion, which is also supported by the precedent of the overthrow of Primo de Rivera by the armed forces. Whether they would do so again is, of course, highly conjectural, but there are several related questions that can be answered with more assurance. These are: What degree of political unity exists among the armed forces? What, if any, are their grounds of discontent with the regime? How strong are their ties with it? And what, if any, alternative regime would they support?

As regards the political unity of the armed forces, the answer must be a mixed one. Two important factors work in favor of their unity. Probably because of the heavy preponderance of the army over the navy and air force, there seems, for one thing, to be relatively little interservice rivalry in Spain. For most political purposes, the army is the armed forces. In the second place, there is a certain solidarity among the officers of all the services; that is important because in a political sense only the officers count. The vast majority of the enlisted men are draftees serving for two years or less; apparently they have developed no corporate political feeling or significance. In contrast, the officers' *esprit de corps,* while rooted in social rather than political soil—that is, in the class feeling that is strong in Spain—has been greatly nourished by memories of the Civil War, an essentially political struggle over issues still relevant today, in which the army played the leading role on the victorious side.

On the other hand, there are other factors that make for disunity among the military. Some of these apparently reflect only personal differences or rivalries, but personalism is strong in Spain as it is in Spanish America. While many of

---

6 *Le Monde* (Paris), July 18, 1958; one of four articles.

the army generals in the government are working, or at least hoping, for an early restoration of the monarchy, the navy's top man, Admiral Luis Carrero Blanco, is apparently an unconditional supporter of whatever Franco wants. Moreover, even within the monarchist groups there are sharp divisions as to timing, type of monarchy, and candidates for the throne. At least one eminent military figure, Captain General Agustín Muñoz Grandes, commander of the Blue Division that fought with Germany against the Soviet Union, is believed by some to regard himself as the proper successor to Franco.

A more basic factor was pointed out in 1959 by *The New York Times* correspondent in Madrid, Benjamin Welles.[7] Formerly, Welles said, two or three generals decided army policy; now at least seven would have to agree, including Muñoz Grandes and six lieutenant generals. Of these, two were at that time cabinet ministers: Antonio Barroso (War) and Camilo Alonso Vega (Interior, i.e., Gobierno); three were area commanders: Miguel Rodrigo Martínez (Madrid), Pablo Martín Alonso (Barcelona) and Antonio Castejón Espinosa (Seville); the sixth was the former High Commissioner in Spanish Morocco, Rafael García Valiño. Finally, there are persistent but unverifiable rumors of growing differences, such as have occurred recently in a number of other countries, between senior and junior officers—differences that reflect not only the impatience of the younger and less privileged group, but also a divergence on political questions.

This brings us to the grounds of discontent among the armed forces. Again, the reports are impossible to verify, but the following points appear to be reasonably sound. First, there is widespread unrest among the junior officers over their low pay, which is not offset by the perquisites enjoyed by senior officers and which usually must be supplemented by a second job; hence the description of the junior officers as "week-end soldiers." Their well-heeled seniors, too, are not infrequently part-time soldiers, but for different reasons. An example of life at this end of the scale is provided by the

---

7 *The New York Times*, March 29, 1959.

case of General Barroso, which will be described below in another connection.[8] The dissatisfaction of the junior officers with their lot is said to have been sharpened since 1953 by the contrast with the much higher pay and the comparatively luxurious way of life of the American military personnel stationed in Spain.

Another and more general ground of discontent has been the pro-Arab policy followed by Franco for several years, above all, his precipitate surrender of Spain's Protectorate over northern Morocco late in 1955. Most Spanish officers detest Arabs and were shocked by the loss of the Protectorate. For nearly half a century it had been ruled virtually as a colony; during that time it was, like Cuba in the nineteenth century, the army's special province. Morocco held a special place in army sentiment, for it was from there that army conspirators launched their attack on the republic in 1936. It had long provided employment for a large part of the army and the best field for young officers, including Franco in his day, in their quest for fame and promotion. Its loss came as a shock to the army for both sentimental and practical reasons. No open resistance has developed, but the resentment remains. One well-informed observer has reported that army leaders are determined not to tolerate any further retreat, either from the few small "places of sovereignty" (such as Ceuta and Melilla) that Spain has retained on the Moroccan periphery, or from its other possessions in Africa.[9]

According to other sources, late in 1957, when an irregular "army of liberation" from Morocco attacked Spanish Ifni on the west coast, the Spanish forces in that area reacted without consulting Madrid and have continued to maintain a critical attitude towards the home government, not unlike that of the French forces in Algeria during the crisis of 1958.[10] All arguments from analogy are dangerous, but the

---

[8] See pp. 140-142.

[9] André Fontaine, in *Le Monde* (Paris), July 15, 1958.

[10] Edgar S. Furniss, Jr., *France, Troubled Ally: De Gaulle's Heritage and Prospects* (New York: Harper, for the Council on Foreign Relations, 1960), pp. 317-348.

North African situation has plainly created discontent in
the army. Whether it will have serious consequences or not
depends partly upon the way in which Franco meets the increasing pressures from Moroccan and other Arab quarters.
There is also said to be some army unrest on other
grounds, mainly through the influence of other social groups.
The middle class, from which the majority of Spanish officers
come and with which they maintain close ties, has many
targets for its dissatisfaction, among them, inflation, the
regime's neglect of the middle class, and the long, unrelieved
monotony of official propaganda; all of which adds up to a
feeling that the time has come for a change. Another source
of infection is nationalist resentment, to which the Spanish
armed forces are particularly susceptible, against the apparently growing dependence of the regime on foreigners—
first, it is charged, by becoming the "satellite and pensioner"
of the United States under the bases-and-aid agreements of
1953, and then, in 1959, by reshaping its economic policy at
the "dictation" of the International Monetary Fund, the
Organization for European Economic Cooperation, and the
United States. However readily such charges may be
shrugged off, they bear a surface plausibility that makes them
particularly dangerous to the once fiercely nationalist Franco
regime. They could be especially effective among the officer
class whose traditional nationalism has in most cases not been
watered down, as Franco's has, by the responsibilities of political power. Though they help him exercise his power, the
regime is, after all, his, not theirs.

This catalogue of military discontents, actual or potential,
is a formidable one. Yet, as matters stand at present, they do
not seem strong enough to break the powerful ties that bind
the military to the regime. One of these is Franco's authority
as generalissimo, backed by his prestige, still unrivaled in
the armed forces, and by his secret police, very efficient in
ferreting out dissent. Another is the stake the armed forces
have in the regime, both individually and collectively. Many
senior officers hold important and lucrative posts in the cabinet, at slightly lower levels in the ministries and provincial

governments, and in autonomous agencies such as INI and its various enterprises. If there were a change of regime, and especially if a liberal or left-wing government were set up, all these posts and perquisites would presumably be forfeited and the armed forces as a whole downgraded, as happened in the 1930's.

Finally, the armed forces do not live in a social vacuum. The nexus of their relations with two other supporting groups—the Catholic Church and the oligarchy—reinforces their own ties with it. The nexus is strongest among the senior officers, but discipline and the hierarchical spirit enable them, for most purposes, to speak for the armed forces as a whole. Their relationship with the church depends partly upon personal connections with leading members of the clergy, partly upon a community of conservative outlook and interests with the ecclesiastical hierarchy. In recent years some church leaders have been critical of the regime on various grounds, including, among conservatives, its alliance with the United States. Even so, these criticisms have not been leveled specifically at the armed forces, which everyone knows did not have the final word about the new policy. On the whole, insofar as one can generalize about two such complex groups as the army and the Catholic Church in Spain, it would seem that they still maintain the *entente cordiale* that was sealed by the hierarchy's benediction upon the Nationalist cause, which was the army's cause, in the Civil War.

A similar community of general outlook tends to unite the army with the oligarchy of big bankers, businessmen, and landowners. In this case, however, there are stronger ties of a personal and material character, through marriages between members of the two groups and participation by military men in business. The latter phenomenon has become a feature of the Franco regime, partly as a consequence of the growing employment of influential military men in government-controlled industrial and other economic enterprises.

A case in point is that of General Barroso, Franco's Minister of War since 1957. Now a rich man and the very picture of a successful soldier, Barroso has served in the army since entering the Infantry Academy in 1908. Before attaining the rank of brigadier general in 1943, he had served extensively in Morocco and had spent several years in France; after graduating from the Ecole Supérieure de Guerre, he served as military attaché in Paris from 1934 to 1936. Again named to this post after the Civil War, he held it during the German occupation, and showed himself, as always, able, energetic, and resourceful. From the close of World War II until his appointment in 1957 as minister of war, he held a variety of assignments, including that of head of Franco's military household. There have been rumors of his participation in anti-Franco intrigues; he was certainly one of three generals who, on July 1, 1956, protested to Franco on the army's behalf against giving the Falange control of his administration, as it was feared he planned to do. Whatever influence the protest may have had, Franco downgraded the Falange when he finally reorganized his cabinet early in 1957 and appointed Barroso as one of his new ministers.

General Barroso, whose army salary is small, is said to have made his fortune since the end of the Civil War. His interests are important and varied. He is chairman of the board of directors of Telefunken Radiotécnica Ibérica; he is said to hold stock in this firm for German interests. He is also a member of the board of directors of its subsidiary, Fábrica Tubos Eléctricos. He is also on the boards of two other companies, Standard Eléctrica, S.A., one of the largest electrical equipment firms in Spain, and Vías y Construcciones, a railway construction firm. He has a luxurious apartment in Madrid, an estate in the Sierra de Gredos, where there is fine fishing in the mountain streams, and a summer home in San Sebastián, which kings and caudillos have made Spain's most fashionable summer resort. Barroso and his wife frequent high society; their two daughters and a son are married to wealthy and prominent people.

Like many other senior officers, Barroso is said to be a strong monarchist. When he and his two fellow generals made their protest to Franco about the Falange in July 1956, so Madrid rumors run, they reportedly proposed establishing a military directorate which would hold a national referendum to choose between monarchy and republic, with the stipulation that, if the monarchy won, a king (the chief pretender, Don Juan de Borbón) would be crowned and would take over power forthwith. (The republicans were apparently not expected to win this referendum; at any rate, the rumors do not say what was to be the next step if they did.) If such a proposal was in fact made, Franco turned it down, and Barroso and his fellow officers let it go at that. Much as many of them may desire a change, their fundamental assumption seems so far to be that this must await Franco's consent and cooperation. In the meantime, they are making the best of the situation, and they are not doing badly.

The Church

The political role of the Catholic Church in present-day Spain is highly important on many counts, including its close connection with the Franco regime, its virtual monopoly of religious activity, its strong influence on education and the general cultural life of the country, and the deep-rooted devotion that it enjoys among many Spaniards. Its strength is unevenly distributed, being greater in the north than in the south and stronger in the small towns and countryside than in the large cities, but it has strong points everywhere. As a religious organization, it has no real competitors anywhere.

The absence of competition cannot be explained solely in terms of the historic persecution of dissent. To be sure, there has been abundant repression. Every schoolboy has read about Torquemada, the Spanish Inquisition, and the burning of heretics in the *auto de fe*. Any such drastic enforcement of conformity went out of use a century and a half ago, and yet even today there are fewer than thirty thousand Protestants among Spain's thirty million inhabitants. In the late nineteenth and early twentieth centuries anarchism was much more severely repressed than Protestantism. Yet it won many more converts. It seems still true that, as has so often been said, Spaniards are Catholics or nothing. The strong

devotion that so many give the church more than anything
else makes it a major power group under Franco, as it has
been in Spain for fifteen centuries past.

Since the broader position of the church is discussed in
detail elsewhere, let it suffice here to recall only the main
facts and considerations that shape its political role. Let us
begin by asking what is meant by the Catholic Church in
Spain, or the Spanish Church, as it is often called. In the first
place, this church is not exclusively Spanish, but a part of the
universal Roman Catholic Church whose head is the Holy
Father. This elementary fact is politically significant in Spain
because the papacy has taken and takes clear-cut positions on
important problems of public policy. Second, while the
church literally consists of all its members, laity as well as
clergy, our concern here is primarily with its leaders, as it was
with the officers in speaking of the armed forces. The reason
is fundamentally the same, for the church, too, has a hierarchical organization and maintains a high degree of discipline and respect for authority among its members.

In the third place, the church receives financial and other
support from the state. It does not have the same power as
the armed forces to deal with deserters, but the state gives it
almost as much protection against hostile forces. Other faiths
are barely tolerated on condition that they stay out of the
public gaze, and the handful of Protestants are constantly
harassed and badgered. There is less religious freedom in
Spain today for non-Catholics than in any other European
country.

In the fourth place, the church does not form a monolithic
bloc. The divisions in the church, which are numerous, are
significant for relations between church and state, which are
also closer in Spain than in any other country of Western
Europe. These relations are now governed by a concordat
signed between the Spanish government and the Vatican in
August 1953.

In Spain, as in all Catholic countries, the divisions within
the church begin with the two major groups of clergy, secular
and regular. The secular clergy is the recipient of the gov-

ernment's direct financial aid to the church. It includes the parish priests and heads up in a hierarchy of bishops and archbishops presided over by the Archbishop of Toledo, as Primate of Spain; all of the hierarchs are in effect appointed by the government.[11] Just as the parish priests are closest of all groups to the Spanish people at large, similarly the hierarchy is the closest of all to the regime. The regular clergy, on the other hand, is divided among various religious orders, such as Dominicans, Franciscans, Jesuits, and others, each of them international in organization and obedience; in varying degrees each of these orders is ultimately responsible to the papacy in Rome. Further divisions among the Spanish clergy have been fostered by the spirit of regionalism. In the separatist Basque country, for example, many priests opposed Franco during the Civil War and have made trouble for his regime ever since. And a highly publicized clash in late 1958, between the Abbot of Montserrat and the Captain General of Barcelona, was apparently brought on by the Abbot's defense of Catalanism. Mid-1960 brought fresh signs of the same kind in both regions: in May, as already noted, the revelation of a young Catalan Catholic group engaged in anti-regime activities; in June, the publication of a letter, signed by more than three hundred Basque priests, which was highly critical of the operation of the regime in that area on several grounds.

In addition, there are church organizations consisting largely of laymen which concern themselves with secular affairs. Leading examples are Catholic Action and Opus Dei, both of which are international in structure and operate under papal supervision. There are important differences between these two,[12] but they are alike in one respect: while neither is committed as a body to the support of the regime, in the public mind both have become identified with it through the participation of their individual members in

---

[11] Since 1941 the appointment of each prelate has been made from a government list of six nominees, reduced by the Vatican to three, among whom the government makes the final choice.

[12] See Chapter VII, pp. 262-279.

Franco's government. On the other hand, the Christian Democrats, a political group of Catholic inspiration, are identified with opposition to the regime. Their opposition is, however, weakened by their division into two wings and tempered by the conservatism of the right wing.

If one strikes a balance among all these diverse and to some extent mutually conflicting elements called the Spanish Church, it seems clear that they still constitute one of the Franco regime's major supports. Nevertheless, since the conclusion of the Concordat of 1953, there have been many signs that some important elements in the church would like to dissociate the church from the regime. Even the hierarchy, the ecclesiastical sector most closely identified with the regime, has been openly critical of some aspects of its policies, though not of the regime itself.

This discreet withdrawal seems to be due mainly to the increasingly acute problem which church leaders describe as the "apostasy of the working class." They are deeply disturbed by this trend. Many of them are sincerely convinced that this large-scale secession not only represents a loss of souls but also reflects the failure of the church to do its duty by the workers. They also fear the damage these millions of apostates may hereafter wreak upon the church under a regime less friendly than Franco's. The fear may be justified. Some left-wing enemies of Franco, looking forward to a change of regime, are prophesying that the sufferings of the church under the republic and during the Civil War—the sacking of churches and monasteries, and the murder of priests and nuns, not to mention hostile legislation—were but a foreshadowing of the martyrdom that may await it in the future.

Whether the forecast proves accurate or not only time can tell, but one thing seems certain: anticlericalism, long familiar in Spain, is again rampant there, among intellectuals and perhaps even more among the urban working class, whose size has increased greatly since 1939, both absolutely and relatively. To be sure, anticlericalism is a common phenomenon in strongly Catholic countries, but in this as in most other matters Spaniards are uncommonly violent. Moreover, in addition to the familiar grounds of traditional anticlericalism, the Spanish Church now suffers in the popular mind a special opprobrium from its close identification with Franco's dictatorship.

From the point of view of self-protection, this situation faces the church with a dilemma: Franco, defender of the faith, gives it security now, but in the long run its identification with his regime may bring it to disaster. Hence the course, which many of its leaders have adopted, of promoting the church's dissociation from the regime, without, however, involving it in subversive activity. The latter course might prove suicidal, while the former holds out some promise as an insurance policy against the wrath to come.

The Oligarchy

Strictly speaking, there is no such thing as an oligarchy in Spain in the usual meaning of the rule of a few, for Spain is under the rule of one. The term also connotes a higher degree of unity and coherence than exists among its diverse elements. As leaders in banking, industry, and commerce, and big landowners, they have many divergent and sometimes conflicting interests. Nevertheless, from the political point of view, there are good grounds for following the common parlance and speaking of the Spanish oligarchy as a unit. Its basic economic interests interlock in a number of ways, above all through the high degree of control which the banking community has achieved over the other segments of the oligarchy. The economic nexus is also reinforced by personal ties. Large landowners, including members of the nobility, have gone into business and banking. Conversely, since landowning has many attractions for Spaniards, including social prestige, the banker or businessman who prospers is likely to acquire a *finca,* or country estate, if he did not own one in the first place. In a political sense the various elements composing the oligarchy are unified by important common interests: in the maintenance of order and security; in the protection of their privileged position; and in gaining greater freedom of enterprise than the Franco regime has so far allowed them, without sacrificing the aid and protection they receive from it.

The importance of the oligarchy's political role in the Franco regime is due mainly to two factors. One is its economic power, which is great on the Spanish scale. Within the restricted but still broad area of the Spanish economy that remains in private hands even after allowance is made for government intervention (which is extensive), dependence on aid from the United States (which has been substantial since 1953), and foreign investments (which are small), the various sectors of the oligarchy dominate Spain's economic life. Organized labor offers no real challenge to their control. Independent labor unions do not exist, the right to strike is denied, and the syndical system, which groups together employers and workers under government supervision, allows much more freedom to management than to labor.

A second factor is the strength the oligarchy derives from its interrelations with two other groups supporting the regime, the armed forces and the church. It is these that give it most of its political influence, for its own numbers are few, it has no mass support, and it lacks the moral authority of the church and the physical force of the army. In its relations with the other two groups, however, the power of the purse is a persuasive argument in favor of its views and interests, and for most leaders in the army and some in the church the oligarchy represents the culmination of a desirable social system.

Three features of the political role of the oligarchy call for special comment. First, as already noted, control of its economic interests is concentrated to a high degree in the banking community, which in turn is dominated by the five largest commercial banks. This fact is politically important because grave financial and economic problems have recently been, and will continue to be, of great concern to the government and people of Spain. The banks possess the best expertise in the country on these problems, and on them they speak for most of the oligarchy.

In the second place, in economic as in other matters, the oligarchy proposes and the regime disposes. The latter not only has ultimate control over the whole economy but also exercises direct control over large sectors of it—for example, over the banking community through a national banking council dominated by its government members, and over management-labor relations through the syndicates. In addition, the government has carried out large-scale incursions into the traditional field of private enterprise, especially industry. The leading example is INI and its enterprises, such as the big steel plant at Avilés.

In the third place, despite large-scale government intervention in economic affairs and Franco's repeated attacks on capitalism, his regime has in fact given substantial protection and encouragement to capitalist enterprise, which has fared better than labor under his aegis. He has also shown respect for the opinions of its spokesmen. The latest evidence of his attitude is provided by his decision, announced in July 1959, to adopt a new economic policy of liberalization and stabilization. This policy was strongly urged by the banking community, and its effects, at least at first, are likely to be of more immediate benefit to the oligarchy than to any other group in Spain.

Yet Franco's acceptance of this sweeping economic reform cannot by any means be regarded as a victory for the oligarchy alone. It was in line with similar recommendations that came to him from other and quite different sources, for example, from Suanzes, director of INI and former high priest of statism, and Solís, spokesman for the Falange. The fact is that, as all informed Spaniards recognized, the economy was headed for a disaster from which it could be saved only by economic reform buttressed by large-scale foreign aid, and the solution recommended to Franco and accepted by him was the only one that would obtain the necessary foreign aid. In short, the reforms of July 1959 did not by any means signify that Franco had turned over the management of the nation's economy to the oligarchy.

On its part, the oligarchy still nurses the discontents that have grown apace among many of its members in the last few years and have made it, like the army and the church, something less than an unconditional supporter of the regime. For the oligarchy, there have been three main grounds of discontent. One is a growing conviction of the incurable ineptitude of the regime in economic matters, based on its twenty-year record of bungling and heightened by the failure of the widely heralded promise of reform and recovery with which the cabinet of February 1957 took office. This conviction will no doubt be dispelled if the stabilization plan of 1959 achieves its major purposes, but it is still too early to assess its results definitively. In the meantime the fear persists that the regime's mismanagement may lead to a social and political upheaval of which the oligarchy would be one of the first victims. Such apprehensions have multiplied as a result of Franco's persistent refusal to give greater stability to his regime and its component parts, including the oligarchy, by institutionalizing his system, or even to give it a better chance of surviving his own departure by making some clear-cut provision for the succession.

Finally, there is resentment against Franco's continued patronage of anticapitalist doctrines and of the Falange. Most members of the oligarchy seem to share the rather widespread Spanish view that, once Franco is gone, the Falange will quickly disintegrate. On the other hand, they believe that, so long as Franco remains in power, there will always be the danger that in a crisis he may bring the Falange back into the seats of power, to the great detriment of the oligarchy. As a consequence, while on balance the oligarchy is still counted among the supporters of the regime, many of its members are hoping and some are openly working for a change, preferably to the monarchy.

The Falange

Ever since the fiasco of its bid for power during an inner crisis of the regime, between the summer of 1956 and February 1957, the Falange has been written off by most commentators as a failure.[13] The Falange has indeed declined since the early years of the regime, but it has not fallen either from so great a height, nor to so low a depth, as is generally assumed. If today it is only Franco's instrument, it has always been just that. And it is still one of his major instruments. For one thing, the Falange has never lost its political monopoly as Spain's only legal party. It still reaches a wide audience through its publications, such as the Madrid newspaper *Arriba,* to which Franco's right-hand man, Admiral Carrero Blanco, has been a frequent contributor.

What is probably more important, since even the Falange has no real political freedom, is the fact that the party still has about one million members and that its bureaucracy controls eight million workers in a total population of just under thirty million.[14] In addition, every government official must still belong to it. Membership may be only nominal for many individuals, but on the whole Franco makes it something much more than nominal through his patronage of the party; that patronage has continued unchanged in other respects even though he has sharply cut the Falange's role in his cabinet since 1957. Its loss of power, combined with other circumstances, has lowered its prestige and influence among the general public. Nevertheless, so long as Franco esteems and uses the Falange as he does, it cannot be written off as a political force. As Arrese's replacement by Sánchez-Arjona in 1960 suggests, along with the decline of the Falange's political role there has been a change in the type of its representation in the regime's top echelons from the militant doctrinaire to the prudent organization man.

---

[13] For example, Herbert Matthews' generally excellent book on Spain never mentions it except in disparaging terms, of which "phony" and "scarecrow" are fair examples; cited, pp. 84-86.

[14] *The New York Times,* May 15, 1958.

A more serious matter than the Falange's loss of prestige, at least from Franco's point of view, has been the sharp decline in its value as a source of support for the regime. How this has come about is relevant to any inquiry into its present strength and political role. The answer will be clearer if we recall the synthetic manner of its birth.

As it assumed its definitive form early in the Spanish Civil War, the Falange was literally Franco's creation. In calling it into being, he illustrated one facet of his aptitude for manipulating the component elements of Spanish society, sometimes under the device of "divide and rule," at other times under that of "unite and rule." Illustrations of the latter technique include his forced mergers of management and labor in vertical syndicates, and of the comparatively respectable Guardia Civil, or national police, with an organization, the notoriously corrupt Carabineros or customs patrol, for which the Guardia Civil had only contempt. But the prime example is his shotgun wedding of three disparate and unwilling groups to produce the Falange, which took its name from one of the three. As we have seen, these were: the original Falange, founded by an aristocrat, José Antonio Primo de Rivera; the left-wing JONS, or National Syndicalist Workers Juntas; and the right-wing Requetés, an organization of monarchists of the reactionary Carlist or traditionalist school.

In 1937 Franco forced the three groups to unite, supposedly as a war measure. They were unable to resist since their only leader of some national stature, José Antonio (as he is commonly called), had been put to death by the Republicans at the beginning of the war. Since most of the Requetés were busy fighting—they were among the best soldiers on the Nationalist side—control of the new party fell to the other two groups; for the most part the original Falangist core prevailed. This was due partly to Franco's patronage, partly to the eloquence of the united party's chief propagandist, young Dionisio Ridruejo—poet, intellectual, and intimate friend of the martyred José Antonio. Ridruejo and other talented and dedicated members of the Falange joined in presenting it in the most attractive light. Under the stress of the Civil War and the almost equally trying years just after its close, many Spaniards joined the party in the belief that it was pointing the way to a new and better Spain. There were probably many more who joined it under pressure or merely for the pleasure of being on the band-wagon.

The extraordinary mélange that was the original Falange, and what happened to it in later years, has recently been summed up by Ridruejo, who has now broken with the party and has become an open opponent of Franco's regime; never-theless, his summation is just, as well as exceptionally well informed:

Falangism [he writes] was an assemblage of diverse and con-tradictory elements, such as traditionalist thought and revolu-tionary syndicalism, aristocratic neoliberalism, whose origin can be found in Ortega [y Gasset], and European fascism, which in its turn . . . was one of the most contradictory complexes that our times have known and contained both nationalist and im-perialist tendencies. . . . We Falangists tried—that is, we thought we were trying—to form a synthesis of sentiments customarily attributed to rightists (patriotism of the traditional cut and ele-ments of Catholic culture) with others attributed to the left, such as revolutionary social justice and a tendency towards eco-nomic collectivism.[15]

For several years Ridruejo remained in the vanguard of the Movement. He even fought with the Blue Division against the Soviet Union—his answer to critics who taunted him with being a man of words, not of action. He was also a partisan of the strongly pro-Axis Foreign Minister Ramón Serrano Suñer; some say that the latter's dismissal turned Ridruejo against the regime, and he did in fact protest against it in a letter to the Caudillo. As regards his secession from the Falange, a quite different explanation has been given by Ridruejo; it is worth reproducing since it applies

---

15 "Respuestas de Dionisio Ridruejo al periódico 'O Estado de São Paulo,'" *Ibérica* (New York), July-August 1959, p. 3; an interview originally published in a Brazilian newspaper.

to others as well. Among his fellow seceders were some who had been the Falange's most active leaders in its early years. The survivors are now referred to as the "Old Guard," and some of them now belong to Ridruejo's Social Democratic group (it cannot legally be a party). Explaining the break with the Falange, Ridruejo has recently said:

Too late some of us discovered that the kind of synthesis [that we attempted in the Falange's early years] could not be achieved without maintaining a dialectical tension between the party's different elements, that is, without democratic freedom. Otherwise the balance would inevitably swing to one extreme or the other. And since the Falange could not be, because it did not wish to be, a movement in favor of the working class, it necessarily ended up by becoming a movement against that class, that is [a movement] in the service of the conservative forces—"the assault guard of the reaction," as its own founder [José Antonio] had feared.[16]

Ridruejo's explanation is accurate in the main, but it is subject to one important qualification. The Falange's role in relation to the working class has not been performed "in the service of the conservative forces"—a term which in this context clearly means the oligarchy—but in Franco's service, which is quite a different matter. Its activities benefit the oligarchy when he chooses, and only then. In fact, its main function in his regime has become that of a counterpoise to the oligarchy in the never-ending game of balance-of-power politics that he plays within Spain. To be sure, Franco himself is mainly responsible for the decline in vitality, as well as in power and prestige, that has prevented the Falange from keeping up with the times and has made it an anachronism in the eyes of many Spaniards. It is also true that Franco has thereby lowered the party's potential serviceability as a nucleus of support for his regime. Most Spaniards have now found other attachments—right-wingers in monarchy, left-wingers in socialism or communism, and moderates in a *rapprochement* with the countries of Western

---

16 Same.

Europe, in the hope of reshaping the policy of Spain along lines similar to theirs.

Nevertheless, the Caudillo still keeps the Falange strong enough to be serviceable to him in many ways. As a bureaucracy, it is most useful in regulating labor relations through the syndical system. It also has value as a potential sword of Damocles to keep the oligarchy in line. In this connection, there have been recurrent rumors, perhaps inspired by Franco, that the Falange may make its way back to power through the syndicates. A broad hint to this effect has been given by the Falange's head, Secretary-General of the Movement, José Solís Ruiz. In a speech delivered at Seville in March 1959, he described the syndicates as forming, together with the armed forces, the "vanguard" of the regime.[17] The Falange organ *Pueblo* went even further, suggesting that the syndicates might become the channel for popular participation in the whole process of government.[18]

Many observers think that the Falange's hold on the syndicates is precarious and would fail in a minute but for Franco's support. It seems in no immediate danger of losing that. Indeed, unless his words and deeds belie his intentions, the Falange will continue indefinitely to play its twofold role. Franco has continued to give lip service to Falangist principles of state socialism and also to play up the party on important public occasions. One such was his notable address to the Cortes in May 1958 in which he made it clear that his successor, whoever the putative king might be, must accept and perpetuate the principles of the Movement, of which the Falange is still the corporate representative. Another recent occasion at which he gave the Falange the place of honor was the dedication, on April 1, 1959, of the monument to the heroes of the Civil War in the Valley of the Fallen—a monument as dear to Franco's heart as the Escorial was to Philip II's. And, significantly, the occasion was highlighted by the removal to the valley from the Escorial of the remains of José Antonio, founder of the Falange.

---

17 See *Arriba* (Madrid), April 15, 1959, for the complete text of the speech.
18 *Pueblo* (Madrid), March 12, 1959; article entitled "Puntualizaciones."

Chapter V

THE DISLOYAL OPPOSITION

IN FRANCO SPAIN all opposition is necessarily disloyal since freedom of speech, press, and assembly do not exist and there is only one legal party, the Falange, of which Franco is the head. More or less clandestine opposition is, nevertheless, widespread. A man who for many years was one of the regime's staunchest supporters, José María Pemán, publicly warned Franco's complacent right-hand man, Admiral Carrero Blanco, in 1959: "If you think you discern a feeling of confidence and security in the Spanish people, I assure you that your estimate and divination have deceived you. . . . No one in Spain feels easy about the future." [1]

In the broadest sense, the Spanish opposition falls into two groups. One comprises those who fear that the regime will not be maintained; the other, those who fear that it will. The former, made up of beneficiaries of the present order, want to change the leadership because they think it has outlived its usefulness and become a liability; in the main they wish to preserve the essential features of a regime that has been useful to them. Something has been said of their views in Chapter IV. Here I shall advert to them only in connection with the monarchy, which to them, though not by any means to all its advocates, is a save-the-regime device. This chapter will deal mainly with the second group, those who wish to make substantial changes in the present regime,

---

[1] Quoted in Luis Araquistain, "La sucesión del general Franco y el comunismo en España," *Cuadernos* (Paris), July-August 1959, p. 70.

if not to revolutionize it. Only organized movements will be discussed, for only they have any chance of success. But it should be remembered that in highly individualistic and chronically discontented Spain, every Spaniard is in effect a one-man opposition party.

Thunder on Left and Right

At the end of November 1958 an international sensation was created by the news that at least eighty foes of the Franco regime had been arrested in the past three weeks. Almost all these new political prisoners were reported to have two things in common: they were Socialists and under forty years of age.[2] They differed widely in other respects, particularly in place of residence, social background, and occupation. Most regions of Spain were represented in the list, from Madrid to Zaragoza and Barcelona in the northeast, San Sebastián and Vitoria in the northwest, and Granada and Seville in the south. Some of those arrested belonged to rich and distinguished families, while others were self-made or still self-making. Their occupations ranged from lawyer, psychiatrist, and university professor to industrial worker. Three unusual or unique features marked the affair. It was the largest round-up of political prisoners since the serious disturbances of early 1956 among the workers of Catalonia and the north. The brutal police methods formerly employed were exchanged on this occasion for correct treatment of the prisoners. And at first the government's usual charge of communism was muted on this occasion.[3]

Two months later another sensational incident gave evidence of unrest in a quite different political and social sector.

---

[2] *The New York Times*, December 1, 1958.

[3] A very different account of these arrests is contained in the Spanish government's book explaining and defending them: *What Is Happening in Spain? The Problem of Spanish Socialism* (Madrid: CEDESA, 1959). For example, it states that only fifty-one Socialists were arrested and that their ages ranged between thirty and sixty-three, and it pins the Communist label on the whole Spanish Socialist movement. It confirms the press reports in regard to occupations and places of residence.

On January 29, 1959, a group of nearly one hundred Spaniards, belonging to an organization called Unión Española, had assembled to hold a dinner, with speeches, at one of Madrid's principal hotels, the Menfis. The main speaker openly attacked the Franco regime, to the enthusiastic applause of his listeners. Almost all members of the group were lawyers, men of substance, and over forty years of age. The speaker was fifty-year-old Joaquín Satrústegui, man of affairs and president of the fashionable Cruz del Campo country club. And the point of his speech was the urgent need for a prompt restoration of the monarchy.

Because of the grave economic and financial crisis that faced the country, these two political incidents combined with the intervening Swiss bank scandal of December 1958 to reveal a crisis of confidence in the regime. Through the early months of 1959 the country buzzed with speculation about the chances of survival of an authoritarian regime that had come to such a pass after twenty years in power, and assorted opposition groups thought they heard opportunity knocking at the door. As it turned out, the government weathered the crisis. The armed forces stood firm, and extensive foreign aid, known to be "in the bag" by May and formally announced in the stabilization plan of July, helped to restore its depleted treasury and bolster its battered prestige.

Nevertheless, the stabilization plan may prove only a stop gap, and in any case the opposition forces highlighted by the crisis of early 1959 will still remain. The crisis gave them a fleeting opportunity, or so it seemed, but it did not create them. Some of their organizations, such as the Socialist party, are old; others, like Unión Española, are new. All are seriously handicapped by the law which makes it a criminal offense to engage in political activity through any channel other than the government-controlled Falange. In order to circumvent this prohibition, opposition groups either go underground or pretend not to be political parties.

The number of such groups is only too large. Lack of unity is one of the opposition's chief weaknesses. Another is its lack of weapons, which are monopolized by the police and the armed forces. The quality and number of these weapons have risen since 1953, thanks to the U.S. military aid program. No rebellion, however, was planned in the crisis of 1959. It is not the only way of ejecting Franco, and at present it seems the least likely one.

What other ways are there? For one thing, there are some who still hope that Franco may be induced, by various kinds of persuasion or pressure, to modify his regime without quitting it. Among the pressures mentioned have been foreign ones. Some Spaniards hoped that political as well as economic conditions would be attached to the life-saving foreign aid that his regime received in connection with the stabilization plan. This was not done, and the resolute noninterventionism of the principal Western powers makes this a rather forlorn hope.

Again, Franco might withdraw voluntarily, with or without special inducements. This is unlikely but not inconceivable. Franco has said more than once that he intends to keep his present position and power as long as he lives, but who knows whether he means it? It is the only thing he could say, whatever he plans. And his plans may change.

A much more probable way would be for the Spanish armed forces to turn against him. They could send him packing without firing a shot, as they did Primo de Rivera in 1930, and Alfonso XIII the next year. They might do so if the opposition should continue to grow in volume and intensity, for they are not unresponsive to public opinion, especially as expressed by the upper echelons of secular society and of the church. The armed forces would be most unlikely to take any action either against Franco personally or against the regime, unless they were offered an acceptable alternative. As it happens, an alternative highly acceptable to many Spanish military leaders is now being offered by the monarchists, with substantial support from other sectors of the opposition. Most of these leaders are believed to prefer a restoration of the monarchy under Franco's auspices, but he does nothing but talk about it as a remote eventuality and one wonders whether their patience is as inexhaustible as his.

Finally, and perhaps most important of all, the opposition is the beneficiary of a new state of mind which has grown up in Spain in the last few years. This is the feeling that the time has come for a change in a regime which has failed to keep up with the changing times. The feeling is shared not only by the many Spaniards who have always detested the regime, and by the new postwar generation to which the regime seems at best an anachronism, but also by many of its former supporters. While applauding it for having given Spain two decades of internal peace and order, his disillusioned backers are deeply disturbed by Franco's stubborn refusal to assure them of long-range protection by modifying and institutionalizing his regime and sharing his power. To them he appears less and less a man honestly convinced of his providential mission and more and more a power-hungry cynic whose motto has become "Après moi, le déluge." Even if they do not dislike him, they fear the storms that may come after his unprepared departure. This fear has opened up an emotional gap between Franco and many of his former supporters—in the church and the oligarchy as well as the armed forces—which, if it continues to widen, may bring success within the grasp of the hard core of the regime's unconditional opponents.

In short, the political situation in Spain contains elements of instability that are great enough to justify an assessment of the present strength and prospects of the opposition to the regime. This will be considered first, but briefly, with reference to the class structure of Spanish society and then, at greater length, from the point of view of political parties or groups.

The Opposition and the Class Structure

The Spanish upper classes have always been the chief beneficiaries and supporters of the Franco regime. In the main the relationship still holds true today. Nevertheless, elements in all three of the main upper-class sectors—especially the oligarchy and the church hierarchy, and to a less extent the military hierarchy—have shown a tendency to draw away from the regime and even to oppose it. These are the elements that have come to believe that the continuance of the regime in its present form may in the long run prove harmful or even disastrous to them. This is at present a minority view in all three sectors, but it is believed to be spreading. Its acceptance does not, however, imply commitment to a plan of concerted political action by the upper class. Rather, oppositionists in this class give positive expression to their views through any one of several political groups. Most of them are associated with one of two widely different monarchist groupings, while some are republicans and others favor a new military dictatorship.

What is commonly called the middle class is so lacking in cohesion that it will be referred to here as the middle groups. Prior to the advent of the Franco regime these groups—consisting mainly of the bureaucracy, professional men, intellectuals, and teachers—were the stronghold of political liberalism. Their predisposition to oppose the Franco regime has been strengthened by their sufferings under the inflation, which have been greater than those of most other Spaniards. The potential of their opposition has been low because of their lack of cohesion, their vulnerability to reprisals, and the reluctance of most of them, except a limited number of intellectuals and university students, to brave the perils of active opposition.

Since 1939 the composition of the middle groups has been altered and further diversified by the rapid growth of one of its original elements, one that had previously been minuscule. This is the group called *burguesía* in Spain, in this context roughly equivalent to "small business" in the United States. Politically the *burguesía* is difficult to classify. About all one can say is that it is not an adventurous group; most of its members would apparently like to assimilate themselves to their wealthier counterparts in the oligarchy and hence are presumably responsive to the latters' currently critical attitude towards the regime.

The two main labor groups, urban and rural, are widely different from a political point of view. In case of a crisis leading to a general breakdown of law enforcement, the farm laborers and peasants might stage another *Jacquerie* like those of the 1930's; in any except such abnormal times they are, as a group, political ciphers, manipulated by the local *caciques* (bosses) and parish priests. On the other hand, the urban, industrial, and mine workers have been a major political force, notably under the republic and through the country's two principal labor organizations, now outlawed, the CNT (National Labor Confederation) and UGT (General Union of Workers). They will doubtless again become a major political force when political freedom is restored in Spain.

The workers' present political attitudes are the subject of widely conflicting reports. Some informed observers say that their prevailing attitude is one of apathy induced by their fear of police brutality and by their absorption in the never-ending struggle for food and shelter. Insofar as they have political views they are, according to one view, inclined to tolerate the regime, if not to support it; though their situation is hard, it has never been anything else, and the regime has done something to alleviate it—more than it has done for the middle groups—through providing the workers with consumer cooperatives and cheap housing. In sharp contrast, other informed observers assert that the occasional strikes and frequent slowdowns and acts of sabotage, all of which are illegal and expose the workers to heavy penalties, are an expression of a deep political discontent and that this is making Spanish labor a fertile field for Communist propaganda. According to this view, only the certainty of severe repression by the police, backed up by the armed forces, is keeping the workers in line. By sitting on the lid of labor unrest the regime is building up steam for an explosion that will some day rock it and the nation.

The view that a great deal of masked political unrest exists among the urban workers is the more plausible because they have more reason than other classes of Spaniards to conceal their discontent. Much harsher methods are employed against dissidents among the workers than against those higher in the social scale. Nevertheless, on the main question the evidence is so conflicting that the only thing we can be sure of is that, politically speaking, the urban workers do not form a solid block but are almost as fragmented as the middle class. Since the 1930's anarchism has declined. Some say that communism is stronger than ever before except during the Civil War. All agree that socialism is still the strongest of the three. And further complications are introduced by regionalism, which, as it happens, is most active in two of the regions in which industry and labor organizations are most highly developed: Catalonia and the Basque provinces. When all these labor fragments get together, their tendency is not to form a single block but to bifurcate, as they did before and during the Civil War, when the bitter rivalry between the two main groups, the CNT and the UGT, facilitated the penetration and ultimate domination of the Republican government by the Communists.

To sum up, class divisions and conflicts certainly exist in Franco Spain and to a marked degree. But, since there are also divisions and conflicts within each class, a more instructive approach to the question of opposition to the regime is one that follows groupings along political lines, which in turn often cut across class lines.

The Opposition Groups

It cannot be too often repeated that in Franco Spain there is only one legal political party, the Falange, and all other political parties are outlawed. Nevertheless, several such parties or groups do exist. By various means and in varying degrees of intensity they oppose the Franco regime. And they range through the entire political spectrum, from Anarchists and Communists on the left, through Socialists, Christian Democrats, and liberal monarchists in the middle, to authoritarian monarchists on the right. Almost all antedate the Franco regime. The only important exception is the Christian Democratic group, and even this can trace its ancestry back to the Catholic coalition of the Republican period, the CEDA (Confederación Española de Derechas Autónomas). They therefore represent a renewal of old associations rather than brand new political creations, which would be much more difficult to establish in the face of repression.

The enforcement of the ban by Franco's efficient secret police is on the whole effective as well as rigorous, although he prudently provides his loquacious fellow countrymen with a safety valve by allowing a high degree of individual freedom of speech even in public places such as cafés, the traditional communication centers of Spanish society. To the regret of those who knew them in the old days, many of the cafés in the center of Madrid and other cities are being squeezed out by more profitable enterprises, above all, by Spain's burgeoning banks.

Opposition parties, being illegal, operate either underground or disguised as "discussion groups," but in one way or another they contrive to function and they have shown a growing vitality. While the widespread opposition labors under severe handicaps, its energies and hopes are, in fact, channeled through organized political parties or groups. The existence of these speak-easy parties, which dispense bootleg political ideas, is well known to every Spaniard who is not deaf and blind.

The channeling of the opposition through several widely disparate groups has advantages and disadvantages. On the credit side, it establishes the opposition on the broadest possible base by providing something for every taste, and it gives the opposition groups a better claim than Franco to the mantle of Spanish tradition. This is important in a country whose people take naturally to a multiplicity of parties and respond readily to the appeal of tradition.

Nevertheless, these advantages carry with them a built-in disadvantage, one that could prove fatal: the handicap of disunity. Like its social classes, the political groups in Spain are not only separate and often antagonistic, but are also split within themselves. Internal cleavages exist in a high degree in all three of the most important opposition groups: monarchists, Christian Democrats, and Socialists. As in the labor movement, diversity is also intensified by regionalism, and opposition to Franco is strongest in Catalonia and the Basque provinces, the two most particularistic regions—that is, the ones that find it most difficult to cooperate with other regions.

Franco has exploited this situation through his usual divide-and-rule tactics and with the unintentional cooperation of his opponents who, by dividing on their own initiative, help maintain his rule. While it lasts, this situation has positive attractions for him. The present semipublic, semiorganized, and disjointed opposition groups are less dangerous to him than if they all went underground and joined in a unified resistance movement. As things now stand, they can let off some steam, but it is very difficult for them to take effective action; they can do nothing legally and they do not have the means for revolt, even if they have the will, which is doubtful. All the while, Franco can keep an eye on them, and he retains the legal right to swoop down on them whenever he likes, as he did so conspicuously in the case of the Socialists, in 1958 and 1959. Yet, these opposition groups are by no means futile even now, and they could become a serious threat to the regime in certain eventualities.

The Monarchists

The monarchists are by no means the largest opposition group in Spain. Properly speaking they are not a group but an agglomeration of factions. And many of them could hardly be described as unconditional opponents of the Franco regime. Yet they have the first claim on our attention because the restoration of the monarchy has of late proved increasingly attractive to the varied and growing opposition forces in Spain. Among them many dislike it and would agree to it reluctantly if at all. Yet, it has, at least in present circumstances, a much better chance of success than the chief alternative solutions, the restoration of a republican govern-

ment or the replacement of Franco by a military junta.
The most interesting outgrowth of the effort to make
monarchism the nucleus of a concerted opposition movement
is represented by Unión Española, whose sensational banquet
at a Madrid hotel resounded across Spain. But before looking
more closely at Unión Española, we must take a bird's-eye
view of the monarchist movement from which it stems.

The leading claimant to the throne of Spain is Don Juan
de Borbón, born in 1914, third son of Alfonso XIII. The
first son died in 1938; in 1945 the second son, a deaf mute,
renounced his rights in favor of Don Juan; and in 1941,
shortly before his death, Alfonso XIII had already made a
similar renunciation, which he repeated in his will. Don
Juan therefore embodies the claims of the principal or "Alphonsine" royal line in Spain, and his prior claim is recognized by virtually all Alphonsine monarchists in Spain. He is
regarded by many as Franco's first choice when and if the
time comes to fill the throne, though in his usual canny way
Franco has made no commitment. There has also been much
speculation about the possibility that Don Juan might be
passed over in favor of his son, Don Juan Carlos, born in
1937. Since 1954 Juan Carlos has been receiving his education in Spain, mainly in its military schools, under an arrangement between his father and General Franco. However,
Juan Carlos is reported on high authority to have rejected
the suggestion unconditionally out of loyalty to his father.
"I will do whatever Papa tells me," he said. And, more forth-
rightly, "I will never accept the crown during his lifetime."

There are also claimants from two other lines, the Carlist
or Traditionalist, and the Habsburg. The Habsburg line is
excluded by the Act of Succession of 1947, which stipulates
that the king must be a Spaniard. In the nineteenth century
the Carlists lost bitter civil wars over their claim, but are
nevertheless a force to be reckoned with. Concentrated
mainly in northern Spain, above all in Navarre, they are
the only monarchist group with a substantial popular following, and they have excellent fighting qualities, which made
them an indispensable support of the rebel side in the Civil

War. In addition, the Carlists justify their other name, Traditionalists, by their unswerving devotion to ultraconservatism in politics, ultra-Catholicism in religion, and ultranationalism in all things. All this strikes a responsive chord among like-minded Spaniards outside their own group who are disturbed by the propensity that Don Juan has shown for concession and compromise and by his reputed cosmopolitanism and Anglomania. Don Juan served in the British navy in the 1930's; since 1947 he has lived at Estoril, in Portugal, among an international set of exiled royalty and their hangers-on. His critics seldom remember in his favor that the only reason he did not fight on the rebel side in the Civil War was that Franco rejected his services.

Consequently, while Don Juan is the main focus of the monarchist movement in Spain, he has had to tread warily in order to placate those who could either keep him from the throne or render it untenable. These include, besides Franco and the power group devoted to him, the Alphonsine monarchists, the Carlist monarchists, and the chief opposition groups in Spain. Shortly after World War II, when the victorious allies were making anti-Franco noises, Don Juan joined in the verbal assault, but, when the sound and fury died down leaving Franco more firmly seated than ever, Don Juan mended his manners and he has not forgotten them since. He has indeed become a pensioner of Franco, regularly has two Spanish Foreign Office officials assigned to his court at Estoril, has had several amicable meetings with the Caudillo, beginning in 1948, and, as already noted, is having his son Juan Carlos educated in Spain.

All this may not seem kingly behavior, but consider Don Juan's situation: by the Act of Succession of 1947, which created a throne but left it vacant indefinitely, Franco put Don Juan on tenterhooks, and he has kept him there ever since. During Franco's lifetime no one can become king of Spain without his support, barring a revolution and civil war, for which Don Juan and his followers have no stomach. With Franco's support the heir apparent could count on winning that of the regime's principal adherents, many of whom are monarchists. Given this situation, Don Juan has had no choice but to bend to the wind or else renounce all hope of recovering the throne.

As for the Alphonsine monarchists, Don Juan's problem has been not in winning their adherence, which was assured by his father's blessing, but in restraining the more impetuous among them, as in the case of Unión Española. To maintain and broaden his contacts in Spain, Don Juan has set up a rather elaborate machinery, which includes a Privy Council (Consejo Privado) of about thirty members, most of whom live in Spain. Several of its members represent him there in various roles. In 1959 these were the Conde de Los Andes as his personal representative, the Conde de Fontanar (until his death early in 1960) as his political secretary, and José Yanguas Messia as his liaison with clandestine groups, as well as two retired lieutenant generals, Alfredo Kindelán as president of the Privy Council and Carlos Martínez Campos, Duque de la Torre, as tutor to the Pretender's son, Juan Carlos.

Quite aside from their titles, this is a distinguished as well as an able group. At the beginning of the Civil War Kindelán's prestige with his fellow officers enabled him to play the key role in obtaining the supreme command of the movement for Franco. Among those who know him well, Martínez Campos is highly respected for his judgment and integrity. And Fontanar was an exponent of the landowning aristocracy's better qualities and a prominent member of the banking community. Nevertheless, luster and talent are not enough without numbers, and the Alphonsine monarchist group is said to comprise only a paltry ten thousand members. Hence it has been earnestly seeking support or cooperation from other groups, particularly the Carlists and certain opposition groups.

The effort has met with limited but perhaps significant success in both groups, despite the fact that the former are reactionary and the latter are comparatively liberal. In early 1957 a splinter group of some two thousand Carlists announced their acceptance of Don Juan as the rightful claimant to the throne on a visit to Estoril. Another ten thousand followed suit during a pilgrimage to the shrine at Lourdes in October 1958. But the bulk of the Carlists, believed to number about seventy thousand, have not yet come over to him. In an effort to convert them and other conservatives as well, the pro-Don Juan Carlists have founded an organization bearing the rather formidable name of Legitimist Traditionalist Communion, happily simplified as CTL, which operates partly through personal contacts and partly through publications and is assisted by members of the Catholic lay institute Opus Dei. To complicate the picture still further, the CTL is also pro-regime. While this gives it exceptional freedom of speech and movement, it also tends to alienate from Don Juan the opposition groups whose support is no less necessary—certainly if he is to be a successful king and possibly if he is to be king at all.

The opposition groups most ardently courted by Don Juan and his lieutenants are the Christian Democrats and the Socialists. In both cases the courtship has been going on for over a decade and its history has been a minuet of alternate advances and retreats, with some net gain for Don Juan but nothing like a complete conquest of either partner. The first figure was danced in 1948. Gil Robles, the leading Christian Democrat today, at that time Don Juan's political adviser, went to Paris on his behalf and obtained for him the support of Indalecio Prieto, exiled Republican leader, and his important faction of the Spanish Socialist party. Shortly thereafter, however, Don Juan held his first friendly meeting with Franco, whereupon Prieto, incensed, withdrew his support. So it has gone ever since. For lack of a better alternative, a considerable number of Socialists have been drawn to Don Juan's side over the years, but ever and anon many of them are alienated as he trims his sails to placate Franco or the Carlists or both. The great bulk of the Socialists were so offended by Don Juan's recent course that in mid-1960 they refused to join in a declaration, to which the other non-Communist opposition groups were ready to subscribe, favoring the prompt restoration of the monarchy.

The case of the Christian Democrats has been similar, except that the conservative majority, led by José María Gil Robles, regards the restoration of the monarchy as inherently desirable, provided it is limited, rather than as a choice of evils, as do some Socialists. Even Gil Robles, though still a supporter of Don Juan, is less close to him since he began his *rapprochement* with the Carlists. According to a well-informed source he threatened a rupture when he heard in the summer of 1958 that Don Juan was about to accept the throne on Franco's terms, which included the perpetuation of the antiliberal principles of the Movement. Thereupon, the account continues, Don Juan drew back and the restoration project was dropped—for the time being, at least. The other main group of Christian Democrats, the Leftists, led by Manuel Giménez Fernández, support a restoration of the monarchy on condition of its prior endorsement in a free national referendum. In 1960 they were said to be weakening on this issue because of second thoughts about the feasibility of a referendum.

To add to the confusion, there is still a third faction of Christian Democrats—the splinter group of extreme rightists led by José Rodríguez Soler. Though devoted to monarchy and determined to get rid of the Falange, this group appears to have no other serious differences with the present regime, and many of its members are called "collaborationists."

In view of all these pullings and haulings, one may well wonder why the monarchist movement is taken seriously by anyone but the monarchists. And why, in any case, should it be described as an opposition movement since Franco is committed to the eventual restoration of the monarchy, is pensioning the leading monarchist candidate and educating his son, and has close ties with members of the only other important faction, who were his comrades-in-arms and a tower of strength to his cause in the Civil War?

A part of the answer to the first question is suggested by the second: the monarchist cause must be taken seriously because Franco himself has espoused it in principle. This is one of the two main reasons why the monarchical solution has the unique and, in the eyes of many Spaniards, irresistible attraction of promising a peaceful transition from the present regime to the next. The other main reason is that key figures in both the military and civilian sectors of the regime are even more strongly pro-monarchist than Franco. They would fight, it is believed, rather than acquiesce in another military dictatorship, and few Spaniards want to jump out of the Franco frying pan into that fire.

Even among the regime's opponents, moreover, there is little enthusiasm for an immediate return to republican government, for that idea revives bitter memories of the republic and the Civil War of the 1930's, which most thinking Spaniards on both sides want to allay. The monarchy, on the other hand, was not involved in that struggle, and so there are many who hope that a king would serve as a symbol of national unity. He could, they believe, become an agent of reconciliation for a nation still split down the middle over the Civil War—at least that part of it over forty years of age, including practically all persons in positions of authority both in the regime and in the opposition. This is why many former republicans, such as the late Gregorio Marañón,[4] one of the intellectual leaders and a political architect of the republic, turned monarchist under Franco.

Finally, in Don Juan the monarchists have a better candidate to head the kind of government they desire, a government of national reconciliation. Though not a brilliant or heroic figure, he seems to have the qualities of a conciliator. His own political views are moderate and middle of the road on the Spanish scale. He is earnest, conscientious, simple in his tastes, and, those close to him say, would not let the old aristocracy turn the restoration into a Roman holiday. And he is physically sound and still in his middle forties. The only comparable figure to head a republic is Gil Robles, who is now a monarchist. Though he is widely respected by all but left-wing Spaniards, Gil Robles is handicapped by his identification in the 1930's with the republic (as a right-

---

4 Marañón died on March 27, 1960.

winger, to be sure) and in recent years with one wing of the opposition group, the conservative Christian Democrats; and he is nearing seventy.

The answer to our second question—why the monarchists should be considered an opposition group—must begin with a reminder of the circumstances under which Franco came to power and the terms in which he has posed the problem of a restoration of the monarchy. When Franco was made political as well as military head of the rebel forces early in the Civil War, it was understood by General Kindelán, the prime mover in this, and apparently by the other officers concerned as well, that the arrangement was a provisional one and would lead to a restoration of the monarchy within a reasonably short time after victory had been won. Accordingly, they waited patiently for four years after the end of the war. Then, in 1943, General Kindelán and more than a dozen other high-ranking officers urged Franco respectfully but strongly to proceed with the restoration. In one way or another the pressure from the monarchists has continued ever since, and, while Franco has from time to time jailed or otherwise penalized overzealous members of the group, he has also shown respect for their cause. He has done so from conviction as well as from prudence, for he himself is a monarchist in principle and delays putting the principle into practice only because he has come to regard himself as a providential leader and his continuance in power as indispensable to Spain's welfare.

Hence the terms in which Franco has posed the problem of a restoration. The basic statement of his position is contained in the Act of Succession of 1947, which, it will be recalled, declared Spain a kingdom but left Franco free to designate the king and to fix the time of succession at will. The act thus put him in a better position than ever to manipulate the monarchists and their candidates in accordance with his favorite divide-and-rule and stalling tactics, so that he could go on exercising the plenitude of power at minimum risk. Though it may be only rationalization, he has justified his course by questioning Don Juan's competence

and stressing the present strength of anti-monarchical sentiment in Spain.

Without bothering to read it, we are told, many monarchists at first welcomed the Act of Succession as a victory
for their cause. In fact, however, it played ducks and drakes
with the fundamental principles of monarchy; on this
ground the more alert among them voted "no" in the plebiscite on it and Don Juan condemned the act publicly. Before
long, however, it became apparent that Franco was going to
have his way, and that the monarchists would have to play
the game on his terms or not at all. Most of them, including
Don Juan, chose the former course in the expectation that
the restoration of the monarchy and Franco's retirement
would take place in the near future.

Franco has continued ever since his cat-and-mouse game
with the monarchists, time and again arousing and then
dashing their hopes. The best example of these tactics began
early in 1957 with his appointment of a strongly pro-monarchist cabinet, and ended in May 1958 with a speech in
which he dismayed the monarchists on two counts. One was
his announcement, for the first time, that he intended to
retain power as long as he lived; the other, his formulation
of still another basic condition that would bind the future
king in the form of a statement of the twelve principles of
the Movement. Franco's Twelve Commandments, as the
monarchists sourly called them, had a Falangist flavor that
was repugnant to most Spaniards who were not members of
that party. Neither point was essentially new, but it had been
hoped that the Falange was on its way out and monarchy on
its way in.

Franco's redefinition of his position in May 1958 made
unmistakably clear what had already been suspected: that
advocacy of a limited monarchy, or of the early establishment
of any kind of monarchy, was tantamount to opposition to
his regime. Members of other groups already clearly identified with the opposition now had an added incentive to join
hands with the liberal monarchists in protest against the
perpetuation of Franco's Twelve Commandments. Finally,

the continued deterioration of the Spanish economy created serious alarm in upper-class circles, which feared more and more that if Franco's economically incompetent regime remained in power much longer, the upshot might be a social explosion that would wreck the nation, beginning with the upper classes.

Unión Española

In 1958 the mood engendered by these developments was expressed in the formation of a new group called Unión Española. As its name indicates, it has aimed at a nation-wide union of opposition forces, except the extreme right and extreme left. Accordingly, it drew one of its two principal officers, Joaquín Satrústegui, from the moderate monarchists, and the other, Enrique Tierno Galván, from the moderate left. The principal speaker at the Menfis Hotel banquet in January 1939, Satrústegui, comes from a prominent Basque family but spends a great deal of time in Madrid; he has no business firm of his own, maintains a varied and substantial portfolio of investments, and serves on the management boards of several enterprises; and he has been a Don Juan monarchist for several years.

Tierno Galván is professor of political science at the University of Salamanca but commutes there from Madrid during the term. He explains that he is less liable to political harassment in Madrid; to which it might be added that Madrid is also a more convenient center for his political activities. Formerly a Socialist, Tierno now deplores the "ideological" character of this and all the other political parties of the past. In politics, he maintains, ideologies are impractical and divisive and should be supplanted by "functionalism," by which he means technical programing of a concrete character. It is another of his major tenets that, in the modern world, international cooperation is indispensable and that it is essential for Spain to join in the cooperative efforts that are being made by her European neighbors.

In furtherance of his views Tierno established at Salamanca an Association for the Functional Unity of Europe, which flourished briefly in 1957 until the government suppressed it. He is still referred to as the leader of the Functionalist group and maintains contacts with leaders of other groups of the left, such as Dionisio Ridruejo and Manuel Giménez Fernández, in addition to having joined with the Satrústegui group in forming Unión Española. Some observers believe that, although nominally only second in command and ostensibly no longer a Socialist, Tierno is actually the dominant member of the Unión Española team, and is using it and Satrústegui to pull his Socialist chestnuts out of the fire. Whatever ulterior motives he may have, those who know both men are generally agreed that Tierno has more driving force, tenacity, and depth than his nominal chief.

These two were the principal speakers at the Menfis Hotel banquet, which was licensed by the government as a professional meeting of lawyers but which was transformed into a political sensation. Both speakers attacked the regime for its injustice, inefficiency, and corruption, and both called for a prompt restoration of the monarchy under Don Juan. The Pretender himself was absent and had not even been consulted about the banquet. Its immediate purpose was to initiate a series of similar meetings in other Spanish cities and thus prove both to Franco and his generals, and to Don Juan, that there was a strong grass-roots movement in favor of restoring the latter as head of a limited monarchy.

As explained by its organizers, the long-range purposes of Unión Española were not to provoke a civil war, but to accelerate a peaceful change of regime; to put much-needed starch into Don Juan's flagging campaign for the throne; and to convince him that the liberal path would, and the reactionary path would not, lead him to it. It also aimed to demonstrate to Franco and his generals that serious trouble lay ahead if they persisted in maintaining the regime in its existing form, and to show that responsible civilian elements of both left and right were organized and ready to cooperate in setting up a limited monarchy on terms that would presumably be acceptable to the generals, if not to the Generalissimo.

Hoping that the regime would give him and his cause the political boost of martyrdom by arresting him for his Menfis speech, Satrústegui had arranged his business and family affairs for a long stay in jail. The government did not oblige. It did, however, fine him 50,000 pesetas and Tierno Galván 25,000 pesetas (a little less than $1,000 and $500 respectively, at the current tourist rate of exchange). It also started business reprisals against Satrústegui through his various financial interests, but soon abandoned that shabby method when he threatened to publish an exposé of it abroad.

What is the significance of this affair for the future of Unión Española and the rest of the opposition? Putting it together with the case of Dionisio Ridruejo, described below, one is struck by the relatively wide latitude that the Franco regime in recent years has given those of its Spanish critics who combine a certain prominence in Spain with connections or news value abroad. Spain's isolation of a decade ago has been so far broken down that Franco, still dependent on foreign aid, has to show some respect for opinion in key foreign countries. Foremost among these in recent years has been the United States, and this may help to explain why the regime has been comparatively mild in its treatment of its monarchist critics and has concentrated its fire on the Socialist and Communist sectors of the opposition. Most Spaniards, whether they support the regime or not, are convinced that in the United States the authorities at least, and perhaps the people at large, like Spain's monarchists, distrust Socialists and, of course, abhor all Communists.

So long as the regime maintains its present attitude in this matter, the monarchist members of Unión Española and other groups will presumably continue to enjoy a relative freedom of maneuver that will enable them to demonstrate what potentialities they really have. Unión Española—or some group like it, if it should fail—ought to fare best since it is not merely a monarchist group but the kind of coalition that is needed if the opposition is ever to become effective.

Unión Española may already have failed. Little has been

heard of it since its meteoric rise to fame in early 1959. It seems to have suffered the fate of most cooperative efforts in Spain. Ultraconservative monarchists were highly critical of Satrústegui's attack on the regime, which they characterized as rash and ill timed. They were also suspicious of the left-wing forces represented by Tierno Galván, whose ultimate designs, they suspect, bode no good for the monarchy and the upper classes. Conversely, many republicans look on Satrústegui's speech, and his whole leadership, as evidence that Unión Española is being engineered by the upper classes to protect their privileges by jettisoning Franco because they think he has become a liability to them. Cooperation and trust come hard to Spaniards.

The Christian Democrats

In their basic ideas the Christian Democrats in Spain resemble similar groups in France, Italy, and West Germany. While their closest ties are with their French counterparts, they have, it is said, received their greatest stimulus from the success of Konrad Adenauer's party in West Germany. They are in no sense, however, a branch of an international party. Like similar parties elsewhere, they are Catholics, but in their political activity they are not controlled by the Vatican or the Spanish ecclesiastical hierarchy. In this respect they differ from the other two politically significant Catholic entities in Spain, Catholic Action and the Opus Dei. Another difference is that the Christian Democrats are nothing if not political, whereas the other two groups function in a broader field and are so much more definitely religious in character that they will be discussed in the chapter on the church.

The Christian Democrats are thoroughly Spanish, but they have no direct antecedent party in the pre-Franco period. They somewhat resemble, and in part stem from, the CEDA of the 1930's; its then head, Gil Robles, is now the principal leader of the Christian Democrats. Until the outbreak of the Civil War, the CEDA was Republican and, on the scale of that period, conservative. The Christian Democrats of today are preponderantly monarchist and include a left wing that is as vigorous as the right.

Since parties are forbidden by law, no one can say how many members the Christian Democratic group has. However, informed observers generally agree that it is one of the two largest political groups in Spain, the other being the Socialists. Hence the eagerness of Don Juan and his advisers to win its support. The Christian Democrats would be even stronger but for their failure to pull together and the diversion of much of their potential membership to Catholic Action and its labor offshoot, HOAC (Hermandades Obreras de Acción Católica), which adhere to the belief that the regime can be reformed from within. Many Christian Democrats once shared this belief, but disillusionment has convinced them that there must be a change of regime. This they hope to accomplish by peaceful means.

The two main divisions of the group are the usual right and left wings. Gil Robles, who leads the former, has long been prominent, and yet he remains a rather enigmatic character. Estimates of his character and performance during the ordeal of the republic, when Spain was constantly on the brink of civil war, seem to depend upon the political angle of observation. A left-winger, Ramos Oliveira, describes him as an "ex-pupil of the Salamanca friars, lawyer, . . . leader of the party of the Church and the great Castilian landowners," who "had character of a sort" but "was not entirely competent" for the task he faced, and whose aim was to denature the republic by a peaceful counterrevolution which would be "quite as complete and profound as the most exigent reactionaries could desire." [5] Madariaga, on the other hand, viewing Gil Robles from the middle of the road, sees in him a man of great ability and strong character who accepted the republic in good faith and was completely innocent of the charge of plotting its destruction. These accusations, he maintains, were brought against Gil Robles by "the leaders of the Left," partly from an honest misunderstanding and

---

[5] Antonio Ramos Oliveira, *Politics, Economics, and Men of Modern Spain* (London: Gollancz, 1946), pp. 521-522.

partly in order to justify their own "rash schemes," which helped bring on the Civil War.[6]

Since the Republican period Gil Robles' role has been less decisive, but still of importance as a monarchist and a leader of the opposition to the regime. He became a monarchist in 1937 after the dissolution of the CEDA and all other parties except the Falange. For more than a decade he served as political adviser to Don Juan. He is still regarded as one of his chief supporters, though he ceased to be his adviser after the fiasco of the proposed coalition between monarchists and Socialists, in 1947 and 1948. In recent years he has taken a courageous stand as legal counsel for persons accused of subversive activities. But many opponents of the regime regard his resistance to it as excessively moderate, and his identification with right-wing conservatism as indelible. His course leaves them dissatisfied and puzzled.

The smaller but more dynamic left wing of the Christian Democratic movement is headed by Manuel Giménez Fernández, minister of agriculture and lieutenant to Gil Robles a quarter of a century ago. Age might seem to make both men unlikely leaders of the opposition and it may account in part for Gil Robles' relative quiescence in recent years. Giménez Fernández, on the other hand, is big, robust, articulate and affable, and lively as a cricket. He is also professor of canon law at the University of Seville and a scholar of international distinction.

As rarely happens in Spanish political factions, the gap between the two wings of Christian Democrats represents a difference of policy rather than personal rivalry. Gil Robles and Giménez still maintain their friendly association of CEDA days. Giménez continues to speak of Gil Robles as "my chief" and as the head of all Christian Democrats. But the policy differences between them are real and in May 1959 Giménez recognized this by formally organizing his followers under the name of "Leftist Christian Democrats." The group is said to have branches all over the country, operat-

---

6 Salvador de Madariaga, *Spain: A Modern History* (New York: Praeger, 1958), pp. 426, 435.

ing mainly from university centers, though with backing from the professional and working classes as well. In order to avoid the ban on political parties, the new leftist organization has declared itself an association of study groups.

On most public issues the group led by Gil Robles is much the more conservative or moderate. On the question of sanctions or reprisals after the change of regime, for example, the Gil Robles group would hold these within narrow bounds, mainly confined to flagrant cases and under some sort of statute of limitations. The Giménez group would apparently exclude from the post-Franco inquest no offense, civil or criminal, committed since the beginning of the Civil War in 1936. Another specific point of difference is the restoration of the monarchy. Provided the monarchy is limited, Gil Robles is committed to it unconditionally, whereas Giménez conditions his support on its prior approval in a national referendum to be held by a provisional government which would let the people choose between a monarchy and a republic.

Each of these two groups has potentialities for substantial growth, particularly in case those Catholics who are still hoping for reform within the regime should decide to try for better success outside it. The growing rift between the two wings poses a serious handicap, but in dealing with the Spanish scene one cannot be sure that such things are not more apparent than real. The left group may conceivably have been encouraged by Gil Robles to form a separate organization in order to step up their campaign among labor and lower middle-class groups; these are likely to be fruitful sources of recruits if Franco really carries out the austerity program that he adopted in the summer of 1959.

The Leftist Christian Democrats may become one of the most important forces in Spanish political life. Even if they do not, considerable interest still attaches to its views as expressed in a declaration of principles adopted in 1959. Circulated clandestinely in typewritten form, its main points may be summarized briefly. In church-and-state relations, it advocates the negotiation of a concordat that would give the

Catholic Church in Spain a status somewhat like that of the
Anglican Church in England, enjoying certain protection
and support from the state, but, along with this, establishing
freedom of conscience and public worship for all faiths. In
the economic field, it proposes the nationalization of banking, insurance, and industrial monopolies. Its political and
cultural plank calls for the integration of kindred peoples,
defined as including all those of Spanish speech, plus Portugal and, because of "our European vocation," France, Italy,
Germany and the Benelux countries. In the military field,
"We repudiate every policy of aggression, every militaristic
infeudation, every infiltration of warlike ideas, and every
economic subordination that might imply military collaboration." The United States was not mentioned here or elsewhere in the declaration, but the unfavorable allusion to
the bases-and-aid agreement seems as clear as anything in
this rather cloudy passage.

The Socialists

One of the great unknowns in Spain's political situation is
the actual or potential strength of the Socialists. Many well-
informed observers believe that they are, if not the largest, at
least one of the two largest groups in Spain, the other being
the Christian Democrats. They also believe that if a democratic government should be established in Spain, these two
together could dominate it, though neither would be able to
do so alone.

On the other hand, equally qualified commentators question this estimate of numerical strength (which no one, of
course, can verify as matters stand). They say, further, that
in any case, because of internal dissension and loss of prestige and morale, the Socialists of today are only a shadow of
the party that ranked first among the parties under the republic. According to this view, the Socialists have never
recovered from the destruction of the republic, and they are
now being further weakened both by the general decline of
socialism in Western Europe and by the inroads that are

being made on their actual or potential membership by other groups, from Communists to Leftist Christian Democrats, as well as by their family quarrels.

The prima facie case for this low estimate is strong, particularly because of the rifts within the Socialist camp. These are of two kinds: first, between the Socialists in Spain and those in exile, and, second, among those in Spain. The first of these divisions reflects the general and perhaps inevitable estrangement that has grown up between those who, from choice or necessity, carry on the struggle in Spain, and those others who, likewise from choice or necessity, are conducting it in exile, an exile which for most of them began more than two decades ago. The exiles are important on many counts, especially for the Socialist party. Their number has been estimated at about half a million, of whom nearly 200,000 live in France. They include most of the leaders of the Civil War generation. They contribute largely to financing the struggle, from their own pockets if they have prospered, or through donations by foreign sympathizers. And they have enjoyed far greater freedom of movement and speech than their fellows in Spain. Hence they have understandably maintained their claim to leadership.

This claim has apparently been asserted with particular vigor by the Socialist party's headquarters-in-exile at Toulouse, in southern France. The Socialists in Spain have grown increasingly restive under the control of Toulouse, for they feel that they know best how to manage their own affairs. They are in the thick of the struggle, whereas the exiles have inevitably lost touch with the situation in Spain, despite frequent clandestine communication across the Pyrenees. By 1958 the tension had led to an open break, but the longer-range consequences of this are still obscured by the dissension that has also developed among the Socialists living in Spain.

This dissension has arisen partly over personalities, as so often happens in Spain, but partly also over policies. One policy question is whether to cooperate with other groups, particularly Communists and monarchists. So far there has been a heavy preponderance of Socialist opinion against accepting Communist overtures for what amounts to a revival of the popular front of the 1930's, but opinion has been deeply divided over the question of monarchy. Some Socialists have been won over to the view that a restoration of the monarchy offers the only basis for a peaceful liquidation of the Franco regime. Others refuse to agree without an ironclad guarantee of a prior popular referendum between republic and monarchy. Still others want no truck with monarchs on any terms.

While the assertion that Spanish socialism has been seriously debilitated is therefore plausible, nevertheless impressive evidence to the contrary has been provided—unwittingly, of course—by the Franco regime. In recent years, especially in 1958 and 1959, its campaign against the opposition has been concentrated very largely on the Socialists. It seems safe to assume that General Franco is following the sound strategy of attacking the enemy at what he believes to be his strongest point, and all observers agree that Franco's efficient secret service keeps him well informed about what is going on beneath as well as on the surface in Spain. His special concern with the Socialists has made them the principal victims of his recent round-ups of political prisoners, including the sensational one of November 1958 and the smaller but substantial one of May 1959.

Again, the Socialists are the only opposition group against which the regime has published a book.[7] This publication was intended to prove that the Spanish Socialist party is fundamentally different from the Socialist parties in other European countries, is "irremediably infected with the most malignant virus of revolutionary violence," and serves as a channel for Communist penetration, which, unless blocked, will inevitably lead again, as it did in the 1930's, to civil war, chaos, and Communist domination. Most of the sup-

---

[7] *What Is Happening in Spain? The Problem of Spanish Socialism,* cited. The Spanish government's responsibility for the book, while not indicated in it, is clear from the circumstances of its publication and its distribution to foreign embassies in Madrid.

porting evidence consists of passages about the republic and the Civil War quoted from Salvador de Madariaga's *Spain: A Modern History.*[8]

Apparently this book was published to defend the Spanish government against the international outcry provoked by its large-scale arrest of Socialists in November 1958. Indeed, the protests abroad were loud and came not only from European Socialists but also from many labor organizations, including the AFL-CIO in the United States. At that very time Spain was engaged in a series of delicate negotiations for foreign aid to avert an impending financial and economic disaster; if the wave of criticism set off by the arrests continued to mount, it might have imperiled their success.

As the authors of the book see history and the future, the Socialist party was responsible for the Civil War and for bringing the Communists to power under the republic. Since then Spanish socialism has been dominated by its head-quarters-in-exile at Toulouse. The Spanish Socialists arrested in November 1958 were acting "in agreement with, and on instructions from" Toulouse (p. 110), and "the Spanish Socialists . . . allied to Communism in all subversive actions against Spain . . . [are] ready to contract any alliance provided it may help them to seize power again" (p. 104). Even the foreign protests against the arrest are linked to communism: "With a highly skilled technique, worthy of the Communists, a whole world campaign has been contrived" (p. 120). And in the grand finale we read that the "peace and continuity" that the Franco regime has given the country has "enabled Spain . . . to take part in the tremendous task of . . . strengthening the free world, now threatened by the worst of tyrannies" (p. 112). The book also quotes a statement by the Secretary of the Socialist party-in-exile in Toulouse, to the effect that "since the Party and the General Union of Workers were clandestinely organized in 1944, we have had to grieve for six clandestine committees fallen into

---

[8] Madariaga promptly protested against the distorted quotation of his study, and pointed to the absence of any proof that the Socialists are the same as in the 1930's.

the hands of the police" (p. 111).[9] This is eloquent testimony to the efficiency of Franco's secret service.

The effect of the book is impossible to estimate. While informed readers will not be taken in, it is plausible enough to discredit the Spanish Socialists in the eyes of the uninitiated abroad, and to sow fresh discord among the opposition forces in Spain by reviving memories of the bitter discord that existed among the Spanish republican parties in the 1930's.

The Communists

Communists are arrested from time to time in Spain, and the regime professes to make them, rather than the Socialists, the main target of its antisubversive campaign. The claim is regarded with skepticism, however, by many foreign observers as well as by most Spaniards. Just one recent example. When the Communists were preparing a one-day nation-wide strike, called for on June 18, 1959, as a protest against Franco's dictatorship, they were permitted so much freedom of movement by the public authorities that, according to a newspaper report, "experienced observers" in Madrid suspected "official complicity as a part of a deliberate policy of the regime."[10]

What is its policy? Its aim is certainly not to build up a strong Communist party within Spain and probably not to curry favor with Moscow, but simply to lend some credibility to the idea of a Communist menace in Spain, which the regime exploits to great advantage both at home and abroad. The presence of real live Communists in Spain lends plausibility to its settled practice of smearing all opposition elements as "Reds." It not only applies this term to its present opponents, but also uses it on all occasions, from Franco's speeches to school books, to designate all those who were on the Republican side in the Civil War.

In the long run this is a dangerous game for the regime.

---

[9] *What Is Happening in Spain?* . . . , quoting *El Socialista* (Toulouse), December 18, 1958.

[10] *The New York Times,* June 18, 1959.

By tarring all opposition with communism it strengthens its appeal to the very numerous anti-Franco elements in Spain. The danger is now all the more real because the governments of the principal powers on the democratic side have tended more and more to tolerate and even support Franco. That he is willing to run this long-range risk would seem to indicate great confidence in his ability to keep his Communist cat's paw under control at least for the time being.

Franco's confidence seems justified by the facts. The Communist party in Spain is very small. Though its exact size is unknown, an informed estimate early in 1959 placed its membership at not more than 5,000. Moreover, it is handicapped by the Civil War heritage of hatred it has left among most former republicans. They have not forgotten how the Spanish Communists conquered power with the aid of Soviet arms and used it ruthlessly to destroy their rivals on the republican side.

In an effort to overcome this widespread antipathy the Spanish Communists are now singing a very different tune. In place of their domineering arrogance of Civil War days, they are now all sweetness and light. They offer their cooperation to all genuine opposition elements, of whatever political complexion, in defense of freedom, true democracy, peace, and Spain's national independence and interests. Like all other opposition groups, they make liberal use of whispering campaigns and clandestine publications, printed, multigraphed, and even typed. In addition, they possess a propaganda weapon that gives them a great advantage over all the other groups. This is Radio España Independiente, the most powerful of all anti-Franco radio stations, which is said to have more Spanish listeners than any other station, Spanish or foreign. It broadcasts regularly seven hours a day, and its popularity has increased since 1957, when, with the gradual *rapprochement* between Paris and Madrid, Radio Paris ceased its anti-Franco broadcasts.

Despite its name, Radio España Independiente is neither Spanish nor independent. It operates with powerful transmitters from behind the iron curtain, at Prague and Odessa, and is financed and controlled by Moscow. From time to time it employs Spanish Communist speakers, notably that firebrand of the 1930's, Dolores Ibárruri, "La Pasionaria."

Information about how the Spanish Communists are organized, controlled, and financed is incomplete, and estimates of their numbers vary widely, though the highest estimate is low. They fall into two distinct groups, those in exile and those in Spain. Most of the exiles probably live in France, where a high estimate of 1958 placed their number at 8,000. Tolerated until 1950, their group activities in France have been banned by its government ever since then, and they have been hampered by their own inner discords. Nevertheless, France is believed still to be the principal corridor for the transmission of funds and propaganda materials from iron-curtain countries to Spain. The Spanish Communist party's Fifth Congress (its first since 1932) was held clandestinely in Paris in November 1954. Its Sixth Congress, in February 1960, was, however, convened in Prague, safely behind the iron curtain. Another Communist corridor into Spain which has apparently disturbed Madrid in recent years has been Morocco, where agents of Red China as well as the Kremlin are said to be active. Under Fidel Castro, Cuba has been added to the list of corridors.

Quiescent from 1939 until a few years ago, the small Communist party in Spain is already envied by other opposition groups as exceptionally efficient and well financed, presumably by Moscow. It aims, not at an early conquest of power, but at gaining an audience and winning friends for the cause, and it goes about its revolutionary business in an almost conservative way, for it hopes to make converts among the clergy, the military, and the "nonmonopolistic" *bourgeoisie* as well as among the workers. When its alleged chief, Simón Sánchez Montero, a forty-four year-old Toledo baker, was caught and tried for "military rebellion" because of his part in promoting the one-day strike of June 18, 1959, he jumped at the chance to make a public "confession" which has been described as a "masterpiece of political propaganda" in its ex-

ploitation of the popular theme of national reconciliation.[11]
In addition to its own members and fellow travelers, the
party in Spain is indirectly aided by the 2,500 Spaniards—
veterans of the Blue Division and their families—repatriated
from the Soviet Union since 1956. With very few exceptions
these repatriates eschew politics, but in the popular mind
they are identified with the Soviet Union and their relatively
high levels of education, behavior, and technical performance
are said to have created a favorable impression of the Soviet
system. In these and other ways, including the daily pounding of Radio España Independiente's broadcasts, the party's
propaganda has had a considerable impact on Spanish public
opinion. In its efforts to revive the popular-front idea, however, the party has so far been rebuffed by the other opposition groups.

Apparently the small membership of the Communist party
in Spain is not increasing rapidly. According to those who
claim to know, such an increase is not desired at this time by
the Communist high command. Rather, they say, it is seeking
to build up a small elite group trained primarily, not for a
take-over, which is not expected in the near future, but to
exploit any future opportunities for expanding its influence
in Spain.

Short-term Communist objectives can be inferred with reasonable certainty from the broadcasts of Radio España Independiente. In 1959 it pursued three favorite themes. The
first was, of course, attacks on the Franco regime, described
as the prop of the oligarchy and the exploiter of the masses.
The stabilization plan provided a steady flow of grist for this
mill. A second theme concentrated on attacking the United
States, mainly the bases program, the American military presence, and U.S. support of the Franco regime. The announcement of the stabilization plan was followed by an increased
emphasis on the role of the United States as a prop of the
regime and on warnings of the economic conquest of Spain
by American capitalism. A no less central topic has been

---

11 Silvio Schädler, "Communism in Spain," *Swiss Review of World Affairs*,
December 1959, p. 4.

national reconciliation, to be achieved through the cooperation of all other peace-loving and freedom-loving political
groups with the Communists, to rescue the mass of the Spanish people from tyranny and exploitation at the hands of the
Franco regime and to defend Spain's national interests and
independence against the threat of military, economic, and
political domination by the United States.

A recent illustration is a broadcast dealing with one of the
station's favorite themes, the military presence of the United
States in Spain. Entitled "U.S. Gibraltar in Spain—Cartagena," it was delivered on July 31, 1959, by Enrique Lister,
former commander of the International Brigade in the Spanish Civil War.

In exchange for ten million dollars [Lister began] and, of
course, political help to keep Franco in power a little longer, the
Americans have received the rights to the Cartagena base, which
though not included in the agreements made public in 1953, has
been built up to be handed over to the Yankees. [His conclusion
was in the same vein:] This new Gibraltar has already cost the
Spanish people tens of millions of pesetas and . . . will cost many
more. What is worse is that the existence of this war base will
constitute a permanent menace to the lives of the inhabitants of
the region, a menace that will end only with the overthrow of
Franco and the liquidation of all U.S. bases in Spain.

Communist propaganda has probably done Franco relatively little harm so far. Its effect has been confined largely
to worker and student circles, where Franco would be disliked even if there had never been any Communist attack on
him. On the other hand, its constantly reiterated denunciations of U.S. cooperation with the Franco regime have probably added substantially to the volume and intensity of
anti-American feeling among the Spanish people.

How shall we sum up the significance of communism as
an element in the Spanish opposition today? In the first
place, the Communist party in Spain has remained demon-
strably weak down to the present. Its weakness is not properly measured by pointing out that the party has only about
5,000 members in a population of thirty million, for it is

possible for a handful of Communists to gain effective control of a country as the 2,000 to 4,000 Communists did in Guatemala in 1953 and 1954. But to do so they must penetrate and manipulate the country's government and power groups, and this the Spanish Communists have completely failed to do. They have not even been able to win the cooperation of the other Spanish opposition parties, much less manipulate them.

The most striking proof is provided by the collapse of their herculean and widely publicized efforts to promote two general strikes, on May 5, 1958 (which, ironically, they labeled "Reconciliation Day"), and on June 18, 1959. The second effort ended in an even greater fiasco than the first, despite the remarkable degree of freedom the government gave them in preparing for it. Even Radio España Independiente admitted the Communists' inability to gain the cooperation of other opposition groups for the strike.

On the other hand, the potential of the Communists in Spain is greater than their present strength. They appear to be the most dynamic of the opposition groups. They have the precious advantage of Radio España Independiente, and superior underground organization and financial resources. Above all, the growing *rapprochement* between the democratic powers and the Franco regime is, according to repeated warnings by anti-Communist opponents of Franco, making many Spaniards look to Communist leadership as the only hope of escaping from a tyranny they detest. According to some, the principal danger point is the potentially powerful syndicates, which the Communists are said to be penetrating.[12] However that may be in the long run, the chief present hazard, so far as the United States is concerned, lies in Spanish receptivity to the grossly distorted Communist image of the United States and the Western defense system.

Even if this process continues, we are told, the Communist party would still remain a splinter group. How then could it gain control of the country? As Patrick Henry said,

_____

12 Araquistain, cited, pp. 65-70.

we have no lamp to guide our feet but the light of experience, and in this case the experience is that of the republic and the Civil War. In the last general election under the republic, in February 1936, only six months prior to the outbreak of the Civil War, the Communists elected only fourteen of 472 members of the Cortes; yet within a year after its outbreak they had a stranglehold on the Republican government. The explanation is simple. Fighting for its life, the republic had to have foreign aid and could get it only from the Soviet Union and the Communists in France; and with dependence on communism came Communist control. A repetition of this pattern is highly improbable, but the same cannot be said of the danger that, unless precautions are taken, the regime that follows this one may give expression to the anti-Americanism and neutralism now being fostered in Spain by Communist propaganda.

Finally, up to the present the chief result of Communist activities in Spain has been to strengthen the Franco regime both at home and abroad. Without ever for a moment threatening its security, they have served as a constant reminder of one of the worst features of the Civil War and hence in favor of continued acquiescence in a regime whose motto is "peace and order." Abroad, the Communist presence in Spain has contributed powerfully to the belief that there is no acceptable alternative to his regime. His reputation as an expert on the Communist menace, combined with Spain's strategic location, has cemented his partnership with the United States, and the yields of this partnership in prestige and material aid have done much to shore up his regime at home.

Other Groups

Once an important force, above all in Catalonia and only less so in Andalusia, the anarchists have never recovered from the disaster of the Civil War. They were decimated by their Communist rivals during the war, and again by Franco afterwards. The experience demonstrated the fallacy of anarchism in any contest, and the need for concerted action.

Many surviving anarchists of that generation have gone over to socialism, some to communism, whereas few recruits have been made from the younger generation. As one observer has remarked, anarchism and Carlism seem well on the way to becoming only quaint survivals of the Spanish past. Present indications are that anarchism will be ready for the museum first.

On the other hand, a new party that may have a longer future is forming around Dionisio Ridruejo, former protégé of Naziphile Serrano Suñer. Like several other ex-Falangist intellectuals, Ridruejo is today one of the most effective critics of the regime. Others are Pedro Laín Entralgo, a scientist of high international repute who strove to reform the regime from within until these efforts led in 1956 to his dismissal as Rector of the University of Madrid, and Miguel Sánchez Mazas, who in exile has produced one of the most searching analyses of contemporary Spanish society.[13]

The Social Democratic party, as this new group is called, differs from the earlier Falange in accepting political democracy and Catholicism, but still shares much the same goal of reform in the interest of justice and social integration. In these respects it has much in common with Giménez Fernández and his Leftist Christian Democrats; like the latter, it is not openly subversive, only critical.

In 1959, while still only a skeleton party with no more than a few hundred members, the Social Democrats were said to constitute a kind of elite cross section of intellectuals, professional men, and workers, both young and old, with their two main concentrations in Madrid and Valencia. In the spring of 1959, in the short space of a three-day visit to Valencia, Ridruejo had some two hundred callers, despite police regulations that permitted him to receive no more than a handful at one time.

The regime's treatment of Ridruejo illustrates its highly selective method of handling its opponents. Its treatment of all persons of position and prestige has been relatively mild

---

13 *Informe sobre las causas económicas de la crisis social española* (Geneva, 1957).

in recent years. Ridruejo possesses both. Although charged early in 1956 with inciting a student ferment of revolutionary implications, he was released after a brief sojourn in jail. In 1957 he was arrested again for giving an interview critical of Franco and the regime to a foreign magazine, but was released on bail; when the case came to trial early in 1959, he was permitted to win a moral victory. Though convicted on the charge of disrespect *(desacato)* towards Franco, he was let off with what amounted to an admonition, despite his having taken advantage of his day in court to reaffirm his low opinion of Franco and the regime.

Some commentators have alleged that this case illustrates a trend towards the assertion of judicial independence,[14] for the court not only let Ridruejo speak freely but held the trial in public; allegedly, it also imposed a penalty much lighter than Franco had told it to. Perhaps so. Others maintain that, on the contrary, Ridruejo's mild treatment accorded with Franco's wishes and needs. At the time the Spanish government was in the midst of delicate international negotiations of great importance, and Franco was said to fear that they might be prejudiced by rigorous punishment of a Spaniard of Ridruejo's stature. According to this view, the regime was happy to have the case settled as it was. The conviction of Ridruejo maintained the principle, while the lightness of the sentence averted an international scandal. Both views are plausible, but the second is the more persuasive.

A few months after his trial, Ridruejo again criticized the regime sharply in an interview published abroad,[15] and this time nothing was done about it. Under the Falange's political monopoly, he said, Spain has become a "political desert." If Spain's "decisive forces," the army and the church, did their duty, they would compel a change of regime; if they failed to do so, there would probably be a "national revolutionary protest." Ridruejo openly advocated the establish-

---

[14] François Bondy, *Preuves* (Paris), April 1959, pp. 7-8.
[15] Published in *O Estado de São Paulo;* reprinted in *Ibérica* (New York), July-August 1959, p. 3.

ment of a "democratic regime" in Spain; under it, he declared, the survival of the Falangist party would be "extremely improbable" and the formation of a pro-Franco party "practically impossible." Clearly, the regime now permits its intellectual elite a modest measure of free speech—outside Spain.

Youth and Unification

A critical, much debated, and at present insoluble question is what role the younger generation of Spaniards is likely to play in their country's unfolding political drama. In Spain everybody talks about the problem and everybody thinks he knows the answer, but those best qualified to know give contradictory answers. For example, Vicente Girbau León,[16] a former Spanish diplomat, now in exile, pictures the youth of all classes as virtually unanimous in their determination to replace the present regime with a liberal one.[17] On the other hand, Ridruejo seems completely disillusioned about the younger generation. In a private conversation early in 1959 he expressed the opinion that 95 per cent of all young people in Spain, including university students, care only about jobs, comforts, and security, and are indifferent to politics and hostile to any political movement that might interfere with their individual careers by upsetting the *status quo*.

My own observations tend to support Ridruejo's view, and yet it must not be forgotten that in any nation and in any class or group the political activists are always a minority, often a small one. The significant thing is that there is a small but hard core of opposition to the regime among the students, an opposition that is growing slowly but steadily

16 In *What Is Happening in Spain?* . . . , cited, pp. 115-116, Girbau is described as a Socialist, thirty-seven years of age in 1959, "formerly in the Foreign Ministry of Spain and simultaneously an assistant professor at the University of Madrid," who was convicted of "clandestine pamphleteering" in March 1956, imprisoned for nine months, and then given a passport and allowed to leave Spain.

17 Vicente Girbau, "La rebeldía de las 'generaciones ajenas a la guerra civil,'" *Ibérica* (New York), December 15, 1958, pp. 3-5.

as its members leave the university and begin their careers. Several of the political prisoners rounded up in November 1958 and May 1959 were men in their late twenties and thirties whose opposition to the regime dated from their university days.

One striking point of agreement among university youth has been revealed by recent inquiries, namely, the almost universal agreement that the highest priority should be accorded to effecting a national reconciliation and, as a prerequisite, burying the Civil War hatchet. This expresses a mood or an emotional attitude. It does not provide a basis for concerted action, for the great majority of Spaniards, old as well as young, are crying for national reconciliation. But each group, and almost each individual, insists on having it on his own terms.

The great need of the opposition groups is to achieve a reconciliation among themselves if they are ever to become effective. They almost certainly comprise or speak for a substantial majority of the Spanish people. But they are weakened by divisions similar to those that crippled the republic and contributed to its defeat in the Civil War. Fragmentation remains strong among the exiles, who inherited it from the republic, as well as in Spain. Efforts at unification have recently been made on both fronts. In 1958 they led to the establishment in Spain of Unión Española, and in Paris to the setting up of an organization to bring together several exile groups. Neither has shown much vitality. Moreover, with the passage of time, an inevitable gap in understanding has arisen between exiles and opponents of the regime living in Spain.

Nevertheless, substantial progress towards a common view seems to have been made by the opposition groups within Spain. This prevailing opinion now rejects the belief, so widespread only a few years ago, that organized pressure could bring about a reform of the regime from within; it has now largely come around to the view that the regime itself must be changed. In the second place, many former Republicans, though far from all, now believe that the best solution would be a restoration of constitutional monarchy. However, their enthusiasm for this solution is checked by the uncritical patience with which the chief claimant waits for Franco to hand him the crown. All told, the weakness of the opposition, as a result of its internal divisions, is still one of the strongest props of the Franco regime.

Chapter VI

ECONOMIC FACTS AND FANCIES

SINCE JULY 1959 the problems and hopes of the Spanish economy, and their impact on Spain's political situation, have centered on the stabilization plan, which was launched midway in that month. A product of months-long consultation between Spanish and foreign economic experts, and of many and vigorous urgings by international financial agencies and foreign governments, this drastic plan was accepted by the Caudillo and by some, perhaps most, of his advisers only reluctantly and under the force of grinding necessity. Their reluctance was understandable. The new plan involved a sweeping change in long-established policies and practices. It imposed a regime of austerity. And it was and is fraught with many hazards. The Spanish government had to accept it, nevertheless, as the price of indispensable foreign aid, the best way out of a mounting economic crisis that threatened the stability of the regime.

The trouble was old and deep-seated. Many attributed it to the clash between the facts of Spanish economic life and the dream of autarky conceived in the early ultranationalistic years of the regime. It remains to be seen whether the new plan will prove to be more realistic in terms of the total Spanish picture—political and social as well as economic.

Background of the Crisis

When Franco reorganized his cabinet in February 1957, Spain was already faced with a serious economic situation which had been shaping up inexorably for the past two years. Its most obvious symptoms were sharp and persistent increases in the cost of living, in the adverse balance of Spain's foreign trade, and in the drain on her gold resources and foreign-exchange holdings and the consequent weakness of the peseta abroad. Despite many manifestations of prosperity in certain regions and strata of society, informed observers knew that the Spanish economy as a whole was in deep trouble.

Diagnosticians differed on details, but there was general agreement that the main causes lay in a combination of three groups of factors. The first, a continuing one, includes certain inherent weaknesses in the Spanish economy, due to natural handicaps of soil, climate, and resources. The second was the heavy damage done by two decades of misfortune, from 1930 to 1950, which included Spain's share in the world-wide economic depression, her own civil war, her relative isolation during World War II, and her ostracism from its close to 1950. The third group was made up of grave faults in the economic system of the Franco regime, ranging from excessive controls and too rapid industrialization to pervasive inefficiency, corruption, and favoritism.

No government could be expected to do much, if anything, about the first two groups of ills but the third was manageable, and here the performance of the new cabinet was deeply disappointing. Few doubted the good intentions or theoretical proficiency of the three ministers mainly concerned—Mariano Navarro Rubio (Treasury), Alberto Ullastres Calvo (Commerce), and Pedro Gual Villalbi (minister without portfolio and President of the National Economic Council). There were, however, many businessmen and bankers who questioned their grasp of practical affairs. Ullastres, a university professor of economics and the most vocal of the three, soon became known as "the mystical minister." Such criticism may have been unfair, but in any event opposition from vested interests and other sources, in the cabinet as well as outside, hampered their efforts at reform. These were aimed at arresting inflation, reducing the number and scope of internal controls, liberalizing foreign-trade regulations, and strengthening Spain's international economic ties, especially with her European neighbors.

As the year 1958 drew to a close, it became clear that the reforms as a whole had not succeeded in halting the deterioration; Spain was heading for a financial and general economic crisis that might have grave political repercussions.[1] The only concrete measure of importance that had won unqualified success was a tightening up of the tax system, which had proved a bonanza and made it possible to balance the regular budget in 1959. This success was more than offset by failures, ranging from partial to complete, in all other respects. The "slow rhythm" of the economic reform probably was due in part to the fact that it had to contend with the "inflationist mentality" that had reigned in Spain for many years past.[2] It has subsequently been suggested that the measures taken in 1957 and 1958 may have been responsible for arresting the rise in wholesale prices in the first half of 1959, even before the stabilization plan was adopted.[3] But that was a delayed effect, and during 1957 and 1958 the cost of living had continued to rise, so that by the end of 1958 the mass of Spanish workers were worse off than they had been before the inflationary across-the-board wage increases that had been

---

[1] "Economic Danger Signals in Spain," *The Economist* (London), January 17, 1959, p. 229, provides a fair sample of informed comment on the gravity of the economic situation. Commenting that General Franco's recent year-end report to the nation had made no reference to "an alarming side of the economic picture that thinking Spaniards are worried about," the writer specified these reasons for alarm: (1) Living standards are threatened. (2) The gold reserve has been reduced to the "untouchable" minimum required by law to cover the national currency. (3) Foreign exchange reserves are nearly exhausted. (4) Lack of foreign exchange has forced the government to cut petroleum imports 20 per cent, and the "gravity of the measure is clear: trucks, tractors and fishing boats stand to feel the pinch." (5) "Another sombre development concerns Catalonia's textile industry which has been caught up in a severe recession," with a drop of 25 per cent in sales, and 59 per cent in advance orders, during the past year; 300,000 workers are involved, and while they must be paid for workless days, idleness may disturb social stability.

[2] Banco Hispano Americano, *La situación económica en 1959* (Madrid: Author, 1960), p. 24.

[3] Banco Urquijo, *La economía española en 1959* (Madrid: Author, 1960), p. 69.

ordered in 1956 as a sop to appease their dangerous discontent over the previous low wage scales.

The continued drain of gold and foreign currency had reduced Spain's foreign-exchange reserves to the vanishing point and the trade deficit remained at a very high level. How, then, was Spain to finance essential imports such as tools, machinery, fuel, fertilizers, and raw materials? Without these her economy could not continue to operate, much less expand to meet the needs of a growing population. Clearly, national bankruptcy and a general economic crash were in the offing. One result was a crisis of confidence in the regime, highlighted by the flight of Spanish capital as revealed in the "Swiss bank scandal" of December 1958. This episode concerned the establshment of numbered (anonymous) accounts in Swiss banks by Spanish depositors with black-market pesetas. It involved some Spaniards connected with the regime and their implication was regarded as marking a crisis of confidence in it. Moreover, rumor had it that the Spanish government's exposé of the scandal stopped far short of the truth both as to the sums involved and the very highly placed persons implicated in it; the suspicion heightened the crisis atmosphere. The exact amount of these deposits has never been revealed.

The Stabilization-Austerity Plan

Out of this situation came the sweeping change of Spanish economic policy represented by the stabilization plan of July 1959, backed by a foreign "package loan" of $420 million to help finance the change-over. This resembled programs already adopted by other countries, including Argentina and Turkey, but it was a far cry from the principles of nationalism and statism that Spain had followed, insofar as she had any settled policy, for more than twenty years. Ultimately the plan promised increased production and higher living standards. First, however, it meant imposing an austerity program which, if carried out, could not fail to injure many businessmen, workers and farmers, in addition to vested interests that had grown up under the protection of the older system. Some of these might suffer only temporarily, from lower profits or unemployment, before the readjustment was completed and the expected recovery under the new and sounder system set in. But the damage done to others might be lasting.

Franco and his advisers had realized at last that they had no choice. The realization was borne in upon them by the diagnoses and prescriptions of teams of foreign and domestic specialists called to the bedside of the Spanish patient. The consultations began in December 1958 with the visit of a team from the Organization for European Economic Cooperation, of which Spain was an associate member. Next, in February 1959, came a team from the International Monetary Fund, to which, as to the World Bank, Spain had been admitted in August 1958. While the details both of the consultations and of the debates they aroused in Spanish government circles were not divulged to the public, certainly the general tenor of the consulting physicians' advice was vigorously supported by Ministers Navarro Rubio, Ullastres, and Gual Villalbi, as well as by other leaders, including the spokesmen of Spain's big private banks, which have a large measure of control over the private sector of the economy.

It was an unusual move for the government to consult the Spanish banking community and other groups and individuals in Spain before reaching a decision. Although the reports were not made public, a reliable source states that they were virtually unanimous in recommending a reduction of government controls, greater freedom for private enterprise, a lowering of barriers to foreign trade and investment, and closer ties with Western Europe, as well as a balanced budget and other anti-inflationary measures. One indication of the gravity of the crisis was that the essential features were supported publicly by the head of the Falange, José Solís Ruiz, and privately by the head of INI and one-time high priest of autarky, Juan Antonio Suanzes. The reports from the banking community and others were presented to the National Economic Council, which in turn reported to the cabinet. In support of the reform campaign the noted French economist Jacques Rueff was brought to Spain in February 1959 for both public appearances and closed conferences with financiers, government officials, and others. Rueff's part in planning the De Gaulle government's recent stabilization-cum-austerity measures gave his word great weight.

It was not until July 20, 1959, that the arrangement was completed and announced to the public in connection with Spain's promotion from associate to full membership in the OEEC. This promotion was another step, and a long one,

TABLE 1

Foreign Support for the Spanish Stabilization Program
(in millions of dollars)

Source	Amount
IMF drawings	75
OEEC credits [a]	100
Credits from U.S. commercial banks (Chase Manhattan and First National City)	70
Sales of surplus agricultural commodities under U.S. Public Law 480 [b]	60
U.S. Export-Import Bank loans	30
U.S. defense support grants	40
Funding of indebtedness owed to OEEC member countries [c]	45
Total	420

[a] The OEEC credits took the form of a special credit, advanced through the European Monetary Agreement—successor to the European Payments Union—and was by far the largest it has provided.

[b] The sales under PL 480, while not aid in the form of grants or loans, help to support the stabilization program since the agricultural commodities are paid for in pesetas and require no expenditure of dollars or other foreign currencies.

[c] The funding of the debts to the OEEC countries permitted Spain to pay its commercial and other obligations over a period of four years. This was similar to the arrangements made among the OEEC countries when the European Payments Union was liquidated. It relieved Spain's immediate position but differed from other forms of aid in not putting new funds at Spain's disposal.

Sources: *The Department of State Bulletin*, August 10, 1959, pp. 210-211; International Monetary Fund press release, reprinted in *International Financial News Survey* (IMF), July 24, 1959, p. 1.

towards restoring normal economic relations between Spain and her European neighbors. Whether the economic facts of life would follow suit remained to be seen.

The new arrangements consisted, as I have already noted, of two parts: a foreign "package loan," and Spain's own stabilization plan, adopted as a condition of the loan.[4] Both these terms are subject to qualification. The so-called "loan" included other forms of assistance (see Table 1), and the stabilization plan has also been described, more aptly, as an austerity program.

Although the ultimate aim of all such stabilization plans is to insure a "sound and lasting economic expansion,"[5] their immediate purpose is to promote stability and efficiency. In order to achieve this purpose they require measures that may at first check production and business activity and increase unemployment. But it is assumed that the recession will be temporary and that the economy will then begin to expand on a firm basis.

The Spanish plan conforms to this general pattern. Its purposes are to control inflation, liberalize Spain's international trade and domestic economic system, promote private investments, and enlist the support of other countries and international agencies for these purposes. One basic measure was reform of the foreign-exchange system. In place of the complex system of multiple exchange rates previously in force, under which there had been in practice wide variations from the basic rate of 42 pesetas to the dollar, a uniform rate of 60 pesetas to the dollar was established. In addition, maximum public expenditures for 1959 and 1960 were specified; borrowing by the public sector was

---

[4] For a detailed description of the plan, see "El plan de estabilización de la economía española," *Moneda y Crédito, Revista de Economía* (Madrid), September 1959, pp. 71-111; the documents section of the same issue contains the memorandum of the Spanish government to the IMF and the OEEC proposing the plan.

[5] Organization for European Economic Cooperation, *European Monetary Agreement, First Annual Report of the Board of Management* (Paris: Author, 1960), p. 49: "This slow-down [in the Spanish economy from July to December 1959] should be only temporary, the aim of any stabilisation programme being to ensure a sound and lasting economic expansion."

sharply reduced from previous years; limits were set on credits to the private sector from commercial banks and the Banco de España; and the rediscount rate was raised by one per cent. Provision was made for the progressive elimination of price controls, and wages were to be increased only if there was a corresponding increase in productivity. A coordinated investment program, establishing priorities, avoiding uneconomic projects, and encouraging foreign investment, was to be worked out by the Spanish authorities. Imports on government account were to be limited to approximately 20 per cent of total imports, and provision was made for progressively freeing imports on private account from government control and for revising customs duties on all freed goods.

Finally, there were two transitional measures. First, as a check on liquidity and speculation, deposits of 25 per cent of the value of goods to be imported were required. Second, for a period of three years imports of edible oil and meats were to be subsidized in order to hold prices down; and, as a means of financing the subsidies and preventing price increases in the home market for citrus fruits and certain ores, export duties were to be levied on these products. The subsidies and export duties were to be gradually reduced and eventually eliminated.[6]

Two comments seem in order. In the first place, the stabilization plan is deflationary in purpose; it encourages private enterprise by diminishing state controls; and, through drawing Spain into closer economic association with the West, it exposes Spanish private enterprise to increased foreign competition, although a substantial level of protectionism is still maintained. In the second place, except for Spain itself, the United States and the IMF appear to have played the primary roles in bringing this arrangement to pass.[7] Nearly one-half of the "package loan" was to come from private and governmental sources in the United States, which was presumably the main promoter of the plan. The United States

6 Same, pp. 47-49.
7 The train of events began with the OEEC mission to Madrid in December 1958, but from then on the IMF seems to have been in the forefront.

certainly has had a major interest in seeing Spain's economic house put in order, both with a view to assuring the smooth operation of the bases agreement and because of its major role in keeping Spain solvent.

Apparently the United States and the IMF saw eye to eye on Spain's economic problems. As a leading member of the IMF, Washington has a major voice in its affairs, and it also makes it a general rule not to aid stabilization programs in countries that refuse to meet the conditions prescribed by the IMF. In the Spanish case, as in others, the IMF did not hand over all its promised aid in one lump sum but will dole it out piecemeal, as the prescribed reforms are carried out. The OEEC does likewise; its credit was to be made available in two installments, and the second of these was approved only at the end of 1959, after it had made an independent survey of the progress of the Spanish economy. The two organizations thus hold watching briefs to see that the Spanish government lives up to the austerity program it has adopted as a condition of the "package loan."

Stabilization at Work

The Spanish government began carrying out most provisions of the stabilization plan promptly and vigorously, devaluing the peseta from 42 to 60 to the dollar, tightening up credit, reducing or removing restrictions on trade, and cutting back subsidies to uneconomic enterprises. In the next few months it abolished a whole flock of price-control boards. But would it persevere in its new course? And what would the results be?

In the short time that has elapsed since the adoption of the plan the evidence necessarily remains inconclusive. Moreover, stabilization is not an end in itself. The real test is whether Spain can increase production, efficiency, per capita income, and living standards. And the answer to those questions can hardly be known before the plan has been in operation for two or three years. There have been, however, some progress reports that provide tentative guidelines and much food for thought.

Among these, special interest attaches to a presumably disinterested Swiss observer's comment on the early reactions to the plan. He found, in October 1959, that the opponents of the regime, at first perplexed by the plan, had more and more realized that "the rehabilitation of a ruined economy calls for measures that would have to be taken by any government, and that any future form of government in Spain should be glad to inherit a reformed economic order." It was desirable, from their own point of view, that the requisite austerity measures be imposed by the government that had made them necessary. As for the "broad masses," he noted that they had "received the announcement of the reform with indifference," partly because of the hot weather, but also because they did not believe anyone was going to undertake the reform they most needed, namely, a reform in the attitude of the Spanish upper classes towards social problems.[8]

The annual reports of the principal private banks are always among the best guides to economic developments in Spain. The report for 1959 by the Banco Central, one of the leading commercial banks, presented a comprehensive and frank appraisal of the stabilization plan to the close of that year. On the credit side, it stressed three achievements. First, the plan had been highly successful in reducing the volume of currency in circulation and in balancing Spain's international payments. Currency in circulation had decreased more than 2.7 billion pesetas in the first eleven months of 1959, as compared with an increase of more than twice that amount in 1958 and even larger increases in earlier years. From August to November 1959 foreign-exchange income had exceeded outgo by $81.3 million, as compared with an unfavorable balance of $21.5 million for the corresponding period in 1958. Second, the rise in the cost-of-

<hr>

8 Silvio Schädler, "Spain at the Crossroads," *Swiss Review of World Affairs,* October 1959, pp. 19-20.

living index had been slowed down to 3.5 per cent for 1959 as a whole, and in the closing months the index had remained stable. Third, as compared with 1958, there had been some notable increases in production in 1959, including agriculture (9.9 per cent) and certain industrial sectors (pig iron, steel, nitrogenous fertilizers, cement, and aluminum).

On the other hand, the Banco Central report pointed out some unfavorable developments. The rate of increase in national income in 1959 (3.5 per cent) was far below the annual average for the preceding decade (5.9 per cent). In the closing months of the year, production had declined in some fields, notably textiles. In other fields, especially key industries, production had exceeded consumption and large inventories were being accumulated, because of the very great difficulty of restricting production. (The reference here is to one of the most explosive issues connected with the stabilization plan: the legal prohibition against discharging surplus labor.) It warned that there was a danger that current production would not be absorbed at present prices.

The report concluded its discussion of the plan with two recommendations. The first was that the Spanish government should profit by the example of other countries that had adopted similar plans and relax its controls as soon as an improvement was noted. The second recommendation called for stimulating private investments: in the case of Spanish capital, by lowering taxes and relaxing credit restrictions; in that of foreign capital, by a liberal administration of the new government regulations, discussed below.[9]

Simultaneously, a Swiss observer gave the plan a carefully

---

[9] Another leading bank, the Banco Urquijo, published similar findings on the mixed results of the stabilization plan to the end of 1959. Thus, electric-power production, which had shared in the general recession just after the plan went into effect, showed signs of recovery late in the year; the decline in the volume of railroad traffic and in the aggregate number of working hours of the labor force as a whole still continued; Banco Urquijo, *La economía española en 1959,* cited, p. 73. The same report (p. 86) expressed the view that the plan would be of "great benefit" to Spain's "suffering middle class."

qualified commendation.[10] His chief reservation, however, went to the very essence of the plan. Its basic idea, he pointed out, "is that recovery can be obtained only with a stable currency," but its reforms "touch only a few, and not even the most important, aspects of the economic renewal of Spain." The correction of old faults, he said, will not be enough. Spain's economy, isolated for twenty years, will have to prove itself in foreign competition, create conditions for increasing production and national income, and overcome chronic unemployment.

The adoption of the plan, this observer pointed out, had led to "a real deflationary crisis," mainly in private industry, and to the failure of a number of firms, so far only small ones. The textile industry, already in trouble, was now even worse off and would have to be relieved of the burden of supporting surplus labor. Foreign capital was badly needed, but so far the plan had not attracted much of it. How greatly Spain needed foreign capital had been shown by the achievements, even in the unfavorable climate of the Franco regime, of French and Italian capital in the Spanish automobile industry, and by Swiss, German, and French capital in pharmaceuticals. Nevertheless, Wolff gave the plan full credit for its notable success in the highly important task of righting Spain's balance of payments. He concluded that, on the whole, the outlook was hopeful, provided the Spanish government stuck to its new policies against the resistance which was sure to be put up by vested interests.

Resistance to the stabilization plan, or to some parts of it, has come from many quarters, both outside and inside the regime. In view of the plan's "basic idea" that "recovery can be obtained only with a stable currency," special interest attaches to an editorial protest against this central concept, published in the Madrid newspaper *Ya*, organ of Catholic Action; its editor, former Foreign Minister Martín Artajo, is regarded as a pillar of the regime. A sound economy, he maintained, is the prime condition of a sound currency, not

10 Salomon Wolff, "Economic Reform in Spain," *Swiss Review of World Affairs*, January 1960, pp. 11-18, and February 1960, pp. 5-12.

the reverse.[11] Indeed, he continued, the economy as a whole can be crippled by giving first priority to a sound currency and the balance of payments. By way of illustration, he compared two cases: that of Finance Minister Fernández Villaverde, who, after the Spanish American War, committed Spain to a policy of sound money and deflation and thus prevented his country from sharing in the world-wide prosperity of 1900-1914; and the case of Prino de Rivera, who, in the 1920's, subordinated currency policy to development, with the result that under his government Spain enjoyed "an economic development without precedent" in its history.

The writer in *Ya* also invoked the authority of the Secretary-General of the United Nations. Dag Hammarskjöld, he said, has quite properly warned that economic development may be held back by the excessive emphasis placed today on economic stability and orthodoxy. As if to leave no room for doubt about its target, the editorial concluded by expressing the hope that Hammarskjöld's views might some day reach even the experts of the International Monetary Fund, "that bastion of conservatism in international economic affairs."

There was resistance to the stabilization plan even within the government. It had existed during the preparation of the plan, and it flared up again in October 1959. According to *The New York Times* correspondent in Madrid, the plan was now "beset by cabinet divisions and public uncertainty" and many cabinet members, led by Minister of Industry Joaquín Planell Riera, were either lukewarm or hostile to the austerity measures, fearing unemployment, political unrest, and foreign competition. Franco himself was said to be unhappy over the plan; "from all accounts [he] dislikes the foreign supervision of his financial policies on which international lending agencies have insisted in return for their latest aid." [12]

One of the most explosive issues raised by the stabilization

11 Emilio Figueroa, "La moneda sana, el Señor Fernández Villaverde, y otras cuestiones," *Ya* (Madrid), January 5, 1960.

12 *The New York Times*, November 3, 1959; dispatch from Benjamin Welles, dated Madrid, October 30.

plan is that of its impact on Spain's labor force of some twelve million workers. Spanish employers say they cannot possibly meet foreign competition, as foreseen by the plan, unless they are released from the strait jacket of the present labor laws, so that they can bring labor costs down to a competitive level, especially by discharging surplus or incompetent workers and by simplifying the present highly complicated wage structure. The workers are bitterly opposed to any change that might undermine their job security, one of their most treasured rights. This is also one of the principal talking points of Communist agents, who are trying to spread the idea that the burden of the austerity program will be shifted to the shoulders of labor.

To mid-1960 the government had not given in to the employers on this question of policy; as a general rule, job security still stood. And yet, through business failures and otherwise, unemployment had increased markedly from its level of about 100,000 before the stabilization plan went into effect. By early November 1959, the number of unemployed workers had risen to 250,000, nearly 4 per cent of the nonagricultural labor force. The figure might go substantially higher, some said, to one million or more, for it was generally agreed that the most depressing effects of the austerity program would be felt in 1960 and 1961. The falling scale of operations also reduced the working hours and days of those who had jobs, and there was widespread elimination of the overtime work that for years had enabled many workers to make both ends meet. In November 1959 the government established for the first time a general system of unemployment compensation. It was restricted to workers legally discharged, and the maximum period of payment was six months.[13]

Meanwhile, the deflation brought about by the program

13 Banco Urquijo, *La economía española en 1959*, cited, pp. 74-75. In an analysis of the effects of the stabilization plan on employment the OEEC observed: "It is impossible accurately to assess the employment position, since there are no statistics of employment or hours of work and the information about unemployment is incomplete." OEEC, *Spain, 1960: Economic Conditions in Member and Associated Countries of the OEEC* (Paris: Author, 1960), p. 15.

had not lowered the cost of living. On the contrary, in accordance with its austerity program the government at once decreed several sharp increases in the prices of several key goods and services. The prices of certain imported goods—gasoline, lubricants, and tobacco—were raised to compensate for the devaluation of the peseta; telephone and railroad freight rates and passenger fares were increased to compensate for the abolition of government subsidies to these services. The latter increases were defended on the ground that they shifted the cost from the taxpayer to the user. The defense was theoretically persuasive. Yet, while the increased costs took effect at once, the taxpayer received no immediate relief but only a promise of unspecified relief at some time in the future.

Encouragement to foreign investment was nominally one of the chief purposes of the stabilization plan. To achieve this purpose will require a virtual reversal of the attitudes hitherto taken by both sides. The Franco regime has never gotten over its inbred prejudice against foreign investors, and the latter have shown only a tepid interest in entering Spain on the terms offered by the regime. While no recent statistics on foreign investments in Spain are available, it is known that they are small. In 1958 those of the United States amounted to $68 million, as compared with its investment of $4,314 million in the rest of Western Europe and $27,075 million in all foreign countries.[14] Prior to July 1959 the chief impediments had been the inability to convert earnings into foreign currency and the general limitation of foreign capital to a participation of 25 per cent (in a few exceptional cases the limit was lifted to 49 per cent). Early in 1959 the general rule was relaxed in the case of the oil industry by removing the ceiling on foreign investment, provided the investing entity was not owned or controlled by a government. The Spanish government was slow to give effect

---

[14] The figures are for private direct investment. The investment in Spain was distributed as follows (millions of dollars): petroleum 17, manufacturing 26, trade 5, all other 20. The total for Spain was $31 million in 1950. *Survey of Current Business* (U.S. Department of Commerce), various issues.

to this part of the plan through appropriate legislation. On October 3, 1959, it issued the first of several decrees on the subject, but these did not relax previous restrictions sufficiently to attract foreign investors. One of their chief defects was that they did not authorize any form of investment save by the remittance of foreign currencies to the Spanish Foreign Exchange Office (Instituto Español de Moneda Extranjera). This defect was at last remedied by a new decree of December 24, 1959, which provided that foreign investments might also be made through the direct supply of foreign capital equipment, technical assistance, patents and licenses, as well as of legally convertible peseta holdings or proceeds held in Spain. Foreign shareholding exceeding 50 per cent of total capital was to be permitted with authorization of the Council of Ministers; it was made easier for foreign investors to transfer profits and repatriate capital. The hope was that these measures would bring to Spain in 1960 the influx of foreign capital that had failed to materialize in the latter half of 1959.

In the first few months after the adoption of the stabilization plan the only important new encouragement to foreign investors was in the field of petroleum. Experts agree that whatever petroleum deposits Spain has are probably limited to Spanish Africa, where her tenure is so uncertain because of the explosive African political situation that even concessions to foreigners could not weaken—and, indeed, might be the only way to strengthen—Spain's hold on her colonies. The petroleum prospects there are encouraging, and by the late summer and autumn of 1959 American and other foreign oil companies were engaged in a lively scramble for exploration rights. As early as January 1960 an American firm, Gulf Oil Company, and a Spanish firm were preparing to prospect jointly for oil in Spanish Guinea. In the same month the Spanish government granted concessions to thirteen American companies to prospect in the Spanish Sahara.

Most if not all of the adverse developments that have occurred in the brief period since the adoption of the stabilization plan were foreseen in Spain as well as in the IMF, the

OEEC, in Washington, and elsewhere. Its advocates have taken a calculated risk. Well aware that austerity will entail some recession and some painful readjustments, they nevertheless believe that it will succeed in the end in producing a stronger economy. By 1959 heroic measures were necessary to arrest its headlong course towards collapse. To orthodox Western economists, this plan seemed the best and perhaps the only one that could produce the desired result. Their basic assumption is that, despite its obvious weaknesses, the Spanish economy contains elements of strength that will enable it to respond to such drastic treatment.

The judgment of these experts is one that laymen are not qualified to review. The facts about the strengths and weaknesses of the Spanish economy are, however, accessible to laymen as well as to experts. They will now be reviewed briefly as an aid to understanding a decision that can hardly fail to have a profound effect on the political as well as the economic development of Spain, and hence on her international role, for many years to come.

Basic Features of the Economy

While well diversified, Spain's economy is relatively so unproductive that her living standard is the lowest in Western Europe except Portugal's. For many centuries agriculture, stock-raising, and mining have been her principal sources of wealth; to these manufacturing has been added since the late nineteenth century. In value of product it now ranks first as a result of its exceptionally rapid growth under the forced draft which has been applied to it by the government in the past decade. Yet the older sectors still play a crucial role. Agriculture provides employment for over 40 per cent of the total labor force, as compared with about 20 per cent in manufacturing, and agriculture and mining together account for the great bulk of Spain's exports and will probably continue to do so for an indefinite period.

Despite this salutary diversification and the rapid rise of manufactures to first place in the national economy since

World War II, Spain still had a per capita national income of only about $260 in 1959. This was less than one-half the average for the other OEEC countries, less than one-third the average for Great Britain, and less than one-sixth that for the United States. On a world scale of economic development Spain occupies an intermediate position between the underdeveloped and the advanced groups and her position is near the lower fringe of the intermediate group.[15]

The relative backwardness and vulnerability of the Spanish economy are due to both short-range and long-range factors. Chief among the former is the unbroken chain of misfortunes that befell the Spanish people from 1930 to 1950. Before the depression of the 1930's lifted, Spain was plunged into her extremely destructive Civil War, on the heels of which came World War II, making it impossible to obtain the help from abroad needed to repair her Civil War damage. When World War II came to an end, Spain was almost completely isolated. Already the declared enemy of the Communist world, until 1950 she was ostracized by almost all countries in the free world. The ostracism was not carried to the point of an economic embargo, but France did, in fact, close the Pyrenees frontier for two years and Spain was, as we have seen, excluded from the Marshall Plan.

Even an economic wizard could not have coped with such misfortunes, and Franco, who has always made all the decisions, has never been noted for wizardry of that kind. As soon as the improvement in Spain's international relations, from 1950 on, gave him room and means for maneuver, his limitations became manifest. The chief exhibit is the industrial boom of the 1950's, which was stimulated by the government at very high cost. It absorbed funds that were urgently needed for other purposes and contributed more than anything else to the inflation and other ills that brought

---

15 With 1950 as the base, the index of Spain's gross national product rose to 134 in 1954, 142 in 1956, and 156 in 1958. Its dollar equivalent in 1958 (at the official exchange rate and in 1957 prices) was $11.1 billion. Spain's estimated population at the end of 1958 was 29.8 million. Data supplied by Program and Economic Division, U.S. Embassy, Madrid, February 1959.

Spain to the verge of bankruptcy in the winter of 1958-1959. On the other hand, relatively little was done to rebuild the nation's highways and railroads, which had been wrecked during the Civil War. Improved transportation is one of its most crying needs, for nature has broken Spain up into regional fragments which must be bound together by man if they are to have any unity at all. Yet, as the decade drew to a close, Spain's transportation system was still described as the worst in Europe.

There are also long-range factors that help to explain why Spain lags behind other countries, such as West Germany, that have suffered even greater disasters in the past generation. These long-range factors may be summed up under two headings: the character of the land and the character of the people. The influence of the physical environment on Spain's economic development has varied with the changing requirements placed upon it from one period to another of its history. At all times, however, Spain has been handicapped by the terrain, which is broken and often rugged or barren and lacks navigable rivers, and by the climate, which is hot in summer, generally semi-arid except in the northern fringe, and always unpredictable. Spain also lacks basic ingredients of economic development—petroleum, high-grade coal, and some other raw materials. When purchased abroad, these must be paid for mainly by exporting products of the soil, whose production depends upon Spain's capricious climate and whose sale depends upon almost equally capricious foreign markets. Moreover, some of the chief traditional sources of wealth, such as minerals, for which Spain has been famous since Roman times, are, if not approaching exhaustion, at any rate probably not susceptible of further expansion on a large scale.

The handicaps of the physical environment might conceivably have been overcome with greater success if the Spaniards were a different kind of people. As it is, some of their salient national traits, however admirable from other points of view, have further obstructed the economic development of their country along the lines that other countries, such as

Great Britain, Germany, and the United States, have followed with great success. Outstanding among these Spanish traits, as virtually all observers agree, is an individualism that verges on anarchy and asserts itself quite as vigorously in the economic as in the political field. Some of the most cherished values of Spanish culture impede economic development of the modern Western type, such as *dignidad*, roughly translated as "dignity," and *casticismo*, an untranslatable term that signifies a clinging to the traditional and authentically Spanish way of life.

Other Spanish traits could be cited, but the important point here is that the workings of the Spanish economy cannot be understood except in terms of the psychology of the Spanish people. Until recently the latter has proved unpropitious to all efforts to modernize Spain, through industrialization or otherwise, that have been made since the eighteenth century. For example, the not inconsiderable industrial growth achieved in the generation before World War I was confined to the Basque country and Catalonia, the least Spanish parts of Spain. Now at last the psychological modernization of the elite groups in the country at large is under way. Striking evidence of this fact was provided early in 1959 by the replies of the spokesmen of the Spanish banking and business communities, the management-labor syndicates, autonomous agencies, and others to the government's inquiry on economic policy. With virtual unanimity they replied in terms that would have been expected of similar British, German, or French groups faced with the same economic problems.

It is paradoxical that Spain should at last be catching up with the modern age under Franco, for one of the main pillars of his regime is the traditionalism represented by the cult of Hispanidad. The paradox may be explained by the traumatic experience of the Civil War and the other misfortunes the Spanish people have endured in the past generation. The old value system is giving way to a new one, not only in the elite circles of the business and banking community, but also among the masses—witness the steady stream of migration that continues to pour from the country-side into the urban areas, despite the government's efforts to arrest it and despite the fact that many of the migrants merely exchange the squalor of a village hovel for an even more squalid and less secure shantytown.

Stagnation in Agriculture

Farming is still the mainstay of the Spanish economy, employing nearly one-half the total labor force (49 per cent in 1950, between 40 and 45 per cent in 1959). On balance, Spain is an exporter of agricultural products. The production of foodstuffs normally covers domestic consumption, although by a narrow margin; even in good seasons the carry-over is so small that a single bad season can necessitate heavy imports. Citrus fruits, wine, olives, and olive oil normally constitute the largest single group of Spanish exports, accounting for about 20 per cent of the total, compared to some 15 per cent for the next group, iron ore and pyrites. On the other hand, stock-raising has declined, almost all branches of Spanish agriculture have been sluggish, and in over-all rate of increase it has lagged behind all other branches of the nation's economy as well as behind its population increase. Even if the average for the depression years 1931-1935 is taken as a base, the general index of farm production had risen only 13 per cent by 1957, a year of average weather and crops, as compared with a population increase of 25 per cent over the same period.

There have been some encouraging developments in recent years, such as the extension of rice cultivation from Valencia to Andalusia, and the revival, again mainly in Andalusia, of cotton-growing which had been squeezed out in the nineteenth century by the competition of American cotton. But the new developments have not been on a large enough scale to make any substantial difference in the general level of production. In addition, changes in food habits and an increase in per capita consumption have put an added strain on Spain's none-too-ample productive capacity.[16]

As a result, by 1959 Spain's export position was threatened just as the crisis in her international balance of payments made it imperative to increase exports by every means possible. Unpromising as the outlook for agriculture is, no other branch of the economy holds out a greater promise in this respect. It is perhaps for this reason that the national investment plan for 1959, issued by the government on March 12, 1959, just before the arrival of the IMF delegation in Madrid, allocated to agriculture the tidy sum of nearly 16,000 million pesetas, or almost one-fifth of the total for all sectors of the economy. The stated purpose of the plan is to increase farm exports by $30 million annually.[17]

The new capital funds for agriculture are designed to intensify the efforts, first undertaken systematically in 1952, which have consisted mainly in promoting irrigation and reforestation, the wider use of farm machinery, the domestic production of chemical fertilizers, and the voluntary consolidation of small landholdings. The program has also provided loans to farmers at low interest rates and a guaranteed minimum price for wheat. Of these objectives, only irrigation has represented a major effort, and the results have been substantial. Irrigation projects have been carried out by a government agency, the National Colonization Institute, which also undertakes the resettlement of farmers in new communities and the improvement of transportation and community facilities. Of these projects the most conspicuously successful has been at Badajoz, near the Portuguese border, a once semi-desert area that is now one of the most productive in Spain. Its transformation has been likened to that of California's Imperial Valley. A major project of this kind was inaugurated in Aragon by Franco in early 1959.

---

16 One example is the shift, attributed to the Civil War, in the north of Spain from lard to olive oil for cooking purposes. In the 1950's the increased demand was met in part by imports of soybean oil from the United States, so that olive oil would still be available for export.

17 The Chase Manhattan Bank, *Spain: An Economic Review* (New York: Author, May 1, 1959; mimeographed), p. 13.

Similar but smaller works of improvement dot other dry areas, which make up such a large part of the country. The bringing of some 300,000 hectares under irrigation between 1939 and 1958 was no mean achievement, for such projects are expensive and require much technical skill. According to a recent estimate, the irrigation of wheat fields more than doubles their yields.[18] Nevertheless this achievement marks only a beginning, for 90 per cent of the arable land, most of it in semi-arid regions, still remains unirrigated.

Other major handicaps of Spanish agriculture are the shortages of fertilizers and farm machinery, due in some measure to the government's restrictions on imports and to the diversion of scarce investment funds to less essential purposes. The consumption of fertilizers reached the pre-Civil War level only in 1954; since then it has risen steadily, as domestic production has increased, but even so it has been held below the level of real demand through various government restrictions. Farmers everywhere still complain that fertilizers are scarce and dear. Larger farmers complain even more loudly that farm machinery and replacement parts are almost unobtainable. In 1959 there were only 33,000 tractors in the entire country and the growing of grain is still largely a manual operation: 90 per cent sown by hand, 50 per cent reaped by hand, and 60 per cent threshed by hand.

One further and major handicap to efficient farming is found in the ill-assorted sizes of Spanish farms, and their fragmentation. A layman who reads what the experts have to say on this subject comes away with the impression that no Spanish farm is the right size. Many are too large, creating the problem of the *latifundio*. The rest are too small, giving rise to the problem of the *minifundio*. Still a third problem, overlapping and complicating the other two, derives from the excessive fragmentation of holdings into many small strips.

The typical Spanish farm is divided into a dozen or more small, separate parcels *(fincas)*. In the northwest, where

---

18 In 1958 the average yield in Spain was from 0.8 to 0.9 tons per hectare **on** unirrigated land and as high as 2.5 tons on irrigated land.

fragmentation is most pronounced, the average number ranges from forty or more in the province of Burgos to an almost incredible eighty-four in the province of Soria. The vast majority of parcels are very small: an agricultural census of 1953 showed that of 45.7 million such parcels, 58 per cent contained one hectare or less, and that in not a few instances "farms" were divided into 100 to 500 tiny parcels so widely scattered that the owners never found time to visit all of them, much less to work them. Fragmentation reached its peak of absurdity in one *finca,* in La Coruña province, which measured thirty-two square meters and had three owners: one of the land, one of its only walnut tree, and one who had the right to collect an annual rent of six eggs from the owner.[19] At the other extreme, the census recorded over 46,000 holdings of more than 100 hectares, several of them owned by a single person or corporation. These were the *latifundios,* which have long been concentrated in southern Spain, above all in Andalusia.

The only parts of Spain in which none of these three problems—*latifundio, minifundio,* fragmentation—exists on a significant scale are the Basque country, Catalonia, and the Levante (Castellón, Valencia, and Alicante).[20] In the rest of Spain—about two-thirds of it, including the principal wheat, olive, and wine regions—the net effect of the landholding system is decidedly adverse. The *latifundio* offers certain potential advantages, such as the economies of large-scale production and the opportunity for mechanization and scientific farming. In practice, however, they have been put to relatively little use, and the *latifundio* is typically plagued by absentee landlordism, a proletariat of landless farm laborers and tenant farmers on short lease—little if any better off than the laborers—and the withholding of large tracts of land from cultivation. The *minifundio* affords pride of owner-

---

19 T. Lynn Smith, "Fragmentation of Agricultural Holdings in Spain," *Rural Sociology,* June 1959, pp. 140-149.

20 Antonio Ramos Oliveira, *Politics, Economics and Men of Modern Spain* (London: Gollancz, 1946), pp. 219-222; although written more than a decade ago, this account remains valid in its main points.

ship, without providing a decent living. Fragmentation spreads risks, such as drought or flood, and theoretically it fosters a community spirit. In fact, however, it leads to endless bickering over boundaries, access, and water rights. In addition, it entails a great waste of time, blocks any efficient combination of agriculture with stock-raising, and renders mechanization and scientific agriculture impossible.[21]

Reformers have tackled the land problem time and again throughout Spain's modern history, but never successfully. Land reform was strongly advocated by Gaspar de Jovellanos, Spain's outstanding exponent of the eighteenth-century enlightenment. Vested interests, both secular and ecclesiastical, opposed change so stubbornly that little was accomplished even with the support of the absolute monarchy. A half century later, the liberal monarchy attempted the abolition of entailed estates *(mayorazgos)*, but faulty planning and bad management of the reform only worsened the problem. The agrarian question again received much discussion and some serious study early in the present century, but the first opportunity for thoroughgoing reform came only in 1931, with the establishment of the Second Republic. Again the opportunity was bungled. Disagreement over the principles of an agrarian reform and preoccupation with other matters, such as anticlerical legislation, delayed resolute action until the very eve of the Civil War. By then it was too late.

In the light of this record Franco's failure to make a determined attack on the agrarian problem is not at all surprising. He has, it is true, put some pressure on the large landlords to bring their waste and fallow lands under cultivation and in general to make more effective use of their properties. He could hardly go further without alienating a power group that is one of his principal supports. Yet without going further he can hardly do anything about the problem of the *minifundio*. Nor as regards the problem of fragmentation could he go much beyond the present policy of encouraging voluntary consolidation without upsetting a

---

21 Smith, cited, pp. 148-149.

great mass of land titles and other centuries-old arrangements. Yet the central fact remains that the development of Spanish agriculture, which is still basic to the country's economy, is retarded by the built-in defects of its traditional land system. Any attempt to promote its progress by other means while leaving this system substantially intact, as the government has been doing, is like trying to drive a car with the brakes on.

The Boom in Industry

Throughout its first twenty years the Franco regime gave top priority to industrial development. If statistics of production alone are considered, without taking into account either the soundness of the industries thus developed or the effect of their growth on other sectors of the economy, the regime must be credited with a notable achievement. With 1953-1954 as the base, the index of industrial production rose to 123.2 in 1956 and 145.2 in 1958. As shown by Table 2, the annual rate of industrial growth in this period was steady and far exceeded that in other sectors of the economy.

TABLE 2

Indices of Production, 1955-1958
(1953-1954 = 100)

Year	Agriculture	Fishing	Mining	Industrial	Total
1955	98.9	118.1	107.5	115.9	107.7
1956	105.6	116.6	117.2	123.2	112.3
1957	109.8	119.7	126.1	134.2	120.3
1958	109.6	119.7	127.2	145.2	125.6

Source: The Chase Manhattan Bank, *Spain: An Economic Review* (New York: Author, April 28, 1960; mimeographed), p. 25.

Admiration for this achievement, substantial as it is, must be tempered by two considerations. First, in any less-advanced country that is pressing industrialization resolutely and with the necessary ingredients, the rate of growth is likely to be high. Second, the Franco regime had a sub-

stantial base to build on. Not until 1953 did Spain's industrial production again reach its pre-Civil War high. Under
Primo de Rivera, special encouragement had been given to
basic industries, such as electric power, steel, cement, and
chemicals. Even before that, metallurgy, textiles, leather-
working and cork industries had been well established,
mainly in Catalonia and the northwestern area centering in
Bilbao.

In the Franco period of industrial expansion the greatest
gains have been, first, in the production of electrical energy,
which doubled between 1940 and 1950, and, secondly, in
metallurgy, chemicals, and engineering. The key role in the
expansion has been played by that rather fantastic national
development corporation, the Instituto Nacional de Industria, run by Franco's friend and trusted economic adviser,
Juan Antonio Suanzes.[22]

Created by a decree of 1941, INI combines certain features
both of an executive agency and of a private corporation. Its
director, who exercises broad powers, is appointed by and
responsible to Franco; its governing board (Consejo de Ad-
ministración) is made up of government officials; INI itself
is exempt from taxation, though the subsidiaries which it is
authorized to found or aid are not. On the other hand, it has
many attributes of a private corporation, including the right
to engage, directly or indirectly, in many kinds of industrial
enterprise and to issue stocks and bonds which are registered
on the stock exchange. It is a mixed corporation in the sense
that, while it utilizes government authority, financing, and
operation, some of its enterprises are expected ultimately to
be bought out by private capital. This does not apply, however, to those enterprises which the government regards as
connected with national defense or as essential to economic
autarky; control of these must be retained by INI.

According to the decree of 1941, INI has been designed
to supplement the policy, adopted in 1939, of strengthening
the Spanish economy against the effects of a "traditionally

---

22 See Chapter IV, pp. 128-130.

adverse balance of payments" and to fill the gap left by the failure of private capital to meet national needs. In order to meet these needs and strengthen the national defense, INI was set up to bring about "the industrial recovery of our Nation" by creating new sources of production and fostering those already in existence. In describing INI's purposes, the decree used such general terms as "the support of our racial values," "the political principles of the Movement," and "the development of our economic autarky." [23]

Backed by this broad grant of power and by large government funds, INI had, by 1957, created or acquired a controlling interest in some fifty firms and held a minority interest in a dozen more. Its activities covered a broad range of key fields, including steel, electric power, mining, aviation, shipbuilding, fertilizer production, and many others.[24] Until late 1957 it was financed mainly by grants from the national budget; their total amounted to 19,054 million pesetas or about $500 million by the end of 1956.[25] Since these subsidies came, not from private savings or tax receipts, but from government-created credits, the effect was decidedly inflationary. In an effort to limit this effect, INI was taken off the state budget by a law of December 22, 1957 (several similar agencies, such as the Institute of Colonization and RENFE, the state railway system, were left on it) and required to finance itself. Such was the political influence of INI, however, that it continued to obtain equivalent amounts on the easiest of terms as loans at 0.75 per cent in-

23 Preamble and Articles 1 and 2 of the Law of September 25, 1941, published in the *Boletín Oficial del Estado,* no. 280, October 7, 1941.

24 Instituto Nacional de Industria, *Resumen sobre finalidades y actuación hasta el 31 de diciembre de 1956* (Madrid: Author, 1957). In 350 pages of text, together with several maps and many illustrations, this volume gives a succinct account of each of INI's activities. In addition to those mentioned above in the text, these include several research projects and cooperation with the Institute of Colonization in the Badajoz plan.

25 The conversion into a dollar equivalent is rendered uncertain by the multiple exchange rates of the peseta and the fluctuations in its value, but $500 million seems a reasonable approximation. Total government expenditures for all purposes in 1956 amounted to $1,433 million.

terest from the Banco de España. The inflationary effect of its programs therefore made itself felt as before.

How INI will fare under the austerity program of July 1959 remains to be seen. The odds are that it will be the hardest nut of all for the advocates of austerity to crack. Despite widespread opposition on the grounds that it is wasteful, burdensome, and inflationary and competes with private enterprise, INI has acquired great influence and is now one of the biggest vested interests in Spain. Important persons, including army officers, are on its payroll. The industries that it has stimulated—steel, pharmaceuticals, fertilizers, meat refrigeration, and others—have become so much a part of the economic and social fabric that no government can tamper with them lightly. For example, its largest single enterprise, the steel plant at Avilés, had by 1959 brought about a fivefold increase in that town's original population of some 10,000; almost everyone in the town and the surrounding countryside, as well as consumers of steel throughout Spain, now has a stake in its welfare.

Although INI is criticized by many for competing with private enterprise, others recognize that many of its undertakings would not have been started for a long time, if ever, had they been left to private enterprise. In any case it is INI's declared policy to sell out its holdings to private investors as soon as they are ready to take over. For a long time the latter showed little disposition to do so, but a perhaps significant break came early in 1959, when the Bilbao banks began buying into the Avilés steel plant; they had hitherto boycotted it because it competed with Bilbao's privately owned steel mill, Altos Hornos, the largest of its kind in Spain. Finally, to many Spaniards, opponents as well as advocates of the present regime, private enterprise is no sacred cow. Many more applaud INI's main objective, which is to make the Spanish economy more self-contained or "independent" by strengthening its industrial sector.

Under the stimulus from INI and other sources, Spanish industrial production since 1940 has shown a rapid growth in many lines, as indicated by Table 3.

TABLE 3

Industrial Production, 1940-1958

(1953-1954 = 100)

	1940	*1950*	*1955*	*1957*	*1958*
General Index	61	76	116	134	145
Metallurgy	75	81	118	134	152
Chemicals	33	56	128	167	191
Engineering	46	69	123	147	158
Food processing	70	78	105	109	105
Textiles	74	89	105	114	122
Leather	78	83	111	125	118
Paper	62	85	117	147	157
Electric power	37	69	115	140	157

Source: Consejo de Economía Nacional.

Within manufacturing as a whole the iron and steel industry is basic to the economy and a favored target of government solicitude; it is also fairly representative of the progress and problems of Spanish industry in general. The production of crude steel, which reached its pre-Civil War peak of one million tons in 1929, did not recover that level until 1954. Since then, with financial aid from the United States, the steel industry has made notable progress in modernizing its equipment.

The best but not the only example is the wholly new Avilés steel plant, the largest and most ambitious of INI's many projects.[26] Authorized in 1950 with a capital of 7,000 million pesetas provided wholly by INI, it had two main purposes: to remedy the steel shortage, which was retarding Spain's entire economic development, and to alleviate the strain on the balance of payments by greatly reducing imports of steel. Despite the magnitude of the task—among other things, the marshy site chosen had to be drained, a railroad and a highway relocated, and the course of a river changed—production began in 1956, and by 1959 it had

---

26 Avilés, the name of the town, is commonly used instead of the cumbersome official name of the firm, Empresa Nacional Siderúrgica, S.A.

almost reached the initial planned capacity of 700,000 tons. Avilés is one of the most modern plants anywhere in the world.

On the other hand, the domestic consumption of steel has continued to grow even more rapidly; as a result, Spain's dependence on imported steel has actually increased in recent years and apparently it will continue to do so. Its dependence on imports of high-grade coal has likewise increased, and, as a result, while alleviating Spain's urgent balance-of-payments problem in one way, the expansion of the steel industry has aggravated it in another. Finally, these and other factors keep the cost of production high and internationally uncompetitive. The result is that the cost must be passed on either to the consumer in the form of higher prices, protected by high tariffs, or to the taxpayer through subsidies to the steel industry. This dilemma persists under the stabilization program of 1959.

Spain's engineering industries, ranging from ships and automobiles to small tools, have been developing at an unequal pace. Automobile production, represented mainly by SEAT, an INI firm that turns out a Spanish version of the Italian Fiat, has been producing at or near capacity level; again, as in the case of steel, the cost is high in comparison with other European countries. In 1959, on the other hand, for lack of essential imported materials, shipyards were working at only about 50 per cent capacity. The building trades have been very lively in recent years, accounting for about 45 per cent of total Spanish investment. This has created a brisk demand for goods and services; it has also had an adverse effect since a substantial part of the investment has gone into luxury housing, thus diverting funds from productive purposes. The government has also given extensive aid to low-cost housing; the 1959 budget provided 5,900 million pesetas for the construction of 140,000 units. It also maintains an extensive system of rent controls which, after the first renting, applies even to apartments built without government aid. Public construction was one of the sectors of the economy most adversely affected by the stabilization plan of

1959 in its first year. How Minister of Housing Arrese's reaction to this development led to his dismissal by Franco in 1960 is noted elsewhere in these pages. (See p. 125.)

Mining has been declining in relative importance since the early years of the century, and iron ore exports, for example, are now hardly half as large as in 1913, when they headed the export list. Early in this century Spain was the principal European producer of lead; its output is now less than one-third the 1913 figure, while that of copper has dropped even more sharply. There has been some compensation in the growing extraction of pyrites, which has doubled, and of coal (mostly low grade), which has nearly trebled over the same period. In net result, the rise in minerals output has been much less rapid than in manufactures, though better than in agriculture. Its growth has been held back by a lack of modern machinery and methods, and by wide fluctuations in foreign markets, particularly in the case of pyrites, now one of the largest of all export items. Against the latter hazard potash and mercury exports are protected by international cartel arrangements, which also limit their production.

Transportation and Power

One of the chief obstacles to Spain's economic recovery and development is the sad state of its transportation system, often deplored as the worst in Western Europe. Spain has almost no navigable rivers, except for a short stretch of the Guadalquivir as far as Seville. The 18,000-kilometer railroad system is badly run down. By 1958 nearly 2,700 of the 3,392 steam locomotives were over twenty-five years old, and a few had reached the century mark. Spanish trains have the lowest average speeds in Europe. The main network is operated by a state enterprise, the RENFE (Red Nacional de Ferrocarriles del Estado); in October 1958 the Spanish government initiated a ten-year $1.5-billion program to modernize the RENFE system, mainly through replacing steam locomotives with electric and diesel units.

The highway transport system is even less adequate, and this reportedly is the main reason why the government's efforts to improve transportation are being concentrated on the railroads. Almost the only first-class roads are those radiating from Madrid; even these generally get worse before one has traveled far from the capital, with the notable exception of the highway from Madrid to the summer capital of San Sebastián. On the whole, the highway system has not been restored to the relative state of grace it had reached under Primo de Rivera.

The government's effort to improve the highway system can be measured in different ways. On a per capita basis, Spain spent only one dollar on its roads in 1958, compared with $4 for Italy, $5 for Belgium and the United Kingdom, $15 for France, and $21 for West Germany and Sweden. On the other hand, in terms of expenditure per motor vehicle Spain stood on a par with France at $130, and well ahead of Italy, Belgium, and the United Kingdom, which ranged from $120 to $70.[27] Of course, the number of motor vehicles in Spain is very small; in 1958 it was just over 300,000 of all types, of which 170,000 to 185,000 were reported to be passenger cars, about six per 1,000 inhabitants. Paradoxically, the number of imported cars, including the expensive Mercedes, strikes the visitor to Spain as being large, because there are relatively few automobiles of any kind; presumably such imports will not be encouraged under the austerity regime.

Domestic air services are provided mainly by the government-owned Iberia Air Lines, again a member of the INI family, which relies largely on those old work horses of the air, Douglas DC-3's, for this purpose. Iberia has large modern planes for its international service, which extends to the United States and South America, as well as London, Paris, and Lisbon. Of Spain's merchant fleet, of 1.4 million gross tons of shipping, two-thirds is more than twenty-five years old. In addition to sharing in carrying Spain's foreign trade, it helps make good the deficiency of land transportation be-

---

[27] *The Times* (London), May 12, 1959, p. 9, "Europe's Motorways. . . ."

tween the northwest coast (Vigo-Bilbao-Santander) and the Mediterranean (Barcelona-Valencia-Alicante).

A much brighter picture is presented by the record of power production, though this too has its somber side. Under strong government stimulus the rapid growth of power production that began in the depressed 1940's continued through the next decade, as indicated in Table 4.

TABLE 4

Electric Power Production
(billions of kwh)

Year	Hydroelectric	Thermal	Total
1935	3.0	0.3	3.3
1940	3.4	0.3	3.6
1950	5.1	1.8	6.9
1955	9.0	2.9	11.9
1957	9.7	4.8	14.5
1959	14.7	2.7	17.4

Source: Banco Hispano Americano, *La situación económica en 1959* (Madrid: Author, 1960), p. 114.

If Spain gains access by pipeline to the extensive reserves of natural gas recently discovered in the French Sahara—for which hopes are high in Madrid—a long step will have been taken towards remedying her still serious power deficiency. Even without that, progress will continue to be made if Spain can find the foreign exchange to pay for the coal and oil needed to generate power, or if she can discover oil in her own Sahara. At any rate, the ten-year plan for power development, announced by the Ministry of Industry in 1953, has worked out well. Its 1958 goal of 15.5 billion kwh capacity was achieved on schedule, and its ten-year goal of 22.5 billion kwh by 1963 seems to be in sight. A shift in emphasis from hydroelectric to thermal power has begun. If persevered in, it will reduce Spain's dependence on a marginal and unpredictable water supply and bring in more capacity at a lower investment; but it will increase her dependence on imported coal and crude oil, thereby aggravating her perennial balance-of-payments problem. For a partial solution the government is looking to the development of atomic energy. It has a Junta de Energía Nuclear which in 1959 joined with private industry in setting up a pilot plant in Aragon. By the following summer plans were under way for the construction of two large nuclear power stations.

Money and Banking

While keeping ultimate control over all aspects of the Spanish economy in its own hands, the government assigns to the commercial banks an important though strictly supervised role. As the principal source of investment capital, the commercial banks exercise a large measure of control over the private sector of the economy. Within the banking community there is a further concentration of power, evidenced by the fact that eight of the hundred-odd commercial banks do two-thirds of all banking business. While these eight compete with each other, they also cooperate on vital questions of common concern and generally carry the rest with them, so that the use of the term "banking community" (*la banca* in Spanish) is justified. Next to the government, the banking community is the most important factor in the operation and development of the Spanish economy.

The supervision of monetary and credit policies is entrusted to a council (Consejo Bancario Superior), created by the Banking Law of December 31, 1946, and consisting of representatives of the government, the commercial banks, and the Banco de España. Its role is primarily advisory, for control of credit policies is vested almost entirely in the Ministry of the Treasury (Hacienda).

The Treasury's monetary policies are executed by the Banco de España, the government's banker and fiscal agent with sole right of note issue. In form the Banco de España is a private organization, and its shares are owned by commercial banks and private investors as well as by the government. Nevertheless, it is closely controlled by the government, which appoints its governor and four of the twenty-four members of its board of directors; these five can veto any decision of the board. Until 1958, when it made its first large loans to the private sector (5.5 billion pesetas to various private enterprises), its credit operations were confined very largely to financing deficits in the public sector, mainly by making loans to public agencies and by placing government securities with commercial banks.

The private banks usually keep about one-third of their deposits in state securities, which can then be taken back to the Banco de España for loans of up to 90 per cent of their market value. It is mainly through these operations that the commercial banks expand or contract credit, for they rediscount relatively little commercial paper (in 1958, only 5.7 billion pesetas as compared with 29.1 billion on advances from the Banco de España). For this reason, various efforts to curb credit by raising the rediscount rate have proved largely ineffectual. Another line of attack on the problem of restricting credit was tried out in the National Investment Plan of March 12, 1959, which provided, among other things, for the issuance of "investment bonds" that could not be used as collateral. The effects of this measure are not yet clear.

Expansion of credit to the public sector of the economy was a major factor in the inflationary increases in the money supply down to 1959. These increases amounted to 15 per cent in 1955, 20 per cent in 1956, and 17 and 14 per cent in 1957 and 1958. Within the public sector the responsibility has lain very largely with the autonomous agencies, such as INI, RENFE, and the National Wheat Service, which have been financed, not through the regular budget, but through issuing government securities. Accordingly, in 1958 the Treasury changed over the financing of the autonomous agencies to special budget appropriations, with the exception of INI, which, as noted, is now required to finance itself. Its first effort to sell shares to the public brought in a paltry 900,000 pesetas, but INI raised another 6.2 billion through a loan from the Banco de España. By government order, similar loans of half that amount were also granted to RENFE and the National Wheat Service.

Apparently it was impossible to close all the doors to inflation at one blow. Too many power groups were exerting pressure on too many government offices that possessed a large degree of freedom of action under a dictator who could not keep his eye on everything at once and who in any case was no economist. The stabilization plan of July 1959 was intended to close the doors and keep them closed. It may do so, but, however perfect it may be on paper, its execution still depends on the same political system headed by the same man.

Whatever the precise nature of cause and effect might be, the experts were convinced that easy credit as reflected in the rapidly increasing money supply was a major factor in the price inflation that began to plague Spain in 1955 after four years of relative stability. From 1953 to the end of 1958 the money supply (notes in circulation and deposits) increased almost 100 per cent, as compared with increases of only 26 per cent in the combined index of production (agriculture, industry, mining, and fishing) and 32 per cent in real national income. As a result, during the same period wholesale prices advanced 52 per cent and the cost of living 48 per cent.

The Condition of Labor

Three-fourths of this sharp rise in the cost of living occurred after general wage increases were decreed in 1956 in a move to appease labor discontent. By the end of 1958 the benefit of the wage increases had been wiped out by the inflation they had helped to stimulate, and the groundswell of discontent began to mount again. As before, it was acute among the middle groups as well, but its potential threat to public order and the stability of the regime was greater among the workers because they were more numerous, less divided, and (it was commonly believed) more willing to run risks.

Even among the workers the threat was only a potential

one, for the government keeps them well in hand through a combination of the syndical system with economic sanctions and, whenever necessary, with physical force. The combination is likely to prove unbeatable so long as the police and the armed forces remain loyal to the regime.

Spain's labor force of some twelve million men and women, as I have noted earlier, is not organized in the Western type of trade-unions; rather, it is regimented in a syndical system comprising also management and government. The latter keeps the other two members of the trinity under its thumb. The twenty-three national syndicates regulate the whole range of labor-management relations. The essence of the system is summed up in two complementary prohibitions: labor is denied the right to strike and management is denied the right to fire its employees. The architects of the system boast that, thanks to these two prohibitions, it has put an end to the "anarchy" and class warfare that mark relations between capital and labor in other Western countries. Through the government's intervention in the public interest, they claim, the syndical system has assured peace, order, uninterrupted production, and evenhanded justice to both sides.

In the opinion of unbiased observers, the system has actually proved much more advantageous to capital than labor. Open resistance to the system has come almost wholly from labor, in the form of slowdowns, sabotage, demonstrations, and even strikes. Here economic and police sanctions come into play. Economic sanctions have become steadily more effective as over the years an increasing share of the workers' compensation has gone into social security benefits; a recalcitrant worker forfeits these benefits, his seniority, and even his job. This grim prospect keeps most of the workers in line. Those who still rebel against the system thereby become law-breakers subject to police action; but the threat of such action is usually enough. In any case the workers lack the financial resources to maintain a long strike. As there are no free labor unions in Spain, so there are no union funds for strikes.

Management has also been restive under the restrictions of the syndical system, which since 1956 has also been sharply criticized by church leaders on doctrinal grounds. Adverse foreign comment on the labor situation in Spain appears to carry more weight with the Madrid government than in earlier years. At any rate, in April 1958 a first dent was made in the syndical system by a new decree permitting a limited range of collective bargaining. However, the final decision still rested with the government, and labor was still denied the right to strike. One effect of the measure has been to decentralize wage controls, thus forestalling any new general increases like those of 1956.

Then came the stabilization plan of July 1959. At no point was its impact more revolutionary than in the field of management-labor relations. The plan has faced the regime with a dilemma. The employers insist that they cannot raise the efficiency of production unless they are given the right to dismiss incompetent and surplus workers. Yet, if they are given this right, the workers can hardly be denied the right to strike. The result would unquestionably be a resumption of that "class warfare" which Franco claims has been abolished by his syndical system.

One year later the dilemma remains unresolved. The regime is apparently making a very human but unpromising effort to evade or postpone the real issue. On a visit to the United States in October 1959, Laureano López Rodó [28] told reporters that employers would probably be permitted to discharge up to 5 per cent of their employees on grounds of incompetence, subject to the requirement of hiring an equal number of new employees. That could be only a partial solution at best, for it does not touch the problem of redundant labor. At about the same time, José Solís, Secretary-General of the Movement, was saying privately that new industries would solve the surplus labor problem. He did not explain how these new industries were going to be developed under the regime of austerity, which in fact was

---

[28] Prominent government official and member of Opus Dei. See Chapter VII, pp. 275-276.

increasing unemployment at that very time. Nor did he have any solution for the problem of incompetent labor. He merely expressed an unyielding opposition to giving the workers the right to strike, on the ground that the character of the Spanish people is such that this would inevitably lead to widespread violence.

Foreign Trade and Foreign Investment

Spain's foreign trade is small in comparison with that of other European countries or in relation to her total economy. Foreign investments in Spain are microscopic. Nevertheless, both factors now have an importance out of all proportion to their size. The imbalance in Spain's foreign trade is at the root of her perennial balance-of-payments problem, a principal source of the economic crisis of 1958-1959. Foreign investments are believed by many experts to be her best hope of finding a way out of her economic afflictions.

Since 1953, when the bases agreement was made, the United States has become one of Spain's two principal trading partners; the other is Great Britain. Western Europe, however, has always accounted for the bulk of Spain's trade. It seems likely to continue to do so unless the creation of the Common Market and the Free Trade Association forces a reorientation. Spain's European neighbors provide much the best outlet for her exports; in the late 1950's, for example, they took 60 per cent of all Spanish exports compared with only 10 per cent bought by the United States. On the other hand, in those years Western Europe provided only 40 per cent of Spain's imports, as compared with 25 per cent supplied by the United States—a figure which is, of course, explained by the U.S. aid program. The rest of Spain's trade (about one-fourth of the total) is carried on mainly with Latin America and countries of the sterling area outside Europe. Since 1956 a very small trade has developed on a barter basis with several iron-curtain countries, principally with Poland, which has supplied Spain with much-needed coal in exchange for fruit. Rumors which began to circulate at that time about Spain's recovering from Moscow some $500 million in gold sent there by the Republican government early in the Civil War, as part of some broader deal between the Kremlin and the Pardo Palace, were, as it turned out, nothing but a mare's nest.

Spain's balance of payments, so often unfavorable in past decades, has seldom presented such an alarming problem as in the 1950's. Between 1951 and 1958 imports doubled while exports stagnated. This imbalance has been attributed to the government's neglect of traditional export industries (mining and agriculture) in its mania for manufactures, and also to the growing pressure of internal demand and unrealistic exchange rates. The headlong effort to industrialize stimulated the demand for raw materials, fuels, and capital goods that could only be obtained abroad.

The source of the trouble, many experts insist, lay not in a lack of controls but in their excessive number and faulty administration. One of the major purposes of the stabilization plan has been to simplify, rationalize, and liberalize this elaborate and highly restrictive system, consisting, until then, of numerous restrictions on both imports and exports, a highly complicated system of exchange rates, special arrangements such as barter deals, and, with most countries, bilateral trade and payments agreements. When first negotiated, these clearing agreements had served to stimulate exports, but by the late 1950's their net effect was adverse on both foreign trade and the domestic economy. The straitjacketing of Spain's trade, for example, often forced importers to buy essential raw materials and machinery in high-cost countries; this in turn raised Spanish costs of production, to the detriment of both domestic consumers and export potential.

The system, faulty in itself, was badly administered. It was bedeviled by a tug-of-war among rival economic interests within the regime; by the lack of an adequate staff of trained technicians, in part a consequence of Spain's long isolation; and by the failure at the top to insist on defining sound measures and then enforcing honest compliance with them. The combined effect of these three factors turned the economic reform of February 1957 into a false dawn. After the mountain had labored greatly, it brought forth the mouse of a nominally uniform rate for a devalued peseta (reduced from 36 to 42 to the dollar), but the multiple rate system soon crept back piecemeal and the peseta continued to slip. At the end of 1958 the various peseta rates for imports ranged from 25 to 126 per dollar, and for exports from 31 to 57. A similar effort was made in 1958 to narrow the trade gap by raising the rates of the *Fondo de Retorno*, in effect taxing imports to subsidize exports. This measure, too, proved ineffectual. The trade gap remained almost as wide as before, and at the end of 1958 the peseta reached a new low of 62 on the Tangier free market.

To add to the chaos, fraud was rampant. Despite strict and omnipresent government controls, or perhaps because of them, smuggling reached a new high. A comparison of Spain's customs records with those of her trading partners indicated that at least one-fourth of all Spanish trade was contraband. This was not possible without wholesale connivance on the part of officials. In the business world corruption was justified as the only means of survival under a government which was both corrupt and inefficient. Many firms had three sets of books, one for the management, one for the stockholders, and one for tax purposes. Spain's rising tide of foreign tourists (four million in 1959) joined in the fraud, to the serious detriment of Spain's balance-of-payments position. As the value of the peseta declined, the number of tourists rose, but the government's foreign-exchange income from the sale of pesetas to them diminished, for many of the tourists took advantage of the black-market rate of as much as 62 pesetas to the dollar rather than buy at the legal rate of 42.[29] The breakdown of law enforcement was like that of prohibition days in the United States, except

29 By special arrangement a tourist rate of 52 (raised in April 1959 to 56) was available, but many tourists either did not know about this or were unable to take advantage of it or simply preferred the black-market rate.

that in Spain's case it seriously weakened an already shaky economy.

One of the most disturbing developments was the growth of Spain's trade deficit, as illustrated by Table 5. After a gradual but substantial rise from 1952 to 1955, the deficit nearly doubled in 1956, when it was equivalent to about three-fourths of the total value of Spanish exports in that year. Even greater deficits piled up in the next two years, despite the efforts of economic reformers in the new cabinet of February 1957.[30]

TABLE 5

Foreign Trade, 1951-1959
(in millions of dollars)

Year	Exports	Imports	Net
1951	482	424	+ 58
1952	458	572	− 114
1953	482	596	− 114
1954	464	614	− 150
1955	446	617	− 171
1956	442	767	− 325
1957	476	862	− 386
1958	486	873	− 387
1959	503	794	− 291

Note: Exports are valued f.o.b. and imports c.i.f. In its *Balance of Payments Yearbook* the International Monetary Fund, using exchange records rather than customs statistics, gives import data on an f.o.b. basis; this valuation shows a somewhat different pattern of imports.

Source: *Monthly Bulletin of Statistics* (UN), August 1960, pp. 98-99.

While U.S. aid, averaging a little over $200 million a year from 1956 to 1958, filled much of the gap, a substantial deficit still remained, which had to be covered by drawing on Spain's slender holdings of gold and convertible currency. These holdings were reduced by about $50 million in each

---

[30] However, a large reduction in imports in 1959 produced a substantial decline in the deficit and an improvement in the foreign-exchange position after the adoption of the stabilization plan.

of these three years, and amounted to only $65 million at the end of 1958.[31]

Spain was now virtually bankrupt. Her liabilities amounted to $68 million ($12 million to foreign banks and $56 million under payment agreements), and additional liabilities totaling $50 million were to fall due in 1959. This situation probably contributed more than anything else to Franco's decision to submit his regime to the surgery of the stabilization plan. Extensive foreign aid, in addition to what the United States was already giving, had become imperative and there was no other way to get it.

In the opinion of most economists, extensive foreign investments were also essential for the long pull. The Spanish government had overextended itself with its ambitious investment program, which, based largely on inflationary credit, would now have to be cut back. Yet, unless the Spanish economy was to stagnate, the gap must be filled by large amounts of investment capital from some other source. Since Spanish private capital was not up to the task, the obvious and only answer lay in encouraging foreign investment, as the stabilization plan recognized.

The United States and the Spanish Economy

Since 1953, through trade and aid—both interconnected—the United States has come to play a crucially important role in the Spanish economy. What has been its effect? And what have been the principal controversies of an economic character between the United States and Spain?

The U.S. aid program is a complex of many different kinds of operations which can be summed up in two main categories: military and economic. Our chief concern here is with the latter, but the two are closely interrelated, for economic aid has been justified largely in military terms,

---

31 IMF data in millions of dollars, available for 1955-1957, show a decline in Spanish official holdings of foreign exchange from 92.73 to 5.21, and in official holdings of gold from 75.58 to 44.18, in that period; International Monetary Fund, *International Financial Statistics.*

and military aid has economic consequences.[32] But for the military program there might perhaps have been no economic program at all, and it would certainly have been smaller and of a different kind. As a result, any assessment of the influence of the United States on the Spanish economy must take into account the program of U.S. military assistance to Spain, amounting to an aggregate of some $374 million through fiscal year 1960, as shown by Table 6. This is, of course, quite apart from the cost of the base construction program, discussed in Chapter II.

TABLE 6

U.S. Military Assistance to Spain, 1950-1960
(in thousands of dollars)

Fiscal year	Programs	Deliveries
1959	31,008	56,713
1960	24,563	58,942 [a]
Total, 1950-1960	431,581	374,236 [a]

[a] Estimated.

Note: Data include valuation at acquisition cost of excess stocks included in military aid. This valuation overstates the budgetary costs to the United States but reflects approximate values from the point of view of Spain.

Source: U.S. Department of Defense, Office of the Assistant Secretary of Defense, International Security Affairs, *The Military Assistance Program: Programs and Deliveries by Area and Country, Fiscal Years 1950-1960*, release of February 26, 1960 (Washington: Author, 1960; mimeographed).

The program of U.S. economic aid to Spain has been designed primarily to support the bases program by strengthening the Spanish economy. Its scope is broad and its content and emphasis have varied from time to time. In the main, the emphasis has been on supplying raw materials and foodstuffs, but substantial aid has also been given to manufactures, transportation and irrigation. Except for the credit of $62.5 million established by Congress in 1950, as related in Chapter I, the U.S. aid program in Spain dates from the bases agreement of 1953, which obligated the United States to provide economic and technical aid along with $350 million

---

[32] For the kinds of military aid furnished, see pp. 70-72, 82-83.

worth of military aid over a four-year period. The obligation was duly fulfilled and the program was continued and expanded, especially on the economic side. By the end of 1959 U.S. nonmilitary aid commitments to Spain aggregated nearly $930 million, as shown in Table 7; this total excludes the gifts of American Catholics through Caritas, which, though important, are nongovernmental. In addition the United States has sold or agreed to sell $392 million worth of surplus

TABLE 7

*Postwar Nonmilitary Aid to Spain by
the United States, 1951-1959*
(in thousands of dollars)

Program	Amount
ICA (and predecessor agencies):	
Defense support (obligations)	469,450
Technical cooperation (obligations)	5,515
Development Loan Fund (loans signed)	22,600
PL 480:	
Title I, Sec. 104 (c), peseta grants for common defense (planned)	9,910
Title I, Sec. 104 (g), peseta loans to Spanish government (agreements)	196,730
Title II, emergency and relief grants (authorizations)	4,186
Title III, donations through private agencies (authorizations) [a]	121,644
Export-Import Bank loans (authorizations, inc. cancellations and participation by others at own risk)	99,204
Total	929,239

[a] Through June 30, 1959.

Sources: U.S. International Cooperation Administration, *Operations Report*, Data as of December 31, 1959 (Washington: Author, 1960), pp. 14, 52, 56; *U.S. External Assistance: Obligations and Other Commitments* (Washington: Author, 1960), p. 16.

U.S. President, *The Eleventh Semiannual Report on Activities Carried on under Public Law 480, 83d Congress, as Amended* (Washington: GPO, 1960), pp. 14, 57, 68, 76.

U.S. Export-Import Bank, *Eximbank Reports* (September 11, 1959); *Report to the Congress, June 30, 1959* (Washington: GPO, 1959), pt. 2, p. 124.

agricultural products under Title I of Public Law 480, for which Spain pays in pesetas.

Both these kinds of aid had their impact, first and foremost, on the crucial weakness of the Spanish economy, the strained balance of payments. But more than just dollar aid is involved. The sale of surplus farm products and the provision of defense-support grants in the form of goods generate peseta balances which are used for a variety of purposes inside Spain, as agreed between the two governments. For instance, as Table 7 shows, the United States lent back to the Spanish government almost $200 million worth of pesetas acquired from the sales of PL 480 commodities. Table 8 shows the movement and use of the various peseta deposits during fiscal year 1959.

As Tables 7 and 8 may suggest, the problem of describing the American aid program and assessing its value is by no means simple. Several different U.S. agencies have a hand in the program, and it includes categories as disparate as grants, ordinary loans, and "soft" loans and sales that are in some unascertainable degree gifts. Also, its terminology is often confusing. One of the principal categories of economic aid, for example, is called "defense support"; this use of the term is justified on the ground that the aid in question supports the defense program, and yet there is no form of aid that does not support that program in some degree. When the United States ships surplus agricultural products to Spain, the transactions are called sales because Spain pays for them. But these shipments are also aid because Spain pays in pesetas and not in dollars and the United States gives back or lends a large proportion of these pesetas to the Spaniards. Since defense-support aid is matched by counterpart pesetas which are legally owned by the Spanish government but are used in ways agreed on with the United States government—largely for the construction of the American bases but also for other uses—one can see how complex the process of American aid to Spain has become and how difficult it would be to put a precise measure on it.

TABLE 8

Peseta Accounts Generated by U.S. Programs in Spain
(pesetas in thousands of dollar equivalents)

Fiscal year 1959	Counterpart funds [a]	Section 402 [b]	PL 480, Title I [c]
Balance, July 1, 1958	19,733	3,893	68,859
Deposits during FY 1959	29,163	14,796	25,459
Withdrawals during FY 1959:	32,084	6,607	31,391
To U.S. account	3,916	—	—
For Spanish use	28,168	6,607	31,391
Balance, June 30, 1959	16,812	12,082	62,927
Purposes of withdrawals for Spanish use:			
Direct military support	12,703	4,814	—
Food and agriculture	—	156	10,825
Industry and mining	228	160	18,943
Transportation	14,883	1,383	—
All other	354	91	1,623
Total	28,168	6,607	31,391

a Counterpart pesetas are generated by U.S. grant aid under the mutual security program. While these funds are owned by the Spanish government, their use must be approved by the United States, which may also acquire some portion of them to meet its own needs in Spain.

b Section 402 of the Mutual Security Act of 1954 (PL 83-665) provided that a specified amount of the total funds appropriated under the Act should be used to finance the sale for foreign currencies of surplus agricultural commodities. The foreign currencies received are owned by the United States and are made available to the purchasing country for purposes stated in the Act. In the case of Spain, a portion of the funds appropriated each year for defense-support aid has been used to supply agricultural products under Section 402.

c PL 480, Title I sales of surplus agricultural commodities provide pesetas that are owned by the United States and made available to a number of U.S. agencies for use in the purchasing country. The data in this table represent the portion of the sales proceeds allocated to the ICA for its programs in Spain.

Source: U.S. International Cooperation Administration, *Counterpart Funds and ICA Foreign Currency Accounts*, Data as of December 31, 1959 (Washington: Author, 1960), p. 62.

A breakdown of the fiscal year 1959 program by agencies will both make the whole program more meaningful and illustrate the difficulty of measuring it.

First, the International Cooperation Administration (ICA) was charged with administering both defense support and technical cooperation. For the former Congress had appropriated $50 million for the fiscal year ending June 30, 1959. (It may be noted in passing that, as on every previous occasion since 1953, the appropriation exceeded the sum asked for by the executive branch; Spain had good friends in Congress.) The defense support program provided mainly for supplying agricultural commodities (cotton and soybeans) and industrial raw materials (coal, steel, scrap, copper). The technical cooperation program of $1.1 million was similar to those in other European countries, with emphasis on participant training; more than three hundred Spaniards have been trained in the United States in each recent year.

Second, the recently established Development Loan Fund (DLF), designed to aid basic economic development through "soft" loans, provided $14.9 million to RENFE for rails, ties, and switches, and $7.7 million to the Colonization Institute for earth-moving equipment.

Third, under the Public Law 480 program, several kinds of aid were made available to Spain in fiscal year 1959. The first, "Title I" aid, gave Spain the right to purchase up to $100 million worth of surplus agricultural products, paying in pesetas instead of dollars. This is a good illustration of the difficulty of determining the exact amount of U.S. aid. In form these transactions were sales, yet the terms were so easy that they were partly gifts. The prices were low; payment in pesetas meant a saving of dollars, to the great benefit of Spain's balance of payments; finally, the United States agreed to lend a portion of the pesetas it received back to the Spanish government for development purposes. By 1959 Title I sales had become one of the most important features of the economic program. They went a long way towards filling Spain's yawning trade gap, and the Spanish government resold the products to Spanish consumers at a profit. In fiscal year 1959 the United States lent the equivalent of $49.1 million of the pesetas it had received from its Title I sales. The other two forms of PL 480 aid were "Title II," relief shipments by the U.S. government, and "Title III," donations through charitable organizations such as the American Red Cross and CARE; the authorizations for fiscal year 1959 under these titles were $2.1 million and $11.9 million, respectively.[33]

Fourth, the Export-Import Bank, which, as agent for loans under the credit of 1950, had been the first in the Spanish field, authorized one new loan in fiscal year 1959, for $4.4 million to INI's Avilés steel plant for rolling-mill equipment,[34] and disbursed $9.0 million on prior loans. At the end of fiscal year 1959 the principal still outstanding on the Bank's loans to Spain amounted to $19.2 million and the undisbursed balance was $30.1 million.[35]

The package aid arrangement, agreed to in connection with the stabilization plan, supplied the framework for American aid in fiscal year 1960 (beginning July 1, 1959). The arrangement provided additional sources of aid and also gave assurance that the bilateral programs of the U.S. government would continue. The amount programed for military assistance to Spain in fiscal year 1960 was less than that for the previous year, but actual deliveries were slightly higher. Congress appropriated $45 million in defense support funds for essential commodities, $5 million more than had been requested by the executive branch, and the ICA continued its technical cooperation program at the $1 million level. In a shift in aid from government agencies to private firms, the Development Loan Fund provided $3.9

33 U.S. President, *The Eleventh Semiannual Report on Activities Carried on under Public Law 480, 83d Congress, as Amended* (Washington: GPO, 1960), pp. 62, 74, 76.

34 While U.S. policy generally precludes loans to government-controlled agencies operating in a field appropriate to private enterprise, it may be recalled that it is INI's declared intention ultimately to sell out many of its various projects to private investors, and Avilés is one of these. In 1958 the Export-Import Bank also authorized a credit of $6.8 million to a privately owned Spanish steel company, Fábrica de Mieres, S.A., for the construction of a blooming mill and other improvements at its plant in the province of Asturias.

35 U.S. Export-Import Bank, *Report to the Congress*, June 30, 1959 (Washington: GPO, 1959), p. 124.

million to the Unión Eléctrica Madrileña for the construction of a power plant on the Tagus River; another loan, of $350,-000, financed the purchase of equipment for a firm making electrical products. The Export-Import Bank's activities were stepped up in fiscal year 1960; six loans authorized by the Bank in the period July 1959 to June 1960 amounted to $49.1 million, all to private firms: $17.9 million for the expansion of power facilities, $13.6 million for aviation companies, and $17.6 million for fertilizer plants.

Without the political as well as financial support of the United States, moreover, Spain would in all likelihood never have been able to obtain the participation of the International Monetary Fund and the other parties to the stabilization plan. In short, throughout the stormy period that began in 1956 and reached a climax early in 1959, the United States played a leading and perhaps indispensable part in keeping the Spanish economy afloat. Franco and his aides were chary in acknowledging the value of this aid. Instead, as the crisis deepened, what one heard was complaints that the United States was not helping enough and that it was even under an obligation to make up to Spain for excluding her from Marshall Plan aid of a decade earlier.[36]

There were also numerous Spanish complaints against specific aspects of American policy and its execution. Among the primarily economic ones, two stood out: one, that the United States was responsible for inflation in Spain; the other, that the United States was dumping its surplus cotton in Spain under the guise of aid but actually for the purpose of stifling its renascent cotton-growing.

The first charge might seem plausible unless one looks into the facts. The United States had, in fact, foreseen the danger of inflation arising out of the bases-and-aid arrangement, and from the start it had taken a number of pre-

---

[36] Outstanding examples are the article by Alberto Martín Artajo, "El primer lustro de los convenios hispanoamericanos," *Revista de Estudios Políticos* (Madrid), March-April 1958, pp. 5-18, and his speech to the same effect before the American Chamber of Commerce in Madrid, on February 5, 1958; see Chapter II, pp. 74-75.

cautions that should have been effective if the Spanish government had pulled its weight. So far as possible it handled supply problems in such a way as to avoid creating shortages in the Spanish economy; such shortages as occurred were fully compensated by its aid program. Pertinent figures released by the American embassy in Madrid in October 1958 showed that in fact the effect of the U.S. program had "clearly been anti-inflationary." [37] These figures were given no publicity by the Spanish government or its controlled press: the former was apparently content to let the Americans be blamed for an inflation which grew out of its own errors.[38] From the start the United States had also taken the precaution of insisting that peseta counterpart funds generated by the bases program should be segregated, and either sterilized or used for productive purposes.[39]

The charge regarding cotton was equally plausible and somewhat better grounded. The United States has in fact disposed of a large amount of its surplus cotton in Spain under the aid program. It was easy to defend this measure;

---

[37] "Anti-Inflationary Effect of U.S. Program in Spain," October 1958, one page; mimeographed. The conclusion was supported by the following data, in millions of U.S. dollars, for the period through June 30, 1958:

Estimated Cumulative Peseta Expenditures	
Base Construction	87.6
Other Defense Dept. Expenditures	78.9
Embassy Expenditures	9.0
	175.5
Estimated Aid Arrivals	
Defense Support (excluding Technical Assistance)	275.7
PL 480, Title I	280.0
	555.7

About 75 per cent of "Other Defense Dept. Expenditures" was accounted for by "accommodation exchange" for military personnel and the rest by public vouchers. Spain has objected, without success, to the former practice, under which the United States in effect recovers in dollars a part of its aid.

[38] In Spanish banking circles, however, it was recognized that the net effect of the American aid program through 1959 had been anti-inflationary and beneficial to Spain; see Banco Urquijo, *La economía española en 1959*, cited, p. 279.

[39] For a general indication of the purposes for which they have been used, see Table 8, p. 243. As noted in Chapter II, the distribution of these funds was altered to Spain's advantage in 1958.

if cotton had not been provided in this way without costing Spain scarce foreign exchange, many of its textile mills would have had to close down. This reasonable defense could have been offered with better grace, however, if the United States had not at the same time refused to aid the current revival of cotton-growing in Spain. This refusal came with particular ill grace from a government which was preaching to the Spanish authorities the need to achieve a sounder economy by curbing their industrial effort and stimulating the production of raw materials. Most observers on both sides of the Atlantic attributed this inconsistency to the cotton lobby in Washington, which, in this matter, appeared to be more than a match for the Spanish lobby, itself no weakling. Many Spaniards, both in the regime and outside, were unhappy about this situation, but they did little about it except to cite it as another example of the (to them) well-known "Anglo-Saxon" hypocrisy. On the other hand, U.S. policy placed no obstacles in the way of any Spanish government efforts to expand the growing of cotton.

On the whole, the aid program has worked about as smoothly and successfully as could reasonably be expected; the major question, after the adoption of the stabilization plan, concerned its future. There is no doubt that it has a future. While U.S. aid has been described from the start as "temporary," the United States is so closely identified with the stabilization plan that, quite aside from its interest in the bases, it could not, for reasons of prestige, stand idly by and let it fail. The question is rather of the form that the aid program will take in the future.

By the autumn of 1959 well-informed Spaniards, including the Ambassador in Washington, José María de Areilza, and the Washington correspondent of the Madrid newspaper *ABC*, had come to the conclusion that direct grant aid of the ICA type was on the way out. They now pinned their hope on compensating increases from other sources, such as Public Law 480, the Development Loan Fund, and the Export-Import Bank. To them, significant straws in the wind were the increasing difficulty of securing appropriations from the Congress for direct grant aid, and the widely heralded announcement on October 20, 1959, by Vance Brand, Director of the DLF, that henceforth the Fund would normally grant credits only for procurement in the United States.

Early 1960 found leading members of the Spanish banking community prepared for the change. They could talk with equanimity about the approaching end of the first period of American aid to Spain. They were hopeful that it would be followed without interruption by a second period in which the aid would take the form of private capital investments as well as government-sponsored loans.[40] On the whole their mood was one of temperate optimism as they viewed Spain's new international position. They seemed to have nothing to worry about except on the home front.

---

40 Banco Hispano Americano, *La situación económica en 1959,* cited, pp. 34-35; Banco Urquijo, *La economía española en 1959,* cited, p. 280.

Chapter VII

THE CATHOLIC CHURCH
IN SPAIN

THE LEADING ROLE of the Roman Catholic Church in the Spain of General Franco is typified by the grandiose Civil War monument in the Valley of the Fallen which he built and, on April 1, 1959, inaugurated. It stands in rugged country, some thirty-five miles west of Madrid, near the geographical center of Spain, with the valley at its feet and the Guadarrama mountains as a backdrop. Like its near neighbor, Philip II's austere sixteenth-century monastery palace of El Escorial, it is a monument not only to a military victory (Philip's was a victory over France), but also to the Catholic faith.

The vast new memorial consists of three distinct parts held together by the links of religion. As the visitor approaches the main entrance, he sees first a towering granite cross, 500 feet high, which dominates the valley. At its base stand giant sculptured figures of the four Evangelists and the four cardinal virtues. Passing this, he enters the second unit, a huge subterranean basilica, hollowed out of the granite mountain, 900 feet long and nearly 200 feet high at the crossing of the nave, with an adjoining crypt designed to receive the remains of 150,000 war dead. Just beyond the basilica lies the third part, a Benedictine monastery which will house a new Center of Social Studies dedicated, according to Franco, to the regime's purpose of uniting national and social interests under spiritual guidance.

Thirty-seven Spanish bishops took part in the inaugural ceremonies, and their high point, aside from two addresses by Franco, was a funeral service conducted by the Primate of Spain, Cardinal Archbishop Pla y Deniel of Toledo. In his principal address Franco described the monument as "a great temple raised to our Lord" in gratitude for having given "Spain" the victory over "Anti-Spain" in that "true Crusade," the Civil War of 1936-1939. "In the whole course of our Crusade," he explained, "there was much that was providential and miraculous." At the very outset, for example, when "our forces" were desperately short of weapons, a whole shipload of arms and munitions unexpectedly fell one night into their hands, like manna from heaven. The same kind of providential aid was repeated time and again throughout the struggle, and, significantly, without anyone's having planned it so, the great battles of the war were won on the most solemn feast days of "our Holy Church." [1]

In Franco Spain the importance of the Catholic Church is not only great but pervasive. It runs through almost the entire range of policy, foreign as well as domestic. From the point of view of Spain's foreign affairs, which are our primary concern, there are three reasons why it merits special scrutiny. First, the church is an essential factor in the stability of the regime and thus, by derivation, in the execution of the bases agreement of 1953. Second, the credibility of the regime's chosen role as a leader in the Western defense against communism depends to a large extent on the demonstration of the vitality of the church in Spain. In the third place, the Catholic Church itself is an international institution, and its Spanish branch is closely related to, and hence in some measure influences and is influenced by, its ties with the rest of the church. The most important of these are, of course, its ties with the Vatican, but there are also other ties between Spanish Catholics and Catholics in other countries through subsidiary channels such as Catholic Action, the

---

1 Text of the address, in *Levante* (Valencia), April 2, 1959, which also gives the text of his second address inaugurating the new Center of Social Studies.

Christian Democratic political groups, the religious orders
—Jesuits, Benedictines, and others—and the secular institute
Opus Dei.

While one must exercise great caution in generalizing
about so complex a structure as the Catholic Church in
Spain, it is safe to say that Spanish Catholicism is *sui generis,*
for Spain has long exhibited in an exceptionally high degree
the general tendency of the Catholic Church throughout
modern history to take on a national coloration in each
country. In Spain this tendency has been nourished by many
circumstances ever since the sixteenth century. Most recently
it has been reinforced by Spain's relative isolation in the
period from its Civil War to the end of its ostracism by the
United Nations in 1950. Since then, the tendency has been
gradually reversed. Spain's emergence from political and
economic isolation has been paralleled by a similar movement in the religious field. The most striking evidence of
this is the tendency of the "new leadership" now developing
in the Spanish Church to look to the Vatican for guidance
and to base its program squarely upon papal pronouncements. If Spanish Catholicism is not becoming less Spanish,
it is certainly becoming more Catholic.

Spain and the Vatican

The traditional strength of the Catholic Church in Spain
is symbolized by the title of "The Catholic Monarchs" *(Los
Reyes Católicos),* by which Ferdinand and Isabella have been
known ever since Spain was first united through their marriage. In contrast to the title "His Britannic Majesty," the
kings of Spain have borne that of "His Catholic Majesty"
(Su Majestad Católica). Except among anticlericals, one of
the proudest boasts of Spaniards is that their country has
been one of the chief bulwarks of the universal church, and
they point with particular pride to its dominant role in the
Council of Trent and the Catholic Counter Reformation of
the sixteenth century. The view that only Catholics can be
true Spaniards has deep historic roots.

Papal authority has always had strong support among Spaniards. Ignatius Loyola, a Spaniard, was the founder of the Society of Jesus, which became the right hand of the papacy. Spain's relations with the Vatican have been close; yet her rulers have often followed their own line rather than Rome's, for example, in the expulsion of the Jews, in the establishment of the Spanish Inquisition, and in inducing a succession of popes to give the Spanish crown extensive powers over the church in the Spanish dominions overseas.

For more than a century, relations between Spain and the Vatican have been regulated most of the time by concordats. One concordat, negotiated in 1851, remained in effect until 1931, when the monarchy was replaced by the Second Republic. It declared Catholicism the state religion of Spain; it provided toleration for other faiths but did not recognize them nor permit them to worship in public. It also gave the church a virtual monopoly over marriage and burial, and a strong position in education. The church's position was further consolidated when, after a brief republican experiment, the monarchy was restored in 1876. By the twentieth century the monarchy maintained an annual budget for the support of the church.

This status, which still exists today with slight modifications, was wiped out for a time by the Second Republic, the culmination of a parallel, century-long development of anti-clericalism in Spain. The fight over the status of the church broke out as soon as the republic was established in 1931. In typical Spanish fashion, neither side was willing to compromise its position. The Vatican counseled the Spanish clergy to exercise patience and moderation, but they would not listen. And the anticlericals hurried the republic into a punitive program that contributed to its undoing, and to their own, by alienating many of its supporters, provoking its opponents to violence, and diverting attention from more urgent matters. The Concordat of 1851 was denounced and the Jesuit order was suppressed, though individual Jesuits were permitted to remain. A new constitution was adopted which separated church and state, and the hold of the church over education was broken by prohibiting the religious orders from teaching. Divorce was legalized and made easy, and crucifixes were removed from all schools. Even the strongly pro-Republican historian of this period, Ramos Oliveira,[2] describes the republic's anticlerical program as fatally misguided: misguided because it created bitter strife over issues that should have been compromised, postponed, or left alone; and fatal, because it split the Republican forces and alienated both the middle class, which was generally pro-church, and the masses, who were disillusioned by the republic's failure to provide them with substantial economic and social benefits. In addition, the failure of the republic to put any real check on the burning of churches and convents and the murder of priests and nuns shocked many moderate anticlericals, while it provoked clericals to violent counteraction.

Thus, when the Civil War broke out in July 1936, nearly all the church leaders espoused the rebel cause and accepted at face value Franco's claim that his forces (which included Moslem Moors from North Africa) were waging a holy crusade. No concerted or formal declaration to this effect was made by the clergy until the war had been going on for a year. Then a pastoral letter, dated July 19, 1937, signed by all but three Spanish bishops (those of Vitoria, Tarragona, and Orihuela), and addressed to "all the bishops of the world," officially endorsed the Franco cause. The letter also advocated, in thinly veiled terms, the restoration of the monarchy. "This war," it said, "was not begun in order to give birth to an autocratic state, and the Spanish episcopacy relies on the prudence of the [insurgent] government to adapt the future configuration of the state to the trajectory traced in the course of past centuries."[3]

Franco disappointed this hope by holding on to power, and church-state relations were not regularized until a new concordat was concluded fourteen years after the end of the Civil War. In the meantime Franco, who is a loyal Catholic

---

2 Antonio Ramos Oliveira, *Politics, Economics and Men of Modern Spain, 1808-1946* (London: Gollancz, 1946), pp. 441, 448.

3 Jean Créach, *Le Coeur et l'épée*, (Paris: Plon, 1958), pp. 285-286.

after his own fashion, re-established the Jesuits in 1938, canceled the divorce law, restored the crucifixes, and, partly under church influence, issued in 1945 the Charter of Spaniards (Fuero de los Españoles), which, however, the church was unable to persuade him to enforce. During this long interval some important and pressing questions were handled piecemeal through special agreements with the Vatican. These were later incorporated in the concordat. Chief among them was the agreement of 1941 which, as noted in Chapter IV, gave Franco the final word in the appointment of archbishops and bishops—a privilege traditionally enjoyed by the Spanish sovereign.

On their part the hierarchy tried to dispel the popular image of the church as Franco's shadow. Cardinal Gomá, Archbishop of Toledo and Primate, in a pastoral letter issued in 1945, declared: "Even when a friendly accord exists between church and state, as is the case in Spain, this should not give rise to confusion as to their respective roles and responsibilities." But such "confusion" did exist from the beginning. It was increased when the hierarchy all but unanimously called on the faithful to vote "yes" in the plebiscite of 1947 on the Law of Succession. Because it committed Spain in principle to the restoration of the monarchy, they approved it, but it also contained a kind of rider endorsing Franco's dictatorship. The identification of the church with the regime was further strengthened in the public mind when prominent lay leaders such as Martín Artajo accepted important offices in Franco's government.

Strange as it may seem, the church's effort to avoid identification with the regime was greatly aided by the conclusion of the new concordat signed on August 21, 1953. In effect, by this agreement Franco traded a measure of his hold over the church for certain immediate political advantages. In completing his negotiations with the United States, Franco sought both to mollify Catholic elements in Spain that were hostile to the agreement on religious grounds and to impress the United States with this evidence of his political prestige and respectability.

Franco's greatest gain from the concordat lay in the Holy See's having entered into an agreement with him. It also inscribed specific gains on the credit side of his ledger. It confirmed the ancient privilege of having in the Tribunal of the Rota two Spanish assessors with jurisdiction over cases presented by Spain. It likewise renewed the familiar arrangement whereby the appointments of prelates are made by joint agreement between the chief of state and the Holy See. Another clause gave the Spanish government the right to fix the boundaries of dioceses and provinces at will and to make them coincide with those of civil provinces.

In return, the church was made the moral director of Spain. It received supervisory power over education, and radio and television facilities were placed at its disposal. An "ecclesiastical patrimony" was created for its financial support, with a kind of escalator clause to protect it against inflation. The clergy were exempted from military service, and church property from taxation. Benefit of clergy was established on a broad base in all civil and most criminal cases. Thus, says one commentator, "The Spanish clergy became an independent community within the national community." [4] This was a far cry from the totalitarian type of state envisaged by Franco and the Falange in the early days of his regime.

Within Spain the Concordat of 1953 was received with thinly veiled hostility by Franco's angry but prudent henchmen of the Falange, and with open hostility by courageous leaders of the opposition, such as Pedro Laín Entralgo and Dionisio Ridruejo. As for the church, some of its leaders took advantage of its newly assured position to press upon Franco measures they had long desired, such as freedom of the press, greater social justice, and the institutionalizing of the regime. These measures had many merits and were advocated by many Spaniards outside the clergy, but for the

---

[4] Same, p. 304. The foregoing summary of the Concordat of 1953 is based largely on Créach, cited, pp. 303-304. A more detailed summary is given in William Ebenstein, *Church and State in Franco Spain*, Research Monograph no. 8 (Center for International Studies, Princeton University, 1960), pp. 41-50.

church they were especially desirable as an insurance against a repetition of the anticlerical outbursts of the 1930's.

In the years since the conclusion of the concordat, church leaders have met with very limited success in their efforts to reform the regime from within. Probably for this reason some of them have intensified their efforts to dissociate the church from it; while not attacking the regime in its entirety, they have been sharply critical of some aspects of it. Their successes, to which many others have contributed, have been confined to such matters as the amelioration of the condition of labor, an improvement that was temporary so far as the general wage increases of 1956 went, and narrowly restricted as regards the reintroduction of collective bargaining. Church leaders have been unable to make any real dent in the censorship or induce Franco to institutionalize his regime. The latter failure has been most disturbing of all, not only to them, but to great numbers of Spanish laymen, because of the fear that it places the nation in peril of a violent upheaval when Franco's rule, in whatever way, finally comes to a close.

Because the church is not a homogeneous unit, the weakening of its support for the regime has not been uniform throughout its constituent parts. Three of its sectors that seem especially significant, from the point of view of the over-all development of Spain, are the secular clergy, Catholic Action, and the Opus Dei. If the center of our interest were different, other sectors of the church body would probably seem more important for Spain's future, for the complex structure of the church contains many other elements which, while apparently less significant at the moment, may possibly count for more than these three in the long pull.

The thoughtful observer should, for example, not overlook the influence of the Benedictines and the Jesuits. Both orders are international and, therefore, in some degree offset the isolationist tendencies that prevail in other ecclesiastical quarters. Beyond that, however, it is hard to identify their public influence at the present time. Among the Benedictines, for instance, attitudes towards the regime vary with personal and regional factors. One of their communities, in effect, aids Franco by serving the monastery in the Valley of the Fallen. Another, at Montserrat, has long been a thorn in the side of his provincial government in Catalonia.

The Jesuits, the prime target of liberals and anticlericals, have conducted themselves with great circumspection since their re-establishment in Spain towards the close of the Civil War. In the public mind, at least, they are not identified with politics in nearly so high a degree as Catholic Action or the Opus Dei. One of their members, Father Sobrino, formerly a lawyer, later cultural relations officer in the embassy in Washington, played an important part in working out the arrangements for handling the thorny religious aspects of the U.S.-Spanish bases program; his moderation and good sense, and the successful operation of the arrangement, have reflected credit on his order.

In its traditional stronghold, that of education, the Society of Jesus is still powerful in the primary and secondary schools; at the university level it has suffered from the inroads of Opus Dei. Its attitude towards the latter has been cool, but (under pressure from Popes Pius XII and John XXIII, we are told) correct. Its leaders profess to be grateful for the competition of the Opus, which, they say, has spurred their order on to greater exertions. The Jesuits feel their present position in Spain is strong, and they look forward to the future with a confidence that combines with prudence to counsel circumspection in the present touch-and-go situation in Spain.

The Secular Clergy and the Regime

Among all sectors of the clergy, the hierarchy of bishops and archbishops is closest to the regime, and the parish priests are closest to the Spanish people at large. Both groups are generally identified with the regime and yet in some measure critical of it, mainly under the influence of Catholic Action and of regional loyalties. The latter have proved more potent among parish priests than within the hierarchy.

Significantly, in 1956, during a period of labor unrest in the Basque country and Galicia, many of the priests sided with the workers, whereas the bishops strongly supported the regime and punished some priests by transfers to other parishes. Except when some such special factor enters in, the priests usually follow the line laid down by their spiritual chiefs. Since the latter in turn are guided by the biblical injunction, "Render unto Caesar the things that are Caesar's," the priests are thus a substantial bulwark for the regime. The typical Spanish village apparently lives under a kind of condominium of church and state, represented by a mayor appointed by Madrid and a priest assigned by a bishop who in most matters is responsive to the wishes of Madrid.

Theoretically, a bishop is largely independent of the civil power. The extremes to which the theory of episcopal independence can be carried in practice by a resolute prelate were illustrated by the actions of Pedro Segura, Cardinal Archbishop of Seville, who for several years openly opposed the regime on various grounds, including the bases agreement with the United States. What is more, Segura gave his opposition a highly personal flavor. Thus, when Franco visited Seville in 1953 for the spring fair, Segura refused to provide him with a chaplain and Franco had to bring his own confessor from Madrid. A few months later, Segura abruptly absented himself from a church meeting in Zaragoza at which Franco had turned up unexpectedly.[5]

Segura was finally eased out of his lofty post only with the alleged aid of the Vatican, and that was granted only after the conclusion of the concordat. Even then the Vatican did not remove Segura, but only induced him to retire after a decent interval by the device of assigning a coadjutor to his diocese on the plausible ground of his advanced age and poor health. In fact, however, Segura had owed his preferment, not to Franco, but to Alfonso XIII, who had brought about his appointment as Cardinal Archbishop of Toledo, hence Primate of Spain. When he was ejected from that post in the

---

[5] Créach, cited, p. 291.

early days of the republic, whose government he likewise defied, the Vatican acquiesced since it was hopeful of bringing about an accord with the republic. For the next few years Cardinal Segura lived in Rome, whence he took a leading part in efforts to bring about a restoration of the monarchy. When Franco's forces took Seville, the Vatican sent him there as Archbishop. Franco in turn acquiesced—he was in no position then to object—and Segura remained there, a thorn in his flesh, for more than fifteen years after the end of the Civil War.

This extraordinary phenomenon could be explained partly by Segura's personal qualities but mainly by the way in which he was elevated to the hierarchy. A repetition of it is still possible but has become highly improbable. Franco has gained the right of nomination, which enables him to screen appointments to episcopal offices; quite aside from his legal rights, the Vatican has shown no disposition to appoint any more Seguras to ecclesiastical office in Spain. The present arrangement tends to produce a pro-Franco hierarchy, or at least to exclude anyone of known anti-Franco leanings. It also tends to induce conformity lower down on the ecclesiastical scale among those members of the clergy who share the natural desire for preferment and have talents to match. Aspirants to higher office know they will, in all probability, never be elevated to the episcopacy if they antagonize the Caudillo.

It is more than a little remarkable that, despite these heavy pressures towards conformity, the hierarchy has carried on and even intensified the effort to dissociate the church from the regime, going so far as to protest against specific abuses of its powers. The grounds of its criticism are various. In 1952, for example, the Archbishop of Valencia made an open attack on the totalitarianism of the Falange and the exploitation of labor which the regime permits. Several prelates joined with Cardinal Segura in condemning the bases agreement with the United States as a Trojan horse that would open the gates of Spain to heresy. When the Archbishop of Barcelona took this occasion to publish a pastoral letter against Protestantism, it was promptly suppressed by the censor. Other complaints from the same high level have been directed against the censorship in general and the domination of university-student associations by the Falange.

The most striking expression of the church's discontent with the policies of the regime was a corporate declaration by the Archbishops of Spain, headed by the Primate, Enrique Cardinal Pla y Deniel, on "The Right and Duty of the Church to Intervene in Social Problems." Dated August 15, 1956, and widely circulated in subsequent months, this declaration was a discreetly worded but definite indictment of the government's social policy for its failure to provide workers with a decent living wage and for its intervention in the country's life in a manner contrary to the teachings of the church as established by papal encyclicals.

Any uncertainty the wording of this declaration may have left about its intent was dispelled by subsequent glosses, notably a series of lectures by an outstanding representative of the new generation of church leadership, Rafael González Moralejo (now Auxiliary Bishop of Valencia).[6] Besides sharpening the critical shaft, the writer made it unmistakably clear that its main target was the government-controlled syndical system, which, as we have noted, fixes the wages of some nine million Spaniards. He also threw a strong light on two important reasons for the protest. First, in recognition of the extraordinary difficulties facing the government when it established the syndical system in 1939, its fatal defects had long been tolerated in the hope of amendment. Now that nearly twenty years had failed to produce any improvement, silence was no longer possible. Second, the syndical system, he continued, was perpetuating social injustice, the maldis-

---

6 Delivered to the Chamber of Commerce of Madrid in April 1957 and published as *El momento social de España* (Madrid: Euramérica, 1959); foreword by Bishop Ángel Herrera of Málaga (see below in the text). An appendix, pp. 173-192, contains the text of the Spanish episcopate's declaration of August 15, 1956, on "The Right and Duty of the Church to Intervene in Social Problems." González Moralejo is the author of other works on social justice, including *La justa distribución de las rentas* (Madrid: Euramérica, 1958).

tribution of wealth, which had divided Spanish society into two mutually antagonistic classes. And this, he maintained, was the main source of "the apostasy of the working class," "the great sin of our century." [7]

Catholic Action, Mainstay and Critic

Monsignor González Moralejo and his patron, Ángel Herrera y Oria, Bishop of Málaga, are members of Catholic Action. Composed of both clerics and laymen, this organization has long played an important and many-sided role in Spanish affairs.[8] Under the Franco regime several of its members have held high government posts, for example, Alberto Martín Artajo, its president before becoming minister of foreign affairs, and Joaquín Ruiz Jiménez, who has served as ambassador to the Vatican and minister of education. Politically overshadowed by Opus Dei since the cabinet reorganization of 1957, Catholic Action is still a major factor in the political as well as cultural and religious life of Spain.

During the period since 1945, the two most eminent members of Catholic Action have been Martín Artajo, of whom I have spoken often in other connections, and Bishop Herrera, its spiritual leader and head of its extensive publishing and educational programs.

Born in 1887, Herrera took holy orders in middle age, after a brilliant career in journalism. After practicing law for several years, at twenty-seven he accepted the editorship of an obscure Madrid newspaper, *El Debate*. Within a few years he had made it one of the most influential journals in Spain. He also established provincial journals and a news agency, and formed around this center a school of young conservative intellectuals, the *"Debate* School," of which Martín Artajo was a member. Having entered a seminary in 1937, at the age of fifty, Herrera was ordained in 1941 and

---

7 *El momento social de España,* cited, p. 84.

8 A separate organization of similar character, the Asociación Católica Nacional de Propagandistas, is so closely related to Catholic Action that the two will be considered together here under the latter name.

made Bishop of Málaga in 1948. Regarded before the Civil War as a pillar of the right wing, he has subsequently taken a position somewhat left of center on social questions. In particular he has pressed hard for a relaxation of the regime's restrictions on freedom of speech and on labor activities.

And yet Bishop Herrera has remained *persona grata* for the regime. This is not surprising, for he sees eye to eye with Franco on some of the most important questions. He is said to have had a hand, through his former protégé, Martín Artajo, in framing the Law of Succession of 1947. He rejects "liberalism" *en bloc* because of the anticlerical connotations of this term in Spain. His view, according to a French interviewer, is that in Spain liberty must be controlled by authority and the people at large, above all the intellectuals, cannot be given a free rein.[9] Accordingly, the freedom of speech he advocates has rather narrow limits and would not extend much beyond the politically conservative Catholic groups.

Catholic Action has its counterparts in many other countries. Their earliest source of inspiration was the admonition of Pope Pius IX, in 1848, to form national Catholic associations for the defense of the church. In Spain this movement, delayed by the mid-century turmoil, began to take shape only in the 1870's, and achieved effective national organization only in 1894. Thereafter its rise was rapid. After weathering the republic, the Civil War, and the pressure of the Fascist-minded Falange, it saw its influence recognized and even augmented in 1945; after the defeat of Nazi-Fascism, Franco, in need of new support in the crisis, chose the leading lay member of Catholic Action, Martín Artajo, to head his reorganized cabinet as minister of foreign affairs. The latter's abrupt dismissal from this post a dozen years later in no way represented a rebuff to Catholic Action, and he continues to be a power in the regime as well as *persona grata* for Franco.

Catholic Action in Spain is in most ways thoroughly Spanish and yet it stands in a special and very close relationship

---

9 Créach, cited, p. 294.

to the Vatican. Its membership, now totaling about half a million, is composed overwhelmingly of Spanish laymen, but its national organization reports through the Primate of Spain to the Pope. Similarly, while it concerns itself with Spanish problems, its approach to these is determined by the Vatican, for its officially declared purpose is to bring about in Spain the application of the principles laid down in various encyclicals and other papal pronouncements, including those of the present Pope, John XXIII, and his immediate predecessor, Pius XII, as well as some older ones, such as Leo XIII's *Rerum Novarum* and Pius XI's *Quadragesimo Anno*.[10]

The range of papal pronouncements is broad, as is that of Catholic Action's activities in Spain. It includes morals and education, the relations of capital and labor, indeed, the whole range of economic and social problems. While its leaders have usually been discreet and moderate in their handling of controversial questions, on occasion they have taken a strong stand when in their opinion Spanish practice has departed too far from papal precepts, as in the activities of the Falange and the syndicates. The one major area of public interest that Catholic Action as a group has never entered is politics. Its individual members are free to enter it. Indeed, so many of them have done so that in the minds of many Spaniards the organization is identified with the regime. But Catholic Action has never ceased to assert that it is and always has been a nonpolitical organization.

The assertion has gained in plausibility from the fact that in periods of political tension there have always been separate but related Catholic groups of an avowedly political character. One such, in the stormy days of the republic, was the Catholic party called Popular Action (Acción Popular), led by Gil Robles, which became the nucleus of his coalition of conservative parties, CEDA. Another is the present Christian Democratic movement. While the latter's membership is said to overlap with that of Catholic Action to a consid-

---

[10] Catholic Action has recently published a collection of these basic documents: *Colección de encíclicas y documentos pontificios* (Madrid, 1955).

erable extent, there is a substantial difference between their respective attitudes towards the regime. The leaders of the Christian Democrats, especially its left wing, wish to change the regime. The leaders of Catholic Action still seem to hope to reform it from within; they are so restrained in their criticisms that they can hardly even be called a loyal opposition. If the organization can be differentiated from its lay leaders, Catholic Action is clearly nonpolitical.

By papal definition Catholic Action carries out a lay apostolate under clerical guidance. This purpose is reflected in its organization and its activities. While its operations are mainly in the hands of laymen, policy is determined by the hierarchy through a governing body, the Supreme Junta, consisting of the bishops headed by the Primate Archbishop of Toledo, and the Junta's executive committee, the Dirección Central, made up of five ecclesiastics and one lay member, and likewise headed by the Primate. The sole lay member of this committee presides over the next lower body, the National Technical Junta, made up of thirty lay members and one clerical member. Thus, it is only at this technical level that laymen begin to predominate. The same pattern continues throughout the organization, down to the local level: laymen preponderate, but ecclesiastical authority, which determines policy at the top, is never absent at any level of any of the branches through which it is carried out. Four such branches or "associations" have been established at various times, for women, young women, men, and young men.[11] The last to be established, in 1940, was the Association of Men. Its having been set up after Franco had banned all political parties except the Falange has created a presumption that this association is a sort of *sub rosa* political party, but there is no indication of its being any more political than any other branch of Catholic Action. In any case, it has been overshadowed by the Christian Democratic groups.

Charity bulks large in Catholic Action's broad program,

11 Emmet John Hughes, *Report from Spain* (New York: Holt, 1947), pp. 56-58.

but its activities in the fields of publication, labor, and education are of greater interest for the purposes of this study. In addition to its weekly *Ecclesia*, Catholic Action controls five influential daily newspapers. One, which probably has a shorter name than any other newspaper in the world, is *Ya*, one of Madrid's two leading newspapers; the others are in Granada, Logroño, Badajoz, and Murcia. When *Ya* inaugurated a new plant in March 1960, General Franco performed the opening ceremony, accompanied by three cardinals, five archbishops, seven bishops, and twelve cabinet ministers.[12]

Control of Catholic Action's periodicals is exercised through a private corporation, Editorial Católica. As reorganized in January 1958, Editorial Católica has as its president Bishop Herrera, with Alberto Martín Artajo and his brother Javier as chief editor and business manager, respectively. Its publication list is by no means limited to devotional subjects. In addition to Monsignor González Moralejo's two books on social problems, already mentioned, it has published such titles as *The Rural Apostolate, The Reasons of the Proletariat, Towards a Sociology of the General Welfare, Jacques Maritain and the Polemic over the General Welfare,* and *The Marxist Doctrine of the General Interest.* Books by members of Catholic Action are also published, either in its name or on the author's own responsibility, through other channels, including commercial firms as well as institutions controlled by Catholic Action.

Labor problems enter into the program of Catholic Action at a number of points and are the main focus of the campaign for social justice which is being waged by many of its members. The most direct expression of its interest is the HOAC, or Hermandades Obreras de Acción Católica (Workers' Brotherhoods of Catholic Action). It is said to have about 100,000 members distributed over most of Spain but concentrated mainly in the urban and industrial areas. As in all other branches of Catholic Action, clerical and lay

---

[12] *The New York Times,* March 13, 1960.

forces combine in HOAC, and each local unit has its spiritual adviser or chaplain. HOAC is not a labor union in the ordinary or Western sense of the term; in that sense there are no labor unions in Spain, for they are prohibited by law, which pre-empts the field in favor of the official labor-management syndicates. Nevertheless, Catholic Action has successfully asserted its right to continue its long-standing activities, begun in 1894, in the labor field, provided these are restricted to fraternal and religious purposes.

Theoretically confined within these limits, HOAC has, in fact, progressively broadened its scope of action until it has come to concern itself with all phases of the labor problem, including wages and conditions of labor, as if it were a full-fledged labor union. For example, HOAC leaders played a major part in a public demonstration of protest against wage cutbacks by two large firms in Seville early in 1959; they have taken a similar initiative on recent occasions in the Barcelona and Bilbao areas. This is, indeed, a necessary outgrowth of the fundamental purpose of Catholic Action, which is to apply in practice the principles laid down in papal encyclicals.

A further consequence has been to bring Catholic Action, and particularly its HOAC branch, into direct conflict with the regime's syndicalist system. For several years past, the issue has been squarely met, and the superior rights of the church asserted, by several Catholic leaders—first by Bishop Antonio Pildain of the Canaries in 1951, and soon thereafter by Bishop Herrera of Málaga and other prelates. The climax came with the joint statement by the archbishops of Spain in 1956, and Monsignor González Moralejo's gloss on it,[13] in which the doctrinal case against the syndicalist system was stated more forcefully than ever before.

Significantly, the government has neither punished nor muzzled its critics on this point. It has even made a slight concession to them by giving labor a voice—though hardly more than a whisper—in syndicate elections and by establish-

---

13 See above, pp. 261-262.

ing collective bargaining under firm government control. On the other hand, it has made no change in the essential features of the system, so that the conflict continues unresolved. In its latest phase the government has actually intensified its punitive action against HOAC whenever the latter has overstepped the bounds assigned it by the government's narrow interpretation of HOAC's proper fraternal and religious role. Some of its meetings have been prohibited or broken up, some of its leaders arrested, and its periodical publications—first, *Tu,* then its successor, *Boletín Verde*—suppressed.

Thus Spain has witnessed the extraordinary spectacle of a government attempting to suppress by force one of the most sincere and deeply felt manifestations, made by one of the groups on which it is chiefly dependent for its support, of the religious principles for which it claims to stand. This would seem to point to the existence of serious and growing tensions within the regime. The dilemma is all the more striking because the demand for social justice, represented by this phase of Catholic Action's program, is felt by many well-informed Spaniards of the center and even the right to be essential to that defense of Spain against Communist penetration which is the declared basic objective of the regime itself. Spain is, indeed, a country of many contradictions.

In the educational field the outstanding achievement of Catholic Action has been the development, at Madrid and Málaga, of the Leo XIII Social Institute (Instituto Social León XIII) and its Social School for Priests (Escuela Social Sacerdotal). Both are the work of Bishop Herrera, and both show the deep imprint of his absorption in the quest for social justice. In 1903 Pope Leo XIII placed Catholic Action under the wing of the Primate; it was, of course, his encyclicals that have inspired Catholic Action in general and the Social Institute in particular.

The Institute's distinctive characteristic is the union of piety with social science. Along with papal encyclicals, the students study the best available works in the social sciences, foreign as well as Spanish, by non-Catholics and Catholics.

Some of the best graduates of the two-year course are sent abroad for advanced study. One such was Monsignor González Moralejo; before becoming Auxiliary Bishop of Valencia, he had studied at Brussels and taught at the Institute's Social School for Priests. At that time he wrote one of the school's first handbooks, *Catholic Action and Social Action: Papal Doctrine* (1949). Most of his subsequent work has been a development of the same theme: that the church, and especially Catholic Action, have the right and duty to intervene in the practical solution of social questions in conformity with Christian principles.

The main function of the Social Institute is to train priests as guides and counselors for lay members of Catholic Action in carrying out their "secular apostolate." The Institute has already had a considerable impact upon the church and the nation at large, contributing greatly to what is called the "new leadership" of the Spanish Church. Since Spain is an overwhelmingly Catholic country, this new leadership holds out hope for the stormy days that lie ahead, through its efforts to change the popular image of the church from that of a pillar of the privileged classes to one of foremost champion of social justice.

The regime has recognized the value of Bishop Herrera's work and, incidentally, seeks to turn this political potential to its own advantage. In dedicating the great Civil War monument in the Valley of the Fallen, General Franco announced the establishment there of a Center of Social Studies dedicated to the investigation and service of social peace and justice, to be headed by Bishop Herrera. Only time can reveal the full implications of this step.

A New Force: Opus Dei

Since the cabinet reorganization of February 1957, another Catholic lay organization, Opus Dei, has acquired in the popular mind the reputation of the regime's collective *éminence grise*. This image is constructed out of three main elements: the atmosphere of economic and political crisis in which the new cabinet was appointed; the assignment of several key posts to known members or sympathizers of Opus Dei; and the mystery surrounding the organization, which has stimulated rumors of an influence on the government much greater than appears on the surface.

According to officials of Opus Dei, this image is completely false. The organization, they insist, takes no position on public questions and leaves each member free to follow the dictates of his own conscience. In a statement published in Madrid newspapers on July 12, 1957, the Secretariat of the Opus Dei declared among other things that "the Opus Dei expressly disavows any group or individual who makes use of the name of the Institute [i.e., the Opus] in connection with his political activities." [14] A prominent member also assured me in private conversation early in 1959 that there is not only no "party line" in Opus Dei but not even any unity of political opinion; on the contrary, its members disagree widely with one another about political questions. Such disclaimers cannot be disproved, and there is some evidence to support them. In any case, whether as a group or through its individual members, Opus Dei plays an im-

14 The proposition that Opus Dei is strictly nonpolitical was developed at length by one of its members, Julián Herranz, in an article (*Nuestro Tiempo*, April 1957), republished in English translation as *Opus Dei and Politics* (Washington, 1957; name of publisher not given), under the imprimatur of Archbishop O'Boyle of Washington. The translation quotes founder Escrivá as saying: "This blessed freedom [of each member "to form his own opinions on world affairs and world events"] ensures that Opus Dei can never be, in the public life of a country, a political party. Opus Dei can harbor all tendencies that are acceptable to a Christian conscience . . ." (pp. 3-4). Herranz adds: "Should extraordinary circumstances . . . call for one and the same political stand to be adopted by all Catholics, only the Church, through Her ordinary Hierarchy, is competent to require this." The role of Opus Dei, he continues, is to give its members "some general ideas" that provide them with "the common denominator" of their "whole political outlook"; but "on this foundation" each member "builds his numerator, his own particular and specific opinion, choosing among the many tenable social or political solutions whichever appeals to him" (pp. 6-7). To this freedom he attributes the "prodigious growth and rapid expansion" of Opus Dei "in the last thirty years . . . among persons from so many countries and different backgrounds" (p. 7). See also Rafael Calvo Serer, "Notes sur un article du 'Times,'" *La Table Ronde* (Paris), October 1959, pp. 3-12.

portant role in the political as well as the religious, cultural, and economic life of Spain today.

This rapid rise to prominence is remarkable. The international organization from which the Spanish branch stems is very young. In no other of thirty-odd countries in which branches have been established has Opus Dei achieved a remotely comparable position. Actually, the phenomenon is less puzzling than it might seem. Opus Dei originated in Spain. It developed there for more than twenty years before papal sanction gave it a firm international basis. And since then it has had a Spanish president and vice-president designated for life. The Spanish environment has been particularly favorable to the special appeal that Opus Dei makes to an elite who wish to carry out an apostolate without abandoning their secular occupations. Moreover, during eight critical years of its early growth, from 1931 to 1938, the Jesuits, who might have checked its rise, were suppressed in Spain.

Founded at Madrid on October 2, 1928, Opus Dei grew out of a series of student meetings which had been held at Madrid and Zaragoza for the past three years under the leadership of an Aragonese priest and former lawyer, Abbé José María Escrivá de Balaguer. Escrivá headed Opus Dei in Spain continuously until he became president for life of the general organization upon its establishment under papal authority, a post that he still holds. Thus the founder of Opus Dei, like the founder of the Jesuit order, to which it is often compared, was both a Spaniard and a man who had had a secular career before taking holy orders.

From the outset, the broad purpose of Opus Dei has been to combat heresy, materialism, and indifference, and to bring about the "re-Christianization" of Spain, especially in the field of education, which was then dominated by the "godless" Institución Libre de Enseñanza and its offshoots. From its founding by Francisco Giner, late in the nineteenth century, until the Civil War, the Institución had been the seed bed of Spanish liberalism. It was, by the same token, anathema to conservative Spaniards. They saw in it the embodiment of those vices, mostly of foreign origin—rationalism, anticlericalism, materialism, cosmopolitanism—to which Spanish conservatives assigned the blame for the woes that had befallen Spain ever since the eighteenth century. The revolt against liberalism throve in the atmosphere of crisis that prevailed just before and during the republic, and it was canonized by the Nationalist victory in the Civil War.

Opus Dei throve with it, though then as now it sought and found the support of the elite, not the masses. In 1930 it added a "Feminine Section." By 1936 it had begun to win support among the hierarchy, and in 1941 the Bishop of Madrid officially recognized it as a "pious union." Soon thereafter it began to gain papal favor, and in 1943 the Holy See accorded it the status of a "communitarian institute." The Nunciature in Madrid investigated it and reported favorably to Rome. And in 1947 Pope Pius XII issued an apostolic constitution, *Provida Mater Ecclesia,* authorizing the creation of a new kind of organization, the Secular Institute. The Vatican then recognized Opus Dei provisionally as the first such institute, granting it definitive status in 1950.

In carrying out the declared aim of Opus Dei—to bring about the observance of Christ's precepts and counsels in daily life—each member has a double obligation: first, to sanctify his own life; second, to carry out an apostolate by persuading nonmembers to do likewise. Membership is open to men and women, lay and clerical, married and unmarried; unmarried laymen predominate, and the men's and women's sections are segregated. The vows taken by its members— poverty, chastity, obedience—are personal, not public, and may be revoked at will. The members wear no distinctive habit or insignia. Far from being required to live in the seclusion of a religious community, they are expected to continue the professional activities and way of life they followed before joining the Institute.

The main purpose of keeping the Opus members "in the world" has been ostensibly to facilitate their mission of regenerating society by maintaining their established, familiar contacts with it. One result, however, has been to create a widespread suspicion that the Opus Dei is following a policy of concealment for some sinister purpose. This suspicion has been exploited to considerable effect by its many critics, who include not only anticlericals and many Falangists but also Jesuits and members of Catholic Action and the hierarchy.

All its many enemies regard the Opus Dei as a reactionary force in both politics and religion. For more than a decade it has been charged with using pressure and intrigue to advance its members, especially in the universities. And since some of its members took high cabinet offices early in 1957 it has been sharply criticized by other Catholic elements for undercutting their efforts to dissociate the church from the Franco regime. When Opus Dei became thus identified with the government, an effort was made in some quarters to represent it as a liberalizing influence, and an article to this effect was published in *Time* magazine for March 18, 1957. Thereupon a group of twenty-five Spanish intellectual leaders, including a former Republican, Gregorio Marañón, and a former Falangist, Dionisio Ridruejo, addressed a letter of protest and rectification to that magazine; in 1959 they were still complaining that their letter had never been published.

Aiming at quality, not quantity, Opus Dei has a relatively small membership; it does not publish the figures, and recent estimates have ranged from 10,000 to 50,000. One prominent member explained to me that Opus Dei is silent about its size, not from any policy of concealment, but simply because it is indifferent to numbers, neither knowing nor caring how many members it has. In any case, its members include persons of prominence, especially in the professions (lawyers, doctors, university professors). From the start it has drawn a large proportion of its membership from academic life. Three of its outstanding leaders are present or former university professors: political scientist Rafael Calvo Serer, often called "the philosopher of Opus Dei," and historians Florentino Pérez Embid, reputed to be its principal political

planner, and Vicente Rodríguez Casado. The latter, besides
holding an important post in the Ministry of Information
and Tourism, is also the head of the Madrid Ateneo, once
a citadel of intellectual liberalism and still one of Spain's
principal cultural centers.

The Opus has succeeded in gaining a strong or controlling
position in many of the universities, though its control is
by no means complete. Indeed, many leading figures in
academic life oppose it and still hold their jobs. It appears
to have extended its influence mainly through its hold over
the making of new appointments and over the national research council (Consejo Superior de Investigaciones Científicas), which dispenses funds for research projects and has
a large publication program.

The Opus also has a quasi-university of its own, the Estudio General de Navarra, at Pamplona. Sometimes called the
only private university in Spain, this institution is not quite
a full-fledged university. But it does offer instruction at the
university level in a large number of fields, including law,
philosophy, history, some of the sciences, pharmacy, medicine, nursing, engineering, and journalism. In addition to
its new school of journalism at Pamplona, it has established
a school of business administration at Barcelona, said to be
highly successful. The students are business executives; only
twenty are admitted at a time, and there is always a waiting
list. Its teachers and equipment are said to be well above
the average for Spain, and it makes free use of foreign mod-
els for both method and content of its courses. The Estudio
General provides substantial aid to needy students. In 1959
one student in eight at Pamplona held a scholarship, and
the tuition fee for the others was low, amounting to 200
pesetas (about five dollars) per month. In many cities it
maintains "residences" (residencias), primarily for the benefit of students.

The influence of Opus Dei has now spread far beyond the
academic and cultural field. It is said to have extensive
financial resources, derived mainly from contributions by
its members; many of them are well-to-do and all are obli-

gated to turn over to the Institute the balance of their incomes after meeting their minimum living expenses. Opus controls the Banco Popular, one of the principal banks, with a branch in Andorra; its operations, particularly in the fields of mortgages and foreign exchange, have aroused growing criticism in recent years. It likewise controls several newspapers (*Alcázar, Madrid,* and *Informaciones* in Madrid; *Correo Catalán* in Barcelona; others in Valladolid and León); and several periodicals (*Nuestro Tiempo* and *Arbor* —organs respectively of the Estudio General of Pamplona and the Consejo Superior—*Punta Europa,* and a picture magazine, *La Actualidad Española*). None of its newspapers has achieved a mass circulation approaching that of Catholic Action's *Ya,* the reputedly monarchist *ABC* (both of Madrid), or *La Vanguardia* of Barcelona; except for its picture magazine, its periodicals are addressed to the elite. In the past few years it has entered the labor field and now gives evening courses for workers.

Its passion for anonymity makes Opus Dei's political influence difficult to appraise. Yet there is good reason to believe that it was substantial even before the cabinet reorganization of February 1957, and it has increased greatly since then. In early 1959 my inquiries indicated that at least seven cabinet ministers and two top officials in the Secretariat of the Presidency (roughly equivalent to the White House staff in the United States) were either members of the Opus or sympathizers. In the cabinet these included two Opus members: Alberto Ullastres (Commerce) and Mariano Navarro Rubio (Finance); three certain sympathizers: Cirilo Cánovas (Agriculture), Alonso Vega (Interior), and Jorge Vigón (Public Works); and two probable sympathizers: Gabriel Arias Salgado (Information and Tourism) and Pedro Gual Villalbi (Minister without portfolio). There was also one doubtful case, that of Joaquín Planell (Industry), whose son, a priest, is a member of the Opus. In the Secretariat of the Presidency the Opus was said to have an "adherent" in the Minister Undersecretary, Admiral Luis Carrero Blanco, and a member in the Chief of the Technical Section, Lau-

reano López Rodó. Both men held very important positions;
Carrero Blanco has long been Franco's right-hand man and
López Rodó was at that time in charge of coordinating
economic policy and planning the administrative reorganization of the government.

These circumstances have understandably induced a widespread skepticism about Opus Dei's protestations that it has
no political "party line" or interest and is exclusively devoted to its lay apostolate. Skepticism has gained ground
through the role of Alberto Ullastres and Laureano López
Rodó, who are simultaneously high government officials and
members of the five-man council which controls the Spanish
branch of the Opus Dei. Moreover, while this branch is
theoretically subordinate to the head of Opus Dei in Rome,
Monsignor Escrivá, who in turn is answerable to a cardinal,
Rome's authority in Spain appears less effective towards
Opus Dei than in the case of Catholic Action. At any rate,
Monsignor Escrivá is said to have opposed the entry of members of Opus Dei into the government in 1957, on the
ground that the Institute ought to stick to its apostolate and
avoid becoming involved in politics. He is also said to have
called Ullastres on the carpet when he visited Italy later
that year. The opposition from Rome was apparently una-
vailing. No member of Opus is known either to have refused
office in Franco's government, or to have resigned from it
under pressure from Rome.

It is, however, one thing to say that the Opus Dei has
become involved in Spanish politics and quite another to determine what significance attaches to this. There is doubt,
in the first place, about the effect on public opinion. It seems
clear, for example, that at the outset Opus Dei's reputation
for austerity had the desired effect of strengthening a morally
discredited regime. But is it true, as many Spaniards assert,
that subsequent events have wasted that asset, to the disadvantage of both the regime and any that succeeds it?

There is some evidence also in support of the twin assertions that Opus Dei takes no corporate position on public
issues, and, alternatively, that it is unable to have its own

way with the regime or even with its own members and supposed adherents. Three examples must suffice. First, one alleged adherent, Minister of Industry Joaquín Planell, is reliably reported to be a leading critic of the stabilization plan, which has been championed by the two most prominent members of Opus Dei and his cabinet colleagues, Alberto Ullastres and Mariano Navarro Rubio. Second, with a view to forestalling criticism of Spain's harsh censorship at an international Catholic press conference, to be held at Santander in October 1960, a commission was appointed in July 1959 to draft a new and less rigorous press law. Yet the only member of Opus Dei appointed to this important commission was Vicente Rodríguez Casado; as an official of the Ministry of Information and Tourism, he is charged with censoring books but has nothing to do with censoring the press.

A third instance relates to the so-called "philosopher of Opus Dei," Rafael Calvo Serer,[15] who is a tireless critic of the regime Opus Dei is said to dominate. His ideas about the restoration of the monarchy are also diametrically opposed to those of Admiral Carrero Blanco, the most influential of Opus' reputed adherents; Calvo Serer insists that the monarchy be restored here and now, whereas Carrero Blanco says it has, in effect, already been restored and is being admirably administered by General Franco. More than this, Calvo Serer demands a kind of monarchy—a "popular and social" monarchy—quite different from the traditional, conservative, authoritarian type desired by most members of Opus Dei. About this point, of course, it is not easy to say where Calvo Serer stands. To persons brought up in a tradi-

---

15 In the *Biblioteca del Pensamiento Actual,* which he edits, Calvo Serer has given Spanish readers a more varied and much more international literary fare than Catholic Action's Editorial Católica. A few samples of the first ninety titles are Etienne Gilson, *El realismo metódico;* Duque de Maura, *La crisis de Europa;* Amintore Fanfani, *Catolicismo y protestantismo en la génesis del capitalismo;* Jorge Vigón, *Teoría del militarismo;* Sir Charles Petrie, *La monarquía en el siglo XX;* Waldemar Gurian, *Bolchevismo: Introducción al comunismo soviético;* Jesús Pabón, *Franklin y Europa;* and Reverend I. M. Bochenski, S.J., *El materialismo dialéctico.*

tion of freedom, Calvo Serer's own definition of the freedom he desires to see established under his "popular and social" monarchy contains more than a strong dose of authoritarianism.[16]

As for the impact of Opus Dei on the Spanish people at large, a visitor to Spain in 1959, after two years of its involvement with the regime, heard a great deal about its political role, which was most often described as ultraconservative. Its educational role was widely commented on and, by many Spaniards, keenly resented because of the ruthlessness with which it allegedly promotes the interests of its own members. Its economic role, best known for its Banco Popular, suspected of large-scale black-market operations through Andorra, was widely condemned. Its religious purpose seemed to be the aspect that was mentioned last and remembered least. "Sanctification" and "regeneration," the ideals of its founder—still alive, but absent in Rome—seemed to belong to that lost world, the more idealistic generation before the Civil War. *Camino*—"road" or "path"—is the title of a simple devotional manual that the founder once wrote for the guidance of his flock.[17] One wonders with what feel-

16 In *La fuerza creadora de la libertad* (Madrid: Rialp, 1958), a collection of articles published between 1953 and 1958, Calvo Serer proposes to establish a monarchy uncontrolled by any effective parliamentary or other representative power. The Cortes would only advise or "criticize," for the chief executive *(presidente o jefe del gobierno)* would depend, "not on the votes of a parliamentary majority," but on the crown, "that is, on the King and his Council of the Realm." In case of a conflict between the Cortes and the executive, the final decision would rest with the king alone. The Council of the Realm would also be only advisory, though Calvo Serer says the king could override it only at his peril. The Council of the Realm is described as elective, but the mode of its election is indicated only in the vaguest terms: its members "should be elected *(elegidos)* in such a way that they would act in the highest interest of the national community," not of the social group to which they belong. There would be neither universal suffrage nor political parties, and liberty must be carefully defined and restricted. (See pp. 341-410.)

17 José María Escrivá, *Camino* (Madrid: Rialp, 1957). A prefatory *Tabla de ediciones* gives the following data: this was the fourteenth and largest (60,000 copies) Spanish edition of this work. A total of 265,000 copies had been printed in the Spanish and other editions; the first Spanish edition (2,000 copies) was published at Valencia in 1939; the second and third editions (5,000 and 8,000 copies) at Madrid in 1944 and 1945. The first of the non-Spanish editions was Portuguese (Coimbra, 1946, 3,000 copies); others included

ings he may now contemplate the green pastures of power to which the path has led them.

Anticlericalism, Indifference, and Protestantism

Just as surely as cathedrals, mystics, and martyrs, anticlericalism is a product of Spanish Catholicism. The phenomenon, familiar enough in Catholic countries, has been more deep-seated, long-lived, violent, and fanatical in Spain than anywhere else. In modern times its most extreme expression has been the burning of churches and monasteries and the murder of priests and nuns. The earliest large-scale outbursts of this kind occurred in the 1830's, the most recent just a century later, shortly before and during the Civil War. Such acts of violence are commonly attributed to the lower orders, but political fanaticism has been displayed by Spanish anticlericals of high as well as low degree, as demonstrated under the republic of the 1930's. Whether or not there was a causal connection, the parliamentary attack on the church was accompanied by storms of iconoclastic mob violence that the Republican government did virtually nothing to check. The first violence broke out in May 1931, and in the last four months prior to the Civil War nearly two hundred churches were sacked and burned.

What are the sources of this extraordinarily virulent anticlericalism? It can be attributed to Communist instigation only in part and only in recent times, for it was fully developed before communism came into existence. By some it has been attributed to the Spanish national character, which for centuries has periodically displayed traits of intolerance, fanaticism, and violence. That easy explanation leaves unanswered the question why this particular expression of these traits did not appear until the early nineteenth century. The

three Italian (Rome, 1949, 1953, 1956), one Mexican (1949), two English (Dublin, 1953, 1957), one "North American" (Chicago, 1954), two Catalan (Barcelona, 1955, 1957), one German (Bonn, 1957), and one French (Paris, 1957), as well as two more Portuguese (1950, 1957), and one in Braille (Madrid, 1956, 100 copies). Evidently, Opus Dei's indifference to statistics was not shared by the publisher of *Camino*.

most plausible interpretation can be found perhaps in a change that took place in the church's role in Spanish society under the impact of the French Revolution and Napoleon's intervention. Until that turbulent period the church had been identified with all classes of society, but in the reaction that followed Napoleon's fall and the restoration of the old regime it emerged as the ally and defender of the privileged and ultraconservative upper crust.[18]

This image of the church as champion of an exploitative, unjust, and anachronistic social system was sharpened by the vicissitudes through which Spain passed in the course of the next century, and it was never sharper than when the establishment of the republic gave free play for the first time to the pent-up forces of Spanish anticlericalism. It is this image that the new leadership of the church is now trying to erase by identifying its mission with the quest for social justice. The effort promises well and seems already to have met with some success, though any judgment must remain uncertain as long as the church is protected by an authoritarian regime.

Indifference may be a greater threat than persecution to the Spanish Church. The tree of faith is nourished by the blood of saints and martyrs, but it withers in the sandy soil of indifference. In at least some segments of Spanish society indifference to the church is widespread and apparently growing. This conclusion cannot be adequately documented; statistics are at best fragmentary and may be inaccurate, and individual observations may be biased. However, this impression is supported by the recent report of an anonymous Spanish priest.[19] In eight large parishes near Madrid, according to him, only 14,000 persons in a population of 105,000 are practicing Catholics. Even among the supposedly more pious country folk, a sampling of eighty towns and

---

18 Richard Herr, *The Eighteenth-Century Revolution in Spain* (Princeton University Press, 1958), pp. 442-444.

19 Sabino Iturri, "Las dos cartas de la Iglesia," *Ibérica* (New York), May 15, 1959, p. 9; an editorial footnote states that Sabino Iturri is the pseudonym of a Spanish priest. In an inquiry made by HOAC in 1957 among 15,000 workers, 90 per cent described themselves as anticlerical and 41 per cent as antireligious.

villages with a total population of 130,000 reported only 52 per cent of the male population as practicing Catholics. In other regions the proportion is still lower, ranging from 30 to a paltry 8 per cent. The figures for Barcelona are particularly striking. Despite the success of the Abbot of Montserrat, Dom Aureli María Escarré, and other prelates of the region in giving a flavor of Catalanism to their criticism of the regime, practicing Catholics constitute only 20 per cent of the population in the center of the city and less than 10 per cent in working-class quarters.

It may be that these and similar figures, even if accurate, are irrelevant; in religion, as in all things, Spaniards show their true colors best in times of crisis and tend to let down in routine situations. Or, as González Moralejo puts it, "the Spaniard is more apt to prove his Catholicism by martyrdom than by silent immolation in his daily life." [20] Nevertheless, apathy rather than hostility is what most disturbs many religious leaders in the attitude of a large part of the Spanish people towards the church today.

One thing Spanish Catholic leaders do not need to worry about is Protestantism, though in fact they seem to worry about it a great deal. In 1959 it was estimated that there were only 30,000 Protestants in Spain (or one per thousand in the total population) more than half of whom were foreigners. The failure of Protestantism to flourish cannot be explained in any important measure by persecution, for the Anarchists, who flourished greatly in Catalonia and other parts of Spain from the late nineteenth century, were persecuted much more rigorously. The familiar phrase, "Spaniards are Catholics or nothing," does not explain the phenomenon, but it is a relevant fact; and it is almost literally true, for the only other non-Catholic groups, Jews and Moslems, are as small, or smaller.

Nevertheless, no Spanish government, except the anticlerical Second Republic, has granted Protestants more than limited toleration, far short of religious freedom. Under the

---

20 *El momento social de España,* cited, p. 157.

monarchical constitution of 1876, Protestants were granted the privilege of worshiping together in private, but were not permitted to identify their churches by any outward markings or to give any other public sign of their existence; they were discriminated against in other ways as well. Since 1945 Franco's Charter of the Spaniards has given them substantially the same measure of limited toleration, under somewhat severer restrictions, mainly relating to marriage, burial, public employment, and schools. Enforcement of these and other restrictions has varied considerably from one part of Spain to another, and from one time to another, but at all times Protestants have suffered greater vexation in Franco's Spain than in any other country in Western Europe, including Portugal, where there is also a personal dictatorship and where, although the constitution separates church and state, it declares that Catholicism is "the religion of the people."

Late 1959 brought with it reports that Franco's government was at last considering a relaxation of the restrictions placed on Protestant and other non-Catholic groups in Spain. The chief impulse was said to come from abroad and to be meeting with a more sympathetic reception than formerly because of Franco's desire to draw closer to the Western powers. Appropriately, support for this relaxation was strongly attributed to Foreign Minister Castiella.[21] If so, things had changed since 1956, when his predecessor, Martín Artajo, defended the restrictions. Catholicism, he is reported to have said, is a great source of Spanish unity; Protestantism is divisive and anti-Franco, and the Protestants "always attack the Pope, the Vatican, the Catholic Church. . . ."[22] In 1959, however, the latter consideration apparently carried less weight in Rome than in Madrid, for the new Pope, John XXIII, was reportedly in favor of lifting the curbs on Spanish Protestants. Since the influence of the Vatican, as well as the Western powers, was then on the increase in Spain, some

---

21 *The New York Times*, September 12, 1959.

22 Quoted by Herbert Matthews, *The Yoke and the Arrows* (New York: Braziller, 1957), p. 155.

relaxation of the curbs seemed not improbable. As usual when Franco was involved, the pace of change was likely to be slow.

The New Pope

The election of Cardinal Roncalli as Pope John XXIII at the end of 1958 aroused great expectations in Spain. His predecessor, Pius XII, had given a measure of support to Franco by entering into the Concordat of 1953 and was also believed to favor Opus Dei and to have protected it against the Jesuits. The new Pope was believed to be cool towards both the Franco regime and the Opus. This belief seems to have been shared by the regime, according to persistent reports that the Spanish Ambassador to the Vatican lobbied vigorously against Roncalli's election and Foreign Minister Castiella put such pressure as he could on the Spanish cardinals to use their influence and votes against him.

The ascertainable basis of the belief was slight. What basis it had apparently rested on the new Pope's alleged friendship with exiled Basque priests in Paris and a poor impression of the Franco regime that he had formed during a visit to Spain in 1950. The new Pope was also regarded as too apolitical to look with favor on the Spanish branch of the Opus Dei as this had developed by 1958.

All this was rather nebulous. So also is the evidence so far provided by his pontificate. The new Pope is said to have given a brief and cool audience to the pro-Franco Primate of Spain and to have said to him, "Now you must be a father to all the people of Spain." Again, at the installation of a new Spanish cardinal, Archbishop Bueno y Monreal of Seville, he asked a Spanish newspaper correspondent, "Are you courageous?" and followed this with the injunction, "Always tell the truth." [23] The group accompanying the Cardinal-elect contained representatives of Catholic Action, but not of Opus Dei; that was taken to reflect the sympathies not only of the new Cardinal but of the Pope.

---

23 *ABC* (Seville), March 15, 1959.

This may be only such stuff as dreams are made of. Equally good evidence pointing in the opposite direction was provided in October 1959 by John XXIII's appointment of a replacement for a Portuguese prelate, the Bishop of Oporto, who had been critical of dictator Salazar's regime.[24] Salazar's dictatorship has been, on the whole, milder than Franco's, but the main criticisms—the hard lot of the workingmen, the suppression of personal freedom—are the same as those leveled at the Franco regime by Catholic reformers within Spain. The Oporto case did not augur well for papal pressure on Franco to put his house in order.

In the long run, pressure to put the Spanish house in order seems more likely to come from leaders of the church in Spain itself. Some pressure has already been exerted by them and they will probably increase it, whatever happens to Franco. There are no political firebrands among them, of course, but some of them constitute a "new leadership" which, as a matter of both conscience and prudence, is bent on reform. This new leadership realizes that, while perhaps Franco will be able to go on ruling to the end as the leader of "Spain" against "Anti-Spain," the church must be the church of all Spaniards, or else a new time of troubles will begin for it when Franco is gone. Many leaders, both clerical and lay, believe that, if a constitutional monarchy or a moderate republic should replace Franco in the course of natural or political events, a broad church-inspired grouping, not dissimilar to the Christian Democratic party of Italy, might emerge as a major force. But in order to bring that about, the church must first demonstrate its attachment to democratic freedoms, justice and order, rather than putting "order" of an authoritarian type above freedom and justice.

Which path the church will choose is highly problematical. Its new leadership, while waxing, still leads only a fraction of its members—probably a distinct minority. The hierarchy is still on the whole a staunch supporter of the present regime and of the authoritarian principle. And much of

---

24 *The New York Times,* October 11, 1959.

the clerical criticism of certain features of the regime comes
from the church's right wing and expresses its displeasure
with Franco for being too modern in his encouragement of
industrialization and for drawing Spain too close to the
United States.[25]

Whether as an inspirer of a broadly liberal and humanitarian party, or as a supporter of a continuation of authoritarianism à la Franco, or as a persecuted faction under a
new leftist regime, the church is bound to exercise a strong
influence on Spain's future political course at home and
abroad, especially in Europe, where its new leaders see Cath-
olic-inspired political forces playing leading roles in shaping
the future of a continent newly aware both of its perils and
its destiny.

---

25 Ebenstein, cited, p. 10.

Chapter VIII

SPAIN AND HER EUROPEAN NEIGHBORS

BY VIRTUE OF geography and culture Spain is an integral part of Western Europe. Nevertheless, she is different in many ways from the rest of Europe, and the character of the Franco regime has made her position in Europe unique. It has also led to an estrangement from most of her European neighbors that is only gradually being overcome.

Spain's position is unique in two respects, and all but unique in a third. Her government is the only one in Europe that has been openly and unremittingly hostile to the Soviet Union and international communism before, during, and since World War II. In the second place, the Franco regime is the sole dictatorship of the Nazi-Fascist crop to survive into the 1960's. In the third place, with the sole exception of Portugal, Spain is the only country in Western Europe that is ruled by a dictatorship. The postwar estrangement between Spain and her European neighbors is rooted partly in the origins of the Franco regime, but even more in its present character, for it is not only a dictatorship in fact but also avowedly antidemocratic in principle, as the term democracy is understood and practiced in the West.

That there has been no similar estrangement between Western Europe and Portugal is not surprising. Salazar's dictatorship was not one of the Nazi-Fascist crop. Rightly or wrongly, it is generally regarded as less obnoxious than Franco's. It has been protected by its close ties with Great

Britain. It cooperated with the United Nations coalition during World War II, largely by making available its important bases in the Azores. And its potential for mischief is much lower than that of Spain, which is far larger and has a much more ambitious foreign policy. Hence Spain's continued exclusion from that largely European organization, NATO, of which Portugal is a charter member.

In Spain the effect of her neighbors' critical attitude has been to provoke a reaction of withdrawal in psychological self-defense. Quite naturally, the reaction was strongest when the condemnation was most general and severe, in the years just after the war. Conversely, as time and tide have abated foreign censure, the Spanish sense of belonging to Europe has reasserted itself with increasing strength and in a variety of ways, both in the regime and among its opponents. Thus, Franco, who had earlier shown himself a master isolationist, in 1957 appointed a new cabinet dominated by "Europeans." Two years later he made important policy changes, at no little political hazard, in order to qualify Spain for full membership in the Organization for European Economic Cooperation.

In a different but no less significant way Franco indicated the new direction of his thinking in his customary year-end address on December 31, 1958. The two events that he described as the most important of the year were both primarily European: the establishment of the De Gaulle regime in France, and the election of a new pope, John XXIII.[1] Simultaneously a clamor for "reintegrating" Spain with Western Europe was rising both in the quasi-independent banking community and among intellectuals and political opposition groups. Among the latter, Tierno Galván's Functionalists are, or at least profess to be, devoted even more wholeheartedly to this goal than to political reform in Spain, though they regard the two objectives as inseparable.

Not surprisingly, in this, as in all other matters, there are many in Spain who dissent, for a Spaniard dissents eagerly.

---

[1] André Fontaine, "L'Espagne, la France et l'Europe," *La Revue de Paris*, March 1959, p. 46.

Again, like Great Britain, Spain lies on the periphery of Europe and has important ties with other parts of the world. Nevertheless, her most vital ties are those that bind her to her European neighbors.

Are Spaniards Europeans?

Spain is, true enough, an integral part of Western Europe, but Spaniards are "Europeans with a difference." For facile foreign generalizers, the difference is usually symbolized by the Pyrenees, attributed to the long Moorish domination of most of the peninsula, and expressed in the cliché, "Africa begins at the Pyrenees." Then, as like as not, the same source says in the next breath that "Spaniards are more Catholic than the Pope." There are, in fact, elements of truth in both generalizations, but they do not help us with our questions: How Moorish are the Spaniards of today? And how European?

This subject has long been debated by Spanish scholars and the debate is carried on today by such learned antagonists as Américo Castro and Claudio Sánchez Albornoz.[2] One result of the intense debate has been to complicate the problem by a new emphasis upon the influence of still another group, the Spanish Jews. Until recently, students laid little stress on Jewish influence in the making of modern Spain. A persuasive case has now been made for placing it on a par with the Moorish influence or even above it, from the late middle ages to the sixteenth century, when the new Spanish policy of converting or expelling both groups of infidels was applied perseveringly, ruthlessly, and with considerable success.

On the main question, while evidences of Moorish influ-

---

[2] See especially Américo Castro, *España en su historia* (Buenos Aires: Editorial Losada, 1948); *La realidad histórica de España* (Mexico City: Editorial Porrúa, 1954); and *Orígen, ser y existir de los españoles* (Madrid: Taurus, 1959); Claudio Sánchez Albornoz, *España, un enigma histórico* (Buenos Aires: Editorial Sudamericana, 1956; 2 v.). Both men have lived in voluntary exile for many years, the former in the United States, the latter in Argentina; Castro's book of 1959 was published in Madrid.

ence still abound, these consist mainly of historical curiosities such as place names and the horseshoe arch. They are far outweighed by those vital factors that stamp the Spanish culture of today as essentially European. Language is one of the best keys to any culture; modern Spanish comes largely from Latin. In religion, another key to culture, most Spaniards resemble most Italians and most Frenchmen in being Roman Catholic or nothing. Similarly, modern Spanish law and Spain's political, educational, and economic institutions developed from the same Roman-barbarian origins, and, despite important divergences, have developed in much the same way as in the rest of Western Europe.

Spain has been an active member of the European family of nations ever since it began to take shape in the fifteenth century. In the sixteenth century, she was the leading European power. Her spokesmen played principal roles in the Council of Trent, which marked an epoch in the history of the Catholic Church; her conquests in the Americas precipitated a price revolution in Europe, with the influx of gold and silver from Mexico and Peru. If her catastrophic decline in the seventeenth century drove her for a time into a kind of spiritual isolation, she was brought back into the mainstream of European affairs in the next century, when the Spanish throne was occupied by a branch of the French Bourbons and the two governments became allies under the Family Compact. From Paris the Enlightenment spread throughout Spain. Cádiz, focal point of Spain's rich trade with her American dominions and of a large part of Europe's trade and thronged with merchants and seamen from all Europe, was one of the most thriving ports in the world.

After the catastrophe of the Napoleonic wars and the loss of most of her American dominions, Spain again drew back into her shell. But the withdrawal was never complete. Indeed, it was confined mainly to the field of power politics: from the early nineteenth century to 1953 she entered into no alliances. Otherwise, to the extent possible, Spain carried on active trade and cultural relations with her European neighbors. From the late nineteenth century through the

1920's, the pace was quickened with the growth of foreign investments—mainly British, French, and German. After the shock of the Spanish-American War the "Generation of 1898" sought to revitalize Spanish society through somewhat the same sort of integration with Europe that is being preached in present-day Spain. Even in the political field there was a trend towards closer bonds with her neighbors, until it was reversed by the outcome of the Civil War and by Spain's isolation, both imposed and self-inflicted.

For a decade after World War II, Spain's relations with most of Europe were badly out of joint in every respect—economic and cultural as well as political. They suffered greatly from her perennial poverty deepened by the world-wide economic depression of the early 1930's and by her own Civil War, from which she has not fully recovered even now. They suffered even more from the revulsion aroused by the regime's original Nazi-Fascist taint and nourished by the maintenance of an iron-handed dictatorship—a revulsion that has been felt even more strongly by Europeans than by others precisely because Spain is a member of the European family. Hence Europe has continued to hold Spain at arm's length even after she had gained a measure of rehabilitation in other circles. Her exclusion has been most pointed in the case of NATO, since this primarily European organization sets itself a political as well as a military goal.

For several years Spain countered her exclusion in two ways. The first, the sour-grapes way, was to pretend that she was isolated by her own choice. In order to make the pretense plausible, spokesmen for the regime embroidered on the fiction that Spain's traditional policy was one of neutrality and isolation. Then, when the West began to thaw a bit, but too slowly to suit the Franco regime, the latter developed another convenient fiction, one which, while opening the door to friendly relations with the West, kept Spain free of commitments to it. This was the fiction that Spain, by virtue of her Moorish past, had an historic mission to serve as a bridge or mediator between the Christian West and Islam.

Recently both fictions have been gathering dust for one very good reason, namely that Spain has made a change of course of somewhere between 90 and 180 degrees in her foreign policy. Begun earlier, the change was first publicly manifested in the bases agreement with the United States. A parallel but slower change in Spain's relations with her European neighbors dates only from the Suez crisis of 1956, but it was greatly accelerated the next year when Madrid saw its initially idyllic relations with the newly independent kingdom of Morocco turn sour. By 1957 "Europeanism" had become the watchword in Madrid. Although not all implications of the term were clear, it meant at least that Spain wanted to normalize her relations with Western Europe. She was no longer playing coy even with NATO. Still insisting that she would not ask to be admitted but must be invited, she let it be known that she was quite receptive to an invitation. On December 21, 1957, the day after Secretary Dulles' visit to Franco on his way home from a NATO meeting in Paris, the Spanish Minister of War, General Barroso, chose the Cortes as a sounding-board to stress Spain's great potential value to NATO.[3]

Since then, Spain has in fact tightened her bonds with her European neighbors in various ways. Still claiming special qualifications for dealing with the Arabs, she now deals with them less as mediator between them and Europe than as a sympathetic European power. Instead of playing a solo broadcast to the whole Arab world, she now performs in a European concert directed mainly at maintaining her links with North Africa.

Spain's efforts to improve her relations with her European neighbors have had their chief focus in the France of De Gaulle and the West Germany of Adenauer. Both have shown signs of a willingness to reciprocate. How far the amelioration may go, and what results it may bring, it would

---

3 *The New York Times*, December 22, 1957. Barroso explained that large naval concentrations could operate from Spain's Canary Islands; her desert areas in West Africa could furnish sites for vital air bases; and her garrisons at Ceuta and Melilla could dominate the approaches to the Mediterranean.

be rash to predict, but they promise to be important if only because Europe needs Spain's help in the Mediterranean. The weakening of the West's position in the Eastern Mediterranean has spread all the way across NATO's North African flank into Morocco, where Europe and Africa almost meet and where Spain holds a position of great strategic importance. North Africa holds out an economic promise as well as a political and military threat, and both Spain and her European neighbors are becoming increasingly aware of their need for each other in meeting the threat and realizing the promise.

Other forces are at work to mitigate the antagonisms of the past two decades between Spain and her neighbors to the north of the Pyrenees. As the weaker party, Spain has more to gain by a reconciliation and her gains would be manifold. As a consequence, the current Spanish wave of "Europeanism" has political, cultural, and economic, as well as military and diplomatic, implications. Many Spaniards, including some supporters of the Franco regime, believe that political conditions in their country would benefit from a return to friendly intercourse with their neighbors. Most Spanish intellectuals look to the latter as their natural allies. And most informed Spaniards in all walks of life count more upon European trade than American aid for a long-range solution to their country's many and difficult economic problems.

The prospect of having to adapt the Spanish economy to the new situation created by the European Common Market of the Six and the Free Trade Association of the Seven has come as a reminder of Europe's economic importance for Spain. In 1954-1957, for example, six of Spain's eight best customers were European countries (Britain, West Germany, France, Netherlands, Belgium, and Switzerland, in that order); together these six took about 60 per cent of her total exports. The other two were the United States and Brazil; both had recently developed an abnormally large trade with Spain under forced draught. The European countries, on the other hand, are Spain's natural trading partners, but the relationship may suffer from the creation of the Common

Market and the Free Trade Association if Spain is left out of both.

The urge to reconciliation is much less strong north of the Pyrenees, but it exists even there. By 1955 several European countries were carrying on extensive cultural programs in Spain. Those of Great Britain and France were the most important, followed by Italy and West Germany. In that year the British embassy already had an active press service and a large cultural section and maintained cultural institutes in Madrid, Barcelona, Seville, and Valencia. France had a smaller press service but a very ample cultural program and exceptionally effective instruments in the French *lycées* of Madrid, Barcelona, and Seville. Special chairs were maintained at the University of Madrid by France, Italy, and Portugal.

While Spain's supply of foreign news came at that time mainly from United Press, under a contract with Spain's own foreign news service, Efe, British Reuters provided some and Agence France Presse a little. The foreign radio programs most frequently heard in Spain were those of Radio Paris and the BBC; Vatican Radio, which regularly relayed an uncensored program through the Radio Nacional de España; and several Soviet bloc radios in Moscow, Budapest, Warsaw, and Prague, in addition to the nominally clandestine Radio España Independiente.

Strategic considerations aside, the motivation of European interest in Spain is mainly economic, based on prospects for trade and investment, and on the need for Spanish products such as citrus fruits, iron ore, and mercury. Great Britain and West Germany have shown a special interest in these possibilities. Likewise, the cooperation of Spain could be useful to France in bringing the new products of the Sahara and Mauritania to market through its African possessions; in North Africa Spain could be a helpful partner to France politically as well as economically.

The Contiguous Neighbors

Ever since the beginning of the eighteenth century, Spain's most important neighbors have usually been the three that are contiguous: Great Britain, Portugal, and France.

If it seems odd to speak of Great Britain as contiguous to Spain, be it noted that the British navy, in effect, made Britain and Spain contiguous by seizing Gibraltar in 1704. By this acquisition Britain gained one point of leverage in the Iberian peninsula. It had gained another one year before by the Methuen Treaty with Portugal. Though confined to commerce, this famous treaty paved the way for the establishment of British preponderance in Portugal, which, continuing to the present, has often strengthened Britain's hand in dealing with Spain.

The frontier between Gibraltar and Spain at La Línea is only one mile long, but it is one of the most contentious miles in Europe. Spain has never given up her claim to Gibraltar, or her efforts to recover it. Britain's retention of the Rock has been a sore point in Anglo-Spanish relations for two and a half centuries.[4] On the other hand, over this long period, Britain has been one of Spain's principal trading partners and, since the nineteenth century, one of the chief investors. Similarly, there have been opposing thrusts of mutual interest and rivalry in their relations with third countries in Europe, Africa, America, and Asia.

One result has been a certain ambivalence in the attitudes of London and Madrid to each other, and in this the Franco period has been no exception. Early in 1944 Churchill, for example, spoke "a kind word" for Spain in Parliament; later in the same year he rebuffed a friendly overture from Franco in terms that were anything but kind. Again, when the Labor party came to power in 1945, its vocal spokesman, Harold Laski, fulminated against Franco Spain, but the lightning never struck. Finally, in 1951 the Labor govern-

---

[4] For a postwar view of this problem by a high Spanish official, see Juan de la Cosa (pseudonym for Luis Carrero Blanco), *Gibraltar, comentarios de un español* (Valencia: Semana Gráfica, 1952).

ment's Foreign Secretary, as I have mentioned earlier, publicly objected to associating Spain with the defense of the West. On the other hand, when the United States insisted on going through with the bases agreement, the British government, now in Conservative hands, was not unwilling to share in its military benefits, while leaving to the United States whatever moral responsibility it might entail.

Today, Britain might acquiesce under pressure in Spain's admission to NATO, but the Labor party is still strongly opposed and the Conservative government is publicly uncommitted. A test case arose in May 1959, when the press reported that France had withdrawn her objection to Spain's admission to NATO and that Spain's early admission had been secretly arranged. When the question was promptly raised in the House of Commons, Minister of State John Profumo sidestepped the issue, taking refuge in a technicality. The question of admitting Spain, he said, was not before the members; hence there had not even been any negotiations on the subject.[5] Even the London *Times,* which deplored the emotional opposition to Spain's candidacy as based on an unrealistic raking up of the past, objected to the irregular way in which the question had now been raised; this could only irritate certain members of NATO and create dissension in its ranks.[6]

The *Times* perhaps underestimated the irritation that these rumors caused in Britain. "Even if the British government were to agree [to Spain's admission]" said one report," "it would then have to face an ugly Parliamentary split," since the Labor party would oppose it resolutely.[7] As evidence of Labor's feelings, its headquarters had already collected nearly $5,000 in individual contributions for the relief and defense of the Spanish trade-unionists arrested in the round-up of November 1958. The same report also quoted an unidentified diplomat (presumably not British) as saying: "My government doesn't want to sit down and

5 *New York Herald Tribune,* May 5, 1959.
6 *The Times* (London), May 6, 1959.
7 *New York Herald Tribune,* May 4, 1959.

talk over all these delicate and intimate matters of Western relations with a Franco representative, and it never will. . . . There is absolutely nothing to be gained militarily by letting Spain in, because the Americans already have a perfectly practical arrangement with them direct."

The Conservative government has, however, made some friendly gestures towards Franco Spain, beginning in 1958, with the first visit to Madrid in many years by a British leader of cabinet rank; the visitor was, significantly, the President of the Board of Trade, Sir David Eccles. As so often in the past, the "Spanish interest" in Britain seems again to be influencing British foreign policy. Presumably, in addition to trade and investments, the Free Trade Association gives London a new motive for taking Spain into account in its plans. Sir David's call was repaid in April 1959 by Minister of Commerce Ullastres, who also talked with Foreign Secretary Selwyn Lloyd and Chancellor of the Exchequer Heathcote Amory. These new discussions—again on the Common Market, the Free Trade Area, and British trade and investments in Spain—yielded no spectacular results. A friendly atmosphere prevailed and Ullastres praised the understanding attitude that Britain had shown ("perhaps more clearly than on previous occasions") in discussing Spain's balance-of-payments problems. Spain has been particularly concerned by her declining market in Britain, which fell about 30 per cent between 1955 and 1958, for her oranges; better grading and marketing by Israeli exporters have cut into this traditional outlet, and a similar loss threatens in the West German market.[8]

Even on the thorny question of Gibraltar, Franco's government seemed for a time to be taking a more conciliatory attitude. A March 1958 report from Madrid stated that high Spanish military officials were considering the possibility of arranging with Great Britain for joint command of the Strait of Gibraltar on behalf of the West.[9] This idea, which would have been inconceivable even one year before, was attrib-

---

[8] *ABC* (Madrid), April 14 and 17, 1959.
[9] *The New York Times*, March 12, 1958.

uted to the mounting Moroccan hostility to Spain, and to the belief among Spanish officials that the possession of Ceuta, if properly exploited, could obtain for Spain an important voice in Western defense planning. Reports of this kind died down in the early months of 1959 as Spain came to better terms with Morocco and developed something like a *rapprochement* with the new regime in France. Simultaneously, the controlled Spanish press renewed its growling about Gibraltar.[10] The government also tightened its border controls at La Línea and continued building up Algeciras, in sight of Gibraltar across the bay, as a rival port of call for ships entering and leaving the Mediterranean.

On the British side there had been no softening. Indeed, the nature of the Franco regime has provided the British with a new justification for keeping Gibraltar. To turn it over to Spain now, they say, would be to deliver a free people into bondage. This argument is not accompanied, however, by any suggestion that Gibraltar would be relinquished to a democratic Spanish regime. Yet the feeling has grown in Foreign Office circles that in the long run Britain and Spain ought to build up a working friendship on the basis of common interests as powers that are peripheral to Europe and have a tradition of great achievement in the new world and a common stake in developing closer ties with America rather than with Europe.

Whether because of this feeling or for other reasons, Foreign Minister Castiella's visit to London in August 1959 to meet with President Eisenhower left him happy over the attitude of the British authorities, although they had not invited him. Foreign Secretary Selwyn Lloyd expressed satisfaction over his presence in London and, in effect, promised to invite him soon to make an official visit. Castiella's reply, according to Spanish report, was "equally cordial," express-

<hr>

10 *Arriba* (Madrid), April 22, 1959. After expressing its regret that the British government had just reaffirmed its refusal to reconsider the status of Gibraltar, the editorial continued: "We also regret to have to break a silence imposed by our desires for harmony. . . . Again it is London that persists in giving cause for lack of understanding."

ing "the fervent wish that Spanish-British friendship may continue to flourish in all spheres." [11] These diplomatic courtesies may have been meaningless. More likely, they reflected a growing desire to achieve a mutually advantageous accommodation. If the division of Western Europe went deeper, it might, some British thinking implied, lead to a new grouping of powers, with Britain, Spain, and the United States in one group, France and Germany in another, and both groups tied together in an Atlantic community.

Salazar's Portugal has been quite important to the policy of Franco Spain. Ideologically akin and politically allied, the two regimes have been close friends for a quarter of a century. Traditional animosities between Spain and Portugal, frequent in earlier times, have not entirely disappeared. Portugal opposed Spain's bid for leadership of the Latin Union (a cultural union of the Latin countries of Europe and America, and the Philippines) in its congresses of 1951 and 1954. With an eye to its claims on Gibraltar, Spain has not given Lisbon the support to which it feels entitled on the issue of Goa.

Despite occasional differences, the two governments on the whole have cooperated closely ever since the days of the Spanish Civil War, when Salazar aided Franco in many ways. Though the two governments are united by a series of treaties stretching from 1939 to the reciprocal defense pact of November 22, 1958, their strongest tie is doubtless the fellow feeling of the two dictators, reinforced by the much older idea of Iberian unity, to which both subscribe. They also have similar if not always identical interests in regard to certain problems—their possessions in Africa and in the mid-Atlantic, and their relations to the European Common Market and Free Trade Area. Their friendship has not been disturbed by the residence in Portugal of the Spanish pretender, for Don Juan is one of the least importunate pretenders in history. Franco may even prefer to see him living in a country where so cooperative a government can keep an eye on him.

---

[11] *ABC* (Madrid), September 3, 1959.

The connection with Portugal has brought Franco many advantages. Besides aiding him in the Civil War, Portugal was for several years after World War II almost his only friend. Salazar's political system is enough like Franco's to lend it a much-needed color of respectability. Portugal has been Spain's chief European link to NATO and has loyally urged her admission to it. And the division of Europe into trade blocs has faced them with common economic problems, even though Portugal has been a founding member of the seven-power Free Trade Association. In 1958 Franco described Salazar as "the most complete statesman I have ever known . . . extraordinary for his intelligence, political sense and humanity. If he has a fault, it is his modesty." [12] Portugal will probably serve as a prop to the Franco regime so long as Salazar remains in power; when he goes, this quiet neighbor may become a center of anti-Franco contagion, as was southern France in the first years after the fall of the Vichy regime.

From De Gaulle I to De Gaulle II

When Charles de Gaulle came to power for the second time, he reversed his previously hostile policy towards the Franco regime and accelerated the movement, already on foot, towards a *rapprochement,* thereby raising France's always great influence on Spain to its highest point in many years. It promises to remain at a high level during De Gaulle's tenure, for it rests on political rather than economic factors, and the political factors are reinforced by the traditionally strong cultural influence of Paris south of the Pyrenees.

As a trading partner of Spain, France ranks third among European nations (fourth, after the United States, among all countries); Great Britain ranks first by a wide margin, and West Germany second. France also lags behind Britain and Germany as a source of investments in Spain. On the other

---

12 *Ya* (Madrid), June 13, 1958; interview with Serge Groussard of *Le Figaro* (Paris).

hand, France provides Spain with more tourists than any other country, and the tourist trade is one of Spain's chief sources of foreign exchange. Each year substantial numbers of Spanish workers eke out their wages by seasonal labor in France. Finally, Spain hopes to share with France in the exploitation of Saharan oil. Yet, neither actually nor potentially does France measure up to Britain and Germany in her economic importance to Spain.

In the political realm, the advent of De Gaulle has made France more important to Spain than any other European country. This is not because of the analogy, in which Franco's supporters at first rejoiced, between his and De Gaulle's coming to power—in both cases on a wave started by a military uprising in a North African dominion which toppled a republican government in the metropolis. As Sir David Eccles is said to have commented, with admirable frankness, the implied parallel breaks down at its most essential point: Franco came to start a civil war, De Gaulle to avert one.

Sir David's pithy comment suggests one of the main reasons why the recent turn of events in France may influence profoundly both domestic political developments in Spain and Spain's relations with her European neighbors. De Gaulle has given striking proof that it is possible, with sound leadership, to solve the dilemma—substantially the same dilemma that has faced Spain for two decades—of transforming the political regime of a deeply divided country without precipitating a civil war. De Gaulle's example has encouraged many Spaniards to hope for a peaceful liquidation of the Franco regime; not the least advantage, as they see it, would be to remove the sole remaining obstacle to Spain's full acceptance as a member of the political community of Western Europe.

For Franco himself, De Gaulle's advent to power has been welcome for quite different reasons—as an added justification of his own regime, and a stimulus to further *rapprochement*. This move, which arose mainly out of a worsening of their positions in North Africa, as well as the West's entire position in the Mediterranean, represented a major shift for both governments. During World War II, it is true, Madrid had been on friendly terms with the Vichy government; after all, Marshal Pétain had been France's first ambassador to Franco after the Civil War. With France liberated, the new antagonism between Paris and Madrid lasted for more than a decade. In 1945-1948 the two governments engaged in a small-scale cold war, and the Pyrenees frontier remained closed for two years. France, which took a leading part in the United Nations' ostracism of the Franco regime, urged still stronger measures against it, only to be restrained by Great Britain and the United States. Even so, Spain was threatened more than once with invasion by a combined force of Spanish exiles and French *maquis*.[13]

Tensions between Paris and Madrid diminished somewhat as the bigger cold war—that with the Soviet Union—developed, but there was no real relaxation until the Suez crisis of 1956. In the meantime, as Franco's accords with the Vatican and the United States made him feel more sure of himself, he had even enhanced the tension by publicly excoriating France's deposition of the Sultan of Morocco in 1953, pressing his pro-Arab policy with redoubled zeal, courting Nasser, and even letting Spanish Morocco be used as a base by France's enemies after full-scale revolt broke out in neighboring Algeria in 1954. This bickering was cut short by the Suez crisis of 1956. After many gyrations, Spain emerged with a new policy which subordinated pro-Arabism to European cooperation. This meant normalizing Spain's relations with France—a task successfully begun by Foreign

---

13 Robert Okin, "Spain in the Post-War World," *Foreign Policy Reports* (Foreign Policy Association), August 1, 1947, p. 125. The frontier was closed by Spain on February 27, 1946, and by France two days later. According to Jean Créach, *Le Coeur et l'épée* (Paris: Plon, 1958), pp. 209-212, the threat of invasion from France began in 1944 and continued until the end of 1946; the would-be invaders were Communists and their principal invasion unit, numbering some 6,000 men, was headed by General Enrique Lister, commander of an international brigade on the Republican side in the Civil War; Franco maintained a defensive force of 100,000 soldiers along the Pyrenees frontier until early 1947.

Minister Martín Artajo just after the London conference on Suez in August 1956.

Although Artajo launched the new policy, he had been too closely identified with pro-Arab and anti-French attitudes to make him a suitable exponent. Accordingly, he was abruptly dismissed early in 1957 and replaced by one of the best-known advocates of "Europeanism," Fernando María de Castiella, who brought to the Foreign Ministry a number of bright young men; all were "Europeans," and many had been educated in France.[14] In August 1957, at San Sebastián and Biarritz, Castiella conferred with the French Secretary of State for Foreign Affairs, Maurice Faure. Reportedly they had a satisfactory discussion of the European Common Market, tensions in North Africa, and France's need for access to the sea through Spanish territory for ore from the fabulously rich iron mines newly opened in Mauritania. The following December Spain's able Permanent Delegate to the United Nations, José Félix de Lequerica, showed himself "one of the most determined and effective supporters of French policy" in the debate on Algeria.[15] In February 1958, for the first time in a quarter of a century, a French parliamentary group, representing all major parties except the Socialists and the Communists, paid a visit of friendship to Spain.

Of two main reasons for Spain's change of policy, one was the appearance of the Soviet specter in the Arab world during the Suez crisis. According to the Spanish government, a second and closely related reason lay in the deterioration of Spain's relations with Morocco. Algeria, the Sahara, and Morocco form a distinct area in which Spanish and French interests have long been intertwined, sometimes in cooperation, more often in rivalry. The importance of these interests has been greatly enhanced in recent years by the combined political threat of rising nationalism and Communist infiltration, and also by the economic promise of early exploitation of the area's resources, particularly oil and iron ore.

---

14 *Le Monde* (Paris), July 18, 1958; article by André Fontaine.
15 Fontaine, "L'Espagne, la France et l'Europe," cited, p. 49.

After coming to power in May 1958 De Gaulle gave a vigorous impetus to the incipient *rapprochement,* begun under the Fourth Republic. Castiella, visiting Paris for a meeting of the OEEC, was given an exceptionally cordial reception by the French authorities as well as much publicity by the press. And in Africa, French military forces in Mauritania cooperated closely with the Spaniards against the Moroccan "Army of Liberation." [16] In June 1958 Franco gave the *rapprochement* a cautious public endorsement. Concord between governments, he said, grows out of understanding between their peoples, and for a long time past Spain had suffered from misunderstanding on the part of many Frenchmen. Friendship and cooperation between the two countries could and should be achieved, but they must lay aside past rivalries and go forward on a new basis.[17] Normalization of relations continued smoothly. On April 30, 1959, De Gaulle strikingly demonstrated his desire for a *rapprochement* by letting Agence France Presse leak the news that France was now ready to support Spain's admission to NATO. Two months later, in June, he proposed, in a public address, the formation of a Western Mediterranean alliance with Spain as one of its members.

This shift came as a great surprise to those who remembered De Gaulle's first government as the one that had taken the lead in trying to force the Franco regime out of power after World War II. Whether he had then followed his colleagues' advice rather than his own inclination, or whether he had soon thereafter changed his mind, from 1950 on, De Gaulle had repeatedly taken a strong position in favor of bringing Spain into the Western defense system, describing her as a "proud and valiant country . . . whose territory is one of the bastions of the West." [18] In June 1957 De Gaulle shrugged off the chief argument against his proposal: "To

---

16 Same, p. 48; *Le Monde,* May 10 and 11, 1958.

17 *Ya* (Madrid), June 14, 1958; interview with Serge Groussard of *Le Figaro* (Paris).

18 *Hoja del Lunes* (Madrid), December 11, 1950; *Le Monde* (Paris), January 9, 1951.

desire to exclude Spain from the Atlantic Community is ridiculous. This has nothing to do with Spain's political regime, about which one may think what one likes." [19] Consequently, when De Gaulle came out in favor of admitting Spain to NATO and including her in a Mediterranean pact, he was only confirming a position he had consistently maintained for several years. Clearly he did not make these proposals because of any sympathy for the Franco regime; there is no evidence that De Gaulle likes it any better now than fifteen years ago. Rather, the explanation lies in his efforts to promote the solidarity of Western Europe and to strengthen its position in the Mediterranean and North Africa. In both cases, the *grandeur* and the interests of France are central to his thinking. De Gaulle attaches so much importance to these objectives and to the potential value of Spain's aid that he has been willing to affront a large body of opinion in France by espousing partnership with the detested Franco regime.

This interpretation of De Gaulle's policy was confirmed by one of his chief lieutenants, Jacques Soustelle, in a conversation with me in May 1959. Soustelle supported the new policy warmly, both in the interest of Western solidarity and defense and because of the special benefits that would accrue to France, particularly by promoting trade and enlisting Spain's cooperation in North Africa. Although Spain's economic potential is low, nevertheless Spain could, he said, be useful in a number of ways: minerals from parts of the French Sahara and Mauritania could be exported most advantageously through Spanish territory, and Spain might receive development rights in parts of the Sahara where oil had been discovered. As regards the character of the Franco regime, he shared the present view of his chief that this consideration was irrelevant, that it was excluded by the rule of nonintervention, and that this was a wise rule.

Naturally, these views were reciprocated in Spain, as illustrated by an interview of mid-April 1959 with General

---

[19] *Le Monde* (Paris), June 25, 1957.

Franco. The General had now cooled to the idea, which he had formerly supported, of a Mediterranean pact. From Spain's point of view, he explained, such a pact would be superfluous. The security of the region was sufficiently provided for by NATO, by Spain's defense arrangement with the United States, and by the good relations that now prevailed between Spain and her European neighbors, above all with France.

The efforts at *rapprochement,* begun on both sides in late 1956, by the spring of 1959 had apparently achieved success. Radio Paris no longer beamed anti-Franco broadcasts at Spain. Spain no longer gave aid and comfort to Algerian nationalists in their struggle with France. The two governments had engaged in military cooperation against Moroccan guerrillas and were talking about partnership on a much broader front. And by her example and the counsels of her chief economic planner, Jacques Rueff, France had contributed to the preparation of the Spanish stabilization plan of July 1959. The atmosphere of mutual cordiality has been maintained. In September 1959, returning from his interview with President Eisenhower in London, Foreign Minister Castiella stopped in Paris for talks with De Gaulle and Foreign Minister Couve de Murville. These were described as "touching more on [general] international problems than on French-Spanish relations," which according to French sources "do not create any difficulties." [20]

According to other reports, the French government has been curbing the activities of Spanish exiles in France, in deference to Franco's wishes and "in exchange for the Spanish vote in the United Nations on the Algerian question." According to one journal, no Socialist or democratic organization of exiled Spaniards "can hold meetings or conferences south of the river Loire," and, as a consequence, two such meetings originally planned for Toulouse had to be moved to Paris and Vierzon respectively. "All of this means," it commented, "that activities of exiled Spaniards have been

---

[20] *The New York Times,* September 6, 1959.

banned in 31 of the 83 French *départements*. Now France is divided into two zones, just as she was after Hitler's victory in 1940." [21]

Whether or not the *rapprochement* develops into an *entente cordiale* will depend in part on the internal stability of the two regimes. If it does so develop, the benefits to Spain may be great. But there are also risks. The chief of these is the tendency of the *rapprochement* to involve Spain in the fate of De Gaulle's Algerian policy.

Other European Nations

Among the other European nations that count in the Spanish scale, the two that weigh heaviest are Italy and West Germany. Spain and Italy have a common cultural and religious heritage, as well as a common interest in the security of the Mediterranean and North Africa. Nevertheless, since World War II their relations have been characterized mostly by rivalry, antagonism or indifference. There is relatively little trade between them, and some of their chief exports, such as citrus fruits, compete in the markets of Northern Europe. Though they have appeared together in the membership lists of virtually all projects for a Mediterranean regional pact, they have more often been rivals than collaborators in this area as well as in Latin America. In 1958, when the government coalition of Christian Democrats and Democratic Socialists was led by Premier Amintore Fanfani, Italy's ambitions in both areas clashed with the interests of France and the United States as well as Spain. [22]

A constant irritant has been Franco's outspoken loyalty to the memory of Mussolini, which he voiced in no uncertain terms as recently as the summer of 1958. [23] On his side,

---

[21] *Ibérica* (New York), October 15, 1959, quoting the daily *Stockholms-Tidningen* and the weekly *Arbetaren*.

[22] *New York Herald Tribune*, September 24, 1958.

[23] Interview, *Le Figaro* (Paris); Spanish translation in *Ya* (Madrid), June 13 and 14, 1958. Franco said he felt "much closer" to Mussolini than to Hitler, for Mussolini was "very human, spontaneous," he had "intelligence and a heart." Franco also said: "I felt a very sincere affection for him. . . . Moreover,

Franco has been wary of Italy because of its strong Communist and Socialist parties. In recent years what reassurance he could find in the governing group in Italy, the Christian Democrats, has diminished as their Spanish counterparts have become more and more critical of his regime.

West Germany is much more important to Spain on both economic and political grounds. Its influence in Spain rests on a firm foundation of centuries-old ties, dating from the reign of the Habsburg dynasty in Spain. In the present century Germany's influence on Spanish thought, quite aside from the impact of Nazism, has been substantial. To give only one example, it provided the training and inspiration for the late José Ortega y Gasset, one of Spain's most seminal minds and a founder of the republic in 1931. Besides intervening in the Spanish Civil War, Nazi Germany exploited this heritage of respect in mounting a major cultural incursion into Spain, and through Spain into Spanish America, with the elaborate and generously financed Ibero-American Cultural Institute at Berlin as one of its chief instruments. The effort backfired; long before Hitler's fall, the Nazi emissaries had made themselves very much disliked by most Spaniards, of all shades of political opinion. This may explain, in part, why German culture has not yet recovered the prestige it enjoyed in Spain before the Civil War.

The situation in the economic and political fields is quite different. West Germany's impressive recovery since 1949 has excited admiration in Spain. What is more to the point, it has, as I have noted earlier, given West Germany a prominent role in the Spanish economy as a trading partner and a source of investments; this latter role may grow greatly if Spain follows through its program for attracting foreign investors. Bonn has also become an important factor in Spain's diplomacy. Since April 1957 it has openly favored Spain's admission to NATO.[24] Franco does not seem to hold it

---

I think I can say that he felt a real friendship for me, and this friendship was mutual up to the last moment."

24 *The Times* (London), April 10, 1957; Bonn was currently negotiating with Spain for the return of German property confiscated or sequestered at the end of the war.

against Chancellor Adenauer that the success of the latter's party in Germany has been a source of inspiration to Christian Democrats in Spain. Adenauer's diplomacy in Spain has apparently been that of a good European and he has resisted pressures to impart an anti-French tone to the friendship between West Germany and Spain. On the other hand, the revelation in January 1960 that Bonn was negotiating with Madrid for the use of military facilities in Spain provoked sharp protests from many quarters in the Atlantic world.

Belgium, Denmark, and Norway have offered the most persistent opposition to Spain's admission to the NATO club. Belgium resents Spain's refusal to extradite the former Rexist leader Léon Degrelle. In Denmark and Norway Protestantism helps tip the scales against ultra-Catholic Franco Spain. In all three countries the strength of Socialist and labor parties is a decisive factor.[25] None of the three has close relations with Spain nor does Sweden. Switzerland is of considerable importance to Spain as a financial center, particularly for flight capital, as evidenced by the "Swiss bank scandal" of December 1958.

Although negligible to Spain in most respects, both Greece and Turkey are valued by its government as members of NATO and for other reasons. Spain's Gibraltar complex has given her a fellow feeling for the Greeks in their controversy with Britain over Cyprus, and Greece has warmly seconded Spain's efforts to promote a Mediterranean pact. In relations with Turkey, the main theme of unity has been common resistance to the Soviet menace.

With the European members of the Soviet bloc, including the Soviet Union, Spain has no diplomatic relations. Recently, however, she has shown signs of softening her attitude slightly by entering into economic and cultural relations with several of its members. The Foreign Exchange Institute,

---

25 *Le Peuple* (Brussels), October 28, 1957, provides a fair sample of this sentiment in an article by left-wing Socialist Fernand Demany; captioned, in reference to Franco, "The Last of the Gauleiters," it concludes that, if Spain is ever admitted to NATO, "we will sign our own abdication of principles and be ready to accept all servitude."

a Spanish government agency, has negotiated trade and clearing agreements with most of the satellites, though not with Moscow. Of late, Spain has bought substantial quantities of coal from Poland and aluminum and cellulose from the Soviet Union in exchange for its own products, especially citrus fruits. Members of the Soviet bloc have recently begun exhibiting their goods at Spanish trade fairs. Since 1955 Soviet scholars and scientists have been visiting Spain to attend international meetings of a technical or professional character, and in July 1958 the first Spanish delegation to visit the Soviet Union in more than twenty years set out for Moscow to attend a meeting of the International Union of Architects.

Spain's softening towards the Soviet bloc has sometimes been attributed to the lure of the legendary Spanish gold, worth upwards of $500 million, which was sent to the Soviet Union by the Republican government during the Civil War. This explanation does not seem very plausible. Although the Spanish government has a good legal case, since it holds the Republican deposit receipts, the Soviet Union refuses to pay, claiming that all the money has long ago been expended. A better explanation of Spain's new attitude is found in her urgent need of new foreign markets. This the Soviet bloc can supply, probably on a much larger scale than at present, and in return it can provide Spain with an increasing volume of its imports.

Spain, NATO, and a Mediterranean Pact

On July 20, 1959, Spain was promoted from associate to full membership in the Organization for European Economic Cooperation. This event was vitally connected with the adoption of the stabilization plan. While the plan envisages a broad reshaping of Spain's economic relations with non-European as well as European countries, its adoption was a prerequisite of her promotion to full membership in OEEC. Moreover, some of its principal features, including the provisions for liberalization of trade and convertibility of currency, were designed specifically to bring Spanish economic policy and practice up to OEEC standards. The risk that the short-run effects on the Spanish economy may be painful has been willingly accepted by many leading Spaniards in the expectation that the end result will be a tightening of their country's economic bonds with its European neighbors.

The effort to bring this about was one expression of the widespread Spanish movement of recent years in favor of "integration with Europe." The movement has been supported on various grounds, depending largely on the type of integration advocated—economic, political, or cultural. In the economic field the reasoning was simple: Spain is naturally a part of Europe but has lagged far behind her European neighbors as they have prospered under freer economic systems and have drawn closer together in the OEEC. The solution seemed equally simple: Spain must assimilate her economic policies to theirs and join that organization.

However, just as Spain finally committed herself to this solution and achieved full membership in the OEEC, the terms of the problem were altered by the division of most of its members into two rival camps, the Common Market and the Free Trade Association. This development may place her at a serious disadvantage if the new groups succeed in their aims. Two of her principal trading partners, West Germany and France, are members of the Common Market, but, even if invited, Spain could hardly afford to join that closely knit group. Most economists agree that it will be at least ten years before the Spanish economy can hope to bear the competition that would be involved. The looser Free Trade Association offers better prospects from this point of view, for even Portugal, certainly no stronger than Spain economically, is a member of it. But Portugal has special ties with the Association's leader, Great Britain, and is not deterred, as is Spain, by important ties with the leaders of the Common Market group. Moreover, the FTA prohibits export subsidies and, as noted in connection with the stabilization plan, Spain will be obliged to subsidize some of her important exports for the first three years of the plan. On the other hand, if Spain joins neither group, she will obviously forfeit the advantages of both, and these may prove valuable if the two groups develop as planned. In a way, Spain is back where she started before joining OEEC, on the outside looking in. The main difference is that she now stands outside two European groups instead of one.

In this situation Spain has welcomed, with good reason, the effort, promoted by the United States in 1960, to supplant the OEEC with a larger economic organization embracing the United States and Canada together with the members of the original body. If the plan for the Organization for Economic Cooperation and Development works out well, it may benefit Spain by forming a kind of bridge between the Common Market and the Free Trade Association, and, as Spanish experts point out, it has already given her a welcome breathing spell.[26] So far, the OEEC—a technical rather than political organization—is the only important European regional body to which Spain has been admitted.

No one can consider Spain's rehabilitation complete until she has gained admittance to organizations of a political character, especially the NATO club. Although NATO includes two non-European members—Canada and the United States—it is very largely West European in membership and sentiment. Except for four confirmed neutrals—Austria, Ireland, Sweden, and Switzerland—which have stayed out from choice, Spain is the only West European nonmember. Hence Spain's election to it remains the acid test of acceptance by her European neighbors.

Why does Spain want to join NATO? What are the prospects of her candidacy? And would her inclusion in a Mediterranean regional group be desirable, either as an alternative or as a supplement to joining NATO?

What advantages would Spain secure by joining NATO, when she has had her defense arrangement with the United

26 Banco Hispano Americano, *La situación económica en 1959* (Madrid: Author, 1960), p. 11.

States since 1953? It is doubtful that joining NATO would give Spain any greater assurance of security, whereas it would nullify or diminish several advantages she now enjoys. For example, Spain would lose both the operational simplicity of her present bilateral relationship with the United States and some of the bargaining power she derives from her special position vis-à-vis the United States. That she nevertheless wants to join NATO [27] is almost certainly due mainly to considerations of prestige, for admission to it would strengthen Franco's hand at home and abroad. In addition, it would aid Spain's efforts to promote trade with her European neighbors and to obtain large-scale foreign aid in bringing her armed forces up to NATO standards. [28]

Outside Spain the division of opinion on admitting her to NATO is wide and deep. It does not follow national or regional lines and yet it is a simple one. It reflects a difference of opinion on whether the question should be decided on military grounds alone, or on political grounds as well. The division over this question in turn reflects a difference of opinion about the purposes of NATO. Those who conceive of NATO as primarily a military defense against military aggression by the Soviet bloc favor Spain's admission. General de Gaulle has stated some of the principal arguments on this side—the need for Western unity, Spain's important strategic position, and the irrelevance of political objections. To these should be added others—Spain's manpower potential and the fighting qualities of her soldiers,

---

[27] The official Spanish position is that Spain is not asking to be taken into NATO, though it is willing to consider an invitation if one is offered. A desire to be admitted has been shown in many ways. Salazar has been urging her admission ever since NATO was established, and articles and speeches complaining of Spain's exclusion are permitted to appear in the government-controlled Spanish press. A recent example is an article on "Europe and Spain" (originally published in *La Liberté*, Fribourg, Switzerland, reproduced in Spanish translation in *Levante*, Valencia, April 5, 1959), complaining against Spain's exclusion from European organizations; following the official Spanish line, it attributed Spain's exclusion to "Moscow and the crypto-Communists of Europe."

[28] For a sampling of Spanish opinion on this question, see a dispatch by Benjamin Welles, *The New York Times*, March 12, 1958.

her natural resources and the strategic importance of the joint U.S.-Spanish bases.

Those who stress NATO's political purpose are uncompromisingly opposed to Spain's admission. A strong comprehensive statement of this view was presented in late 1957 by Denis Healey, a leading younger member of the British Labor party.[29] Quoting the Preamble and Article 2 of the North Atlantic Treaty, which commits NATO to safeguarding "the freedom . . . of their peoples, founded on the principles of democracy, individual liberty, and the rule of law," and to "strengthening their free institutions," Healey described NATO as "unique in diplomatic history." "As the nucleus of the free world's resistance to communist expansion, it represents a moral commitment as well as a military undertaking." As for the Franco regime, he said, "Neither in principle nor practice has it anything in common with the sort of parliamentary democracy which the peoples and governments of NATO have sworn to uphold. The admission of Spain to NATO now would destroy the moral claims of NATO to the allegiance of decent people." "To the peoples of Western Europe," Healey went on, "Franco is not just a repulsive dictator—he is the last of the Nazi Gauleiters . . . put into power by the efforts of Hitler and Mussolini. . . . These memories are an important political reality in Western Europe. They help to explain why European democrats draw a sharp distinction between Spain and Portugal." "These political factors . . . should have an overriding priority in a period when so many people feel that the military threat from Communism is less immediate, or presents itself in a form against which NATO's military efforts offer them little protection." Finally, he asserted, under its agreement with the United States, "Spain is already making the only contribution it can usefully make to Western defense."

Similar sentiments have been voiced ever since the crea-

---

29 "Militarily Useless and an Affront to our Principles," *Western World*, November 1957, pp. 37-41. Along with Healey's article, under the general caption, "Debate of the Month," was one by Senator Michael J. Mansfield, "A Strategic Necessity . . . a Tribute to Western Civilization," pp. 32-36, which presented the case in favor of Spain's admission.

tion of NATO. The opponents of Spain's admission to NATO, be it noted, are not seeking to bring about any form of intervention against Franco, least of all to revive his post-war ostracism. In their view, as expressed by Healey, the boycott was a great mistake since it hurt only the people of Spain and strengthened Franco. What they favor is, according to him, a clear distinction between the Franco regime and the Spanish people, the encouragement of "the freest possible contact between the Spanish people and the outside world," and the avoidance of "any relationship with the Franco regime which is likely to strengthen its prestige or its power inside Spain"—as the admission of Spain to NATO would do.

Whether the debate will be settled in the near future is an open question. The advocacy of Spain's admittance seems to have gained ground since early 1957, when the United States and West Germany came out in support of it. It gained further strength from France's approval of it in April 1959, although De Gaulle's notorious coolness towards NATO creates some doubt as to just what his advocacy of Spain's admission signifies. On the other hand the opposition is still strong and firm. It is believed to include at least the governments of Denmark and Norway, and probably Belgium; and admission to NATO requires unanimous consent of its fifteen members. The opposition also includes the principal minority parties in France and West Germany, where the present governments favor admission, and also in Great Britain, where the Conservative government has not taken a public stand. A firm protest was voiced by Guy Mollet, leader of the French Socialist party, in April 1959. ". . . The goal of the Atlantic Pact is the defense of peace by the peoples of the free world who, in the words of its preamble, are 'attached to the principles of democracy, to individual liberties, and to the reign of law' . . . . It would be a grave error to pretend that one can defend liberty with [the aid of] the adversaries of liberty." [30] A similar protest was voiced

---

[30] *La Documentation Socialiste: Bulletin Hebdomadaire de la S.F.I.O.* (Paris), May 7, 1959.

by Hugh Gaitskell, leader of the British Labor party, in August 1959. "Spain is after all a Fascist country. [Her admission] . . . would completely destroy the idea of NATO being a group of democracies. It would do the alliance very great harm." [31] The depth of the resentment in Western Europe at the idea of embracing the Franco regime was again made plain in early 1960, following the revelation that the government of West Germany had for some time been discussing with Madrid the possibility of setting up German "facilities" or "bases" on Spanish soil. These, it was explained, would provide West Germany, cramped for space at home, with room for storage and training. Communist propaganda naturally claimed that the facilities would also include rocket-launching ramps, which were prohibited to the West German forces by international agreement. Even without this propaganda fillip, the revelation caused a great hue and cry throughout Western Europe. It revived fears of German militarism and recalled bitter memories of Franco's ties with Hitler, and the apparent failure to clear this proposal in NATO reawakened many scarcely dormant suspicions of both Germany and Franco. A typical reaction came from the Copenhagen newspaper *Information:*

The thought of a Bonn-Madrid Axis is so detestable one might think it was fostered by the Kremlin. Adenauer could not find anything worse to do than try to make secret agreements with the only surviving Fascist dictator in Europe.[32]

In more measured terms it was reported from London that this, along with other developments in West Germany, was thought by senior allied officials to have brought about a "serious decline in Western unity." [33] The division in question, it was explained, was one between the United States and its allies, since "many Americans believe their allies, especially in Britain, are making a mountain out of a

31 *The New York Times,* August 30, 1959.

32 Same, February 28, 1960, "West Germany Stirs Old Fears"; dispatch from Bonn.

33 Same, February 28, 1960, "Bonn Said to Peril Unity of West"; dispatch from London.

molehill." Again, there was a clear gap in the preponderance of views, between the United States and its major allies in Western Europe, over the relative weight they attach to NATO's military function and its political purpose. If anything, this episode was a setback to Franco's desire to be invited into the NATO family.

One of the few things that seem clear is that it would require heavy pressure from the larger powers to bring about Spain's admission at any time in the near future. It is also clear that the opposition, based on principles proclaimed by the North Atlantic Treaty itself, is so strong that, even if this pressure were exerted successfully, it would leave a heritage of dissension and disillusionment in the ranks of the Western alliance.

All this has been known for years past, and a less provocative way of bringing Spain into a multilateral alliance for the defense of the West has been sought through a Western Mediterranean pact, such as that which De Gaulle proposed to Italy in June 1959. Behind it lie many considerations besides the Spanish problem. It could, quite conceivably, serve to reinforce a NATO that included Spain, rather than as an alternative to Spain's joining NATO. Nevertheless, its main attraction seems to lie in the latter possibility.

Since World War II the idea of some sort of regional arrangement for the Mediterranean—either for the eastern part of it, or the western, or the whole area—has been put forward many times by various Mediterranean governments, including Spain. It first attracted widespread European attention, however, when French Premier Félix Gaillard proposed it again, in March 1958, in the form of a Western Mediterranean pact. His listing of Spain as a potential member was an early sign of the coming *rapprochement* between Paris and Madrid. Madrid gave Gaillard's proposal a warm welcome, pointing out, however, that it had made similar proposals some years earlier.[34]

---

[34] Same, March 10, 1958. For the historical background of Spain's post-World War II interest in Mediterranean problems, see Carlos Ibáñez de Ibero, Marqués de Mulhacén, *Política mediterránea de España, 1704-1951* (Madrid: Instituto de Estudios Africanos, 1952).

Nothing came of Gaillard's initiative, partly because of the political instability of the Fourth French Republic—Gaillard's government fell the next month—but also because of the coolness of some of the proposed members towards it and the storm of nationalism raging over the North African side of the Mediterranean. De Gaulle's revival of the idea in 1959 brought it back into the realm of practical politics under the auspices of a more stable French government, one that has been working hard for a peaceful settlement of the Algerian problem, the heart of the North African turbulence.

Except that the charter members were to be France, Italy, Spain, and Morocco, the precise details of De Gaulle's plan appear not to have been spelled out. In general, however, the pact would be a regional security arrangement, interlocking in membership with NATO. It would create a Western alliance with its major focus of interest centered in the crucial and vulnerable North African area, and it would satisfy Spain's desire to become a partner with at least some of her European neighbors. From the point of view of the United States, it would relieve it of much of the onus of its bilateral connection with Franco and would further its aim of improving Spain's relations with her neighbors, without forcing Franco's company on any who would prefer to do without it.

The Role of the United States

In the early and middle 1950's the United States' bilateral defense agreement with Spain was regarded as an alternative, not a prelude, to Spain's admission to NATO. It sought and concluded this direct agreement after the hopelessness of the proposal to admit her had been made clear in the first two meetings of the NATO Council. The rejection was so decisive, we are told, that the question has not been formally raised again, though it has been much discussed both in NATO circles and in public forums, especially since 1957. An upturn of interest was stimulated by a change of front on the part of influential leaders in the United States. As early as 1955 both the State Department and the House of Representatives took positions in favor of Spain's admission to NATO, but the Senate rallied to its support only in 1957. In February of that year the State Department made known its view in response to requests from the Senate Committee on Foreign Relations and the House Committee on Foreign Affairs.[35] It is, as so often, unclear just where either the initiative or the decisive impulse came from. In any case, the important thing is that the U.S. executive's advocacy of Spain's admission to NATO now had the explicit endorsement of both houses of Congress, thus making it for the first time a truly national policy.

The new policy was sent forth in virtually identical letters, of February 25, 1957, addressed by Assistant Secretary of State Robert C. Hill, on behalf of the Secretary of State, to the chairmen of the Senate and House committees.[36] The letters reaffirmed the Department's advocacy of Spain's admission. But since 1955 it had become clear that "a number of the member nations" were "not yet prepared to agree to Spanish membership in NATO." Consequently, the best course the United States could follow for the present was to work for improved relations between Spain and the NATO powers, "in order to tie Spain as closely as possible into plans for the regional defense of Western Europe, and thus

---

[35] *Expressing the Sense of the Congress that Efforts Should Be Made to Invite Spain to Membership in the North Atlantic Treaty Organization*, Report no. 206 of the House Committee on Foreign Affairs, 85th Cong., 1st sess. (Washington: GPO, 1957); and *Favoring Admission of Spain as a Member of the North Atlantic Treaty Organization*, Report no. 212 of the Senate Committee on Foreign Relations, 85th Cong., 1st sess. (Washington: GPO, 1957).

[36] House Committee Report no. 206, cited above, pp. 3-4, letter from Assistant Secretary of State Robert C. Hill, for the Secretary of State, dated February 25, 1957, replying to an inquiry from Chairman Thomas S. Gordon of the House Committee on Foreign Affairs, dated February 7, 1957. The Assistant Secretary's letter stated: "The United States favors Spanish membership in NATO. However, Spanish admission to NATO depends upon the willingness of all member nations to accept Spain as a member. This requires improvement in relations between Spain and certain NATO powers, which is primarily the responsibility of Spain and the other countries concerned." The letter is likewise contained in Report no. 212 of the Senate Committee, also cited in n. 35.

to create a climate favorable to eventual Spanish participation in NATO." The Department's statement made it clear that, while the executive favored the admission of Franco Spain to NATO, it did not believe this was urgently required or feasible for the present. Consequently it gave priority to improving Spain's relations with the European members of NATO, since only in this way could the opposition to her candidacy be overcome.

This policy has remained unaltered down to the present writing. Presumably, it goes far to explain the United States' support of the stabilization plan. Whatever efforts Washington may have made in this delicate matter, they have been rather modestly rewarded, for the principal improvement in Spain's relations with her European neighbors has taken place in the economic field. In the political field, her principal gains have consisted in the endorsement of her NATO candidacy by West Germany and France, but in both countries strong minority parties are still adamant in their opposition to it, and the significance of France's support is open to question because of De Gaulle's attitude towards NATO itself. Moreover, the opposition is also still strong in other European members of NATO. In short, the success of the new U.S. policy of 1957 has not been impressive.

Finally, there remains the question of Washington's attitude towards the projected Western Mediterranean pact. While the late John Foster Dulles is said to have looked on the idea with favor, particularly in the form proposed by Premier Gaillard in 1957, there is no evidence of a concerted effort to press for its realization, perhaps because one of its many prerequisites—an enduring settlement of the Algerian problem—has been lacking. In the general form in which it has been discussed, the idea of a Western Mediterranean pact has much to commend it. In addition to stabilizing the situation of the western half of North Africa, such an arrangement might provide an acceptable way out of the dilemma of Spain's relation to NATO and a useful means of strengthening her ties with several of her European neighbors.

Chapter IX

ARABS AND LATIN AMERICANS:
THE SPANISH BRIDGE

IF THE READER wonders why Spain's relations with two disparate areas—the Arab world and Latin America—are treated together, there is an easy answer: Spain herself has linked them through her ambition to be an essential "bridge," or mediator, between Europe and the Arabs and between Latin Americans and Europe.[1] Spain has important ties with both areas, and they in turn have some things in common with each other, above all, the fact that both are underdeveloped areas seething with social unrest and nationalism. Perhaps, then, the beams and planking exist for building a bridge, but can Spain erect one?

So far, she has not proved equal to the task. In both areas she has had some successes but greater failures. At present the odds are growing against her "bridge" policy. Nevertheless, the idea and the effort merit our attention, for the United States also has vital interests in both the Arab world and Latin America, and there has been a constant interplay between Spain's "bridge" policy and her relations with the United States.

Since World War II the Spanish government has given priority to the Arab world over Latin America. Its earlier and strong stress on Hispanidad was crippled as a political policy by the defeat of the Axis, whereas the postwar rise of

---

[1] For a study that links the two, see Rodolfo Benumeya, *Hispanidad y arabidad* (Madrid: Cultura Hispánica, 1952).

nationalism and independence in Arab lands has given a new focus to Spain's traditional interest in the Mediterranean area and Africa. According to a scholarly study published in 1952 under Spanish government auspices, "Spain's permanent policy, conditioned by its geographic position, has had to be both Atlantic and Mediterranean, but essentially the latter, and . . . hence African." [2] Spain's Arab policy centers on Morocco, traditionally of capital importance to its policies abroad and at home.

Morocco and Spain, 1470-1950

The population of Morocco, some ten million, is only one-third as large as Spain's, and in the past half-century France has controlled much more of it than Spain. Nevertheless, for both tangible and intangible reasons, Morocco has been of paramount importance to Spain.

To begin with Spain's security interests—the Strait of Gibraltar between Algeciras and Ceuta is only fourteen miles wide, one-third the distance between Calais and Dover. In consequence, Morocco has always been a useful corridor for trade and travel in time of peace, but a potential menace in the hands of an unfriendly power. The Spaniards have never forgotten that Morocco was the starting-point of the great invasion of 711, followed by a centuries-long subjection. Even after the Christian reconquest of Spain was completed in 1492, its southern coasts continued to be ravaged by Moroccan raiders over the next three centuries. Now that Morocco has regained its independence, and the spirit of nationalism and the instigations of communism are abroad in Arab lands, Morocco once more looms in Spanish minds as a potential threat. These anxieties have been increased by President Eisenhower's announcement, on his visit to Mo-

---

2 Carlos Ibáñez de Ibero, Marqués de Mulhacén, *Política mediterránea de España, 1704-1951* (Madrid: Instituto de Estudios Africanos, 1952), p. 21; the institute is a dependency of the government's Consejo Superior de Investigaciones Científicas.

rocco in December 1959, that the U.S. naval and air bases there will be completely evacuated by 1963.

But this is not all. An expansionist Morocco is a growing threat to Spain's remaining possessions on the Moroccan periphery: Ceuta, Melilla, and the other "places of sovereignty" in the north; to the west and south, Ifni, the Spanish Sahara, and Spanish Guinea. Here Spain's economic interests are strong, above all in the Sahara, where it has recently conceived high hopes of matching the fabulous resources of natural gas, oil, and minerals recently discovered in the French Sahara and Mauritania, as well as of benefiting by the French discoveries. All these dreams could be shattered by a new Moroccan attack like that of 1957 against Spanish Ifni, especially if it were aided by other Arab states or by new states of Black Africa.

The ties between Spain and Morocco are of long standing. In ancient times, lands on both sides of the Strait of Gibraltar were held successively by the Phoenician, Carthaginian, Roman, and Byzantine empires. In the early middle ages, the Visigothic kingdom in Spain held an outpost at Ceuta. Twenty-two years before the last Moorish kingdom of Granada was extinguished in 1492, Spain had already acquired African Melilla, which it has held uninterruptedly to this day. African Ceuta, taken from the Moors by Portugal in 1415, first came under the rule of a Spanish king in 1580, when Philip II ascended the Portuguese throne; since 1688 it has been a Spanish possession.

Her long-established ownership of these "African Gibraltars"—Melilla, Ceuta, and three smaller "places of sovereignty" (Peñón de Vélez, Alhucemas, and the Chafarinas Islands)—enabled Spain, though a minor power, to salvage something for herself when Morocco was dismembered by the great powers in the decade preceding World War I. Fortunately for Spain, the great powers principally concerned fell out over the division of the spoils. France, backed by Great Britain under their *entente cordiale* of 1904 in her designs on Morocco, drew Spain in as a junior partner,

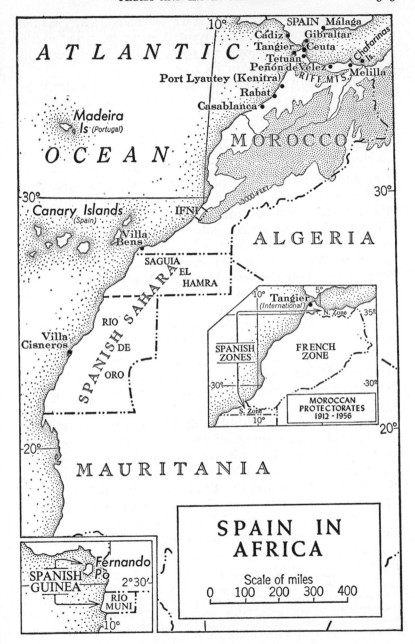

ATLANTIC

SPAIN Málaga
Cádiz Gibraltar
Tangier Ceuta
Tetuán
Peñón de Vele
Port Lyautey (Kenitra)
Rabat
Casablanca
Chafarinas Is.
RIFF MTS.
Melilla

Madeira
Is (Portugal)

OCEAN

MOROCCO

30°   30°
Canary Islands
(Spain)   IFNI
3000 FEET

Villa
Bens   ALGERIA

SAGUIA
EL
HAMRA

RIO

Villa   DE
Cisneros

ORO

SPANISH SAHARA

Tangier
(International)
10°   5°
N. Zone   35°
SPANISH   FRENCH
ZONES   ZONE
30°   30°
S. Zone
10°
MOROCCAN
PROTECTORATES
1912 - 1956
20°

20°

MAURITANIA

Fernando
Po
SPANISH   2°30'
GUINEA   RIO
MUNI
10°

SPAIN IN
AFRICA

Scale of miles
0   100   200   300   400

through a treaty of the same year.[3] Germany, who had her own ambitions in Morocco, resisted strongly, twice to the point of threatening war: in 1905, and then, despite the Algeciras settlement, again in 1909.

When the dust settled, Spain, too weak to be feared by the great powers or to line up with either side, was in possession of one of the two Moroccan protectorates.[4] Spain's smaller share was divided into two widely separated parts. Along the Atlantic coast facing Spain, she held a thin strip of northern Morocco, but its best port, Tangier, had been carved out as an international zone. Spain's Southern Protectorate, lying far to the south, beyond the French Protectorate, contained a great deal of sand and a handful of inhabitants. The French Protectorate embraced three-fourths of Morocco, as well as its principal cities.

At first glance Spain might seem to have gained little but the prestige of sharing the Moroccan booty with the great powers. In fact, northern Morocco has great strategic importance for potentially it dominates the approaches to the Strait of Gibraltar on both east and west. Moreover, the Spanish zone was not wholly devoid of natural resources. By dint of developing the nearby iron mines, Spain had built up Melilla from a poverty-stricken town of 3,000 in 1900 to a thriving modern city of 50,000 (90 per cent European) by 1930.

Morocco became a symbol of Spanish prestige, partly as a result of this long train of events, but mainly because of its identification with the politically powerful Spanish military. For the army, Morocco filled, as we have noted, the gap left by the loss of Cuba and the Philippines. Its restless people, especially the hill tribesmen of the Riff, provided steady employment for Spain's armed forces. In Morocco the officer class found its best opportunities for field experience and promotion (illustrated by General Franco's own career) and

---

[3] José María Campoamor, *La actitud de España ante la cuestión de Marruecos (1900-1904)* (Madrid: Instituto de Estudios Africanos, 1951).

[4] Tomás García Figueras, *La zona española del protectorado de Marruecos* (Madrid: Instituto de Estudios Africanos, 1955). Both protectorates were established in 1912, first France's, covering the whole country, by a treaty with Morocco, and then Spain's, by a treaty with France.

also for more peaceful pursuits in many posts from that of
high commissioner on down.

Though Spanish military operations sometimes failed, the
hard-won victories made them a greater source of pride than
if they had been uniformly successful. The best illustration
is the war of the Riff, waged from 1921 to 1926 against formidable forces skillfully led by Abd-el-Krim. The war began
disastrously for Spain, with a crushing defeat at Anual and
the massacre of four-fifths of a Spanish army of some 20,000
men. Within Spain the shock of this disaster provoked bitter
recriminations between civilians and military, and against
the meddlesome monarch, Alfonso XIII. One immediate
result was the establishment of the dictatorship of Primo de
Rivera in 1923 and the erosion of monarchy, which led to
its almost casual overthrow in 1931.

In the meantime, Primo handled the Moroccan crisis
with skill to salvage an apparently hopeless situation. The
achievement was all the greater because his heart was not in
it. Unlike most of his fellow officers, he was in favor of liquidating the whole Moroccan venture, and he even proposed
exchanging Ceuta for Gibraltar, if Britain would agree. But
the army would have none of this scuttle-and-run policy, for
its pride and prestige were too deeply involved in Morocco.
Through restoring cooperation with France and shifting to a
vigorous offensive, he brought about the final defeat of
Abd-el-Krim in 1926, and then by his program of reforms
created a new spirit of accommodation between Spaniards
and Moroccans. This achievement, maintained without serious disturbance for a quarter of a century, is the principal
source of whatever plausibility attaches to Franco's bridge-
to-Islam policy.[5]

The main fruits of Primo's success were reaped by the
Spanish army.[6] By 1936, only ten years after the elimination
of Abd-el-Krim, Franco and his fellow conspirators were so

---

5 Even Salvador de Madariaga, who seldom has a good word to say for
any dictator, describes Primo de Rivera's Moroccan policy as a "brilliant success"; *Spain: A Modern History* (New York: Praeger, 1958), p. 351.

6 For information on this point and on Republican plans for reform in
Morocco, see Manuel Azaña, *Una política (1930-1932)* (Madrid: Espasa-Calpe,
1932), pp. 379-392.

confident of the army's control of Morocco that they launched their assault on the republic from Moroccan bases and employed Moorish contingents in Spain, where they helped him destroy the republic. As a mark of gratitude and trust, Franco kept a bodyguard of Moors with him for the next twenty years. This was bridging the Islamic-Christian gap with a vengeance.

Against this background it is easy to understand why, within Spain's strongest power group—the armed forces— sentiment as well as prestige was by mid-century deeply engaged in the Moroccan venture. Since 1955, when circumstances forced Spain to abandon its Moroccan protectorate with unseemly haste, this engagement has become a serious liability to Franco. His prestige in Spain suffered the worst shock ever administered to it, a shock that was fraught with the greatest potential danger, among the military, whose sentiments and self-interest had suffered grievous injury.

Morocco and the Bridge to Islam

Franco's policy of making Spain the interpreter of the West to Islam has sometimes been described as an adjunct to his basic policy of seeking an alliance with the United States. According to this view, the idea of Spain's special mission in the Arab world was to be exploited as a means of enhancing Spain's value to the West, thus strengthening Franco's bargaining position whenever the United States came to him in quest of bases, as he was sure it would. Chronology speaks in favor of this view. Franco's first public bid for a military association with the United States was made in July 1947. The bridge-to-Islam policy was first announced by Foreign Minister Martín Artajo in a speech of December 12, 1950, and the first major effort to launch it was Artajo's tour of the Near East in April 1952, in the midst of the long negotiations between Spain and the United States over bases.

The principal lesson Artajo brought back from his mission was a greater awareness of the crucial importance of

Morocco in Spain's bridge-to-Islam policy. In her effort to profit by this lesson Spain followed a course that opened a new and dangerous phase of antagonism with her old rival in North Africa, France. During his tour of Egypt and other Arab countries the Foreign Minister made warm professions of Spain's friendship for their peoples and underlined them by omitting from his itinerary Israel, which Spain had not and has not recognized. At the same time, true to his government's "bridge" role, he proffered its good offices for the settlement of the current dispute between Great Britain and Egypt and for the inclusion of the Arab League in the Western defensive system (of which, incidentally, Spain herself was not yet a part). The Arab response was rather chilling. The Secretary of the Arab League commented that Spain's attitude towards the Arab world would be judged by her behavior towards Morocco. So far Spain had maintained her Moroccan protectorate intact, without making any concessions to rising Moroccan nationalism.

Two new developments in French North Africa soon offered Spain what seemed a golden opportunity to profit by this lesson in how to win Arab friends and also to get back at France for past injuries. In 1953, without consulting Madrid, the French government ousted an uncooperative Moroccan Sultan, replacing him with one more to its liking, in the face of growing unrest and turbulence. In late 1954, Algerian nationalist forces began a long and bloody fight against France in the name of an independent Algeria.

Spain grasped eagerly at these opportunities to court the Arabs by opposing France. Franco's government offered the ousted Sultan asylum in the Spanish zone, continued to recognize his authority there, and ignored the French puppet who had replaced him at Rabat. When France backtracked and restored Sultan Mohammed V in 1955, Madrid claimed its full share of the credit for his restoration. Likewise, during the first three years of the fighting in Algeria, Spanish Morocco served the insurrectionists as a corridor for the shipment of arms and the transit of reinforcements, and as a base of communications. The Spanish government was undeterred by the fact that its new course ran counter to the interests of numerous Spanish elements in Algeria.[7] In any case Franco was playing for higher stakes.

He did not win them. Whether he could ever have won is doubtful. True, he made some fleeting gains, as when, in a ceremony at Tetuán (January 21, 1954), the Spanish High Commissioner received a declaration in which Moroccan notables of the Spanish zone condemned France and endorsed Spain's policy.[8] At any rate, France defeated Franco at his own game. Reversing its course, in December 1955 it publicly committed itself to recognize Morocco's independence. As was only natural, this action was taken without advance notice to Madrid.

Franco was caught far off base. On November 30, 1955, just a few days before the momentous announcement in Paris, he had issued a statement of his own to the effect that, while Morocco must, of course, become independent some day, that day still lay in the indefinite future. "It would be dangerous," he warned, "to assume that the Moroccans are capable of keeping peace and order in their country." Only two weeks later, on December 13, the pressure of the French coup forced him to reverse himself and commit Spain to the immediate independence of Morocco.

Even after this rout Spain resorted to delaying tactics, attempting to prescribe certain special arrangements in her former zone. All her efforts were in vain. At a tripartite conference of France, Spain, and the Sultan, the independence of Morocco was formally proclaimed on March 2, 1956, and on April 7 an agreement for the transfer of authority in the

---

[7] Some estimates place the Spanish proportion in the total *colon* population of about one million at between 40 and 20 per cent. A prominent leader of the *colon* uprising of January 1960 bore the name of Ortiz. Most of the Spaniards in Algeria have been assimilated by the French community; some are Republican refugees and presumably still anti-Franco.

[8] Vicente Girbau, "The Foreign Policy of Franco Spain (II)," *Ibérica*, October 15, 1959, p. 11; the second of a series of three articles. An editorial note describes the author as "formerly an official in the Spanish Ministry of Foreign Affairs, [who] went into exile last year [1958] to escape police persecution," and as one of the foremost younger leaders of the democratic opposition; same, September 15, 1959, p. 4.

Spanish zone was signed in Madrid by Franco and the Sultan. The break was not immediate or clean-cut. As late as early 1959 there were still 60,000 Spanish and 25,000 French troops in Morocco. The essential fact remained that Morocco had won, with Franco's assent and without striking a blow, the independence for which he had declared it unfit only four months earlier. Moreover, Morocco emerged with a regime quite unlike his, for it became a kingdom with a king, a somewhat representative assembly, and competing political parties. Finally, Spain had also failed to obtain a firm definition of its boundaries with Morocco.

The fiasco could hardly have been more complete. The reverse had been suffered in Spain's chosen field of Arab relations and at the hands of her rival, France, of whose ineptitude in Moroccan affairs she had been unsparingly critical, especially over the past two years. All that Spain salvaged was her "places of sovereignty"—primarily, Ceuta and Melilla in the north, and Ifni on the west coast—and a tenuous hold on her barren Southern Protectorate. Her failure to secure a clear definition of the new boundaries was soon to make trouble for her as Moroccan nationalism turned to territorial expansion.

Yet it seems excessive to criticize Franco, as some have, for not forestalling France by sponsoring Morocco's immediate independence.[9] This would have been a contradiction to the principles on which his own regime is based. How could he affirm the Moroccans' capacity to govern themselves while denying that of his own people? At times a resolute statesman can and does ignore such inconsistencies with impunity, but Morocco's proximity and its long-standing ties with Spain would have made the contradiction too glaring. When he finally acted, Franco could at least plead that he was doing so under *force majeure*.

In another Arab-Western conflict, the Suez Canal crisis of 1956, Franco was again a prisoner of his own ambitions. Out of it, Spain could chalk up one political gain. Her participa-

---

[9] For example, the article by Vicente Girbau, cited, pp. 10-11.

tion in the London conference on Suez marked the first time
since 1936 when she had taken part in a top-flight international conference.[10]

Spain's attitude towards the Suez crisis passed through two
stages, only to wind up in a third.[11] At first, Spanish sympathies, as reflected in the controlled press, were all on the
side of Nasser, whom, in line with her pro-Arab policy,
Spain had been courting for the past two years, while quarreling with France over Morocco, grumbling as usual against
Britain over Gibraltar, and deploring the very existence of
Israel. This stage soon came to an end. As the spreading crisis
raised the specter of Soviet penetration of Egypt and the
Arab world, Spain shifted to a more neutral stand, maintaining it down to the London conference, where Artajo tried
once more to play the role of mediator. But the "bridge"
collapsed under the weight of the bases agreement with the
United States. In any case, Secretary Dulles, who believed
that "he who is not with us is against us," gave Artajo's
neutralism short shrift.

As soon as the London conference was over, Artajo
stopped off in Paris to begin a *rapprochement* with France,
as part of a new course designed to tighten Spain's bonds
with Western Europe. Morocco was one of the main subjects
of discussion between him and the French Foreign Minister,
Christian Pineau.[12] He is reported to have urged that Morocco should henceforth be a bond of union between France
and Spain, which should cooperate to keep it from falling
under the influence of "international communism." The
new orientation has been steadily strengthened since Suez,
though under a new foreign minister more definitely associated with "Europeanism," Fernando María de Castiella.

---

10 Spain had taken part in the International Civil Aviation Conference
at Chicago in 1944, a technical meeting.

11 *La Documentation Française, Chroniques Etrangères* (Paris), no. 175,
September 25, 1956, "Espagne," especially pp. 8-13, "L'Espagne et l'affaire de
Suez."

12 Same, pp. 14-15.

Expansionist Morocco, the Maghreb, and Black Africa

The course of events in Morocco and more generally in North Africa since the establishment of Moroccan independence has tended to deepen Spain's *rapprochement* with Western Europe. Until the latter part of 1957, it is true, this underlying trend was obscured by Spain's very human effort to picture her Moroccan fiasco as a success. Upon the declaration of Morocco's independence, the Spanish authorities attempted to coax the notables of their zone into making a public acknowledgment of gratitude to Spain for giving them their freedom. They failed, but for the next two and a half years Madrid tirelessly repeated its boasts of maintaining excellent relations with independent Morocco and doing a much better job in this than France.[13] Of course, Spain, unlike France, was not enmeshed in the never-ending problem of Algeria or in the disputes over the U.S. bases in Morocco. What use will be made of the bases by Morocco disturbs Spain, but that is a question for the future. Until it is settled the United States and France, not Spain, will be the nationalists' main target.

On the other hand Spain has been the chief sufferer from the Moroccan urge for territorial expansion. Her west-coast enclave of Ifni was invaded on November 23, 1957, by an irregular Moroccan force of some 8,000 men, styled "the Army of Liberation," ostensibly in support of a revolt by Ifni tribesmen. Ostensibly also, the attack had not been authorized either by King Mohammed V, in the United States at the time, or by the regent, Crown Prince Moulay Hassan. In any case, the true purpose of the attack seemed clear when the Crown Prince offered to use his influence to end the "revolt" if Spain would hand over its Southern Protectorate to Morocco.[14]

---

13 For a brief treatment of French policy, see Edgar S. Furniss, Jr., *France, Troubled Ally: De Gaulle's Heritage and Prospects* (New York: Harper, for the Council on Foreign Relations, 1960), pp. 229-231.

14 *The New York Times*, December 5, 1957. King Mohammed blamed Madrid for the Ifni trouble on the ground that it had kept "a part of our national territory," presumably the Southern Protectorate, and had "aban-

The choice of Spain's Southern Protectorate as a target was quite understandable, for it is much larger and more strategically located, and Morocco had a clear title. A sandy waste of some 740 square miles, the Ifni enclave is completely hemmed in by Morocco except for some forty miles of coastline.[15] Acquired by Spain in 1860, Ifni bears no relation to the post-1904 protectorate, and Morocco cannot claim it on the ground of Spain's having surrendered its protectorate in 1956. The Southern Protectorate, on the other hand, could be claimed on that ground, and Spain had retained it in 1956 on the argument that the kingdom of Morocco was unable to maintain order there. This in effect conceded that the territory belonged to Morocco and must be turned over to it sooner or later. Although the Southern Protectorate is likewise a sandy waste, its area (10,000 square miles) is far larger, and it has the advantage of adjoining the Spanish Sahara, with its hopeful prospects for oil. Some day oil may be discovered in the Southern Protectorate, and meanwhile it could serve as a base for expelling Spain from its Saharan colony. Moroccan designs on the Spanish Sahara, and on most of French Mauritania as well, were made fairly clear early in 1958, when Mohammed V and other political leaders hinted broadly that their country's territorial rights extended as far south as the Senegal River.[16]

Spanish reinforcements quickly assured the safety of Ifni, but Madrid soon gave in on the main point, the surrender of the Southern Protectorate. In return it asked Morocco to agree on a definition of their common boundaries and to promise to respect the adjoining Spanish possessions; so far as can be ascertained, it failed to gain either point. The relinquishment of the Southern Protectorate, which was due partly to the weakness of its case and the expense of defend-

doned a method of peaceful solution" of the question; same, December 10, 1957.

15 Hermenegildo Tabernero Chacabo, "Ifni, la obra de España," *Ejército* (Madrid), March 1958, pp. 3-10. The author, an infantry colonel, was at the time attached to the office of African affairs (Dirección General de Plazas y Provincias Africanas).

16 *The New York Times,* March 21, 1958.

ing a remote desert area, is said to have been encouraged by the United States so that in this instance it was Washington that served as a "bridge" between Christianity and Islam.

Yet even this concession did not restore Spain's good relations with Morocco, for the ceremony of transfer brought on a new crisis. On April 1, 1958, Foreign Minister Castiella notified Rabat that Spain was ready to make the transfer. When the Crown Prince, on his way to accept it, tried to take the most convenient road, which ran through Spanish Sahara, he was turned back at the border on the ground of his not having obtained permission for his armed escort, numbering about 1,000 men, to accompany him through Spanish territory.[17] On the home front, this incident lent substance to rumors that the Spanish army in North Africa was beginning to take a critical and independent attitude towards the civilian government at Madrid, not unlike that of the French army in Algeria towards Paris. In any event, the incident brought Spain's relations with Morocco back to the boiling-point, and Moroccan extremists kept the borderlands in a ferment for several months. Here the recent improvement in Spain's relations with France paid off, for French troops cooperated in a police action that restored relative peace and security by the end of the year. It recalled, on a smaller scale, their joint action against Abd-el-Krim in the 1920's.

The *rapprochement* between Spain and France was both deeper and narrower than the casual observer might believe. In both countries it had its roots in national needs, and in France it was not the work of any one party; the Fourth Republic had begun it and De Gaulle carried it on. Its limited scope was brought out by Spain's refusal, in September 1959, to join an international consortium headed by France in exploiting the rich iron ore reserves of French Mauritania. The consortium, Mauritanian Iron Mines Company, or MIFERMA, included British, West German, and Italian interests, but France controlled it with 55 per cent of the stock,

---

17 Same, April 13, 1958.

nearly half owned by the government. A railway outlet to the Atlantic through Spanish West Africa was needed, and in return for permission to build it Spain was offered a participation of between 5 and 8 per cent in the consortium. After long haggling, Spain declined. Concrete points of disagreement included the location of the coastal terminus (Spain wanted it built at her own Villa Cisneros, whereas France and the consortium insisted upon French-owned Port Etienne); and the percentage of Spain's share. But Benjamin Welles of the *Times* was probably right in suggesting that more important than specific disagreements was the still vigorous sense of rivalry between Spain and France in Africa.[18]

The subsidence of friction on the Moroccan-Spanish frontier was accompanied by a clearing of the atmosphere between Rabat and Madrid. Apparently troubles at home contributed greatly to pacifying both sides. In Spain's case they were related mainly to the economic crisis of 1959; in Morocco's, they were partly economic but still more political. Rabat's decision, in December 1958, to hold to the old rate of the franc after France devalued it from about 420 to 494 to the dollar was a severe shock to its precarious economy. And Morocco's political stability was shaken by an uprising that began in the ever-restive Riff, whence it spread quickly to the center and south, and by the near-chaos created by bitter quarreling between and within the two principal parties.

To make matters still worse, Spain was suspected of stirring up the Riff tribesmen, for the purpose either of restoring the Protectorate, or else taking revenge for the attack on Ifni. Proof was seen in the granting of refuge to several hundred defeated tribesmen, first in Ceuta and Melilla, then at Málaga. However, when the Spanish government cited the right of asylum, which Morocco had formally recognized,[19] the matter was dropped. There may well have been complicity on the part of individual Spanish officers, but

---

18 Same, September 27, 1959.
19 *Le Figaro* (Paris), January 24, 1959.

none has been proved on the part of the government. On the contrary, by early 1959 Franco had reverted to his earlier policy, upset by the Ifni episode, of promoting friendly cooperation with Morocco so long as it had a government he could live with. One such government was the new cabinet headed by Sid Abdallah Ibrahim, a moderate, who visited Madrid in April 1959.

Spain could also not avoid being concerned over foreign influences within Morocco. Whether or not the Algerian Front de la Libération Nationale had had a hand in the tribal effervescence, Spaniards regarded it as a powerful force in Moroccan politics; and there was unquestionably growing Berber resentment against the dominant Istiqlal.[20] Communist agents, usually Arabs, were also active, as were agents from other Arab states. The largest group of persons from Western countries were the military personnel of Spain, France, and the United States, who numbered about 100,000 in early 1959.

Franco's government has often been reminded that Morocco is now playing an active international role in relation to Black Africa south of the Sahara, as well as to the Maghreb and the Arab League. In March 1959, Mohammed V publicly coupled Black Africa and the Maghreb in a way that cannot have been very pleasing to Spain, or, for that matter, to France. At a reception for a mission from the new republic of Guinea, he placed special stress on the ties between Black Africa and North Africa. Discussing the movement for the liberation and unification of Africa, he said: "This unification will promote close cooperation between Black Africa and the Arab Maghreb in political, economic, and cultural fields. The Sahara has never been an obstacle between Morocco and Black Africa. . . . The Sahara is a highway, not a barrier." This brought him to his climax: "The riches of the Sahara are the property of the peoples who border on it." This sounded a clear warning to Spain and France, especially since the Moslem population south of the

---

20 Lorna Hahn, *North Africa, Nationalism to Nationhood* (Washington: Public Affairs Press, 1960), p. 194, on Berber resentment.

Sahara is estimated at over forty million.[21] In conclusion, however, the King qualified this claim by adding that of course the riches of the Sahara could be developed with the cooperation of third parties.[22]

Morocco Moderates Its Course: United States and Spain Evacuate

This was perhaps music of the future. Immediately, however, the advent to responsibility of the moderate Ibrahim cabinet, in place of the Balafrej one, was followed by a renewed cordiality in Morocco's relations with Spain. Apparently the new Foreign Minister exerted a calming influence at the meeting of the Political Committee of the Arab League, held at Beirut in early April 1959.[23] His visit, immediately thereafter, to Madrid was marked by the establishment of a permanent mixed commission of the two countries to study any problems existing between them and propose solutions.[24] A number of comments on this visit stressed the importance of Moroccan-Spanish friendship for the entire Maghreb.[25] On the other hand, the revived cordiality between Madrid and Rabat did not imply any slackening in Morocco's role in affairs of the Arab world, for it was taking part at the same time in an Arab conference at Cairo on oil, and the Crown Prince was about to pay an official visit there. Morocco has since shown increasing interest and activity in Arab affairs, marked by the meeting of the Arab League at Casablanca later in 1959 and the visit of the King to the Middle East in 1960; but these growing ties could hardly be said to have affected Spain's interests, except perhaps negatively in creating a firmer general Arab backing for demands which Morocco might later make on Spain.

---

21 Vernon McKay, "External Political Pressures on Africa Today," American Assembly, Columbia University, *The United States and Africa* (New York: Author, 1958), p. 73.

22 *Arriba* (Madrid), March 7, 1959; dispatch from Tangier.

23 Same, April 15, 1959, citing *At Tahrir.*

24 *ABC* (Madrid), April 16, 1959.

25 Same; dispatch from Tangier.

Foreign Minister Ibrahim's visit to Madrid was followed by an accelerated withdrawal of Spain's military forces from Morocco. From a peak in early 1959 of 60,000, these had been reduced by mid-September to about 11,000.[26] The matter was not easily brought to the point of final settlement, partly because Spain was not prepared publicly to accept the principle of total evacuation according to a fixed schedule. But, after the new Moroccan government headed by the King himself as premier came to power in May 1960, the Spanish withdrawal did proceed quietly on Madrid's own initiative. France was not happy about the rapid evacuation of Spain's forces, for it increased the pressure on her to withdraw, or at least greatly reduce, her own military forces, which still numbered about 25,000 men—a strength which she wished to retain there until the conflict in Algeria was terminated. On the other hand, Spain's action was in line with the U.S. policy of gradually evacuating its Moroccan complex of air and naval bases.

For Franco, the United States' decision was a decidedly mixed blessing. It had the great advantage of increasing his bargaining power by enhancing the value of the Spanish bases to the United States; the Moroccan air bases had represented about one-half the strength of the Strategic Air Command's Sixteenth Air Force, and now only the Spanish half would remain available to it. Similarly, the loss of the United States' naval installations at Port Lyautey (renamed Kenitra) and elsewhere in Morocco would increase its dependence on its naval installations in Spain. On the other hand, the prospect that an unfriendly Moroccan regime might use these bases against Spain, especially against Ceuta, Melilla, and the Spanish Sahara, was a disturbing one. Franco accordingly redoubled his efforts to reach a good understanding with Morocco, in furtherance of the double purpose of protecting Spanish interests there and on its periphery, while simultaneously maintaining Spain's role as bridge between the Arab world and the West.

---

26 *The New York Times,* September 13, 1959.

Why Spain's Bridge Role?

The reasoning behind Spain's ambition to play a "bridge" role is perfectly clear. But can it succeed? And has it been worth the effort? Spain can not hope to play a military role of any significance in the Arab world. Aside from an occasional deal, such as the exchange of Spanish rice for Egyptian cotton, her economic relations with the Arab states have been tenuous. She might perhaps gain some Arab votes in the United Nations, but this is peripheral to the regime's basic interests—its alliance with the United States and its *rapprochement* with France. Nor is the "bridge" role any longer a useful counter in its relations with the United States.

One plausible explanation is that after the Suez crisis Franco, deeply disturbed over Communist penetration of the Arab world, hoped to help stem the tide by proving to the Arabs that there is still a bridge between their world and the West and that Spain is that bridge. A second explanation is that the "bridge" gambit represents a bid for popularity and prestige within Spain. Like the peoples of certain other once imperial countries, the Spaniards do not easily reconcile themselves to the thought that ancient grandeur and glory are gone, never to return. That they would return was an article of faith for the Franco regime in its early years.[27] To fill the vacuum of prestige Spanish myth-makers have cast Franco as the peerless prophet who from the earliest days of World War II had foretold the coming division

---

[27] Literary expressions of the imperialist idea in the Franco period abound. A fair sample, vintage 1943, is the following, which would lose much in translation: "*Fuera torpeza insigne, y más en este 1943 hirviente, en que todo pueblo ha de sentirse cazador de horizontes, propugnar una política puramente espiritualista. El Imperio entraña fines y medios terrenales.*" This occurs in the chapter headed "Nuestro imperio" in José Corts Grau, *Motivos de la España eterna* (Madrid: Instituto de Estudios Políticos, 1946), p. 45. A few other works of this type are Ricardo del Arco y Garay, *Grandeza y destino de España* (Madrid: Esceliser, 1942), and *La idea de imperio en la política y la literatura española* (Madrid: Espasa-Calpe, 1944); Eleuterio Elorduy, *La idea de imperio en el pensamiento español y de otros pueblos* (Madrid: Espasa-Calpe, 1944); Fernando María de Castiella and José María de Areilza, *Reivindicaciones de España* (Madrid: Instituto de Estudios Políticos, 1941).

of the world between Communists and anti-Communists; by an extension of this myth, he has been pictured as employing his gifts of serenity, second sight, and racial aptitude to bridge the gap of comprehension between the Arab world and the West.

Illustrations are provided by Radio Madrid's round-up of Spanish press comments on Franco's appraisal of the crisis of July 1958 over Lebanon and Jordan. Published as an interview in *Ya*, Franco's estimate was sharply critical of the "colonialist" West, whose course "reflected more mistakes than tact," though of course his chief target was, as always, the Soviet Union. *Madrid* objected to "outworn colonialism," which explains the paradox that "Soviet Russia, the real threat to the independence of those nations within reach of its claws, attracts these nations because of the lack of understanding on the part of the West." [28]

Mediterranean and Turkish Pacts

Another and broader expression of Spain's interest in Mediterranean affairs is the idea, discussed above, of a regional pact for the area. The Spanish government first expressed the idea strongly in the early 1950's, partly as an extension of its "bridge" policy, partly as an alternative to membership in an inhospitable NATO. Since then Spain's interest in the pact has alternately waxed and waned. Speculation about this idea was stimulated, whether intentionally or not, in April 1959, when the new agreement with Morocco was followed by a visit to Madrid by Adnan Menderes, Prime Minister of Turkey.

The controlled Spanish press greeted Turkey as the "heir of Byzantium" in the defense of the West against the Slavs and praised it for the courage and firmness with which it plays its role of "sentinel." It stressed the common interest of Spain and Turkey in the Mediterranean, where each is

---

28 Monitored broadcast, July 24, 1958.

the guardian of an important strait, and "the intensity and sincerity of their anti-Communist sentiments." [29]

Public opinion in Spain and abroad attached more significance to the Menderes mission than was justified by the rather routine terms of the published treaty of friendship to which it led (April 16, 1959).[30] Some Paris newspapers saw Spain becoming a "Mediterranean meeting ground," and *Le Monde* reported from Athens that Greece might be invited to cooperate with Turkey, Spain, and Morocco in "a secret plan which would be a solution [of the problem] of the Mediterranean Pact." [31]

In the midst of these negotiations I had an opportunity to discuss with General Franco both the situation in North Africa and the related question of the projected Mediterranean pact.[32]

In reply to a question about the prospects for Spain's relations with Morocco, General Franco said that they were bound to be difficult for some time to come: first, because Morocco was suffering from the excess of nationalism common to all newly independent countries today; and second, because King Mohammed V had made the double mistake of permitting communism and the political-party system to take root in his country. Moreover, there is a perpetual source of trouble of many kinds in the tribes of the Riff, where the King's writ does not run. Nevertheless, the King now realized that the precarious internal situation in his country made Spain's friendship important to him. Fortunately, the stabilization of Morocco's internal situation no longer depended upon the pacification of Algeria; there were only two possible ways of settling the Algerian problem, both of which would be extremely difficult: either integration with France or complete independence. As for the proposed unification of the Maghreb, that was a dream which

---

[29] *Arriba* (Madrid), April 15, 1959.

[30] *ABC* (Madrid), April 17, 1959.

[31] Same.

[32] The conversation, technically an audience, was held on April 15, 1959, in General Franco's office *(despacho)* in the Pardo Palace.

would certainly not be realized in the visible future, if only because Morocco and Tunisia knew that in any such union they would be dominated by Algeria, which holds the central position and is much stronger.

To my question, "What is your present attitude towards the establishment of a multilateral association or regional group along the lines of the projected Western Mediterranean pact which was so much discussed about two years ago?" Franco answered without hesitation or qualification that he was opposed to any such arrangement. North Africa, whose participation is essential to such an arrangement, could not be brought into it. Morocco once favored it, but no longer does, and the Algerian problem, which must be settled first, was still wide open. Also, no such pact was needed by Spain, which was finding its bilateral relations with France, Italy, and the other Mediterranean powers satisfactory and adequate. Finally, the defense of the Western Mediterranean was, he felt, already sufficiently provided for by NATO and by Spain's agreements with the United States. Lack of time prevented a similar exploration of the Eastern Mediterranean aspects of the question, but it seems reasonable to believe that Franco would have been even more unwilling to bind Spain to a pact with that comparatively remote region than for its own immediate area.

As regards Morocco, there seems to be sufficient ground for Franco's cautiously sanguine views. His negative attitude towards a Mediterranean pact may have been due to a foreknowledge that France and West Germany were about to come out in favor of Spain's admission to NATO, as they did only a fortnight later; for Spain, membership in a Mediterranean pact has always been in some measure a substitute for membership in NATO. Continued indifference to it may, in any case, be nourished both by the general strengthening of Spain's international position since 1958, and by the prospect that, in any Mediterranean pact worthy of the name, Spain's freedom of action would be seriously limited by the divergent policies and interests of her associates.

This limitation would be felt most of all in the pursuit of

Spain's "bridge" policy, which enables her government to gain prestige at home without running serious risks abroad, through the simple device of making grand gestures that involve no commitments. As a lone-hand policy, it appeals to many Spaniards, both supporters and opponents of the regime, who deplore Franco's abandonment of Spain's traditional isolationism. And while it is particularly pertinent to Spain's relations with Morocco, their fluctuations do not weaken the regime's attachment to it. Late in 1959, for example, domestic tensions and Communist-bloc intrigues in Morocco created in high Spanish circles the fear that "another Korea" might be in the making across the strait. Nevertheless, the mouthpiece of the still influential Martín Artajo chose this time to remind its readers: "We may not be a great military or economic power, but no one can discount our mission as a bridge between Europe and Africa and Latin America." [33] And in his regular end-of-the-year message to the Spanish people, General Franco paid his customary tribute to the "bridge" policy.

Spain and Latin America: Neo-Hispanidad

Our examination of the Latin American end of Spain's hypothetical bridge between it and the West would be a lengthy one if cultural and social influences formed the central theme of this book. Instead, because its focus on Spain's quasi-alliance with the United States gives a high priority to the theme of political, military, and economic relations, what needs to be said about the Spanish bridge to Latin America can be said briefly. Latin America played an important role throughout the United Nations' proceedings about Spain from 1945 to 1955; since then it has continued to be a significant factor in the relations of the United States with Spain; and today it shows signs of becoming a seriously adverse factor in them.

Purged by Foreign Minister Artajo of its pro-Axis and

---

[33] *Ya* (Madrid), quoted in *The New York Times*, November 15, 1959.

Yankeephobe connotations, since 1946 Hispanidad has ostensibly been aimed not at hegemony over other Hispanic nations, but at cooperation with them. As defined by the director of the Instituto de Cultura Hispánica, its objective is the formation of the Hispanic nations as a cultural, economic, and spiritual bloc. In the economic field, he explained, it postulates a common market; in the spiritual field, a campaign to strengthen the moral fiber of Latin America by sending Spanish priests there, in accordance with the wishes of the Pope and the plan already set on foot by the society known as Obra de Cooperación Sacerdotal Hispanoamericana.[34] Two months later in accordance with this plan, an agreement was concluded with the Dominican Republic under which members of the Spanish clergy were to help establish model communities on the frontier between that country and Haiti. Some observers saw in this an effort on Trujillo's part to strengthen his relations with the Catholic Church, lest its disapproval undermine his regime as it had those of Perón and other dictators.

Other official statements make it clear that Hispanidad, though greatly changed, still has a political purpose. A recent decree declares that "the Hispanic community of nations has the ineluctable duty of interpreting Hispanidad as a system of principles and norms destined to the better defense of Christian civilization and to the ordering of international life in the service of peace."[35] Later the same year, on Columbus Day (now officially styled "Hispanidad Day," formerly "Day of the [Spanish] Race"), in a speech at the Instituto de Cultura Hispánica, Foreign Minister Castiella stressed the common economic interest of Spain and Latin America because of their underdeveloped economies and the danger of Communist penetration of Latin America; in the latter connection he hinted broadly that Spain could render the United States important aid in combatting communism in Latin America.

---

[34] Speech of Blas Piñero, January 27, 1958, entitled "The Mystique and Policy of Hispanidad."

[35] *Boletín Oficial* (Madrid), February 8, 1958; decree of January 10, 1958.

In general, Hispanidad enjoys much greater vitality in Spain than in Latin America. As the mother country of eighteen of the twenty Latin American nations, Spain enjoys special advantages, arising from the community of language, literature, and traditions. On the other hand, she is handicapped both by a remnant of anti-Spanish feeling in her former colonies and by the recent rise of *indigenismo,* a blend of Indianism and nativism, generally xenophobe but containing a special bias against Spain. Recently this bias has been strengthened by the trend against dictatorship in Latin America.

The United Nations Ban

Latin America's most important actions since 1945 in relation to Franco Spain were taken in the United Nations and principally concerned two questions: the ostracism of Spain, and the independence of Morocco. The exclusion of Spain had not been formally decided when the founding conference met in April 1945 to adopt a United Nations Charter. The decision was taken at San Francisco and the initiative came from a Latin American, Luis Quintanilla. On his motion, the conference unanimously adopted a resolution that closed the door of the United Nations to Franco Spain by declaring that "states whose regimes have been established with the help of military forces belonging to the countries which have waged war against the United Nations" could not be regarded as meeting the membership requirement of "peace-loving."

Significantly, Quintanilla represented Mexico, which has always been in the forefront of Latin American hostility to Franco's regime. During the Civil War, Mexico had openly aided the Republican side. After the war it became the seat of the Republican government-in-exile and the principal American haven for Republican refugees. Today it is the only Latin American country that has never recognized Franco's government. The basic source of its unwavering antagonism lies in Mexico's unique role as the first country in Latin America to be transformed by a thoroughgoing popular revolution of a type that is today spreading to other countries in that area.

The adoption of the Quintanilla resolution was the first of a series of anti-Franco actions taken by the United Nations with Latin American support during its first five years, only to be reversed in the next five, again with Latin American support. As a leading authority has said, the Spanish question was "one of the most dramatic to come before the United Nations" in that decade. None was "closer to the hearts of the Latin Americans." And their changes of position on it were exceptionally significant for the way in which it was handled and finally settled.[36]

After Spain had been denied membership by the San Francisco conference, the Spanish question next came up in the meetings of the Security Council and General Assembly in 1946, in the form of proposals to take some kind of positive action against the Franco regime. The solid front of Latin America against Franco broke down over this issue. A majority of the Latin American governments again took the anti-Franco side. For many in Latin America, as elsewhere, it was still urgent to eradicate the last vestiges of Nazi-Fascism, of which Franco Spain, they believed, was one. Some of the Latin American spokesmen went so far as to reject the very principle of nonintervention. In a curious alignment within the Security Council, Mexico and France sided with Poland and the Soviet Union in favor of a Polish resolution branding the Franco regime a threat to international peace and security and calling for a complete severance of diplomatic relations with it. The resolution was defeated. The United States, though still definitely anti-Franco, threw its weight in the General Assembly to a Belgian compromise resolution that recommended the recall of chiefs of mission from Madrid, not a severance of diplomatic relations. Even this proved too strong for nearly one-half of the Latin American states: only eleven voted for it, while three abstained

---

36 John A. Houston, *Latin America in the United Nations* (New York: Carnegie Endowment for International Peace, 1956), p. 88.

and six opposed it. The only votes cast against the resolution were the six from Latin America.[37]

Chief among the opponents of the Belgian resolution was Argentina, which played a major part in splitting the Latin American group wide open on this issue. Juan Perón, who had just consolidated his position by a decisive victory in a free election and was at the height of his prestige in Latin America, had a fellow feeling for Franco. His own regime was tainted with Nazi-Fascism, and Argentina's own admission to the United Nations had been strongly opposed outside Latin America, where a family feeling worked in her favor. As for the principle of nonintervention, Argentina had long taken the lead in asserting it.[38] This gave greater validity to Perón's insistence that the same principle be applied to Franco Spain.

All in all, Franco had no more valuable friend than Perón in the first few years after World War II. His support was the more valuable because in that stage of its career the Perón regime seemed to belong to the category of "popular liberation" movements which in Latin America have typically been antagonistic to the Franco regime.

From Repeal to Spain's Admission

When the Spanish question next gave rise to a major controversy in the General Assembly, the Latin American governments completed the shift they had begun in 1946. This time the question was whether to repeal both the recall-of-ambassadors resolution of 1946 and a companion measure that had excluded Spain from the specialized organizations such as UNESCO. When the proposal first came to a vote in 1949, it was supported by twelve of the Latin American states, but failed to obtain a two-thirds majority. In 1950, however, after the outbreak of the Korean War, it was adopted by the General Assembly, by thirty-eight to ten,

---

[37] Same, pp. 90-93.

[38] Arthur P. Whitaker, *The United States and Argentina* (Cambridge: Harvard University Press, 1954), pp. 96, 224-225.

with sixteen of the affirmative votes being cast by Latin American states; Guatemala, Mexico, and Uruguay cast negative votes, and Cuba abstained. Latin America thus contributed decisively to repealing the ban that it had taken the initiative in imposing only five years earlier.

The change of attitude was due, no doubt, to many factors, which varied from country to country. Basically, however, the Nazi-Fascist issue had inevitably lost its overriding urgency, and many Latin Americans were no longer willing to support measures against the Franco regime that undermined their own treasured principle of nonintervention. Likewise, the sharpening of the cold war had convinced many doubters that this was no time to weaken the West by continuing the controversial and obviously ineffectual ban on Franco Spain. Finally, soon after the war the political atmosphere in Latin America had changed, to Spain's advantage. Public interest had become absorbed in domestic problems, especially economic development, so that the Spanish question was pushed far into the background. And in several countries, notably, Venezuela, Colombia, and Peru, liberals had lost ground to conservatives, or to dictators, whose predilections were in favor of Franco.

The same developments help explain why the great majority of Latin American states also took a position favorable to Spain on the independence of Morocco, which was repeatedly debated in the General Assembly between 1951 and 1954. Although France was most directly concerned, the Latin Americans were well aware of Spain's important stake in Morocco. Despite their normally strong anticolonialist stand, on this occasion a large majority of Latin American delegations departed from it in an effort to bring about a compromise settlement. The resulting break between them and the Arab-Asian bloc, with which they had often cooperated on other issues, was a measure of the problem Spain had taken on in attempting to build its various bridges between East and West.

Since the admission of Spain to the United Nations in late 1955 was part of a package deal, it is impossible to isolate those factors that concerned only Spain and Latin America. However, the great majority of Latin Americans now approved—some reluctantly, others with enthusiasm—the admission of a member whom all had blackballed a decade earlier. Their votes did not necessarily imply approval of the Franco regime, but only support for the view that the United Nations should be as nearly as possible universal. Incidentally, by approving the package deal the Latin American bloc had also voted to reduce substantially its own relative weight in the United Nations. From almost one-half its original membership, their share has declined to less than one-fourth. In any case, now that Spain had at last gained entry, her individual relations with each Latin American government became more important than any group action they might take in the United Nations.

The Newest Phase

Since 1955 Spain's position in Latin America has deteriorated, mainly through the disappearance of most of the dictators who had been Franco's principal points of support. Perón, who fell in the year of Spain's admission to the United Nations, was followed by Odría of Peru, Rojas Pinilla of Colombia, and Pérez Jiménez of Venezuela, and, in January 1959, by Batista of Cuba.[39] By 1960 the three surviving dictators ruled the smallest and least influential countries in Latin America; the most notorious of the survivors, Trujillo of the Dominican Republic, had been signally honored by the Spanish chief of state.

Clearly, the recent tide in Latin America has been running against the regimes that, like Franco's, basically represent authoritarianism supported by the armed forces and by a subservient oligarchy of the well-born and well-to-do. Antagonism towards the Franco regime on this score, naturally sharpest in the recently dictator-ridden countries, reached a peak in Cuba, where Franco was widely believed

---

[39] Edwin Lieuwen, *Arms and Politics in Latin America* (New York: Praeger, for the Council on Foreign Relations, 1960), pp. 55-58.

to have aided Batista with arms and fighting-men against the revolution. Shortly after his downfall in January 1959, one of the Cuban revolutionary leaders threatened to carry the war to Spain and begin its liberation. At first less outspoken, in December 1959 Fidel Castro protested vehemently against President Eisenhower's visit to Franco. When he followed this up with a radio attack on Spain, and the Spanish Am-- bassador interrupted the broadcast to protest, Castro gave him twenty-four hours to get out of Cuba and also recalled the Cuban Ambassador from Madrid.

The broad Latin American significance of these and later clashes between Cuba and Spain will be completely misunderstood if they are regarded as reflecting only Castro's growing attachment to the Sino-Soviet bloc. In respect to this Communist affiliation his regime stands alone in Latin America and is generally reprobated in the rest of it, whereas his attitude towards Spain is widely and warmly shared. The support for it is more likely to increase than to diminish, for it is typical of the hostility that is felt towards the Franco regime by important elements now rising to power in Spanish America. Far from being made up wholly of wild-eyed radicals and illiterate peasants, much of their strength comes from the generally moderate middle groups of society.[40]

The record of the past decade points to the same conclusion with regard to Latin America as in the case of the Arab world. Spain's ambition to be a bridge between them—and, more broadly, between Islam and the Christian West—has lost its substance as a policy to become a dramatic pose. In the early 1950's the policy had some merit as to both function and bases. By 1960 it had become largely a propaganda device used to support Franco's prestige at home, where it fed the national appetite for dignity and compensated in some measure for Spain's exclusion from NATO.

Outside Spain the pretensions of her bridge policy have become a handicap to both Spain and the United States, when they have any effect at all. In the Arab world, where

---

40 John J. Johnson, *The Middle Groups in Latin America* (Stanford University Press, 1958), throws new light on these groups and their political role.

the tone is set by Nasser's neutralism backed by massive Soviet aid, as in the building of the Aswan dam, Franco's rhetoric has aroused expectations that he cannot fulfill without straining his ties with France and the United States. In Latin America the United States is the chief sufferer by his ambitions. Franco's boasts of Hispanidad only remind Latin Americans of Washington's close association with a military dictatorship that is detested by their own rising liberal elements as the personification of the very forces from which they are struggling to free their own countries.

Chapter X

A SUMMING UP:
PROBLEMS AND PROSPECTS

By MID-1960 Spain's partnership with the United States had been in operation for nearly seven years, and its continuing significance for both governments had been confirmed by President Eisenhower's visit to General Franco. By this time Spain had also lived for nearly a year with her venturesome stabilization-austerity plan of July 1959, which promises great things for the Spanish economy if it succeeds, but is fraught with danger to the regime if it fails. As much as any point of time can, this offers a useful occasion to recapitulate and look ahead.

Any such summing up cannot be a mathematical or scientific operation, for it is bound to be biased by the individual's assumptions and value judgments. So that the reader may make due allowance for these and correct them, when necessary, by substituting his own, let it be said at once that the role of Spain as an ally is appraised here from the point of view of an American, with emphasis on its value to U.S. policies and purposes, and on the assumption that the criteria to be applied must measure more than the military usefulness of the joint air and naval bases in Spain, and more than the political, economic, and other factors that seem likely to enhance or diminish their worth. In addition, I shall also give weight to ethical considerations, for reasons that have been so well stated in a recent study that I am happy to make them my own:

. . . Americans continue to believe deep-down that force by itself is not power; that ideals and values are among the essential components of strength in a democracy. Our own actions are made what they are—effective or frustrated—in large part by the degree to which they are in conformance with what we basically believe to be right. Similarly, our relationships to other countries are inevitably affected by the values they uphold as well as by their estimate of ours.[1]

The Changing Face of Spain

Spain presents different faces to different observers. A prominent British Labor M.P. says of the Franco regime that "most of the evils for which free men loathe communism exist in Spain today, even though, like Dollfuss's Austria, it is a 'dictatorship softened by slovenliness.'" [2] On the other hand, in the minds of its own adherents it evokes images of Molière and Abraham Lincoln. Commenting on Spain's admission to the United Nations after ten years of exclusion, one leading newspaper wrote:

There were friends of our country who remembered the remorse of the French Academy with respect to having excluded Molière from their group. On his statue are these words: "His glory was lacking in nothing; he was lacking to ours." [3]

In early 1960 it was reported that, "in talking with his counselors recently, General Franco has likened himself to a Spanish Abraham Lincoln who had 'emancipated' his country from Communist slavery and has since devoted his life to 'binding up its wounds.'" [4]

Some of the changes are the work of time. The passing of a generation was signalized by the death in 1955 of José Ortega y Gasset and in 1960 of Gregorio Marañón, two

---

1 *The Mid-Century Challenge to U.S. Foreign Policy,* Panel I Report of the Rockefeller Brothers Fund Special Studies Project, America at Mid-Century Series (New York: Doubleday, 1959), p. 7.
2 Denis Healey, "Militarily Useless and an Affront to our Principles," *Western World,* November 1957, p. 38.
3 *ABC* (Madrid), July 18, 1956.
4 *The New York Times,* March 27, 1960.

leaders of Spain's greatest cultural flowering since the eighteenth century. Changes of another kind were accelerated after 1950 as the country began its material recovery from two decades of depression, civil war, isolation, and ostracism. By the end of the decade Spain had been blessed with supermarkets and motels. *Fútbol* had become the national sport, and, except for a dwindling old guard of *aficionados,* bullfights were for tourists.

And the tourists came in droves, as never before in Spain's history, some four million of them in 1959 alone. The largest groups were French, but they also came in substantial numbers from Germany, Great Britain, the Low Countries, Scandinavia, the United States, and Spanish America. They flocked to the Costa Brava, north of Barcelona, and to Torremolinos and the "Spanish Riviera" in the south, as well as to older havens in Mallorca and the Cantabrian coast around San Sebastián. As, however slowly, Spain improved its roads and the tourists improved their Spanish, they began to stray from the beaten path of the coastal periphery and the Toledo-Segovia-El Escorial circuit around Madrid, to permeate all parts of the interior and mingle with the generally hospitable and communicative Spaniards. This influx was doing more than all the cultural exchanges and missions and foreign books, newspapers, and magazines combined—more than the disembodied radio transmissions, even including the seven-hours-a-day pounding of the Communist Radio España Independiente—to break down the traditional cultural isolation of the mass of the Spanish people.

The Spaniards are also on the move, not so much to foreign countries as within their own. The government encourages both emigration and seasonal migration abroad, to combat unemployment and obtain foreign exchange. Otherwise foreign travel is still difficult for the ordinary Spaniard because of restrictions on passports and foreign exchange. Migration from one part of Spain to another, however, has achieved mass proportions since World War II. In general, the movement has been from rural to urban-industrial areas and from south to north. The result has been overcrowding in some areas and a shortage of labor in others. So serious had the situation become by the end of 1958 that an Interministerial Commission was set up to deal with it. At its first meeting, in March 1959, the commission identified the following as the four principal "zones of immigration" and congestion: the two most industrialized areas, Barcelona and "the north" (Bilbao-San Sebastián-Avilés-Vigo); Madrid, which, besides being the political and financial capital, is beginning to industrialize; and the southern valley of the Guadalquivir River (Córdoba-Seville), where growth has been stimulated by irrigation projects and by the air and naval bases of San Pablo, Morón, and Rota.[5]

There is also a growing mobility in the field of education, both secondary and higher. In the traditional universities, the children of barons and butchers, of physicians and peasants, nowadays brush shoulders, and the proportion of women students has risen sharply. There is also a whole new system of "workers' universities" *(universidades laborales)*, residential schools that provide technical training of highschool level. And whether from either type of university or from a secondary school, the young man or woman must now obtain a degree or diploma of some kind to qualify for almost any skilled occupation, whether in industry, commerce, or agriculture, in one of the professions or in government service.[6]

These and other evidences of a new horizontal and vertical mobility suggest that the integration of Spanish society is making rapid progress with a consequent blurring of inherited distinctions based on class and region. Some commentators assert that "the very concept of *forastero* ["foreigner" from another part of Spain] is disappearing. There are no longer any *forasteros*."[7] Such beliefs and expectations seem premature. Though perhaps weaker than a generation ago,

---

[5] *ABC* (Andalusia edition), March 17, 1959.

[6] J. Vega Pico, "Carreras para todos," *España Semanal* (Madrid), March 1, 1959, p. 3.

[7] "Viajar por España," *ABC* (Andalusia edition), March 8, 1959.

regionalism is still strong, and other divisions within Spanish society have, if anything, probably become more pronounced; in any case they are so deeply rooted that it would take much more than a generation to change them. So far, the main result of the greater mobility in the postwar period has been to weaken old ties and loyalties without forging new ones in their place. The society on which Franco has imposed his authoritarian system of rigid controls has tended to become, in contrast with that system, increasingly fluid and unstable.

Stabilization, Instability, and Don Juan

The stabilization program of 1959 has given a new shape to the urgent problems of Spain's future. Its full economic effects can hardly be felt until it has been in operation for two or three years. There may be a further lag of a year or two before its social and political effects are clear.

The essence of the program is the imposition of temporary austerity in order to achieve a permanent increase in production and in the standard of living. Thus baldly stated, the program would seem a bargain to anyone, but the case is not that simple. Austerity is certain and immediate, whereas higher production rates and better living standards are sure to be delayed. Moreover, the austerity weighs most heavily on those least able to bear it, the mass of workers and white-collar employees, since they have no reserves to cushion them against its impact. If carried out thoroughly and in good faith, austerity will also impose sacrifices on members of privileged groups who, while far less numerous, are in a much better position to resist or evade its effects. In short, the adoption of this program has committed the regime to a race between austerity and production. Will production increase fast and far enough before the social and political ferment yeasted by austerity provokes an outburst?

While it is too early to draw firm conclusions, up to mid-1960 the stabilization plan seemed to be fulfilling expectations, for better and for worse. It maintained its prompt and decided success in righting the balance of payments, providing more foreign exchange, sustaining the devalued peseta, and checking inflation. On the other hand, the ill effects of austerity were still being felt: business was stagnant; unemployment was increasing slowly but steadily; and in the important Catalan industrial area the take-home pay of skilled workers was reported to have been cut in half by the elimination of overtime and incentive bonuses,[8] which by long custom had come to seem a part of normal compensation.[9]

No less serious for the long pull was the failure of the program to attract foreign capital on any considerable scale or to stimulate private enterprise within Spain. One flaw in the carrying out of the program has been the failure to create confidence in the government's "determination to remove obsolete controls and let business forge ahead." [10] Even a new or several new injections of foreign aid can only be a palliative. The basic question, to which no answer has so far been given, is whether the regime can and will apply the policy of austerity to itself by reforming an obsolete system of excessive controls and favoritism to which it clings from habit, national pride, and the influence of vested interests.

Another tentative conclusion must be that the stabilization plan is strengthening the identification of the Franco regime with the right wing, which first began to take definite shape with the cabinet reorganization of 1946, though some of its outlines had appeared earlier. According to its proponents, the plan would ultimately benefit all sectors of society. Its first and surest beneficiaries, however, were the banks and the big business interests of which they were the focus, whereas the incidence of austerity fell mainly upon small business and labor. If we may believe a commentator hostile to the regime, this incidence was aggravated by other meas-

---

[8] *The New York Times,* April 3, 1960.

[9] A conservative source has estimated that bonuses and overtime received by all Spanish workers had declined by 40 per cent during 1959; Banco Urquijo, *La economia española en 1959* (Madrid: Author, 1960), p. 281.

[10] *The New York Times,* April 19, 1960.

ures adopted by the government in the latter half of 1959. Chief among these were a sharp increase in indirect taxes, which bore more heavily on the masses than on the upper classes, and the granting of income-tax exemptions to owners of stock in some two hundred companies including "practically every one of the firms in which the most outstanding members of the financial and military oligarchy have invested." [11] Also, the total armed forces budget for 1960, as finally approved by the Cortes, showed an increase of 8 per cent over 1959. Significantly, much the largest increases in the new budget were assigned to the forces immediately charged with the maintenance of public order; 16 per cent for the Civil Guard, and 34 per cent for the Directorate General of Security.

The continuation of the conservative trend is not, however, a foregone conclusion. Some close observers think it quite possible that, rather than risk a deepening of the economic recession and the unrest it is breeding, the government may retreat from stabilization, revert to inflation, and justify its course by invoking the Falange doctrine of "social justice." There is as yet no substantial evidence to support this prognostication. But neither is the government proving that it has the will and the ability to effect the internal liberalization which is essential to the success of its new economic policy. Rather, the impression it has been giving since early 1960 is so much one of hesitancy and indecision that by early summer the Madrid wags were saying, "What this country needs is a strong government."

If the unbalanced sharing of austerity continues, it may provoke a new wave of unrest surpassing that of 1956-1957. It has not yet done so, but a growing apprehension on this score has colored the interpretations of General Franco's revival of negotiations with the Pretender Don Juan. Their meeting, the first in five years, took place near the Portuguese frontier on March 29, 1960. Speculation about it was all the more lurid because it had been postponed abruptly

---

11 Steparius (pseud.), "A Government Against a Country," *Ibérica* (New York), February 15, 1960, pp. 3-8.

—officially, because of excessive publicity. The rumor that the Caudillo had suffered a heart attack was promptly denied; his indisposition was attributed to carbon-monoxide poisoning, caused by a defective exhaust pipe in his car.

The public communiqué stated that the Pretender's son, Don Juan Carlos, who had completed his military training in Spain, would now continue his education at the University of Madrid under Franco's watchful eye and with the guidance of an advisory board headed by a monarchist member of the faculty. It added that this arrangement did not in any way prejudge the question of succession or of normal transition of the dynastic obligations and responsibilities. This phrase has been widely and perhaps correctly interpreted as safeguarding the Pretender's prior right of succession. However, since the commitment is not explicit, it seems more logical to conclude that Franco's seeming promise to Don Juan actually changed nothing and that he still has as free a hand as ever, within the terms of the Act of Succession, to pick both a king and the time to install him. Yet it is incorrect to say that nothing has changed.

Since the communiqué was so inconclusive, rumors have continued to fly thick and fast. The most plausible is that Franco had at last been persuaded to agree to an early restoration of the monarchy because he and his advisers had become disturbed over the danger of a political upheaval in Spain, not immediately but in case Franco should die or be incapacitated. Consequently, the rumors continued, he had decided to guarantee a smooth transition and the continuity of his regime by himself presiding over the restoration of the monarchy at an early date.

The question of the continuity of the regime is the real issue. All evidence shows that Franco is still uncompromisingly determined to perpetuate the essential features of his regime. Nothing that has happened since his speech to the Cortes of May 1958 in which he restated the principles of the Movement, has indicated any weakening of his determination. On the contrary, shortly after his meeting with Don Juan in March 1960 it was reported that Franco was preparing a final "fundamental law" for this purpose.[12] And in May, during a visit to Barcelona, he made a fighting speech in which he declared that he would continue on his present course without change.[13]

The proposed law would unquestionably require the maintenance of the present corporate state. This would mean, among other things, the perpetuation of the ban on political freedom and specifically on political parties; the retention of the Falange's political monopoly; and the preservation of the present syndical system, which not only prohibits free labor unions and the right to strike but also shackles management and labor together in one great government-controlled organization. It would also mean the perpetuation and widening of the breach between Spain and Anti-Spain, for there are many Spaniards, both monarchists and republicans, who would accept a limited monarchy but would never settle for an authoritarian pseudomonarchy that is only a thinly disguised continuation of the Franco regime.

Consequently the chief significance of their meeting is that, to all appearances, Don Juan has at last agreed to a restoration of the monarchy on Franco's terms. If this is so, then the agreement represents the culmination of the long process of Don Juan's conversion from open criticism of the regime, just after World War II, through a period of prudent reserve, to his present collaboration in perpetuating its essential features.

It has been suggested that Don Juan never intended to abide by this agreement once he has been crowned and that he entered into it only because his supporters, losing patience with his long political inactivity, had sent him an ultimatum to bestir himself.[14] This suggestion is plausible, for Don Juan must have known that the agreement would offend most of his supporters unless they understood that he

---

12 *The New York Times,* April 10, 1960.

13 "Caudillo Among the Catalans," *The Economist* (London), May 28, 1960, p. 873.

14 Silvio Schädler, "General Franco and Don Juan," *Swiss Review of World Affairs,* June 1960, pp. 12-13.

had his fingers crossed when he made it. Moreover, he has subsequently renewed his public protestations of liberalism in the Spanish-language edition of *Life* magazine; he even sent a marked copy of it to General Franco. This course of action marks Don Juan as either extraordinarily naïve or exceptionally subtle. In either case Franco is likely to prove more than a match for him. Reportedly, the question of banning this issue gave rise to a heated cabinet discussion, which Franco brought to a close by saying, "Gentlemen, if the Count of Barcelona [Don Juan] wishes to commit political suicide, I shall not prevent him. Let the magazine be sold." [15]

While Franco is probably fully capable of dealing with Don Juan, his insistence upon a restoration on the terms he has prescribed must be set down to a pride in his own creation that has blinded him to the realities of the situation in Spain. Or, to put it another way, his stubborn insistence on perpetuating his regime unchanged may reflect that same craving for immortality that is believed to explain his erecting the stupendous and extravagant monument in the Valley of the Fallen. His most recent course tends to confirm the view that he is a skillful tactician but a poor strategist, a consummate politician but no statesman.

The Present State of the Opposition

The initial effect of the stabilization plan of 1959 was further to enfeeble the faint of heart among the opposition by bringing reinforcement to the Franco regime just when some of them were hoping its bankruptcy would help them topple it. Subsequently their morale has revived as it has become clear that, instead of coasting to an easy victory, the government's greatest difficulties in making a success of the plan on the home front still lie ahead. Its difficulties are political as well as economic, for rising unrest over the economic stagnation and inequitable distribution of the benefits

---

[15] Benjamin Welles, in *The New York Times*, June 28, 1960.

and burdens of prosperity promises a rich harvest for the opposition groups. They are well placed for gathering in the sheaves. Their wide variety of political faiths, ranging from monarchist to Communist, gives them a foothold in every sector of Spanish society and two of them, the Christian Democrats and the Socialists, are reputedly strong enough to constitute major parties if and when political freedom is re-established.

The opposition groups are no doubt bestirring themselves to exploit the opportunity along the lines described in earlier chapters. In the nature of things, reliable information about their current activities is fragmentary. But it will at least contribute to an understanding of their present state if we review certain conditioning factors about which we are better informed. Those that will be considered at this point are the influence of regionalism and Communist propaganda, and the attitudes of the church and the younger generation. Two other major factors, the armed forces and the oligarchy, will be considered below in another connection.

As a source of opposition to the regime, regionalism is probably weaker now than it was two decades ago, though it is still not negligible. And yet, to the extent that regionalism has been abated by the centralizing tendencies at work in Spanish society, the opposition to the regime has actually been strengthened. This may seem paradoxical, but the reason for it is clear. The greatest weakness of the opposition has been its inability to unite, and one of the chief sources of disunity has been regionalism, since the opposition in each region works alone and for its own goal, and the goals are different.

The two major examples are, of course, the Catalans and the Basques. Their respective regional movements have always been independent of each other, but the differences between them are probably greater now than at any time since they took their modern shape in the nineteenth century. The Basque movement aims at political autonomy if not complete independence. It is comparatively well financed by contributions from wealthy Basques within and outside

Spain.[16] And it keeps in constant touch with the Basque "government in exile" in nearby Bordeaux, headed, until his death in 1960, by José Antonio de Aguirre, a hero of the Civil War and a highly respected Republican leader in exile. The Catalan movement, on the other hand, aims not at a political separation from Spain but only at cultural freedom and economic autonomy. It has been described recently as cowed and divided, with no stomach for a fight. Apparently it derives little financial support from rich Catalans at home and none from abroad.[17] Yet, for all this, Catalanism is still a vigorous force, as shown by the demonstrations in Barcelona during Franco's visit in May 1960. And some observers think it significant that the leaders were not Communists or anarchists but young Catholic professional men.

While the cutting edge of Spanish regionalism has been dulled, it is still strong, and Spain—one of the first European countries to start on the road towards unification in the fifteenth century—will be the last to achieve a true national synthesis. The day is still far off when the Basque provinces and Catalonia will feel towards Castile even the qualified identification that marks the attitude of Scotland and Wales towards their senior partner in the United Kingdom. Nevertheless, there is among large numbers of people in all parts of Spain a growing disposition to think of themselves first as Spaniards and only secondarily as belonging to a particular region. This change, inseparable from the modern way of life, has been greatly accelerated in the past quarter-century. The Civil War mingled people from all parts of

---

[16] The late Jesús de Galíndez, a Basque exile whose mysterious disappearance and presumed murder late in 1954 created an international sensation and who was a member of the faculty of Columbia University at the time, was said to have collected a half-million dollars for the Basque government in exile. Señor Aguirre, its head, declared that Galíndez's accounts were in order. The kidnaping and murder of Galíndez was attributed to Dictator Trujillo of the Dominican Republic, against whom he had written a book. Despite the friendship between the Trujillo and Franco regimes, and despite the important role of Galíndez in the anti-Franco Basque movement, there have been no serious suggestions that the Spanish government was implicated in his disappearance.

[17] *The New York Times,* March 27, 1960.

Spain in both armies and made them more conscious of their Spanish (not their provincial) character by associating them with foreign soldiers, such as the International Brigade, the Condor Legion, and the Italian divisions. Then came the long, heavy, unremitting pressure of the Franco regime towards nationalization and centralization.

As elsewhere, the radio has played its part in eroding the granite walls of particularism. If one may trust the testimony of many educated Spaniards, the press has contributed little to develop a national consciousness, or to anything else, for censorship has made it dull beyond endurance. Yet even the sports section conveys the national idea after a fashion, for football is now Spain's national sport.

When to all this is added the large-scale migration that has been going on within Spain, it seems possible that historians may some day say of Franco, as they have of an Argentine tyrant, Juan Manuel de Rosas, that with all his faults he still helped greatly to build a nation. To Rosas, the "intellectual exiles" from his tyranny also represented "Anti-Argentina," but in the end it was they who prevailed, overthrowing him after twenty-three years of rule and going forward to make modern Argentina.

Among all the potential forces of opposition, the element of greatest uncertainty is the younger generation. If we accept current Spanish usage, which employs this term to describe those who were still in their teens at the end of the Civil War, it will be difficult to discover any attitude towards public affairs common to all members of this group, or even to any large fraction of it. In other words, the younger generation in Spain is an age group, not a state of mind. Moreover, in this age group the only part that corresponds at all closely to the younger generation of tradition—restless, courageous, questing, full of ideas and ideals, determined to "turn the rascals out" and make things over—is the university students, or some of them. Yet, so far as can be learned, there is no concerted opposition movement among the students. As elsewhere in Spanish society, the elements of opposition within the universities are weakened by internal divisions and by an apparent apathy on the part of many students.

On balance, however, it would be imprudent to discount the Spanish university students as a potential force of opposition. Latin countries have a tradition of student political activity that not even dictatorships can eradicate, and the principle of intellectual freedom, latent in Spanish universities even under the present regime, is a perpetual threat to authoritarianism. Youth grows impatient with a regime that already seems an anachronism and which its chief is nevertheless seeking to freeze and perpetuate. And the corporate life of a university provides a framework of unity that could help bring about a merger of divided opposition forces in time of crisis. It is by no means impossible that the university students of Spain may emulate the example set early in 1960 by those of South Korea and Turkey.

The Catholic Church in Spain can certainly not be listed among the forces opposing the Franco regime. Yet, in recent years, its attitude towards it has been sufficiently critical to weaken the tie forged between them during the Civil War, to dim the image of the church as an all-out supporter of the regime, and even to give some encouragement to those who are openly opposed to it. Moreover, Catholic laymen dominate both wings of the Christian Democratic movement, which constitutes one important segment of the political opposition.

The church's criticisms relate to specific problems of great importance, particularly the syndical system, the maldistribution of wealth, and censorship. On the first two points it has been voiced by the highest ecclesiastical authorities in the form of the archbishops' collective pastoral letters, the first of which was published in 1956. The latest, issued early in 1960, underlined the suffering of the workers, as a result of the stabilization plan, through growing unemployment and the reduction in take-home pay.[18] Protests against the rigid censorship have come from individual churchmen of high

---

[18] *Hispanic American Report*, April 1960, p. 80; dated January 15, the pastoral letter was published on February 6, 1960.

rank, including Bishop Ángel Herrera of Málaga, a leader of Catholic Action and a noted social reformer.

Since 1957 the growing political influence widely attributed to the secular Opus Dei, though denied by it, has somewhat blurred the line of demarcation between church and regime. Nevertheless, it would seem that on the whole the distinction has been maintained and is growing, as most church leaders apparently desire. Moreover, the church is meeting with some success in its parallel effort to erase the picture of itself as the ally of the oligarchy, an image that took shape in the nineteenth century. To avert the danger of becoming identified solely with the growing middle classes of society, its "new leadership" is working with good effect to establish it as the champion of social justice, as defined by papal encyclicals, with a special concern for the working masses. In short, the church in Spain is striving to become again, as it was until the eighteenth century, the church of all the people.

These developments augur well for the adaptation of the Spanish Church to a liberal type of regime if one should be established after Franco passes from the scene. They also suggest that the church might in certain circumstances even help speed the transition, as Catholic leaders have recently done in several predominantly Catholic countries, such as Argentina, Colombia, and Venezuela. Finally, they have made less likely a recurrence of the ferocious anticlericalism of the 1930's. The trend towards dissociation from the Franco regime has received encouragement from Catholic Church leaders in Western Europe but apparently less so in the United States.[19]

The strength of the Catholic Church in Spain has been recognized even by the Communist party. At its Sixth Congress, held at Prague in February 1960, it overruled complaints from some of its members and included in its new program a provision for subsidizing the Catholic Church

---

[19] William Ebenstein, *Church and State in Franco Spain*, Research Monograph no. 8 (Center for International Studies, Princeton University, 1960), pp. 19-20.

after a Communist take-over.[20] This holding out of an olive branch is an outgrowth of the revived "popular-front" tactics which seek temporary alliances with all shades of the opposition, without thereby abandoning long-range Communist aims. The new "line" has attractions even for anti-Communist members of the opposition in Spain, both because of its ostensible support of democratic values and because of the feeling among anti-Franco forces that the democracies have deserted them by giving material and moral support to the regime and that again, as during the Civil War, only the Kremlin is willing to help them.

This is a dangerous state of mind. By developing its social mission, the church is doing much, but not nearly enough, to combat it. Politically, the church is at best neutral. Many observers feel that this situation provides a fertile seedbed for communism. Reportedly the Communists are making headway even in Catalonia, where the strong remnant of traditional anarchism has lost out to the Communists because of their great superiority in financial resources, organization, and propaganda.[21]

These advantages have enabled the Communists to become an influential factor in the opposition, not only in Catalonia but in Spain at large. But it is important to define the nature of their influence. As a party they are still weak and unpopular, and likely to remain so. On the other hand, as field agents for following up and driving home the radio propaganda that pours in from iron-curtain countries, they are assiduous and effective. And, since that propaganda follows the popular-front line, is skillfully designed to please and incite all the potential enemies of the regime, and often bears no mark of its Communist origin, it arouses a widely favorable response in non-Communist as well as Communist circles. As a result, while their own party is still weak, the

---

[20] Radio España Independiente, February 17, 1960; monitored broadcast of a speech by Fernando Claudín, a member of the Executive Committee. The party's stand on this question had been anticipated at its Fifth Congress, at Paris in 1954.

[21] *The New York Times,* March 27, 1960.

Spanish Communists are helping substantially to strengthen other opposition groups in Spain.

The Future of the Opposition

What are the prospects of the Spanish opposition? And, if Franco should fall, what would happen in Spain? Would the Communists take over? These questions are of great and immediate concern to the United States, because of their bearing on the use of the military bases and Spain's role in the defense of the West, and because of the fact that the bases agreement will come up for renewal in the near future.

The prospects of the opposition depend upon so many variable factors in Spanish affairs, both domestic and foreign, that any prediction must be highly tentative. But we are on firmer ground in establishing priorities among these factors, and I am convinced that the one which will most profoundly affect Spain's future in the years just ahead is the stabilization program initiated in 1959. It is crucially important not only because the welfare of the nation's economy hinges on it; the present conjuncture has likewise made it the touchstone of almost every aspect of Spanish life—political, social, and psychological, as well as economic.

If the stabilization program is a decisive factor, it is also a highly uncertain one. As we have seen, it began with a resounding success in the field of Spain's external relations but has recently shown such strong signs of bogging down on the home front that its entire future is in doubt. At present it seems almost equally possible either that the program will eventually succeed, or that it will fail as the economy continues to stagnate, or else that a harried government will scuttle the program and run for the illusory cover of another round of inflation.

Let us make a trial run of the political prospects in each of these three eventualities. Our starting-point is the premise that Franco's present position in Spain is a strong one, but that it is in need of further strengthening, and that it could deteriorate rapidly.

If the stabilization plan succeeds in time to allay the present unrest over its results on the home front, the opposition will have little or no prospect of improving its position for some years to come. Rather, its relative strength will probably decline as the powerful vested interests that have grown up under the regime, and which were beginning to regard Franco as a liability in the dark winter of 1958, rally around him with redoubled devotion in his hour of triumph. Franco's position will then be secure for a long time, provided he maintains his regime in substantially its present form. This is detested by many Spaniards but it combines two features that make it unbeatable so long as things are going well. One feature is the protection, amenities, and other benefits it confers on the power groups which in turn support it. The other is the open-ended character that Franco has given his regime by maintaining its provisional character (which he has maintained for more than two decades) and by keeping everyone guessing as to what kind of regime will succeed it. He thereby provides a safety valve for political discontent, through the encouragement his system gives to wishful thinking among the malcontents. Until the final decision about the future of the regime is made and announced, each group of malcontents can hope that, when it comes, it will be the one it wants.

True, the range of choice in this matter was confined to monarchy by the Act of Succession of 1947. But there are so many possible varieties of monarchy that the range is still wide enough to accommodate most tastes, and Franco has not yet finally committed himself to any specific variety. At times he has seemed on the verge of doing so, and he has stated certain principles—those of the Movement—that the future monarch must bind himself to follow. Yet he still retains a wide latitude of choice. In his own interest he would be foolish to give it up, for by doing so he would strengthen the opposition to his regime, no matter which of the possible types of monarchy, or which of the possible candidates for the throne, he might select. His handling of the question over the years indicates that he is aware of this danger.

Consequently, if the stabilization plan succeeds, Franco may be expected to continue his regime in substantially its present form for several years. As likely a cut-off date as any is 1967, when the Young Pretender, Don Juan Carlos, will be thirty years of age and hence eligible for coronation under the Act of Succession, whereas Franco himself will be seventy-five and perhaps ready for retirement. There is of course the impediment of the prior right of the Old Pretender, Don Juan, but that is a detail that Franco could be trusted to take care of. Also, it is possible that, rather than wait for 1967, Franco will place Don Juan himself on the throne, if occasion requires and the state of the opposition permits. In this case, however, we may be sure that Franco, who does not trust that "Anglophile cosmopolite," would keep the reins of power in his own hands. In any case, as these examples suggest, if stabilization succeeds, Franco will continue to make the decisions for years to come and the opposition forces will go on playing the same ineffectual role that they have played heretofore.

If, on the other hand, the stabilization program either fails or is abandoned in favor of a return to inflation, the opposition will flourish and will probably take over, sooner or later—sooner, if the program is adhered to in the face of deepening economic recession; later, if recourse is had to another round of inflation, which would bring a passing wave of prosperity but only postpone the day of reckoning. The political permutations and combinations that might occur in either case are so numerous and complex that only the most obvious alternatives can be considered here.

In order to clear the ground, let me begin by excluding certain possibilities which, in my opinion, are highly improbable. These are: a Communist take-over, the outbreak of anarchy or civil war, and the establishment of a republic. My reasons for excluding the first are implicit in what I have already said about the weakness of the Spanish Communists. Anarchy and civil war, including one of the type that brought Fidel Castro to power in Cuba, are ruled out because the forces of order are too strong and, for reasons to be given below in another connection, will be united, and because the horror of another civil war is still widespread and deep. A republic might be established later on, but it would be barred at first by the bad name this form of government acquired in the 1930's, by the violent hostility to it among the main power groups in the present regime, and by the lack of strong support for it among the present opposition forces.

The establishment of another military dictatorship to succeed Franco seems unlikely except for a transitional period, but highly probable for that. There is no second Franco in sight. Several of his generals are said to aspire to succeed him, but their clashing ambitions are counted upon to prevent any of them from doing so. Similar rivalries would be one of many obstacles to another type of military dictatorship that has been much talked about since it has had some success in other parts of the world—a nationalistic, demagogic dictatorship of junior officers impatient for advancement. A junta might be a solution of such personal rivalries at either level, but not of the problem of government; plural executives seldom work well for long periods, least of all among the military. And civilians, of the regime as well as the opposition, are heartily tired of dictatorship; even now their attitude is clearly, though discreetly, expressed in the clamor for the "institutionalization" of the regime. As a transitional device, however, a military dictatorship is not only possible but might prove indispensable, as it did in Argentina after Perón's fall.

The transition would be to a regime designed to safeguard and serve the three principal power groups of the present regime—army, oligarchy, and church. The form of government would probably be a monarchy of a type very unlikely to be set up by Franco, if he restored monarchy at all: a limited monarchy. That the monarchical form would be chosen is assumed mainly by elimination: no other form is widely supported either in the regime or in the opposition, and it has wide support in both.

The expectation that this particular type of monarchy

would be chosen rests on an assumption about the way in which the Franco regime would be supplanted. It is assumed that the major break would consist in defections among the power groups mentioned above, which have been the present regime's main support. The growth of their individual strengths and interlocking ties makes them potentially the greatest constellation of power in Spain, in case Franco loses his grip. The motivation of their break with him would be complex but would have a simple core: the belief that he had outlived his usefulness and that his continuation in power threatened to bring on a political and social upheaval of which the privileged classes would be the first victims. This apprehension was spreading in the uneasy winter of 1958. The adoption of the stabilization plan checked it, but it would spread again if the plan failed or if the regime reverted to the inflation that brought on the crisis of 1958.

A new regime of the kind I have suggested would arouse no enthusiasm and much resentment among the majority of the Spanish people, but the opposition to it would probably not be sufficiently strong to prevent its establishment and maintenance for a considerable period. As a way-station to a more liberal regime it might even be accepted with some alacrity by the numerous middle groups whose growth has been stimulated by the rapid industrialization, bureaucratization, and urbanization of the Franco period. Antagonism to the new regime would be strongest among the workers, but the constellation of power described above ought to be able, as De Gaulle has been able in France, to manage refractory labor groups without precipitating civil war. In one important respect the Spanish task is easier than De Gaulle's, for the Communists are far stronger in France than in Spain. In any case, the new regime will inherit, and may be expected to use, the machinery and techniques developed by Franco for keeping labor in line. Regionalism might pose a more serious problem than labor, but, as we have seen, the cutting edge of regionalism has been dulled in the past generation. In addition, virtually every plan for this kind of regime that I have heard about makes some concession to regional interests and sentiments.

My conclusions, therefore, are that the prospects of the Spanish opposition are dim if the stabilization plan succeeds, but bright if it fails or is abandoned for a new round of inflation; and that there is no good ground for the assertion, propagated by the present regime, that Spain's only choice is between Franco and anarchy or civil war leading to communism. On the contrary, peaceful alternatives exist, and the most likely of these is a limited monarchy weighted in favor of the present principal power groups—army, church, and oligarchy. Such a regime might not last more than a decade or two, but that is another story.

Spain's Role in World Politics

Three subjects dominate international relations today, both within the United Nations and outside: the cold war, colonialism, and economic development. All three involve Spain and her relations to the United States.

By virtue of the bases agreement, Spain has, ever since 1953, been lined up on the side of the West in the cold war. So far, the United States has remained her only partner, and Spain has not been accepted into any Western European regional arrangements of a military or political character. Three ways of associating Spain actively with her neighbors have been under discussion: the formation of a Western Mediterranean pact; Spain's admission to NATO; and a bases arrangement between Spain and Germany.

The proposal for a Western Mediterranean pact, which has substantial merits from the point of view of both the United States and Spain, is in a state of suspended animation. The turbulent situation in North Africa, particularly in Algeria, raises many doubts about its feasibility, and even its desirability is placed in question so long as there is a chance of Spain's being accepted in NATO.

Spain's admission to NATO has been publicly espoused by Portugal, the United States, West Germany, and France, in that order, and several other governments are known to favor it. Great Britain is publicly uncommitted, while Denmark and Norway have blocked the unanimous consent required. Strong minority parties in Britain, France, and West Germany continue to offer unremitting opposition to this proposal.

The main grounds of opposition are that both the origin and the character of the Franco regime make its admission incompatible with the declared aim of NATO to defend freedom and democracy, and that Spain is already making her maximum contribution to the defense of the West through her agreement with the United States. The Spanish government desires an invitation to join NATO both for reasons of prestige and in order to obtain foreign aid in modernizing its armed forces to bring them up to NATO standards. The U.S. government has supported Spain's admission partly in order to gratify its ally and partly as a way of getting its NATO partners to share in the cost of modernizing the Spanish armed forces. It may also wish them to share the political responsibility for its special ties with the Franco regime. Apparently most of the NATO governments have been ready to do so out of deference to the United States and in the interest of European unity. Nevertheless, opposition outside government circles is so strong and so widespread that the cause of European unity might well be set back rather than advanced by this step so long as the Franco regime remains in power. The question clearly involves a head-on collision between military considerations and political and moral purposes. Its solution also depends on differing appraisals of the nature of the Soviet Communist threat—on whether it is more a military or a political threat—and hence of the best means to resist it.

The same emotions which surround the question of Spain and NATO were, as we have seen, deeply aroused early in 1960 by the revelation that the West German government had been discussing with Madrid the possibility of establishing what were variously styled German "facilities" or "bases" on Spanish soil. These reports, first denied and then acknowledged, illustrated the complex crosscurrents that surround any seemingly simple proposition that Spain under its present regime should somehow be integrated into the common defenses of the West.

On the problem of colonialism, Spain's position is either clear-cut or equivocal, depending on whether it is viewed from Madrid or from some other capital. To non-Spaniards, Spain is clearly a colonial power since she has her "Gibraltars in Africa"—notably Ceuta and Melilla—and her possessions on the West coast—Ifni, Río de Oro, and Spanish Guinea. Moreover, the *rapprochement* with France since 1957 has meant a closer association with one of the two leading colonial powers. On occasion Spain has even spoken up for France in United Nations debates on the Algerian question.

If we are to believe Madrid's assertions, Spain's position these days is definitely anticolonial, but is maintained with the moderation and serenity achieved by marrying compassion for the colonial peoples to patience with their misguided masters. It is fascinating to observe the insouciance with which the Franco regime has discarded its "revived will to empire" of yesteryear to don its new mantle of anticolonialism. To lend plausibility to the change, it has not only given up its Moroccan protectorate but has converted its African colonies into Spanish provinces; as for its "Gibraltars in Africa," these, it insists, are not and never were colonial possessions but "places of sovereignty," as Spanish as Spain itself. Madrid's new anticolonialism makes even its support of its new-found friend, the France of De Gaulle, somewhat capricious. Thus, when the second uprising of the *colons* in Algeria began in January 1960, Madrid, overestimating their chances of success, smiled upon them through the controlled Spanish press.

Generally, however, Spain's new anticolonialism is expressed with moderation and prudence. For the United States, its significance lies mainly in its application to the Arab world and Latin America, and in both areas it can be useful to Washington. It represents today the chief surviving remnant of the pro-Arab policy so highly featured by Foreign Minister Artajo in the early and middle 1950's. Towards the Arab countries Spain is still a bridge, but the gap to be bridged is now identified in terms of colonialism and anti-colonialism rather than Christianity and Islam. In its concrete expression, Spain's policy coincides substantially with that of the United States: it encourages legitimate aspirations for independence and development, but lays much stress on moderation and a due regard for the rights of others, even colonial or former colonial powers. Meanwhile, Spain keeps her own colonies.

Towards Latin America, Spain has effected a remarkable redefinition of her concept of colonialism. In its brasher years the Franco regime pictured the United States as subjecting Latin America to a new kind of colonial servitude through investments, bases, the Pan American system, and so forth. Now that all this has been reversed, Madrid's attitude might be very helpful to the United States if only the Franco regime were more highly regarded in Latin America. Both there and in the Arab world Spain sounds the tocsin against a Communist penetration that could be the advance agent of the worst kind of colonial imperialism, domination by the Soviet Union.

With regard to the problem of economic development, Spain's role is a dual one. As an underdeveloped country, she has been the recipient of foreign aid of various kinds over the past decade, mainly from the United States, but also, beginning in 1959, from the IMF and OEEC. On the other hand, Spain has assisted—on a very small scale, to be sure—the development of countries still more underdeveloped than herself, particularly in her African sphere. It now appears that this second role is to be given more prominence, for by 1960 the OEEC was in process of being supplanted by a broader Organization for Economic Cooperation and Development, with Spain as one of its twenty members; one of its major functions is to be the promotion of economic development in Africa and Asia. It is questionable how much necessitous Spain can do to help others, but at least its government has broken out of its isolationist shell and is showing a strong desire to engage in international cooperation, usually along lines that run parallel to American policy.

Spain's Direct Interests and American Policy

Spain's problems in her relations with the Arab world come to a sharp focus in Morocco, where her current policy of cultivating a *rapprochement* has met with some success. The United States has an interest and a certain amount of leverage in supporting it through its temporary possession of bases in Morocco. But what will happen after they are evacuated in 1963? A number of disagreeable things could happen even before then in Morocco, where the situation is rendered highly unstable by many unresolved problems as well as by the agitation of extreme nationalist and left-wing elements.

A resumption of Moroccan pressures similar to the attack on Ifni late in 1957 could, for example, have highly embarrassing consequences for the United States as well as Spain. What would Washington do if Rabat launched an attack on the Spanish enclaves in Morocco, the "places of sovereignty," or invaded the more southerly Spanish possessions, in which American companies have begun to explore for oil? Franco has said he will not give up another inch in Africa, and if he does not stick to this he may lose the support of his army. If he does stick to it, he may become embroiled with Morocco. By supporting Spain against Morocco, the United States might alienate the whole Arab world; yet by failing to support Spain it might alienate Franco and imperil its bases in Spain. The problem is not one that the United Nations or NATO or the projected Western Mediterranean pact is likely to solve. The fact of its existence suggests that U.S. ties with Spain may be more of a liability than an asset in its dealings with the Arabs and North Africa.

By mid-1960, Spain's relations with Latin America were worse than ever before in the twentieth century, except for a brief period after 1945. Spain still holds the affections of many individuals in Latin America, especially among conservative groups. But Franco's only two friends in power are Trujillo of the Dominican Republic and Somoza of Nicaragua. The row that took place early in 1960 between Fidel Castro and the Spanish Ambassador to Cuba does not seem to have done Spain much harm outside Cuba; neither did it help. More important, the general trend towards regimes of the popular liberation type in Latin America, if continued, will almost certainly make the general atmosphere in that area still more unfavorable to the Franco regime. If U.S. ties with Franco were ever a real asset to it in Latin America— which is very doubtful—the asset has now wasted away.

The role of the Soviet bloc in shaping Spain's current situation is of great importance. If there were no Soviet threat and hence no cold war, there might well be no Franco regime, for the cold war has been its mainstay at home and abroad. But for it, there would have been no American need for bases in Spain. Fortunately for Franco, the cold war seems unlikely to come to an early end. This makes it possible for Franco to give an unstinted endorsement—as he did in the exchange of letters with Eisenhower in August 1959— to the policy of relaxing international tensions, though this is about the last thing Franco would want to see happen. In endorsing it, he underlined the President's proviso that, until the tensions are safely relaxed, an adequate defense posture must be maintained—and the bases in Spain are an essential element of that posture. Consequently, no discord exists in the basic policies of Spain and the United States towards the Soviet Union. None seems likely to develop, for the only conceivable change on either side would be the adoption of a less-relaxed attitude on the part of Washington. Nothing could please Madrid more than that.

Compared with the cold war, all other topics of common interest in the relations of the United States and Spain with the Soviet bloc pale into insignificance. The small-scale trade that has developed between Spain and the iron-curtain countries gives Washington no qualms so long as Spain's exports consist of such unwarlike materials as oranges and so long as Spain does not recognize East Germany and does not admit Soviet bloc agents into Spain. Admitting them is something Franco would be most unlikely to do in any case, even in return for the suppression of Radio España Independiente, which is causing him real trouble, for this would be only to exchange the frying pan for the fire.

Another question involves the once fabulous and now seemingly mythical gold hoard of some $500 million which was sent to the Soviet Union by the republic for safekeeping. Spain's own efforts to regain it having proved sterile, sources close to the Caudillo have hinted that the United States should help Spain recover it. The question is so obviously not even academic, since neither government can do anything about it, that Washington's failure to oblige has caused no heartburnings in Madrid. On the campaign against communism, the two governments generally see eye to eye, though they often disagree on how best to strengthen the free world.

As regards Western Europe, both governments have made a sustained effort ever since 1957 to tighten Spain's ties with her neighbors, or, as some put it, to reintegrate Spain with the Western European community. As regards the community at large, the chief gain so far has been to achieve Spain's membership in the OEEC, now to be the OECD. There has also been some increase in Spain's cultural and economic relations with Western Europe, but in the political field the only marked improvement has been in its relations with West Germany and France. How far this cooperation is likely to go, and what its concrete advantages may be, remains uncertain. With Great Britain there has been some improvement of relations, but the Labor party is unremitting in its hostility to the Franco regime. And whichever party is in power, the perennial question of Gibraltar is always certain to serve as in irritant.

The nub of the problem of reintegrating Spain with Western Europe is, of course, NATO. Her admission to that organization would not prove that she had been restored by her European neighbors to good standing, but her exclusion proves that she has not. The issue provides a minimum test of her acceptability as a partner. If she cannot gain admittance to a military-political organization whose primary purpose, like Spain's self-declared mission, is defense against the Communist threat, then it is obvious that she has not been rehabilitated in any general political and moral sense.

The pros and cons of Spain's admission to NATO have already been discussed, and our only concern here need be with the bearing of this question on the U.S. policy of promoting Spain's reincorporation into the Western European family of nations. This policy has been pressed with vigor, with some success as regards economic relations, but to no avail in the political field. Should it be continued? Or is it time to let it lapse?

One factor that should be given more weight is that there is apparently no compelling military or strategic reason why the defense arrangements with Spain should be integrated with those of Western Europe through NATO. There is, of course, much to be said on both sides of the question, but many experienced military men, including Americans, are known to believe that on balance the present bilateral arrangement is preferable both for its simplicity and flexibility and because it is already linked to NATO through the United States' participation in it.

The second point is that, by bringing Spain into NATO, the European nations, which are benefiting from Spain's contribution to Western defense, would thereby share with the United States the political and moral responsibility for the association with the Franco regime which makes this contribution possible. On the other hand, while the United States should gladly share this responsibility with anyone who is willing to help bear it, it has no right at this late date to insist on being bailed out by its allies. By insisting too much with the reluctant, it may imperil its own more basic policy of promoting Western European solidarity.

Finally, the way in which the United States moved or drifted into championing Spain's admission to NATO points up the futility of its original efforts, in 1951-1953, to treat its quasi-alliance with Spain as a limited liability arrangement. The logic of the relationship has broken down these limitations. It has turned the Franco regime into a remarkable combination of partner, pensioner, and, as the NATO case shows, protégé. There is no convincing evidence that the present relationship, which is already complex enough, would be any more manageable if it were somehow handled through NATO channels.

The Washington-Madrid Nexus

For the United States, the bases agreement of 1953 was both a relatively late addition to its far-flung defense system and an important new departure in its policies. For the first time since its diplomacy had rediscovered Spain in 1936, Washington adopted a policy towards it that was independent of and contrary to the policies of Great Britain and France. In addition, the new policy brought with it numerous and unforeseen implications. Concluded as a limited liability arrangement for exclusively military purposes, by 1960 the bases agreement had expanded into a quasi-alliance whose liabilities, though still limited, had now become political and economic as well as military. And those liabilities had grown to be much heavier than anyone had apparently expected in 1953.

For Spain, the partial partnership with the United States meant her emergence from the isolation of the past decade and the beginning of a slow process, still incomplete, of restoring the Franco regime to international good standing. From it the regime has drawn indispensable military aid, economic support, and, increasingly, political acceptance without sacrificing any of its authoritarian props at home. The new tie with the United States has, it is true, cost Franco some part of an illusory freedom of maneuver, notably in Spain's ambition to serve as a bridge between Islam and the Christian West. But Franco had less need of freedom of maneuver, once he was assured of American support.

The concrete results of the partnership have been more

important to Spain, and particularly to the Franco regime, than to the United States. The economic aid it brought to Spain, substantial in earlier years, was decisive in 1959. Along with other benefits, Spain has received valuable instruction in economics, together with the wherewithal to apply it in the crucially important stabilization plan. Politically, the tie with the United States has been of the greatest value to the regime. It has reinforced its hold on the loyalty of Spain's chief power group, the armed forces. It has helped it cope with the country's economic difficulties. It has draped Franco in the mantle of partnership with the free world's greatest power. Militarily, it has increased the danger of a Soviet attack on Spain in case of a general war; aside from that, Spain's military gain has been great, particularly in improved equipment and training. And if or when the partnership is dissolved, the bases will be entirely hers.

For the United States, the economic consequences of the alliance have been of little moment. By 1959 the money cost of the aid programs had probably totaled slightly more than one billion dollars, and the cost of the bases a shade less than half that sum. This six-year aggregate, while not trifling, imposed no strain on an annual budget of about eighty billion dollars. As for trade and investment, the alliance has not had any large or lasting effect on either. The capacity of the United States to absorb Spanish products in any considerable volume, and that of Spain to attract American investments on a large scale, remain to be demonstrated. Militarily, all the experts seem to agree that the United States has derived very substantial advantages from the Spanish link in its armor of oversea bases. Politically, the Spanish bases have been useful in enabling the United States to yield gracefully to neighboring Morocco's demand for the evacuation of its bases without seriously weakening its posture in that area.

On balance, however, its partnership with the Spanish dictator is a distinct political liability to the United States, as have been its associations with other authoritarian regimes —to mention only very recent instances, Pérez Jiménez in

Venezuela, Batista in Cuba, Syngman Rhee in South Korea, and Adnan Menderes in Turkey. The Spanish tie is a liability in many countries, including Spain itself, where it may seriously prejudice American relations with any successor regime. The issue has a high propaganda potential and the Communists are making the most of it with the aid of their Radio España Independiente, which beams its anti-American venom to Spain seven hours a day, year in and year out.

The future of the partnership with Spain, it would seem, depends primarily on the military value of the bases, and that in turn depends on the development both of missile strategy and of prospects for a general limitation of armaments. So far as Soviet policy is concerned, one of its main demands is for the liquidation of the U.S. bases overseas, including those in Spain; but it has not offered any counter-concessions that would make this a likely eventuality. Before a change occurs in the expansionist Soviet ambitions, missiles will probably supplant bombers as a decisive instrument of long-range strategic warfare. That will not necessarily entail any essential changes in the partnership unless or until the United States should decide to base its retaliatory missile force solely within North America. In that event the United States would presumably have little or no need of Spanish or other oversea bases to deter a central strategic war, and Spain and other oversea allies of the United States might be, unfortunately, even more dependent than they are now on the deterrent capability of the United States in case of a limited as well as a large-scale attack by the Soviet bloc. But, if only because of the present state of missile development, such a decision seems unlikely in the next few years; other considerations might delay it even longer. It is more probable, at least in the short run, that U.S. oversea air bases will merely be replaced or supplemented by rocket-launching bases, in which case the alliance with Spain will remain an important factor in the defenses of the free world.

In any event, the principal naval base, at Rota, will remain valuable as long as the United States maintains a fleet in the Mediterranean. The development of the submarine-launched Polaris missile, which is approaching the operational stage, may even enhance Rota's value in any situation short of an all-out Soviet offensive against the free world; in that event, one or two well-aimed Soviet missiles could put Rota out of business in a few minutes. This is a calculated risk that will henceforth affect the value of all fixed installations. In situations short of all-out war, U.S. access to Rota and other bases in Spain can help to deter or check the expansion of local or limited aggressions in the Western Mediterranean, in North Africa, or in West Africa north of the bulge. In sum, the prospects are that the value of the Spanish bases to the United States will remain substantial for a good many years to come.

An unfriendly Spain could make the bases untenable, and this hazard brings to the fore the political prospects of the Washington-Madrid alliance. As matters stand today, there is little doubt that the United States will seek to renew the bases agreement in 1963, at the end of its initial ten-year period. And in view of the great value of the alliance to General Franco, and the improbability of his regime's being strong enough to dispense with it by that time, he may be expected to agree to its renewal after the customary haggling.

But what if a change of regime should take place in Spain, either before or after 1963? The answer will depend primarily on the character of the new regime, though factors external to Spain would affect it too. If the new government should be controlled by the main props of the present regime, but gradually broadened and liberalized, the odds would be strongly in favor of a continued close association. Otherwise the issue is uncertain.

In this connection, readers in the United States should heed the warning, all the more effective for its quiet tone, recently sounded by a leading Spanish writer, not an exile, who knows the United States well and likes it. Discussing "the obvious deterioration of the American image in Spanish minds" since 1954, and its possible consequences, he writes:

Paradoxically, the United States appears to be praised and supported now by quite a few of its old (pro-Nazi) opponents and by other people who in fact strongly dislike it; meanwhile, anti-American feeling is growing among the potential real friends of the United States.

The likelihood is that in the near future, if nothing is done to prevent it, a large part of the influential people in Spain will not be friendly to the United States. Yet they could be. The Western defense system, which of course is very important, ranks high among the present issues; but I cannot help thinking that though bases can be very valuable assets if surrounded by a friendly, willing and reliable country, there is some chance that the future may be subordinated to a precarious present.[22]

Despite the censorship and other authoritarian controls, which make it difficult to get at Spanish public opinion except through fragmentary samplings, the major prospects are fairly clear. Some observers feel that a post-Franco regime, democratic in character, will not resent the U.S. alliance with Franco, but will be grateful for the minor gains of individual security and for the major economic assistance that have accrued to Spain during this period of unprecedented U.S.-Spanish association. Others believe that a new regime will swing towards the neutralist left, will be hostile to the U.S. partnership with Franco but not towards basic democratic values. Such a regime would probably exact an early evacuation of the bases but would not join a grouping hostile to the United States and to Western Europe. The least likely eventuality, at present, is the emergence of a Communist regime. Even that of a popular-front government including the Communist party is improbable. The Communists have a well-organized and well-financed organization; they have the invaluable help of Radio España Independiente; and they have the advantage of complete irresponsibility in exploiting the social and economic sufferings of the Spanish people. Still, there is a widespread distrust of their purposes and claims, and a fear of totalitarian-

22 Julián Marías, "Spanish and American Images," *Foreign Affairs*, October 1960, pp. 96, 98-99.

ism of the right making way for an even more ruthless totalitarianism of the left. This feeling is stronger among the generation which lived through the Civil War than among the new generation.

While the ultimate aim of the Communist party in Spain as elsewhere is to secure the victory of communism under the leadership of the Soviet Union, the party has shown great tactical flexibility in adjusting its slogans to win as wide support as possible, and its present posture, confirmed at the Sixth Congress in early 1960, is closely patterned on the popular-front tactics of the mid-1930's. Specifically Communist aims are passed over in silence, and the cooperation of Socialists, anarchists, Republicans, liberals and even the reformist clergy is ardently sought. While the Communists, who strive to become the anti-American party everywhere, are constantly attacking the United States and its policy towards Spain through their radio broadcasts, they seem to feel that it will not gain them much support in Spain to press the anti-U.S. line to an extreme. So, for example, the new party program calls for "the abolition of military bases," but also urges "the desirability of collaboration between the two states on a mutually beneficial basis. . . ." They qualify this by insisting that the party's "central ideas" are "peaceful coexistence, the renunciation of war as an instrument of foreign policy, and disarmament." [23]

As a guide to the Communist appraisal of Spanish opinion, this statement reflects the general Communist campaign to capture "peace," "democracy," and "freedom," by putting forth a "minimum program" designed to make possible "an agreement among all the anti-Franco forces." After explaining that it had been deemed necessary to elaborate "a concrete alternative" in order to avoid the "vacuum" that many Spaniards fear might follow the disappearance of the Franco

---

[23] Radio España Independiente, February 17, 1960; monitored rebroadcast of a speech delivered on February 15 by Fernando Claudín, member of the Executive Committee of the Communist party of Spain at its Sixth Congress, in Prague.

regime, the spokesman for the Central Committee continued:

> The alternative we propose is not a Communist alternative. It is not even a left-wing alternative. It is a national alternative . . . a minimum program on which we [i.e., "all the anti-Franco forces"] can all agree.[24]

Weasel-worded though it is, the statement was clearly hostile to the U.S. bases program, and it was clearly expected to win popularity. From other sources, we know that the bases and the whole military arrangement with the United States are much disliked by many people in Spain, anti-Communists as well as Communists, on the right as well as on the left. Those who oppose the alliance only because it has served as a prop to the Franco regime might accept it once the regime had been changed. But to some of them it is so indelibly associated with the present regime that they would never be reconciled to it. Still others have opposed it from the start, deploring any departure from what they call Spain's traditional policy of isolation or noninvolvement. And Spain has certainly not been immune to the contagion of the new neutralism of the cold war, which is perhaps a by-product, in part, of Spain's growing contacts with Western Europe, which has its own spectrum of neutralists. The United States cannot decide which Western European influences are to play upon Spain; even Franco cannot do that.

Although the Spanish government has taken no pains to publicize the fact, most Spaniards understand that their country has derived important material benefits from its cooperation with the United States. A wider awareness of this might dissuade them from terminating the arrangement, although it would be rash to assume that Spaniards are less capable than Moroccans of sacrificing such benefits for the satisfaction of getting foreign forces out of their country. In short, neither the continuation of the bases program, nor

---

[24] Same, February 12, 1960; monitored rebroadcast of a speech by Santiago Carrillo, February 10, on behalf of the Central Committee of the Communist party at the Sixth Congress.

its termination, can be regarded as a foregone conclusion in the event of a change of regime in Spain.

A Course of Action

The United States must, unfortunately, base its policy on guesswork about what a people now muzzled may do in a hypothetical situation that may not arise for years to come and which may develop along more or less gradual or more or less turbulent paths. On the other hand, since the strategic balance in the cold war will apparently require it to seek access to bases in Spain for an extended, perhaps an indefinite, period, the United States should plan its policies so as to retain access to them as long as they are needed and as long as Spain agrees. Its policy should also aim to place relations between the two countries on a sounder footing in the years ahead.

Because of the very important assistance that the United States is providing to help the Spanish government put its economic house in order, it is justified in exerting every legitimate pressure to bring about a thoroughgoing application of the principles of austerity and reform to the Spanish government itself and the public sector of the economy, as well as to the people of Spain and the private sector. The United States can properly place the Franco government on notice that its willingness to provide continued assistance will be strongly influenced by that government's own efforts and that it will not indefinitely bail out or coddle a regime that does not mend its ways. Amendment has been promised and a beginning of it has been made. Much remains to be done, and signs of faltering have already appeared. As a result, constant outside advice, encouragement, and pressure will still be needed. Its use seems fully justified, for, as we have noted, by early 1960 the leaders of Spain's own banking community believed the time was near at hand when the Spanish economy would be able to stand on its own feet, with loans and foreign private investment providing additional support for its expansion.

For another thing, it is to be hoped that preoccupation with the negative and narrow themes of military defense and anticommunism will not be allowed to dominate relations between the United States and Spain in the years ahead as they have in the past decade. The potentialities for a more broadly based relationship exist. Americans have had a long tradition of literary and learned interest in Spain; while the counterpart has been lacking in Spain until recently, the interest in American literature and social sciences is growing. For many years Spanish has been one of the most widely studied foreign languages in the United States, and in Spain the study of English is on the increase. While something has been done to develop these potentialities through the U.S. cultural relations program in Spain, which has had some able administrators in the past decade, the program needs to be greatly expanded and upgraded from its present role of tail to a military kite.

The chief growth in this field must, of course, come from private sources, and it can never develop freely so long as Spain is ruled by an authoritarian regime. But through an augmented official program, properly conceived, Washington can help even now to stimulate an increase in people-to-people communication, and this can be expected to accelerate as the shackles are removed from Spanish intellectual life. In the end Spain should be in the forefront of the United States' cultural relations in Europe.

The most urgent problem for U.S. policy has arisen directly from the bases program. From enlightened self-interest, as well as from principle, the United States should endeavor to reduce the unnecessarily swollen political and moral liability that it has incurred through its increasingly close association with the Franco dictatorship. There are at least three things it can and should do.

First, the United States should revert to its cool and correct attitude of 1953 towards the Spanish dictator, in conformity with the attitude it has officially adopted in its dealings with Latin American dictators. That is all that is required by international decorum, and the fact that in this case there is a quasi-alliance makes no difference. There is no foundation in reason or history for the notion that allies must be bosom friends.

In the second place, the United States should strive to persuade other nations to share this liability provided it can do so without making a bad situation worse. Things are made worse by its continuing advocacy of Spain's admission to NATO. The widespread antagonism in Europe towards the Franco regime makes this equivalent to throwing another apple of discord into the ranks of an already divided Western Europe. NATO has troubles enough of its own without this. At some future stage it may be possible to find a solution through a Western Mediterranean pact, with Spain as a member. Since this would be a new organization and in it all other members would be voluntarily associated with Spain, there would be no such controversy as the NATO question has provoked.

Finally, the United States should make clear its disappointment with the failure of the Spanish government to give effect to the principles of "individual liberty and free institutions" which it endorsed by signing the economic aid agreement of 1953 with the United States. As a member of NATO, the United States should abandon its present position on Spain's admission to that organization and let it be known confidentially both to the Spanish government and its NATO allies that it will no longer press for this so long as the present contradiction persists between the character of the Spanish dictatorship and the declared purpose of NATO to defend freedom and democracy.

This is as far as the United States can go without violating the rules of the United Nations and its own traditional policy of nonintervention; and these steps do not constitute intervention. They do not even come as close to intervention against the Spanish dictatorship as the United States has already come to intervention in its support by furnishing it with military, economic, and political aid. What the United States can do is suggested by a recent study, already quoted at the beginning of this chapter. Discussing the type of problem with which we are concerned, the authors say:

> To press specific forms of democracy upon countries whose ideas run in other directions can obviously be self-defeating. . . . We cannot . . . hope to effect an immediate transformation in a regime which has developed along lines hostile to freedom. In such a case our task must be conceived as a long-range one of persuasion, assisted by the force of example and by the whole weight of America's record and achievements.[25]

After seven years of limited partnership the Madrid government remains quite unmoved by the weight of America's example, record, and achievements, and by whatever persuasion these may have exerted. If the goal of winning Spain for full-fledged partnership in a society of free nations is to be achieved at some future day, the effort of persuasion must obviously be more consistent and comprehensive. If American policy fails to make clear to all our country's basic dedication to the principle of "freedom in justice" that President Eisenhower proclaimed on his visit to Madrid in 1959, our alliance with the Spain of Franco will continue to strengthen his dictatorship, weaken our position and confuse our friends in the free world, provide grist for Communist propaganda, and store up trouble for us in our relations with the Spanish people long after the Franco regime has passed into history.

---

[25] *The Mid-Century Challenge to U.S. Foreign Policy*, cited, p. 7.

BIBLIOGRAPHICAL NOTE

READERS WHO WISH to know more about Spain and do not command its language would do well to begin with the latest edition of Salvador de Madariaga's *Spain: A Modern History* (New York: Praeger, 1958), which deals largely with the twentieth century, bringing the story down through the bases agreement of 1953 with the United States. The author, a leading Spanish intellectual, self-exiled and highly critical of the Franco regime, tries to be fair; his strictures on the Spanish Socialists of the 1930's provided most of the ammunition for a book against them published by the regime in 1959 (noted below). No such balance is sought by another useful work, Antonio Ramos Oliveira's *Politics, Economics and Men of Modern Spain, 1808-1946,* tr. by Teener Hall (London: Golancz, 1946); kind to some of the left-wingers pilloried by Madariaga, it is more informative on social and economic problems. Another one-volume history, more recent and better balanced than either, is Harold Livermore's *A History of Spain* (London: Allen and Unwin, 1958; New York: Grove, 1960).

For readers of Spanish, Emilio González López, a Republican exile, brings the story down to 1958 in his *Historia de la civilización española* (New York: Las Américas, 1959), and Américo Castro has recently capped his rewriting of Spanish history since ancient times with another volume, *Origen, ser y existir de los españoles* (Madrid: Taurus, 1959).

Further exploration of the recent history of Spain, both domestic and diplomatic, requires a reading knowledge of Spanish. Those who possess it should consult M. Fernández Almagro, *Historia política de la España contemporánea* (Madrid: Ediciones Pegaso, 1956); Gaspar Gómez de la Serna, *España en sus episodios nacionales (Ensayos sobre la versión literaria de la historia)* (Madrid: Ediciones del Movimiento, 1954); Maximiano García

Venero, *Historia de las relaciones internacionales de España* (Madrid: Ediciones del Movimiento, 1942; 2 v.); and José María Cordero Torres, *Relaciones exteriores de España (Problemas de la presencia española en el mundo)* (Madrid: Ediciones del Movimiento, 1954). Carlos M. Rama, *La crisis española de siglo XX* (Mexico City: Fondo de Cultura Económica, 1960), appeared too late to be utilized in the preparation of this study.

The list of recent works of a general character dealing wholly or largely with the Franco period is headed by Herbert L. Matthews, *The Yoke and the Arrows: A Report on Spain* (New York: Braziller, 1957). The work of a top-flight journalist *(The New York Times)*, who already knew Spain as a correspondent with the Republican forces during the Civil War, it is more comprehensive and judicious than a comparable product of French journalism, *Le Coeur et l'épée: Chroniques espagnoles* (Paris: Plon, 1958), by Jean Créach, former correspondent of *Le Monde* in Spain. The latter concentrates heavily on politics and reflects the monarchist sympathies that are said to have led to the termination of the author's assignment in Madrid. The British companion-piece is V. S. Pritchett's *The Spanish Temper* (New York: Knopf, 1955). The best brief appraisal of the Franco regime's first twenty years is Mildred Adams' "Twenty Years of Franco," *Foreign Affairs*, January 1959, pp. 257-268.

Outstanding among accounts of the Franco regime in World War II are: Carlton J. H. Hayes, *Wartime Mission in Spain, 1942-1945* (New York: Macmillan, 1945), an enlightening account of the author's activities and observations as American ambassador to Spain; a similar work by the British ambassador, Sir Samuel Hoare (Viscount Templewood), *Complacent Dictator* (New York: Knopf, 1947); an exceptionally well-informed and perceptive *Report from Spain* (New York: Holt, 1947), by Emmet John Hughes, a member of the staff of the American embassy in Madrid; a briefer but judicious analysis is given by Willard L. Beaulac, counselor of embassy under Hayes, in *Career Ambassador* (New York: Macmillan, 1951); and *Appeasement's Child: The Franco Regime in Spain* (New York: Knopf, 1943), by Thomas J. Hamilton, *The New York Times'* correspondent in Spain, 1939-1941, is another full-length portrait.

Works by Spaniards are legion, and, despite the constrictions of censorship and self-censorship, they are well worth sampling, if only because they show how the regime would like to appear to Spaniards and foreigners. From the point of view of Franco's foreign policy, the most striking change that has taken place in their character is the moderation in recent years of the earlier spirit of vaulting ambition, accompanied by the emergence of a note of self-justification. Of special significance are Fernando María de Castiella and José María de Areilza, *Reivindicaciones de España* (Madrid: Instituto de Estudios Políticos, 1941); José Corts Grau, *Motivos de la España eterna* (Madrid: Instituto de Estudios Políticos, 1946), a collection of articles first published from 1943 to 1945; José María Cordero Torres, *Aspectos de la misión universal de España* (Madrid: Artes Gráficas Helénicas, 1944); Rafael Calvo Serer, *España sin problemas* (Madrid: Rialp, 1949); Luis Carrero Blanco (Franco's right-hand man, writing under the pseudonym "Juan de la Cosa"), *España ante el mundo (Proceso de un aislamiento)* (Madrid: Ediciones Idea, 1950); José María Doussinague, *España tenía razón (1939-1945)* (Madrid: Espasa-Calpe, 1949), arguing that "Spain was right" all along in its anti-Soviet policy; Florentino Pérez Embid, *Ambiciones españolas* (Madrid: Editora Nacional, 1953); and Luis de Galinsoga, *Centinela de occidente* (Barcelona: Editorial AHR, 1956).

The condition of Spain and its problems have been presented by General Franco in his collected speeches. A volume appropriately entitled *Franco ha dicho: Recopilación de las más importantes declaraciones del caudillo. . . .* (Madrid: Editorial Carlos Jaime, 1947) brings together a selection up to the end of 1946. Less comprehensive topically, but extending to 1957 and more detailed, is the three-volume collection, *Francisco Franco, pensamiento católico, la cruzada anticomunista, pensamiento económico* (Madrid: Centro de Estudios Sindicales, 1958).

Two works already outdated, which interpret Spain's international role in terms of geography, are *España, geopolítica del estado y del imperio* (Barcelona: Editorial Yunque, 1940), by Jaime Vicens Vives; and *España, potencia mundial: La omnipotencia geográfica española* (Madrid: Imprenta de Magisterio Español, 1949), by José Díaz de Villegas y Bustamante. In his book, Vicens Vives, a foremost Spanish intellectual and lately a leading critic of the regime, has nothing to say about Spain's role as a pro-Arab or anticolonial power, and much to say about its imperial role in the Mediterranean, Africa, and elsewhere; it is sharply critical of the United States' "dollar imperialism" in

Latin America and argues that this will be held in check by Pan Hispanism. He died in 1960.

Interpretations of the history of Spain abound, as do discussions of the related but even more controversial theme of Spanish national character. A good starting point for the study of both has been provided by Ángel del Río, now of Columbia University, in *El concepto contemporáneo de España: Antología de ensayos (1895-1931)* (Buenos Aires: Editorial Losada, 1946). Two quite different works by British authors are deservedly given the highest ratings in their respective fields by Madariaga: Havelock Ellis, *The Soul of Spain* (Boston: Houghton Mifflin, 1913), a wise essay and a labor of love; and J. A. Pitt-Rivers, *The People of the Sierra* (London: Weidenfeld and Nicolson, 1954), a scientific community study. Between these two in scope and character lie two books by another British subject, Gerald Brenan: *The Spanish Labyrinth* (New York: Macmillan, 1943), and *South from Granada* (New York: Farrar, 1957). A minimum list of Spanish works would include Ángel Ganivet, *Idearium español* (1896), Miguel de Unamuno, *En torno al casticismo* (1902), and José Ortega y Gasset, *España invertebrada* (1922), all of which are universally recognized as classics and have appeared in various editions; the first and last are available in English translation. Some students of Spain would add to the list Ortega's earlier work, an address, *Vieja y nueva política* (Madrid: Renacimiento, 1914). The list should also include works whose authors are, or were at one time, identified with the Franco regime, such as Pedro Laín Entralgo, *España como problema* (Madrid: Seminario de Problemas Hispanoamericanos, 1949; 2 v.), and Florentino Pérez Embid, *El símbolo de Santiago en la cultura española* (Madrid: Editora Nacional, 1955). In between (chronologically speaking) lies Salvador de Madariaga's interesting comparative essay, *Englishmen, Frenchmen, Spaniards* (London: Oxford University Press, 1928).

No continuous account has been published of relations between the United States and Spain since the former rediscovered the latter in 1936 after a third of a century of oblivion. For the first three years we have F. Jay Taylor, *The United States and the Spanish Civil War* (New York: Bookman Associates, 1956), and for World War II the works of Hayes, Hughes, Hamilton, and Hoare (Templewood) noted above, to which should be added Herbert Feis, *The Spanish Story: Franco and the Nations at War*

(New York: Knopf, 1948). Feis' observation post was at Washington, not in Spain, but he was exceptionally well informed, he saw the Spanish scene in broad perspective, and his acute analysis still stands up well. For most of the period 1936-1945, much instruction can be derived from the *Memoirs of Cordell Hull* (New York: Macmillan, 1948; 2 v.) and from *The Time for Decision* (New York: Harper, 1944), by Sumner Welles, who opposed the U.S. government's policy of nonintervention towards the Spanish Civil War as strongly as Hull supported it. In most cases, however, there is little grist for our mill in works by or about the highest officials in the United States and Europe, including President Roosevelt, Prime Minister Churchill, and Generals de Gaulle and Eisenhower.

The history of the period since 1945 is marked by the same dearth of data at and near the summit. The dearth is even greater on the American than on the Spanish side. For example, the former has yielded nothing to compare with Foreign Minister Alberto Martín Artajo's speech to the Cortes on the bases agreement of 1953, which was published by the Spanish Foreign Office and is discussed at length in the present study, or his article "España y los Estados Unidos de América," *Punta Europa*, no. 27, 1958, pp. 61-73. Stanton Griffis, *Lying in State* (New York: Doubleday, 1952), deals in part with Spain; the author was the first U.S. ambassador to Spain after the recall of chiefs of mission by UN members in 1946. Relations with Spain after 1948 are not discussed in Harry S. Truman's *Memoirs* (New York: Doubleday, 1955-1956; 2 v.); and Spain is not even listed in the index of Robert J. Donovan's *Eisenhower: The Inside Story* (New York: Harper, 1956), although the conclusion of the agreement with Spain was one of the more important acts of the Eisenhower administration in its first year. Even in unofficial circles there has been little systematic study of the subject; articles of the type of the anonymous "Franco's Foreign Policy," *World Today*, December 1953, pp. 511-521, are highly exceptional.

As a result, one must rely on such aids as *The United States in World Affairs* (Council on Foreign Relations, annual), and *Hispanic American Report* (Stanford University, monthly, edited by Ronald Hilton), which has a regular section on Spain; on articles and news items in *The Department of State Bulletin;* and on newspapers and periodicals. Among the latter, the most useful have been the *Swiss Review of World Affairs* (Zürich),

The Economist (London), and *Revista de Estudios Políticos* (Madrid). Among newspapers, *The New York Times* has been indispensable, though the *New York Herald Tribune* and *The Christian Science Monitor* have yielded many nuggets, as have the London *Times* and *The Observer*, the *Manchester Guardian*, *Le Monde* and *Le Figaro*, as well as *ABC, Ya, Arriba, Informaciones, Madrid*, and *Pueblo* (all of Madrid), and occasionally other newspapers such as *La Vanguardia* of Barcelona, and *Levante* of Valencia.

The only general account of relations between the United States and Spain in the postwar period is Carlton J. H. Hayes, *The United States and Spain* (New York: Macmillan, 1952), which stops short of the crucial bases agreement of 1953. Occasional references to Spain are found in works of a general character, as in *A History of the United Nations Charter: The Role of the United States, 1940-1945* (Washington: Brookings Institution, 1958), by Ruth B. Russell; *NATO and the Future of Europe* (New York: Harper, for the Council on Foreign Relations, 1958), by Ben T. Moore; and *The United States and Africa* (New York: Columbia University, 1958), published by the American Assembly.

The whole history of an important aspect of cultural relations from early colonial times is told with enormous erudition in Stanley T. Williams, *The Spanish Background of American Literature* (New Haven: Yale University Press, 1955; 2 v.).

Recent Spanish opinion about the United States is discussed in Bogdan Raditsa, "Ferment in Franco Spain," *Commentary*, June 1959, pp. 500-507; Arthur P. Whitaker, "Anti-Americanism in Spain," *Orbis*, Fall 1959, pp. 313-331; and Julián Marías, *Los Estados Unidos en escorzo* (Buenos Aires: Emecé, 1956), and "Spanish and American Images," *Foreign Affairs*, October 1960, pp. 92-99.

The present study is based on the assumption that Spain's relations with the United States ought to be considered in the light of its international role, broadly conceived, as well as the worldwide responsibilities now borne by the United States. The quickening, under the Franco regime, of Spanish interests in the Mediterranean and North Africa is reflected in many publications. Four of fairly recent date and general scope are: Rafael Gay de Montella, *Valoración hispánica en el Mediterráneo* (Madrid: Espasa-Calpe, 1952); Carlos Ibáñez de Ibero, Marqués de

Mulhacén, *Política mediterránea de España, 1704-1951* (Madrid: Instituto de Estudios Políticos, 1952); José María Cordero Torres, *El africanismo en la cultura hispánica* (Madrid: Silverio Aguirre, 1949); and Ángel Flores Morales, *Africa a través del pensamiento español* (Madrid: Ediciones Ares, 1949). Spain's rather recent and tenuous pro-Arab policy has found expression mainly in periodical literature; a more substantial monument, which relates it to Pan Hispanism, is Rodolfo Gil Benumeya's *Hispanidad y Arabidad* (Madrid: Cultura Hispánica, 1952). Spain's ancient connection with Morocco is much better represented: for example by José Díaz de Villegas Bustamente, *España en Africa* (Madrid: Instituto de Estudios Africanos, 1949); José María Campoamor, *La actitud de España ante la cuestión de Marruecos (1900-1904)* (Madrid: Instituto de Estudios Africanos, 1951); and Tomás García Figueras, *La zona española del protectorado de Marruecos* (Instituto de Estudios Africanos, 1955). Lorna Hahn, *North Africa: Nationalism to Nationhood* (Washington: Public Affairs Press, 1960), is useful for background purposes.

Spain's interest in Spanish America has been subsumed for more than a quarter of a century under the cult of Hispanidad, a term given currency by Ramiro de Maeztu's *Defensa de la Hispanidad,* first published in 1934. Among the mass of Spanish publications on this theme, special mention should be made of Manuel García Morente, *Idea de la Hispanidad* (Madrid: Espasa-Calpe, 1947), Rafael Gil Serrano, *Nueva visión de la Hispanidad* (Madrid: Talleres de "Prensa Española," 1947), Luis Villaronga, *Hispanidad, catolicidad* (Madrid: Gráficas Aragón, 1951), and Alberto Martín Artajo, *Hacia la comunidad hispánica de naciones: Discursos de Alberto Martín Artajo desde 1945 a 1955* (Madrid: Ediciones Cultura Hispánica, 1956).

Doubtless for prudential reasons, the very great concern that Spaniards feel over their country's relations with its European neighbors has found no adequate expression in printed form. Relatively innocuous aspects such as cultural relations and, quite recently, economic relations have been so treated, but not questions of *haute politique.* Only rarely does one see even so modest an essay in this field as the article by María Dolores Gómez Molleda, "España en Europa: Utopía y realismo de una política," *Arbor* (Madrid), February 1955, pp. 228-240. The Gibraltar question is an exception, for obvious reasons; Luis Carrero Blanco, again under the pseudonym "Juan de la Cosa," addressed himself to it in *Gibraltar, comentarios de un español* (Valencia: Semana Gráfica, 1952). But for the most part one must look to non-Spaniards for substantial discussions of Spain's European relations, and even they treat the subject not in books, but in articles, of which leading examples are E. J. Debau's "L'Espagne, forteresse européenne," *Revue des Deux Mondes* (Paris), December 1951, pp. 540-548, and André Fontaine's "L'Espagne, la France, et l'Europe," *La Revue de Paris*, March 1959, pp. 43-54.

Among recent accounts of the Spanish political system, which must be presumed to be not unacceptable to the regime, are "Un estado con signo: Nota sobre los principios políticos fundamentales," *Punta Europa* (Madrid), no. 22, 1957, pp. 48-69, by Vicente Marrero; and an anonymous study, "Texto [y glosa] de los principios del movimiento nacional," *Arbor* (Madrid), nos. 151-152, 1958, pp. 323-522. The earliest authoritative exposition was given by Juan Beneyto Pérez in *El nuevo estado español* (Madrid: Biblioteca Nueva, 1939). Two commentaries on key features of the regime were provided by José Luis de Arrese in *La revolución social del nacional sindicalismo* (Madrid: Editora Nacional Gráficas Uguina, 1945), and *El movimiento nacional como sistema político* (Madrid: Imprenta de la Delegación Nacional de Sindicatos, 1945); the author, a Falangist, has been in and out of high office over the past two decades and again went into retirement early in 1960.

The Falangist view is also stated by Raimundo Fernández Cuesta, in *Continuidad falangista al servicio de España* (Madrid: Ediciones del Movimiento, 1955). A political handbook of different orientation is José Ruiz Huerta's *Manual de iniciación política* (Madrid: Imprenta Huérfanos de Oficiales del Ejército, 1946). Monarchist views have had their most persistent expression in the works of Rafael Calvo Serer, reputed "philosopher of Opus Dei," whose ideas of the "new popular and social monarchy" were not too distasteful to the regime to permit their inclusion in one of his latest books, *La fuerza creadora de la libertad* (Madrid: Rialp, 1958). The opposition forces, as the regime wished or was willing to have them appear, are described in *What is Happening in Spain? The Problem of Spanish Socialism* (Madrid: CEDESA, 1959), and in separate histories of Basque and Catalan nationalism by Maximiano García Venero published at Madrid in 1944 and 1945. The opposition expresses itself in print in various vehicles, but nowhere to better effect than in the monthly journals *Cuadernos* (Paris) and *Ibérica* (New York).

Except when the government wishes things to appear otherwise, the best over-all views of the Spanish economy are provided by the annual surveys of the Banco de España and the principal private banks. Among the latter, those most extensively used in the present study were the surveys of the Banco Urquijo, the Banco Hispano Americano, and the Banco Central. Because of the large scale of its operations, the reports of the Instituto Nacional de Industria (INI) should also be consulted, though they lack the focus and perspective of the bank surveys. Whenever possible, Spanish economic reports have been checked against reports from other sources, and this has been done particularly in the case of foreign-trade figures and customs revenues. Useful non-Spanish sources range from statistics on imports and exports and more or less routine reports of government offices, such as the British Board of Trade and the U.S. Department of Commerce, to special reports of international agencies and private foreign banks and articles in journals such as *The Economist* and the *Swiss Review of World Affairs*. A most useful survey that reached me at a late stage in the preparation of the book is Organization for European Economic Cooperation, *Spain, 1960: Economic Conditions in Member and Associated Countries of the OEEC* (Paris: Author, 1960).

Economic data for most of the Franco period are sampled in "Aspects de l'économie espagnole (1940-1957)," *La Documentation Française: Notes et Etudes*, January 14, 1958. The regime's earlier goal of autarky, to which it dedicated INI but which it would now like to forget, is the subject of Miguel Capella's *La autarquía económica en España* (Madrid: Editorial Vimar, 1945). An appraisal of the accomplishments is provided by Manuel de Torres, *Juicio de la actual política económica española* (Madrid: Aguilar, 1956). The possibilities of promoting Spanish exports to the United States are explored in detail in *Proyecto de plan para el incremento de las exportaciones españolas a Estados Unidos*, edited by Jaime Alba, Counselor of the Spanish embassy in the United States (Washington, 1958; mimeographed, 2 v.). A very recent and remarkably outspoken analysis of social aspects of labor problems in Spain is provided by Antonio Perpiñá Rodríguez, *Hacia una sociedad sin clases* (Madrid: Euramérica, 1959). Useful periodicals include *The Economist* (London), *El Economista* (Madrid), and *Cuadernos de Información Económica y Sociológica* (Barcelona).

William Ebenstein's *Church and State in Franco Spain*, Research Monograph no. 8 (Center for International Studies, Princeton University, 1960) is invaluable on that subject and, though brief (53 pages), covers admirably every aspect of it that is of general public interest, except perhaps Catholic Action (Acción Católica) in Spain. Further reading might include E. Allison Peers, *Spain: The Church and the Orders* (London: Eyre, 1939); R. Duocastella, *Problemas sacerdotales en España* (Madrid: Cáritas Española, 1959), which stresses the shortage of priests in Spain; Pedro Cantero, *En defensa de la unidad católica en España* (Zaragoza: Instituto "Fernando el Católico," 1953); José Luis Aranguren (one of Spain's leading intellectuals), *Catolicismo y protestantismo como formas de existencia* (Madrid: Revista de Occidente, 1952), and *Catolicismo: Día tras día* (Barcelona: Noguer, 1955); Rafael González Moralejo, *El momento social de España* (Madrid: Euramérica, 1959), notable for its criticism of the syndical system and as the work of a leading exponent of the Catholic Church's social mission. *Las hermandades de trabajo* (Madrid: Euramérica, 1959), with a prologue by Abundio García Román, describes the Catholic labor brotherhoods. José María Escrivá, *Camino* (Madrid: Rialp, 1957; 14th ed.), is the famous devotional manual by the founder of Opus Dei. The history of the monument in the Valley of the Fallen is told in *El monumento de Santa Cruz del Valle de los Caídos* (Madrid: Instituto de Estudios Madrileños, 1959), by Dom Justo Pérez de Urbel.

Current interests and problems of the Spanish armed forces are reflected after a fashion in the periodical *Ejército* (Madrid). The wide variation in estimates of their role in the present century may be illustrated by two pairs of contrasts. One consists of the Republican leader Manuel Azaña's chapters on them in *Una política (1930-1932)* (Madrid: Espasa-Calpe, 1932), and Carlos Martínez Campos, Duque de la Torre, "De política y milicia," *Revista de Estudios Políticos* (Madrid), January-April 1947, pp. 71-107. The other is provided by Efeele (pseudonym), *El desastre y los vicios de nuestras instituciones militares* (Madrid: Imprenta del Cuerpo de Artillería, 1901), and Jorge Vigón Suerodíaz, *El espíritu militar español* (Madrid: Rialp, 1950), which won the Premio Nacional de Literatura in 1950. Retired by the republic, Vigón Suerodíaz became the head of the Nationalist artillery in the Civil War, is the brother of Franco's emissary to Hitler in June 1940, and has been minister of public works in Franco's cabinet since 1957.

INDEX